Citizenship, Nationalism and Refugeehood of Rohingyas in Southern Asia

Nasreen Chowdhory · Biswajit Mohanty
Editors

Citizenship, Nationalism and Refugeehood of Rohingyas in Southern Asia

Springer

Burma's independence in 1948, the political demands of the Buddhist and the Muslims from the Arakan Hills were never met. In 1962 when Ne Win seized power, the situation of ethnic and religious minorities became precarious. Consequently, in 1982, the new Citizenship Act made it impossible for Muslims to become full citizens and they were given the status of associate citizen. As for the Rohingyas, they became a stateless community in 1982 when the Myanmar citizenship law excluded them from the list of 135 national ethnic groups.

The situation of Rohingyas became progressively more precarious. For decades, Rohingyas have been subjected to excessive violence. In 1989, the Myanmar government issued a colour-coded scrutiny card for citizens, but Rohingyas were not issued any card. On 21 February 1992, U. Ohn Gyaw, the Foreign Affairs Minister of Myanmar, announced: "Historically, there has never been a 'Rohingya' race in Myanmar? Since the first Anglo-Myanmar War in 1824, people of Muslim faith from the adjacent country illegally entered Myanmar Naing-Ngan, particularly Rakhine State. Being illegal immigrants, they do not hold immigration papers like other nationals of the country". From 1995, as a result of enormous pressure from the UNHCR, the Rohingyas were given a white card that could not be used to claim citizenship as that card did not mention a person's citizenship. Thereafter, the situation of the Rohingyas did not improve at all.

In 2015, the trials and tribulations of Rohingyas became known to the world when it was discovered that hundreds of Rohingyas were perishing in the boats as they were trying to escape persecution in Myanmar. None of the other countries in the region were willing to take in the Rohingyas. The plight of Rohingyas in high seas led to protest by international human rights regime when open graves were discovered in Thailand. This more than any other event revealed the precarious situation of the Rohingya population. For the Rohingyas, there are no safe options. In March 2017, another crackdown of Rohingya Muslims was defended by the Myanmar government as counter-insurgency operations. Social scientists call the Rohingyas "the world's most persecuted minority without citizenship". As for Rohingya women, their situation is even worse. According to one observer, "because of the diversity among Burma's 135 officially-recognized ethnic groups generalizing about them is risky. However, there clearly exists a country-wide pattern to the abuses suffered by Karen, Karenni, Mon, Shan, Kachin, Chin, Arakanese, Rohingya, and other ethnic women". Among the groups mentioned, the Rohingya women are worst off because they belong to a stateless community. A 440-page report by UN Human Rights Council (UNHRC) released in August 2018 details the persistence of crime against Rohingya women in Myanmar. The report includes accounts of women tied by their hair or hands to trees then raped; young children trying to flee burning houses but forced back inside; widespread use of torture with bamboo sticks, cigarettes and hot wax; and landmines placed at the escape routes from villages, killing people as they fled army crackdowns.

Any work on the Rohingyas is a welcome addition to the corpus of literature on forced migration. This particular volume is very timely not only because the problem of the Rohingyas persists but also because thousands of other South Asian population groups are getting displaced in Rohingya-like fashion. To begin with, they are being denied citizenship on the basis of ascribed primordial identities. Once rendered stateless, the "majoritarian" leadership then has the luxury to retain them as precariat and therefore cheap labour or displace them through acts of horrific violence as per their will. In this way, we are ushering in a new dark age that is far more dangerous because of available technologies. This volume has a number of papers by young scholars. This is the target group that should be read and heard as they are the only hope for any corrective measures. These are dire times, and volumes such as this are the need of the hour.

Kolkata, India

Paula Banerjee

References

Belak, B. (2000, October 31). Double Jeopardy: Abuse of ethnic women's human rights in Burma. *Cultural Survival Quarterly,24*(3), 24.

Ibid., p. 4.

Rahaman, M. R. (2017, April 13). Rohingya: The community of no human rights. *The Daily Observer*. https://observerbd.com/details.php?id=68541. Accessed November 4, 2018.

Safi, M. (2018, September 18). Tied to trees and raped. *The Guardian*. https://www.theguardian.com/world/2018/sep/18/tied-to-trees-and-raped-un-report-details-rohingya-horrors. Accessed October 20, 2018.

Acknowledgements

Writing a book is a collective process. The idea of this particular book emerged from a conference panel that brought friends across international borders who have been engaging with the Rohingya refugees and none could have been better than Prof. Nasir Uddin, Dr. Meherun Ahmed and Dr. Shahana Chowdhury in constructing the foundational understanding of the Rohingyas in Bangladesh. Subsequently, Dr. Nasreen Chowdhory and Dr. Biswajit Mohanty were able to build on this idea in various discussions that emerged in Associations for Asian Studies, i.e. (AAS in Asia) in Delhi and later in Bangkok. Nasreen would like to acknowledge Mahanirban Calcutta Research Group, especially Prof. Ranabir Samaddar, Prof. Sabyasachi Basu Ray Chaudhury, Prof. Samir Das and Prof. Paula Banerjee for their continuous support and affection over the years in all academic activities. In the Department of Political Science at the University of Delhi, Nasreen remains grateful to Prof. Veena Kukreja, Prof. Navnita Chadha Behera, Prof. Ujjwal Kumar Singh, Prof. N. Sukumar, Prof. Rekha Saxena and Prof. Madhulika Banerjee. With friends, family needs to be acknowledged as each member contributes to the scholarship in a different way. Nasreen remains forever grateful to her parents Azharul Islam Chowdhury and Nuron Nessa Chowdhury; to her sister Parveen Chowdhury for being the champion that she is. Nasreen is very grateful for the time and space that her sister has given over the years and for keeping her grounded, with love and consistent support; to Junied Alam Chowdhury, I remain grateful; to Amaan Chowdhury, the youngest in the family, I appreciate his love; witty encounters and constant support that are an integral part of all academic endeavours. I truly value his timely intervention in matters that have helped me to further my academic engagements; I'm very grateful to my little brother Samit. To Adlul Islam, my partner, I remain forever grateful for his support at every step of my academic life and otherwise.

In any academic work, research scholars have a critical role to play. Special thanks to Dr. Ramneet Kaur. A heartfelt gratitude to Dr. Sabur Ali M, Dhivya Sivaramane and Namreeta Kumari; Biswajit Mohanty would like to acknowledge three important persons who have inspired this book—Ershad and Anson of

Stephens College, University of Delhi, were the first source of inspiration. Their small endeavour to peep into the harsh reality of Rohingya's life in a short film titled "upavahan", produced and directed by them, compelled me to think about Rohingyas. Ali Johar, a Rohingya who is working for the Rohingya's cause, provided the initial insight about them. Nasreen Chowdhory, mentor, friend and co-author, who plodded me into the book project, was an inspiration for me. I thank them all.

The work would not have become possible without unconditional moral support extended to me by the family members. Babita, my wife, despite her ill health provided all kinds of support. My son Agastya, daughter Shirin and niece Monika were a big help in crucial times.

Thanks are due to my mother Tilottama Mohanty, sister and brothers, Jita, Lipu and Pipili, respectively, and Tutu and niece and nephews, Kandhei, Diya, Ayush and Ayushi, for their constant encouragement. My late father would have become the happiest person to see the publication of this book.

Professor Manoranjan Mohanty and Bidyut Mohanty, my peesa and peesima, constantly nagged me to write a book. It was this nudging that compelled me to write. Thanks are due to my cousins Jinee and Sanju who have helped me in formulating ideas.

A special thanks to our principal Dr Rajeev Agarwal who encouraged me and supported in different ways to complete the project. College colleagues Deba Bhai and Subasini Apa helped me a lot when I really needed it. Thanks to them.

Thanks are due to our DUTA members, Rajib Ray, Mithuraj Dhusia and Najma Rehmani, and the DTF members, Saswati Majumdar, Nandita Narain, Rudrashish Chakravarty, Abha Dev, Sanjay Bohidar, Vijaya Venkatraman, Rityusha, Shaileza, Deo Kumar and Rajbir, for pardoning me for missing DUTA and college dharnas.

The editors of this book would like to express their gratitude to all contributors of the book for painstakingly supporting the effort and keeping the various deadlines despite their busy schedule. We especially would like to acknowledge Ms. Satvinder Kaur and Priya Vyas of Springer, who have been very much supportive all the way from the submission of the book proposal to sending it to production.

The book is dedicated to Azharul Islam Chowdhury and Nuron Nessa Chowdhury.

Contents

Editors and Contributors

About the Editors

Nasreen Chowdhory is an Assistant Professor at the Department of Political Science, University of Delhi. She received her Ph.D. in Political Science from McGill University. Some of her prominent works are "Refugees, Citizenship and Belonging in South Asia: Contested Terrains" (Springer 2018) and "Deterritorialised Identities and Transborder Movement in South Asia" co-edited with Nasir Uddin (Springer 2019).

Biswajit Mohanty is an Associate Professor at the Department of Political Science of Deshbandhu College, University of Delhi. As a member of the CSDS-Lokniti network, he has contributed articles in journals like the Economic and Political Weekly, as well as numerous book chapters. His current research focus is on border and migration studies.

Contributors

Meherun Ahmed is an Associate Professor of economics and joined Asian University for Women (AUW) in fall of 2010. She has received her both Ph.D. and M.A. in economics from the University of Washington in Seattle, Washington, USA. Her research focuses on the micro-economic analysis of household behaviour, with an emphasis on investment in education and health, forced displacement, crisis coping mechanisms, well-being, poverty, as well as labour force supply. Before joining AUW, she was an assistant professor at Carleton College, Minnesota, USA. She has worked for many national and international development agencies and think tanks like the World Bank, the International Monetary Fund, International Organization of Migration and Institute of Micro-finance. She has published in reputed journals and presented her research in numerous conferences.

Nhung Tuyet Bui recently completed an undergraduate degree from Asian University for Women in Bangladesh. She majored in economics and minored in mathematics and finance. Her research interest lies primarily in the areas of micro-finance, economic development and factors behind socio-cultural and economic changes in developing countries.

Nergis Canefe is an Associate Professor and a scholar trained in the fields of political philosophy, forced migration studies and international public law with a special focus on human rights law, war crimes, state criminality and mass violence. She has over 20 years of experience in carrying out in-depth qualitative research with displaced communities and teaching human rights globally. Her research includes working with the Muslim and Jewish Diasporas in Europe and North America, refugees and displaced peoples in Turkey, Cyprus, India, Uganda, South Africa, Bosnia and Colombia.

Nasreen Chowdhory is an Assistant Professor in the Department of Political Science, University of Delhi. She completed her Ph.D. from McGill University, Canada. Her research interests are forced migration and refugee studies, nationalism, citizenship and ethno-nationalist movements. Her significant publications include Uddin Nasir and Chowdhory, Nasreen 2019. "*Deterritorialised Identity and Transborder Movement in South Asia.*" Springer Nature Singapore Pte Ltd., ISBN 978-981-13-2778-0 (e-book) and 978-981-13-2777-3 (hardcover), pp. 227; https://doi.org/10.1007/978-981-13-2778-0; "*Refugees, Citizenship and Belonging in South Asia- Contested Terrains.*" Springer Nature Singapore Pte Ltd., 2018 ISBN 978-981-13-0197-1 (e-book) and 978-981-13-0196-4 (hardcover), pp. 181; https://doi.org/10.1007/978-981-13-0197-1; Nasreen Chowdhory and Shamna Thacham Poyil (2019) "*Transitional Justice: Reconciliation and Reconstruction Process. The Case of the Former LTTE Female Combatants in Post War Sri Lanka.*" In Canefe Nergis (ed.) Transitional Justice and Forced Migration: Perspectives from the Global South. Cambridge University Press; https://www.cambridge.org/core/books/transitional-justice-and-forced-migration-critical-perspectives-from-the-globalsouth/B2B65D943C5E568C54AF5BC5B1A09F3E?fbclid=IwAR2xFRqgykB_UNlvlB_Hl3B8su9aIqtnt7l6-d8hiw9AFJ51Jqs0Q4nvSj4; Chowdhory, Nasreen 2016. She is Guest Editor of a special issue on *Displacement—A 'State of Exception' and Beyond: Issues and Perspectives in Forced Migration in South Asia*, in International Journal of Migration and Border Studies, Volume 2 Issue 2.

Shahana Afrose Chowdhury is currently working as Research and Development Manager at the Kazi Shahid Foundation (KSF); prior to that she was an associate professor and researcher at the Center for Sustainable Development (CSD), University of Liberal Arts Bangladesh (ULAB). She worked as Research Associate at the Trace Analysis Facilities (TAF), University of Regina, Saskatchewan, Canada, on air pollutants analysis. She had done a collaborative research on street food contamination by heavy metals from food, wrapped by the used paper, with Institute of Fundamental Studies (IFS), Kandy, Sri Lanka, and Asian University for Women (AUW). Previously, she was Assistant Professor of Environmental Chemistry at Asian University for Women (AUW), Chittagong, and School of

Environmental Science and Management (SESM), Independent University, Bangladesh (IUB), Dhaka. She also worked as Teaching Associate during her post-graduate studies at Monash University and RMIT University in Melbourne, Australia. She has completed her Ph.D. in green chemistry from Monash University, Australia, and a research master's degree in food additive analysis from RMIT University, Melbourne, Australia. She completed her B.Sc. (Hon's) and M. Sc. in Chemistry from University of Dhaka. Her research interests are green chemistry, medicinal chemistry, environmental sustainability, gender and society, migration, sustainable energy, food safety and nutrition, disaster management, waste management, natural resources management, public health, sustainable agriculture, sustainable development, etc.

Shamna Thacham Poyil is a Doctorate of Philosophy (Ph.D.) scholar in the Department of Political Science at the University of Delhi. Her research focuses on the narrative of statelessness of the Rohingyas and the politics of exclusion where denial of citizenship is used as a strategy for ethno-political nation building in post-colonial Burma, rendering minorities like Rohingyas stateless. Her M.Phil. dissertation titled "Birds of Freedom: Depiction of LTTE militant women in Tamil Cinema" explored the representation of militant women challenging the binary of agency and victimhood. Apart from holding a bachelor's degree in electronics and instrumentation engineering, she graduated summa cum laude from her Master's in conflict studies and peace building from Jamia Millia Islamia, New Delhi.

Meghna Kajla is a Doctorate of Philosophy (Ph.D.) scholar in the Department of Political Science, University of Delhi. She has completed her M.Phil. in political science on the topic titled "Symbols of Hierarchy and Dominance: The Changing Pattern of Dresses in North India". She authored the chapter "Nation-state and its Production of Statelessness: A study of Chin Refugees" and article in Mainstream Weekly "Changing Rights of Minorities in France". Her research interests are post-colonial theory, identity politics, religion, cultural studies and citizenship.

Kaveri is a Doctorate of Philosophy (Ph.D.) scholar at the Tata Institute of Social Sciences (TISS), Mumbai, India. Prior to joining at TISS, she was working with the UNHCR—BOSCO Project as a Child Protection Officer. The nature of her work involved working with children refugees and unaccompanied minors. Her interest and research focus on statelessness and refugee's migration in Southeast and South Asia, including citizenship, human rights, security, identity and contemporary political theories.

Ugyen Samdrup Lhamo has recently graduated from Asian University for Women, Bangladesh, Chittagong with a Bachelor's in Arts. She majored in politics, philosophy and economics and minored in development studies. Her interest in the development of the concept of refugee, identity politics and their assimilation in communities leads her to research about the process of assimilation of Rohingyas, one of the world's largest refugee crises in the host country Bangladesh.

Ritambhara Malaviya obtained her Ph.D. from Jawaharlal Nehru University and is presently Assistant Professor at the Department of Political Science, Kamala Nehru College, University of Delhi. Her areas of interest are in international relations, peace and conflict studies and modern Indian political thought. She has presented related papers at various national and international seminars and published analytical articles on related themes. She worked on the interface between the media, state and discourse on terrorism in her doctoral work, studying the English and Hindi newspapers in India.

Biswajit Mohanty is an Associate Professor in the Department of Political Science of Deshbandhu College, University of Delhi. His research interests are election studies in India and borderland and migration studies. He has contributed articles in several books, newspapers and research journals like Economic and Political Weekly. He has also contributed articles in international journals on border and migration studies. His latest publication is on ecologic border.

Ayesha Tasnim Mostafa is currently working as an executive in Research & Development at the Kazi Shahid Foundation (KSF). She has completed her undergraduate from Asian University for Women (AUW) in Chittagong, Bangladesh. She did her BA in economics (major), and development studies was her minor programme during undergraduate studies. Currently, she is pursuing her master's degree in development studies from BRAC University, Dhaka, Bangladesh. She has done internships at Grameen Bank and works for better Bangladesh. She has also participated in a research project titled "Climate Induced Displacement and Livelihood Choices: Evidence from Slum Areas in Dhaka Metropolitan City", as part of her undergraduate programme. Her research interests are rural development, migration and development economics.

Mafia Mukta is a Bangladeshi freelance journalist, currently working with DW Akademie—Germany's leading media development organization as a freelance on the Rohingya response in Cox's Bazar, funded by German foreign ministry, in the Editorial Management team for the radio magazine Palonger Hota (Voice of Palong). Palonger Hota goes on air from Radio Naf, Teknaf, Cox's Bazar, every Saturday afternoon. In her seven years of experience, she has pursued her career in radio and television, beginning with Rajshahi based Community Radio Padma, later Dhaka's Radio Dhoni and news tv channel News24 as a reporter. She has also worked with a British Council Active Citizen project as a facilitator. Before joining DW Akademie, she has also worked with Fondation Hirondelle—a swiss media development organization, as an editor for their radio contents. She has extensive knowledge and expertise in community-based audio-visual content production along with sufficient technical know-how on audio editing, video camera operation, script writing, production planning and design and so on. Mafia Mukta has completed her Bachelor with honors and Masters in Management from Bangladesh's National University.

Syeda Nafisa Nawal is a Master's candidate at the North South University, Bangladesh. She also works as Partnerships and Communications Manager at the non-governmental organization BRAC. Her research interests mostly lie within the space of human development, spanning across several areas such as micro-finance, nutrition, food systems, migration and urban poverty.

Shamna Thacham Poyil is a Doctorate of Philosophy (Ph.D.) scholar in the Department of Political Science, University of Delhi. Her research focuses on the narrative of statelessness of the Rohingyas and the politics of exclusion where denial of citizenship is used as a strategy for ethno-political nation building in Post-colonial Burma, rendering minorities like Rohingyas Stateless. Her M.Phil dissertation titled "Birds of Freedom: Depiction of LTTE militant women in Tamil Cinema" explored the representation of militant women challenging the binary of agency and victimhood. Apart from holding a Bachelor's degree in Electronics and Instrumentation Engineering, she graduated summa cum laude from her Masters in Conflict studies and peace building from Jamia Millia Islamia, New Delhi. Her recent publications include, The idea of protection: the norms and practice of refugee management in India, Refugee Watch (2019) with Dr. Nasreen Chowdhory and Meghna Kajla; Transitional justice, reconciliation and reconstruction process: the case of the former LTTE female combatants in post-war Sri Lanka with Dr. Nasreen Chowdhory in Transitional Justice and Forced Migration, ed. Nergis Canefe Cambridge University Press 2019.

Sucharita Sengupta is a Doctorate of Philosophy (Ph.D.) scholar in the Department of Anthropology and Sociology at the Graduate Institute of International and Development Studies, Geneva. Before this, she has been working on issues related to migration and forced migration in Asia as part of her work as a researcher at the Calcutta Research Group, India. For her Ph.D., she is working on conditions of life under "statelessness", through the case study of Rohingya refugees in camps of Bangladesh and India. The work intends to explore existing categories within refugee studies that in turn trigger debate on the anthropology of the state and how modern governance is conceived in the light of that. She is interested in studying refugee agency and resilience through the context of the Rohingyas in refugee camps in Bangladesh.

Abbreviations

AI	Amnesty International
ANOVA	Analysis of variance
ARIK	Arakan Rohingya Islamic Front
ARMO	Rohingya National Alliance Organization
ARNO	Arakan Rohingya National Organization
ARSA	Arakan Rohingya Salvation Army
ASEAN	Association of Southeast Asian Nations
ASMP	Association of Social Media Professionals
BDT	Bangladeshi Taka
BRAC	Building Resources Across Communities
BSF	Border Security Force
BSPP	Burma Socialist Programme Party
BWS	Burmese Way to Socialism
CEDAW	Convention on the Elimination of All Forms of Discrimination against Women
CIC	Camp in Charge
CSC	Citizen Scrutiny Cards
DAJI	Development Justice Initiative
EU	European Union
ExCom	Executive Committee
FCRA	Foreign Contribution (Regulation) Act, 2010
FTF-I	Fair Trade Forum India
GOB	Government of Bangladesh
GoI	Government of India
HRLN	Human Rights Law Network
ICC	International Criminal Court
ICCPR	International Covenant on Civil and Political Rights
ICESCR	International Convention on Economic, Social and Cultural Rights
ICG	International Crisis Group
IDPs	Internally displaced persons

IOM	International Organization of Migration
IR	International relations
IRB	Institutional Review Board
LDC	Least developed countries
MR	Measles-Rubella
NDPD	National Democratic Party for Development
NGO	Non-governmental organization
NHRC	National Human Rights Commission
NLD	National League for Democracy
NRC	National Register of Citizens
OAU	Organization of African Unity
RIF	Rohingya Independence Force
RNDP	Rakhine Nationalities Development Party
ROHRInga	Rohingya Human Rights Initiative
RPF	Rohingya Patriotic Front
RRRC	Refugee Relief and Repatriation Commission
RSO	Rohingya Solidarity Organization
SA	Subsistence allowance
SAARC	South Asian Association for Regional Cooperation
SAHRDC	South Asian Human Rights Documentation Centre
SAM	Severe acute malnutrition
SGBV	Sexual and gender-based violence
SLIC	Socio-Legal Information Centre
SLORC	State Law and Order Restoration Council
SUHAKAM	Suruhanjaya Hak Asasi Manusia Malaysia
TRC	Temporary registration card
UEC	Union Election Commission
UN	United Nations
UNDP	United Nations Development Programme
UNHCR	United Nations High Commissioner for Refugees
URNL	United Rohingya National League
US	United States
WASH	Water sanitation and hygiene

Chapter 1
Contextualizing Citizenship, Nationalism and Refugeehood of Rohingya: An Introduction

Nasreen Chowdhory and Biswajit Mohanty

Abstract A definition of a refugee involves an epistemological process, of identifying the politico-spatial contexts of generative conditions: an intertwining of normative and empirical considerations, and the interrelation between the local and the global. This epistemological exercise manifests in the gradual overcoming of methodological territorialism, (Audebert & Dorai, 2010), to contrast with methodological nationalism (Wimmer & Schiller, 2003) towards an understanding of the refugee problem. In the introduction, the authors highlight the evolving definition of refugees' as stipulated in the United Nations' Conventions and Protocol on refugees. Contextualizing within the debates on citizenship, nationalism, and rights of people, the introduction will elaborate on the creation of statelessness of the Rohingyas and raise the following questions: whether the Rohingya issue is a struggle for "the right to have rights"? Is it clash of identity with religion at its core?

Keywords Citizenship · Nationalism · Refugees · Identity · Rohingya

Introduction

The #IBLONG campaign by the United Nations High Commissioner for Refugees (UNHCR), resolved to eradicate the very source of new cases of statelessness and provide protection, completed the halfway mark in November 2019. According to the UNHCR report, forced displacement has increased in the last five years (UNHCR, 2017) and the Syrian conflict has contributed immensely to this phenomenon. The other countries that contributed to the ever increasing stateless pop-

N. Chowdhory
Department of Political Science, University of Delhi, New Delhi, India
e-mail: nchowdhory@gmail.com

B. Mohanty (✉)
Department of Political Science, Deshbandhu College, University of Delhi, New Delhi, India
e-mail: mohantyagastya@gmail.com

N. Chowdhory and B. Mohanty (eds.), *Citizenship, Nationalism and Refugeehood of Rohingyas in Southern Asia*,
https://doi.org/10.1007/978-981-15-2168-3_1

ulation are Burundi, Central African Republic, the Democratic Republic of Congo, Iraq, Myanmar, South Sudan, Sudan, Ukraine, and Yemen. The Rohingyas in Myanmar have significantly contributed to the growing population of stateless people and the present refugee crisis. They are facing a "systematic" violence and systemic discrimination and attack (UNHCR, 2017, p. 4). According to the Joint Response Plan (2019), the Rohingyas have been murdered, imprisoned, tortured, and disappeared and females have been subjugated to various kinds of sexual violences: rape, sexual abuse, forced prostitution and enslavement (Joint Response Plan, 2019, p. 10). The report further states there are "elements of extermination, and deportation" as well as "systematic oppression and discrimination [that] may amount to the crime of apartheid" (Joint Response Plan, 2019, p. 10). According to the Inter-Section Coordination Group Report, nearly 9,08,878 refugees are staying in Cox's Bazar of which 52% of refugees are women and girls who "have been exposed to severe forms of sexual violence in Myanmar before and during their flight to Bangladesh" (Joint Response Plan, 2019, p. 16). They are also facing gender-based violence in camps: forced marriages, domestic violence, trafficking, and other forms of exploitation. In a joint statement issued to the media, after a joint visit by the UN Emergency Relief Coordinator, Mark Lowcock, Head of UN migration Agency Antonio Vitorino and UN High Commissioner for Refugees, Filippo Grandi to the Cox's Bazar refugee camp, stated that "the most appalling brutality imaginable" has been committed to the children. Almost half of the refugee children under the age group of 12 have been deprived of basic education and other facilities (UN News, 2019). In India, they live in very precarious conditions in different parts of the country spreading from north to far south in Andaman and Nicobar Islands and east to west. In its first comprehensive report on the Rohingyas, Chaudhury and Samaddar, state that there would be 10,565 families of Rohingyas all across India (Chaudhury & Samaddar, 2015, p. 2). The Hindu Report estimates that there would be around 18,000–20,000 Rohingyas. Witnessing their appalling condition, the Hindu report by Amin has rightly titled it as "*Nobody's children, Owners of nothing*" (Amin, 2018).

The fundamental questions are: how should we analyse the Rohingya problem in Myanmar? Is it a struggle to have "the right to have rights? Is statelessness a product of clash of identities with religion forming the core of the conflict? The Rohingya's story of persecution in Burma is complex. The complexity begins with contestation over the very nomenclature Rohingyas and extends into the multiple perspectives on generative conditions of their statelessness. The scholars researching on Rohingyas have understood the issues from two different perspectives. From the historical perspective, the scholars are examining the contested terrains of intersectionality of nationality, religion and identity formation and/or construction, and subsequent alienation and loss of rights caused by the clannish and authoritarian state (Cheesman, 2017;

Farzana, 2016; Yusuf, 2018; Kyaw, 2015; Leider, 2018; Tonkin, 2014). The political economy perspective analyses the structural change in the regional economy and the changing internal economic environment on Rohingyas. The scholars argue that the neo-liberal policy adopted by the ruling class has invited the Foreign Direct Investment from China, provided tax benefits, setting up special economic zones in villages and towns mainly inhabited by the Rohingyas. Thus forced eviction of Rohingyas, coupled with the perpetual state violence perpetrated on them, created a conducive atmosphere of permanent no-return to their place of belonging. (Ibrahim, 2016; Sassen, 2017; Wade, 2017).

Mostly, researchers have a narrow focus confining the analysis to Myanmar only. The book by Chaudhury and Samaddar (2018), for the first time, has expanded the scope of analysis beyond Myanmar to include other South Asian states. They have adopted a legal-statist framework to analyse the issue of Rohingyas within the ambit of power relations, influence, and responsibility. For the authors, it is an important method of analysis, amidst the majoritarian democratic regimes prevailing around the world, that assumed responsibility of conducting self lies with the minorities. The second reason for the authors to adopt the legal-statist framework centering around the nation-state is to lay bare the power relationship between the nation-state, burdened with domestic and international responsibilities, on the one hand, and the transnational institutions, "agencies and regimes" without obligations, on the other. The primary responsibility of resolving the refugee crises lies mainly with the nation-states, whereas the transnational agencies are the architects of generative conditions for engendering refugees. The authors argue that the responsibility of the national and supranational bodies to resolve the crises is carried out within a legal framework to fix respective duties (Chaudhury & Samaddar, 2015, p. 14). The authors, therefore, conclude that the stateless persons are the outcome of brutal violence, which the United Nations conventions do not touch. Uddin (2019), similarly taking a statist position, argues it is the state that "accelerates" refugee movement and produces vulnerability—even the local state matters when generating vulnerability within the host countries. The local state acts in favour of the dominant localised power structure without acting responsibly to protect the minorities from the brutalities of the majority Buddhists community (Uddin, 2019, p. 88).

The major critique of Chaudhury and Samaddar's framework is that it does not clarify whether responsibility means accountability of agent or it is about the consequence of action for the future? If it is in the sense of accountability of the agency, then it brings in the question of the power of the agent to be autonomous of conducting self-legislation and self-ownership. It is about the state, which is "able to appropriate itself entirely in the ideal of sovereign's self-responsibility and transparency" (Raffoul, 2010, p. 11). If it is about the consequence of action then it is futuristic. The futuristic actions may be within the boundary of "calculability and control" or within the ambit of "arrival of the arrivant", i.e. "a future that cannot be anticipated; anticipated but unpredictable " (Derrida quoted in Raffoul, 2010,

p. 12). There is a third aspect of being responsible, i.e., one's obligation for the others: "a pre-originary openness to another, and the claim made upon me by this other" (Raffoul, 2010, p. 13). The claim made upon the State by the individual draws from the constitutional practices and any other legal and moral framework available within a nation-state. The constitution guarantees the rights that the State provides or denies to citizens and non-citizens, respectively. There are moral claims on the State to protect the rights of citizens: they may be enshrined in the constitution or not. Our point of departure from Chaudhury and Samaddar's formulation is that the question of stateless is analysed through the framework of citizenship and rights: where protecting the rights of the citizen is constitutional and the moral obligation of the political communities: of the State, individuals and civil society.

The rights discourse is useful for understanding stateless people in the sense that it has a legal as well as moral dimension. When legal techniques facilitate the stateless processes, it may seem ironic that the nation state itself produces illegality to make the legal, as is seen in debates on illegal immigration (De Genova, 2002; Samaddar, 1999). Scholars (such as Balibar, 1988, p. 724; cf. Reed-Danahay & Bretell, 2008) reveal that there are "routine manifestations of citizenship as both participatory and local in character". The everyday practice of citizenship and membership shapes the nomenclature of rights of those who have been dispossessed of their land, their dignity, and the official status. De Genova's (2002) concept of bordered identities appreciates how exclusions, as realized through technologies of exclusion such as border policing and enforcement, also regulates the inclusionary work. The nature of "inclusionary work" is inseparable from the processes of migrant illegalization and the subordination of migrant labour. Thus, through the process of juxtaposing the scene of exclusion to the "obscene of inclusion", the conventional notions of "belonging" and membership allow us to see not only the "necropolitical extremities" of regulatory regimes but also the biopolitical regularities that they produce— the "irregularity" of "irregular" migration (Chowdhory, 2019). Our study moves beyond "methodological nationalism" to include the regional actors and suprastate agencies to understand necropolitical extremities actuated on Rohingya across the Southern Asian nations.

South Asia has been conceptualized as a region of "unity in diversity" or "diversity in unity" (Bose & Jalal, 2004) or by what the states are not (Nandy, 2005, p. 541) or in terms of homogeneity and heterogeneity (Uddin & Chowdhory, 2019). Bose and Jalal (2004) as well as Nandy (2005) claim that the idea of South Asia is a recent invention. What is important for Nandy is that the concept emerged in the 1970s and gained public recognition in the 1980s. The neighbouring countries those were unhappy about India's domination accepted the nomenclature South Asia which seemed neutral than the idea of Indian subcontinent: a domineering and hegemonic conception (see also Gellner, 2013). According to Nandy, "the usage has frozen a cultural region geographically as it left out Afghanistan which had played an important role in shaping the Indian culture and history" (Nandy, 2005, p. 542). Gellner (2013) conceptualizes the northern South Asia instead of South Asia by referring to the presence of different kinds of borders and various responses to the power in the state–society relationship. He concludes that the northern South Asia is marked by unequal levels of control and divergent narratives along with "cartographic anxiety" that controls the movement of people across the border (Van Schendel, 2013, p. 267).

Nandy has not included Myanmar within his conception of South Asia as it may not have fitted into his nostalgic moments and shared histories. Gellner's consideration of Burma logically remains the outlier. Uddin and Chowdhory (2019) have conceptualized South Asia that includes states within the South-East Asian region but does not provide the meeting point of South Asia and South East Asian regions that have a shared past, a colonial history, and post-colonial upheaval of state- and nation-building processes.

In this context, Schendel's work becomes very pertinent. He connects the two through an interstitial region called "Zomia" (Farrelly, 2013, p. 195) or "land without state". Farrelly argues that to understand the post-colonial conflict, development, migration, and refugee, one must investigate through the node of Zomia. In other words, Zomia defines Southern Asia, which is identified by "idealised, borderless, transnational realm of interchange and conversation [that] can be positioned as the anti-thesis of the border-mapping and fence-building world" (Farrelly, 2013, p. 198). India, Bangladesh, Burma, and China fail to control the highland inhabitants because of "state repelling" and "state evading" nature of people. This region has more in common with each other than with the lowland area. Interestingly, the government is taking charge of this area and changing its ecological and political landscape through different means (Farrelly, 2013, p. 199). The refugees are very much imbricated within this project of governmentality expressed through the nation-building and state-building processes of Myanmar in collaboration with the Southern Asian states.

The Making of "The Palestine of the Farther East"

The 2014 Myanmar Census states that there are about 1 million Rohingyas concentrated mainly in Maungdaw, Buthidaung and Rathedaung towns situated along the Bangladesh border (Leider, 2018, p. 2). On the contrary, the Amnesty International survey states that there could be more than the stipulated number. The reason for the less return in the census is the deliberate attempt by the Myanmar authorities to deprive Rohingyas of vital documents and finally pushing them to the state of stateless people (Amnesty International, 2017).

The Rohingyas had been facing discrimination not only with the promulgation of the first Citizenship Act in 1948 after independence but also prior to it. The process began with the contestation over the claims over on the indigenous ethnic groups and their demand for citizenship.

The Arakan is a strip of the coastal plain area situated in the western part of Myanmar along the Bay of Bengal. It touches Bangladesh border on the northwest. The Naf River separates Arakan from the Chittagong region of Bangladesh. The North Arakan is the point of contact with Bangladesh. Historically, irrespective of Hindu, Muslim, and Buddhist rules, Arakan had always remained an independent monarchy (Leider, 2018, p. 2). The ancient political history revolved, first around the Dhanyawadi and later in the sixth century A.D. around Vesali, an urban township on the deltaic flood plain of the Kaladan and Lemro rivers. The name "Arakkhadesa" and the ethnonym "Arakanese" means the land of Arakans: appeared in different inscriptions of the eleventh century. The "Kingdom of Arakan" expression was traced to 1356 A.D. (Htin, 2007, p. 65). Archaeological evidence has been provided by the scholars to suggest that not only Buddhism spread during this time but also a strong political and cultural relation existed between the ruler of Bengal and Arakan (Htin, 2007, p. 59).

Parallel to the Burmese interpretation of the Arakan history runs the Rohingya history. There was no comprehensive and authoritative history available on Rohingya in Burma. It was M. A. Tahir Ba Tha, a native resident of Rohingyadaung village of Buthidaung Township, worked as a bank manager in Myithyikina city, first started highlighting the plight of Rakhine Muslims by writing in the Daily Mirror, Kaba Alin and The Guardian in 1960s (Jillani, 2007). He was subsequently approached by the executive committee members of the United Rohingya National League (URNL) to write a comprehensive and authoritative history of Rohingyas. This book was translated by A. F. K. Jillani in 1998.

According to Ba Tha, Rohingyas are a distinct ethnic group with the Arab and Pathan descendants who arrived in the Rakhine region from Arab and Bengal Sultanate during the seventh century and fifteenth century AD, respectively. Thus, there are two conflicting accounts about the nomenclature of Rohingyas. According to Ba Tha, the term Rohingya is a corrupted form of Rohai and Roshangi, a term used to refer to the Muslim people inhabiting the old Arakan area. The term meant "honest, dutiful, pitiful or kind- hearted to others" (Tahir Ba Tha, 2007, p. 17). He also mentions that the term Rohingya may have been derived from the Magh language, "Rwa-haung-gya-kiya" meaning "a brave tiger", a title attributed to General Wali Khan and General Sandi Khan of the Pathan army, who had invaded Rakhine to return the throne to Narameikhia of Longgeret dynasty, which changed in time to Rwahingyia and subsequently to Rohingya (Tahir Ba Tha, 2007, p. 17).

Ba Tha divides Muslim history of Arakan into three distinct periods. First, the Arabs as traders arrived in Arakan around the seventh century and extended trading activities into Burma and even set up a port city in Arakan known as Akyab (in Persian it means "piece of the river meeting the sea") (Tahir Ba Tha, 2007, p. 7). They married the local women and Islam spread during this time. They served the kings of Arakan and later migrated into the Lemro, Kaladan, Mayu, and Naf valley. The rivers Kaladan, Lemro, Mayu and Naf are Arabic names. The second phase of entry of Muslims was from India. A deep relationship between them developed when Rakhine Magh, an admixture of Tibeto-Burmans and Vesali Hindus (Tahir Ba Tha, 2007, p. 7), had political contact with the Bengal Sultanate when Narameikhia ruled this area. It was Narameikhia who shifted to Mrauk-U an important city around which the subsequent history of Arakan state revolved. According to Azeem Ibrahim, Islam was a significant religion that became very dominant among the descendants of Mrauk-U dynasty (Ibrahim, 2016, p. 39). From the fifteenth century onwards, Islam became very prominent in this area and relation with Bengal remained very warm.

The Arakan kings used Muslim titles. The third phase of Muslim rule was during Mughal rule in Bengal, under the governorship of Shah Shuja, one of the son's of Shah Jahan and brother of Aurangzeb. All this led Ba Tha to conclude, "The Arabs and Pathans army founded the original nucleus of the Rohingyas in Arakan, who arrived from Arab and Bengal Sultanate during the Arakanese kings" (Tahir Ba Tha, 2007, p. 17). He claims that "Rohingyas are a nation" (Tahir Ba Tha, 2007, p. 18).

Tonkin (2014) and Leider (2014) contest the Rohingya history as written by Ba Tha and subsequent authors. Derek Tonkin, with his reading of Census reports from 1872 through 1941 and 1917 district Gazetteer of Akyab, emphasizes that Rohingyas were not the original ethnic group residing in this area. He emphasises on the 1917 Gazetteer compiled by R. B. Smart and claims that the Muslims living in Sittwe, the present capital of Arakan, are immigrants from the Chittagong area. He cites data from the Gazetteer and British authors extensively to prove that the nomenclature Rohingya did not exist in the document. According to him, the Muslims staying here were "overwhelmingly" Bengalis or Chittagongians. He also claims that "Rohingya is a myth created" by "jihadist uprising" and gained acceptance because of support from the military leadership to bring about peace in the region (Tonkin, 2014, p. 3).

Similarly, Leider (2014, 2018) also cites the Dutch, British, Orientalist studies as well as censuses to contest the claim made by Rohingyas about their indigeneity. He claims that the articulation of Rohingya identity is a "Muslim Imaginaire" (Leider, 2018, p. 10). And further suggests that articulating the Muslim identity as Rohingyas and tracing the origin to antiquity would not be robust, instead it would be fair to classify it as "Rohingya movement" which is an ongoing process of identity formation (Leider, 2014, p. 22). The construction of Rohingya identity is a recent history whose material aspect was established during the colonial period. The material condition of the Muslim Imaginaire can be traced back to the arrival of the Bengali Muslim from Chittagong following the British occupation of Burma in 1825 and subsequent commercialization of rice cultivation and the construction of Akyab port by the British. The British initially divided the Arakanese population into the Bengali speaking Muslim groups and Arakanese-speaking Buddhist groups. Within that broad category, they fused the old Arakan Muslim community settled before 1785 with post-1826 Chittagongian migrants. Subsequent censuses—1921 and 1931—differentiated between the old Muslim Community as "Arakan Mahomedans" and racially categorized them as "Indo-Burman". The relatively nascent settlers were called "Chittagongians" and were racially classified as "Indians". The new Muslim immigrants and the old settled Muslims "shared the same cultural idioms and a network of exchanges" (Leider, 2014, p. 12). A broad Muslim identity developed among the Muslims during the same time in the Rakhine area (Leider, 2018, p. 5). The argument raises two questions. First, it is unclear as to how these two groups merged to form the category, Rohingyas? Second, both Leider and Tonkin though explain the construction of identity by the Rohingyas, but they failed to answer the question: why and how did the contested histories got transformed into the extermination of Rohingyas in Burma?

The process of formation of local identity from the broad Muslim identity and subsequent movement for autonomy by the Muslims has a long history dating back to the colonial era where the British authority occupied Burma and ruptured the social harmony by dismantling the monarchy and bringing in a new political economy (Wade, 2017). It seems that the deep-seated animosity between the two had its root in the "idea of ethnic boundaries and enforced territorial ownership" by the British in 1920 (Farzana, 2017, p. 44). Burma was ruled as the provinces of the colonial power from 1887 until 1937. The British introduced dual administration in Burma. In the 1920s, in a limited way, a parliamentary form of government was introduced. In the frontier areas, the traditional system of the ruling was retained, and the monarchy was destroyed in mainland Burma. British favoured many ethnic communities and minority groups who subsequently occupied various positions in the colonial services. These minority groups became collaborators of the British against the Burmese state. This was one of the reasons for the schism between the minorities and the nationalist Burmese.

The changing economy provided the appropriate momentum for antagonism between the two groups. There was a lot of anguish among the Buddhists against the British whom they saw as the destroyer of Buddhism and, on the other hand, against the Muslims who by the early 1920s had become "economic powerhouse, able to pay higher rents than the Myanmar counterparts and to buy up swathes of land in Yangon and the delta, which has been transformed by the colonial power into a hugely lucrative rice bowl" (Wade, 2017, p. 27). The commercialization of agriculture and the construction of the port in Akyab propelled intra-region migration. People from India and China constituted the major portion of immigrants (Farzana, 2017, p. 46). The Buddhist perceived a threat of subordination from the Indians who had invaded their lucrative job market.

In 1937, Burma was made a self-administered colony by the British empire. The Muslim minorities perceived this as an opportune moment to carve out an autonomous region for them. According to Leider, the beginning of the formation of Rohingya identity may have started during 1936 in Maungdaw province with the formation of the first council of teachers known as Jamyyat Rohingya Ulema (Leider, 2014, p. 16). It is surprising to note that Leider, in his 2018 article, has deleted the word Rohingya and has added "ul" to the word Jam'iyyat and Ulema to read it as Jam'iyyat Ul-Ulema (Leider, 2018, p. 7). In July 1938, the anti-colonial sentiment had not only reached its peak, but a strong sentiment against the Muslims had started in Yangon that erupted in the form of violence against Muslims. Subsequently, the attacks erupted all over Myanmar (Wade, 2017, p. 28).

The year 1942 was the watershed in the history of Rohingyas as well as the Rakhine Buddhists. The invasion of the Japanese divided the population into two hostile camps with Rakhine supporting the Japanese and the Muslims supporting the British. With the advancement of the Japanese troop into central Arakan and subsequent collapse of colonial order, a nationalist fervour started among the Burmese. The Burmese wanted to end all favours given to minorities such as Karen, Kachin and Muslims by creating a great Burmese nationality or what is called "Mahabama" (Farzana, 2017, p. 45). The Japanese instigated the Burma Independence Army (BIA) to attack minorities that resulted in violent clashes leading to communal riots. The Muslims were attacked; inhabitants were killed or driven away; and the Muslims fled to India in large numbers. This fuelled animosity between the two communities. Several attempts were made by the Buddhist and Muslim leaders to bring peace, but they did not succeed in establishing it in the area (Tahir Ba Tha, 2007; Leider, 2018).

By 1947, some Rohingyas had been negotiating with West Pakistan about incorporating Maungdaw and Buthidaung of the northern Arakan region into East Pakistan. The negotiation failed as Mohammad Ali Jinnah and Aung San did not concede to their demands. This had a long-term impact on the Muslim population as they were considered as hostile to the new government, outsiders, and disloyal to the nation. This idea got reinforced when the Burmese Communist Party tried to overthrow the newly elected government (Ibrahim, 2016).

The narrative of "othering" by the state had already begun. It got institutionalized and intensified not only with the formulation and enactment of the first-ever constitution in 1948 but subsequent constitutions reinforced the very idea of the "other". Thus, began the "Palestine of the Farther East", a nomenclature that was attributed to Arakan area by a famous Swiss Pali scholar Emil Forchhammer (Forchhammer, 1891). Arakan was the citadel of Buddhism from where it spread to rest of the Burmese territory (Galache, n.d.). Now, it connotes a land of conflict, of violence and mass killing, clash of genealogies and historical narratives.

"The Sovereign Is the Problem"

Knowledge of the inner qualities of any concept begins with its definition. Defining a term serves five purposes. First, it opens new paths for understanding a concept or phenomenon. Second, it unravels the "priorities and power relations" that any definition possesses. Since no definition is politically neutral, definitions try to promote specific values and interests. The analysis of definitions help us to unravel the hidden "normative and political commitments". Third, it also reflects the cultural context, the historical moments and territorial locations of a phenomenon. Each conceptual framework corresponds to values, norms and social and political commitment that the individuals and communities hold. Thus, the function of the definition is not to "secure universal acceptance" but to generate debate and effectively communicate with others on various insights and individual experiences. Fourth, it enables us to acknowledge the tentativeness and contingent aspect of knowledge and force us to reappraise, redefine and reinvent our knowledge constantly. Fifth, the definitions make formulations consistent, sharp and precise. By doing so, it lends internal coherence and relates to the empirical world (Scholte, 2005, pp. 52–53).

Stateless and refugees are such entities. All stateless may not be refugees in strictly legal parlance but all refugees can be stateless depending on several factors. People who are residing within a sovereign state and lack the state protection in terms of loss of rights are called stateless. To gain the status of the refugee, they have to cross the international border or lose their membership of habitual residence. This is strictly a legal definition which is reflected in three important international documents: the Statute of the UNHCR of 1950 (hereinafter Statute), the 1951 Convention relating to the Status of Refugees (hereinafter the 1951 Convention)[1] and the Protocol to the Status of Refugees (hereinafter Protocol).[2] There is a small distinction between the Statute definition of Refugee and that of the 1951 Convention. The Statute defines a "refugee" as any person:

> Who is outside the country of his nationality, or if he has no nationality, the country of his former habitual residence, because he has or had well-founded fear of persecution by reason of his race, religion, nationality or political opinion and is unable or, because of such fear, is unwilling to avail himself of the protection of the government of the country of his nationality, or, if he has no nationality, to return to the country of his former habitual residence.[3]

The 1951 Convention defines the category of the refugee as any person who:

> As a result of events occurring before 1 January 1951 and owing to *well-founded fear* (emphasis added) of being persecuted for reasons of race, religion, nationality, membership of a particular social group or political opinion, is outside the country of his nationality and is unable or, owing to such fear, is willing to avail himself of the protection of that country; or who, not having a nationality and being outside the country of his former habitual residence as a result of such events, is unable or, owing to such fear, is unwilling to return to it (UNHCR 2010, 14).

In terms of determining the difference that exists between the two definitions, it may appear minimal—the 1951 Convention laid emphasis on the political meaning or rather the lack of political rights of a group of people who at any point living within the state structure may feel insecure and may have to leave the country of

[1]Text of the Statute: Annex to the UN doc. A/Res/428 (V) (1950). The text of the 1951 Convention: 189 UNTS 137; entry into forces on 22 April 1954; as of 1 August 1996, the convention have been ratified by 127 states. It should be noted that the two instruments are of different legal status, a General Assembly (GA) resolution establishing the terms of the mandate of the United Nations High Commissioner for Refugees, respectively, a treaty, though some experts argue that the Statute is in substance a treaty on account of its being an implementation of the UN Charter by the GA and therefore binding for all states members of the United Nations, Grahl-Madsen, 1966 at 32 (where the reference is made to the Statute as "an international convention adopted by delegated authority"). The adoption of the Statute by the General Assembly constitutes a decision of the Assembly on the basis of Art. 22 UN Charter, which is in virtue of its being a decision internal to the organization, that is, concerned with the internal working of the organization, hence binding to its member states. See Hartling (1979, 129).

[2]Text: 606 UNTS 267; entry into force on 4 October 1967; as of 1 August 1996, the Protocol have been ratified by 127 states. The continuing importance of the both the 1951 Convention and the Protocol of 1967 has been reaffirmed time and again, by the Conclusions of the UNHCR Executive Committee: Conclusions 42 (XXXVI) (1986); Conclusion 43 (XXXVII) (1986); Conclusion 57 (XL) (1989); Conclusion 61 (XLI) (1990); and the general Conclusion on International protection of 1993, 1994, 1995 contained in resp. UN docs. A/AC.96/821 (1993) and 19; A/AC.96/839 (1994) and 19; A/AC.96/860 (1995) and the 1993 Vienna Declaration and Program of Action.

[3]Art. 6; the Statute comprises and contains other definitions in Art. 6.

habitual origin. But the overemphasis on *political* often leave other aspects of rights like; economic, cultural behind, and therefore subsequent Convention or Protocol attempted to fill this void. Insofar as the Convention definition of the refugee is concerned, it lays down the broad definition in terms of the *year, thus year-marking those events prior to 1 January 1951 might have led to crisis*, which has led to refugee or refugee-like situations. Having said that it should also be contextualized that indeed events prior to 1951 were the events of Second World War, thereby restricting rather than "extending the temporal restriction with a geographical one" (Zieck, 1999, p. 28). She asserts that there is little difference between the Statute and the 1951 Convention's definition. In the Convention, a refugee is defined as any person who "owing to well-founded fear of persecution for reasons of race, religion, nationality, membership of a particular social group or political opinion, is outside the country of his nationality and is unable or owing to such fear, is unwilling to avail himself of the protection of that country of his former habitual residence is unable or, owing to such fear, is unwilling to return to it" Art. 1 A(2) 1951 Convention *jo.* Art. I(2) 1967 Protocol.

However, there are still countries that have not acceded to the Protocol of 1967, and thus, the geographical limitation of 1951 Convention is still applicable. Another aspect of the 1951 Convention definition of a refugee delimits the status to those who have *crossed the international border then they can be termed as a refugee, thus leaving a certain group of people devoid of any status even though they maybe the refugee in every sense of the term.* In most case, a refugee, who does not cross the international border but is seeking refuge or fleeing persecution, is called an internally displaced person (IDP). The internally displaced person may suffer from a lack of protection comparable to those who left the country is expressed by the UNHCR: "frequently the internally displaced person cannot obtain effective protection from their own government, either because it has lost control of a part of its territory or because it perceives them as a threat and supports or condones violations of their rights".[4]

The 1951 Convention, while determining who is a refugee, engages in mostly objective definition of the phrase "well-founded fear of persecution". But scholars like Chimni and others argue that the sole premise of *refugeeness* should not be based on objective criteria alone, as the concept of *fear* is a subjective feeling, which essentially needs to be ascertained through *objective* means. The Convention's mandate protects only those whose "civil and political rights" are violated, which leaves those with socio-political rights at risk. It extends to persons who have been disenfranchised on the basis of race, religion, nationality, membership of a particular social group or political opinion. Having said that, the Convention's importance cannot be undermined. Hathaway (1991, p. v) states, "in the Convention refugee definition is a singular importance because it has been subscribed to more than one hundred nations in the only refugee accords of global scope. Many nations have also chosen to import this standard into their domestic immigration legislation as the basis upon which asylum and the other protection decisions are made".

[4]Statement of the UNHCR on March 3, 1993. UN Doc. E/CN.4/1992/23; Annex to UN doc.E/CN.4/1993/35; Undocs.E/CN.4/1994/44 and Add. 1;E/CN.4/1995/50; E/CN.4/1996/52.

The 1967 Protocol relating to the Status of Refugees (hereafter the 1967 Protocol) removed the "temporal and geographical limitations" contained in the 1951 Convention. No doubt, the Convention was a pioneering document determining refugee status; it was both a product of Cold War politics and had Eurocentric biases that did little for refugees both from and within the developing countries. Also, there was little emphasis to incorporate the geographical imbalance that existed within the framework of definition of "refugee". This meant that most "third world refugee continued to remain de facto, as their flight is frequently prompted by a natural disaster, war, or political and economic turmoil rather than by persecution or at least as that term is understood in the Western context" (Chimni, 2000, p. 8). The Organization of African Unity (OAU) Convention expanded some of the criteria needed to determine who a refugee is? It defines the term refugee as persons fleeing their country of origin due to "external aggression, occupation, foreign domination or events seriously disturbing public order in either a part of the whole of the country of origin or nationality". The addition mainly moves away from the 1951 Convention definition in terms of "well-founded fear of persecution" alone. The standard of persecution has been further determined by stressing those refugee-included persons fleeing civil disturbances, violence and war, etc.

The 1984 Cartagena Declaration recommends a definition along the lines of OAU Convention. The 1984 Cartagena Declaration calls for consideration of the objective situation in the country of origin and the particular situations of the person or group of persons seeking protection as the refugees. This definition requires that two conditions are needed to be declared for the refugee status: that there exists a threat to life, security or liberty; and the threat result from factors such as generalized violence; foreign aggression; international conflicts' massive violations of human rights, etc.

Kibreab (1987) contends that prior to the 1969 OAU Convention governing the specific aspects of the refugee problems in Africa; it was devoid of principles, norms, rules and procedures on voluntary repatriation. There was a strong exilic bias in the way solutions were conceived (UNHCR, 1995). As Coles (1985, p. 202) perceptively observes, "A regional framework already exists in the case of Africa but little or no framework for any other region. In so far as they relate to the solution, the international legal instruments are predicated on the durability or permanency of exile". The 1969 Refugee Convention is one of the binding documents between states that are a signatory to it and the international agency, the UNHCR that explicitly covers some of the issues related to "voluntary repatriation". The UNHCR recognises voluntary repartriation and responsibilities are fixed on both the country of asylum and the country of origin.[5] The Cartagena Declaration also has some provisions in relation to repatriation. The principle includes range of issues, providing appropriate information to refugees, freedom of movement, non-discrimination on any ground, access of returnees to means of subsistence and land and returnees access to the UNHCR. There have been numerous agreements on voluntary repatriation that has

[5]See Article V of the 1969 OAU Convention Governing the Specific Problems of Refugees in Africa; see also CM/ Res. 399 (XXIV) Resolution on Voluntary Repatriation of African Refugees of the OAU Council of Ministers, Addis-Ababa, 1975.

been signed between States (as countries of asylum and countries of origin) and the UNHCR.[6] These agreements[7] concern the more significant voluntary repatriation operations and set out the respective duties and responsibilities, as well as the rights of refugees and returnees. Given their binding nature, these agreements reinforce the legal underpinning of voluntary repatriation in each state. Increasingly, more and more peace agreement seems likely to have these provisions and principles as well.

The nation-state is an important category where "peoplehood" finds a clear expression in state-centric theories. It believes that people are sovereign entities as citizens enjoy equal political, social and economic rights. They also have group solidarity held together by mutual obligations and support. They share a common culture and united through a common destiny (Wimmer & Schiller, 2003, p. 582). The denizens, state and nation are bound by national territory to define each category. The nation-state not only defines citizen but also from time to time create conditions of statelessness and refugeehood. Refugee and statelessness is a process whose generative cause lies in the nation-building project. It begins with, not necessarily in the same order: genocide, forced uprooting of people, ethnic cleansing and domination and subordination processes.

Arendt argues in The *Origins of Totalitarianism* that discourse on the "rights of man" is relevant only as long as one can be acknowledged as "human". The "abstract nakedness of being human" is not revered enough that it, by default, would make any human worthy of rights. The institution of the state is the medium through which an individual can claim the right that he or she is entitled to. The notion of inalienable rights that any individual possesses by virtue of being human renders itself obsolete in the absence of a "nation state" as the spatial and temporal variables that form the margins of citizenship are determined by the nation state. It is here that Arendt's differentiation between "right to human rights" and the "right to be recognised as the right to have …" gains significance. In her theorization of Arendt's work, Benhabib (2004, p. 56) elaborates on this dyad of rights, the first inference of "right" is based on a " moral claim to membership and a certain form of treatment compatible with the claim to membership while second usage of "rights" implies the privilege and prerogative of an individual who belongs to an "organized political and legal" community. Being stateless, to Arendt, is the conjoint repudiation of both these inferences of rights. The indispensability of a stateless individual, according

[6]Such Agreements included: Abkhazia/Georgia/Russian Federation (1994), Afghanistan/Pakistan (1988), Afghanistan/Islamic Republic of Iran (1992), Afghanistan/Islamic Republic of Iran (2000), Afghanistan/Islamic Republic of Iran (2002), Angola/South West Africa Peoples Organization (1989), Angola/Namibia (1995), Bangladesh (1993), Burundi/United Republic of Tanzania (1991), Congo/United Republic of Tanzania (1991). Croatia/Bosnia-Herzegovina (1995), Eritrea/Sudan (2001), Guatemala (1991), Islamic Republic of Iran (1992), Liberia (1996), Mali/Burkina Faso (1994), Mozambique/Malawi (1988), Mozambique/Zimbabwe (1993), Myanmar (1993), Pakistan (1998), Rwanda/United Republic of Tanzania (1995), Somalia/ICRC (1990), South Africa (1991), Sri Lanka (1993), Sudan/Lutheran World Federation (1973), Suriname (1988), Vietnam (1975 and 1988).

[7]See Annex 5 of the Handbook, Voluntary Repatriation: International Protection, UNHCR (1996).

to Arendt, (1951, p. 295) is not that they are differentiated by the application of the same law, as the state does not consider them worthy enough.

It thus creates a dilemma in that the very sovereign who provides the right to the citizen also creates the condition for division within. The sovereign becomes the Problem, to paraphrase the former High Commissioner for Refugees, Sadako Ogata. The state holds immense power to nullify or withdraw rights as defined by the prevailing law within a given territory. It, in the name of violation of sovereignty, prohibits intervention from outside to carry out annihilation of communities, genocides, creation of massive internally displaced persons and refugees.

"Genealogy of Citizenship"

Often the compulsion of state's asylum policies is the result of a conflict between international norms and the idea of providing refuge as essential loosening asylum policies, on the one hand, and national interests tightening, on the other. In most situations, the state attempts to strike a balance between the two: an argument that can be applied only in the context of developed countries. It can be argued that the state essentially determines asylum policies depending not only on national interest but also on security concerns. Some recent literature reveals the interface of immigration and refugeeism with citizenship and democracy. Walzer (1995, p. 24) asserts that membership allows for an "exclusivist membership in the democratic state which is essential for a democratic society". Soguk's (1999) interpretation is different from others. He contests refugee being a negative concept, rather in terms of their capacities to effect disruptive changes in sites of governance. Despite the negative connotation on refugees as a term, this particular author claims and views refugees as a positive-sum that impacts changes in "sites of territorial governance". Both refugees and immigrants transgress political and cultural boundaries and undermine the "democratic and its institutions as the domain of the life of citizen". Their existence in any state and its territory construct and negotiate new identities for democratic space. Thus, despite their ambiguous status which is invisible and uncertain, refugees participate in the "exclusionary legal, cultural, political, and economic practices of a specific kind of democracy", which privilege the citizen as the proper entity of the sovereign state. However, refugees are instrumental in creating tension and make their presence felt in any events of discrimination, despite their improper status, which subsequently makes them more visible than "invisible". Citizens draw raison d'etre from their position within the state based on membership. This puts refugees at a disadvantage vis-à-vis their position in any state. Furthermore, to a certain extent territorial democracy is a specific manifestation of the sovereign territorial state, which clearly contests any space for refugees who are disruptive and fails to reaffirm relations, identities of the territorial, citizen-oriented democracy.

Marshall's (1950, p. 15) theory suggest a mechanism to make "state the servant of individual needs"; that is, the people of the modern state advance citizenship by actively subjecting the state to their demands. However, to make the state/government work, individuals have to be politically active in demanding the material benefits, which constitute the core essence of the economic and social rights described by Marshall, that is the individual, as the citizen of a participatory state is however, economically passive. "There is no more dynamic figure in modern history than the citizen", writes Dahrendorf (1974, p. 673). "Citizenship is civil rights, political participation, social welfare, on the other hand, is identity and recognition". Citizenship is a contentious issue that has much more significance once an individual has crossed the international border. Once in an alien territory, refugees have no rights other than those entitled to under the international law, more specifically stipulated under the international refugee law. The identities of refugees are enmeshed with nationality and belonging within the question of statehood. Citizenship becomes a vital issue that both shapes and governs state's recognition towards their distinctive identity.

Citizenship is not just about having right to enjoy rights (Arendt, 1979) but also about "citizenship as identity". Citizenship means membership in a political community where members are de jure bearer of rights that make them politically, economically and socially equals (Bellamy, 2008, p. 12). Belonging is the first hallmark of being a member of political community. Belonging to a community or the state is the necessary condition for being citizen but not the sufficient condition for enjoying the status of a citizenship or participating in the social, political and economic life of the community. There are various forms of exclusion that the membership brings in: being a dissident, members banned by the state or the community may result in exclusion from the larger political group. There are thus some legal conditions that citizens need to follow or obey: accepting the legitimacy of the state and its rules. The state provides rights to its citizens in return demands the legitimacy of the rule which becomes the sufficient condition for becoming a citizen. The rights provide the ground for equal treatment of citizens by the state and citizens towards their fellow citizens. The rights allow citizens to be part of democratic participation, where democratic participation in a minimal sense means right to vote or taking decisions. The nature of participation is dependent on the citizen's choice and engagement with the state and other members of the political community (Bellamy, 2008, p. 14). The rights as individual entitlement provide an agency to the citizens and are one of the collective goods available to them to shape their life and choices. It is coterminous with the civic duty that each citizen has towards the other and the state. "Hence, the association of rights with the rights of democratic citizens, with citizenship itself forming the right of rights because it is the 'right to have rights'—the capacity to institutionalize the rights of citizens in an appropriately egalitarian way" (Bellamy, 2008, p. 15).

The major criticism of citizenship rights described in terms of "right to have rights" is that it becomes reductive and exclusivist by stressing on the fact that the access to other sets of rights is dependent on membership within a given political community. Theoretically, the right to have rights is not exclusivist because, in a democratic country same sets of rights can be extended to those who may be considered as non-citizens like refugees, immigrants and stateless persons provided that the citizens decide which rights they want to extend to these persons. The right to have rights become human rights if the state provides "succor" to those who have no rights, for instance, asylum seekers, immigrants, refugees and stateless persons (Bellamy, 2008, p. 16).

The ability of the state to denaturalize citizens[8] reminds how citizenship as an institution can be used to constitute new "social hierarchies, wield political control and create new national narratives" (Chung, 2017, p. 436). Following Tilly (1996), citizenship is seen as a "contested institution and cluster of practices negotiated by the state and non-state actors" to demarcate formal membership in the nation state and "accompanying rights, statuses and obligations". It may be proposed that citizenship is a vital construct that enables the incorporation of individuals who are spatially located in a "sovereign territory" to assert their rights. Bosniak (2000a) categorizes the framework of citizenship into four strands: citizenship as a "legal status", as the attainment of "rights", as the prerequisite for political participation and as a mark of "identity". In *Constitutional Citizenship through the prism of alienage,* Bosniak (2002) examines the duality of inclusion-exclusion implicit in the notion of citizenship by engaging with the status of "alien citizens".

The globalized literature tends to be optimistic about the reach of the state in determining nationalized-based rights, as the role of the state is decreasing (Chowdhory, 2019). The traditional argument on citizenship is limited to a "formal national membership", that prioritizes the rights of members over those of non-members. The concept of citizenship rights has expanded from the individual membership-based to include group-based demands and the trajectory of the change overlooks the need to include the category of non-citizens. It has failed to acknowledge the rights of the stateless and non-nationals, aliens and refugees (Sassen 1999a, b). Bosniak (2000b) concurs that previous theories of citizenship overlook the immigrant "alien" context of citizenship. Soysal (2000) argues that "decoupling in citizenship between rights and identity" is necessary to understand claims beyond nationality. Identity-based claims tend to be more particularistic. Therefore, citizenship aims for egalitarianism and further facilitates empowerment, non-citizens like Rohingyas who occupy the disadvantaged zones of restricted membership, citizenship becomes a legally discriminating instrument to propagate inequality. The state, on the other hand, will negate such claims and suggest that the universal norms of citizenship can be challenged and, typically, a *non-citizen* represent the justifiable exception to this universality norm (Bosniak, 2017). Often non-citizens are reduced to "bare life" in the quest to have citizenship rights that focus on territory and state-determined. The non-citizens in liberal democracies may experience rights as citizens but will not conform to the rights, duties and responsibilities of citizens. The prominent feature is the idea of the border and how state appears to play a constitutive role and territorialization of rights. Thus, non-citizens are the ramification and product of state borders and attempts to make claims on the basis of de-territorialized identities.[9]

Socially inclusive and politically democratic citizenship system is possible if "egalitarian and solidaristic principles, practices, and institutions of civil society and

---

[8]See Chowdhory (2018) for more details.

[9]Chowdhory (2019).

the public commons are able to act with equal force against the exclusionary threats" (Somers, 2008, p. 8). Realization of the normative values of citizenship is thus contingent upon prevailing political practices, the existence of democratic institutions and inclusive cultural practices of the state. The "genealogy of citizenship" (Somers, 2018) aptly captures the contingent moments, unraveling of repressed moments and "a story of countervailing power" (Somers, 2008, p. 83). It is an "instituted process" of constantly changing the balance of power among institutional sites. The institutional relationship is the core of citizenship (Somers, 2008, p. 35). The institution where citizenship is instituted is the constitution. It is the epitome of the temporal, ideational and material aspect of citizenship. It is the very site for creation and denial of citizenship.

Rohingyas as an ethno-religious minority group are subjected to discrimination in various dimensions which is often "horizontal inequalities" (Stewart, 2008) manifested in political, social, economic and cultural levels. This inequality is explicitly visible in the form of colour differentiated pink and white "citizen scrutiny cards" that have been generated to Burmese public locating their status of political membership. Kabeer's (2005, p. 23) observation on "horizontal view of citizenship" is visible in the interaction between the "full citizens", "associate citizens" and non-citizens like Rohingyas whereas "vertical view of citizenship" is reflected in the interface that exists between the government and the individual.

The shifting definition of citizenship of Rohingyas and others is coeval with the implementation of different constitutions that have been adopted from 4 January 1948 until 2008. This is also the key to understand the processes of exclusion, discrimination and enforcing statelessness on Rohingyas. Furnivall (1948) provides details of how political reforms and economic transformation in Burma had contributed to the ethnic discord between 1920 and 1940. Burma became conflict-prone with the implementation of the Village Act in 1924, and the Constitution Act of 1937 (Furnivall, 1948). The major ethnic groups inhabiting these areas were Rakhine, Shan, Karen Karenni, Chin and Kachin. In February 1947, General Aung San had signed the Panglong Agreement with Shan, Kachin and Chin ethnic nationalities after which the drafting of the Constitution commenced. This was a symbolic political act between the majority Burmans and ethnic nationalities who recognized Burma as their home. The 1948 Constitution recognized five federated states, namely Shan state, Kachin State, Karen State, Karenni State and the Special division of Chins. Despite the agreement and being part of the Constitution of 1948, the ethnic conflict proliferated in the federative regions (Crouch, 2015, p. 3). The geographical spread of violence in contemporary Myanmar in Rakhine area neighbouring Bangladesh, in Chin, Sagaing and Kachin in the North touching the Indian border and the Shan and Karen district in the East is the pointer to the occurrence of the past ethnic conflicts.

Before Burma got independence, there were debates among different sections of new ruling elites on the kind of constitution to be adopted. The Buddhists saw it as the right moment to create a Buddhist polity dominated by Burmans. Aung San, the chief architect of Burma's independence, wanted an inclusive and federal polity: after his assassination in 1947, his wife also pursued the same principles. Within the army, there was also a debate as well whether to have a military rule independent of civilian rule or remain under the civilian rule. With the assassination of Aung San, the debate was settled in favour of the Buddhist beliefs. During the democratic transition, Buddhism was seen as the guiding moral principle of organizing daily life but seldom it became deeply associated with "Bumeseness". It got deeply anchored in the Burmese psyche in 1962 when the change occurred from civilian to military regimes (Ibrahim, 2016).

The legal status of Rohingyas should be discussed in this context. Burma's first Constitution reflected inclusiveness, but there were biases against the Rohingyas. Under the first Constitution, Burma became "Union of Burma" and it committed to provide citizen—social, economic and political justice, various kinds of liberty including to retain their religious beliefs and equality of citizens (The Constitution of Burma, 1947). The inhabitants of the frontier states areas and Karen states were recognised as citizens. The Constitution had provisions which inherently promoted "bipolar cultural and ethnic terms in many of its provisions" (Parashar & Alam, 2017, p. 98).

Section 10 and 11 specifically deal with the provisions of citizenship. Article 10 states that there would be a single citizenship provision throughout the Union. Article 11 (i–iv) provides guidelines for acquiring citizenship: (i) every person whose "parents belong or belonged to any indigenous races of Burma"; (ii) born within the union or any territories whose grandparents belong or belonged to any indigenous groups; (iii) of parents both of whom had been born and alive during the commencement of the Union; and (iv) born in territories in British Dominion or resided in this territory before 1942.

The Union Citizenship Act, 1948, in Article 3(1) enumerates the Arakanese one among the other indigenous race of Burma, namely Burmese, Chin, Kachin, Karen, Kaya, Mon or Shan residing before 1823 A.D. The Citizenship Act when studied in conjunction with the Universal Citizenship Act then it is amply clear that the Rohingyas were not citizens at the very out-set of post-colonial nation-building process in Burma. It is because the insertion of the term Arakanese need not mean that it includes the Rohingyas and the name Rohingya has not been addressed anywhere in the text.

It is claimed that the Rohingyas can be considered as citizens if the 11 (i), (ii) and (iii) read in conjunction with 3(1) the phrase that reads "and such racial groups those settled in before 1823 could become citizens."

There have been expansive judgements made by the Supreme Court of Myanmar to affirm the status of the Rohingyas as citizens. For instance, the Letto Law Danga v. the Union of Burma (1959 BLR 30 HC) the court upheld that under the relevant sections of 11(i) (ii) and (iii) of the Constitution and section 3 of the UCA 1948 indigenous people of Burma meant those people who share similar culture and ethnic characteristics (Parashar & Alam, 2017, p. 99). Surprisingly, in the case of Hasan Ali and Meher Ali (Criminal Miscellaneous Applications No. 155 of 1959) versus the immigration authorities, the Supreme Court held that the applicants who did not know

Burmese and Arakanese language are ethnically different people hence were not granted citizenship. The Rohingyas were not stateless as they possessed citizenship card issued by the Myanmarese governent following the Citizenship Act provisions. They were allowed to contest the elections until the military coup overthrew the civilian government in 1962.

The military regime under General Ne Win adopted a socialist Constitution in 1974. The Constitution introduced seven states and seven divisions. The ethnic groups had no special status in the Constitution. The ethnic nationalities those were given special recognition in the 1947 Constitution were given the status of States—Kayah, Karen, Chin, Kachin and Shan. Two more states were added, Mon and Arakan. The names of the states were named after the dominant ethnic groups inhabiting those areas (Crouch, 2018, p. 4).

Four years after the adoption of the Constitution of 1974, the first military campaign, codenamed "Dragon King", was carried out forcing about 200,000 Rohingyas to cross the border into Bangladesh. The Burmese government willy nilly took back the refugees under pressure from the United Nations High Commissioner for Refugees and the Muslim countries under Shwe Hintha operation in 1979.

The enactment of the Citizenship Law in 1982 by the Burmese governemnt was the deathblow to the Rohingya's aspiraton to acquire citzenship. The Act created three classes of citizens—full, associate and naturalized—under the *jus sanguinis* principle. Section 39 stated that the "national races", those who have settled before 1823, can become full citizens. The state had complete discretion to allow ethnic groups to become full citizens or not (Craig, 2016). The ruling government popularized the view that Rohingyas are a constructed identity (Leider, 2018). The associate citizens are those who do not qualify for full citizenship but can be qualified if apply for citizenship under the Union Citizenship Act. Under section 23, a central body would determine past applications. Technically, it was very rigid in some cases as it can only give associate citizenship and the person cannot appeal if it is an unsuccessful application form. Those Rohingyas who could not apply were left out of associate citizenship. Naturalized citizenship also could not be accorded to the Rohingyas under section 42 of the Citizenship Law. The section demands people to provide conclusive proof of their entry and residence before January 4, 1948, and of their offspring born within the state. The Rohingyas are not eligible as they could not provide the place of birth, because the family list provided by the governemnt does not show the place of birth of the Rohingyas. The provisions of the Act for all practical purposes made the Rohingyas stateless by vesting overarching discretionary power on the central government to assign citizenship rights to individuals and communities.

The second military campaign began in 1991 that expelled 250,000 Rohingya Muslims. The United Nations brokered an agreement with the government to repatriate the expelled people and allow international agencies to have access to the refugees. In 1995, under the pressure of the UNHCR Burmese military government willy-nilly provided a Temporary Registration Card (TRC) which remained very useful subsequently. However, there was no mention of bearer's place of birth on the card, hence, could not become a legal document for claiming the Burmese citizenship.

The 2008 constitution was very subtle in denying the Rohingyas citizenship by drastically narrowing down the grounds of acquiring citizenship by the Rohingyas. As per Article 345, he/she would be declared a citizen who is born of parents "both of whom" were nationals of the republic when it came into existence or one of the parents was already a citizen when the Constitution came into force. However, the majority of Rohingyas would not meet these requirements, as their parents in all possibilities did not possess any document to show that they were Myanmarese (Parashar & Alam, 2017).

The central government very effectively could curtail several incidents of communal violence between Buddhists and Muslims in the years 1984, 1988, 1994 and 1998. It became very ineffective in preventing violence in 2012. In 2012, violent attacks mainly targeting the Rohingyas spread in Karen state and subsequently to other regions displacing thousands of people by April 2013. A nationwide campaign was carried out by Buddhist monks that demanded anti-Muslim legislation. In 2015, the movement became an important factor in the passage of "Race and Religion Laws" for targeting Muslims. The majority of them constituted the Rohingyas who had lost their citizenship rights became stateless in their "homeland" (Thawnghmung, 2016).

The constitutional changes had far-reaching consequences for the Rohingyas. They were disenfranchised to participate in democratic processes. In the earlier elections, Rohingyas had their representation from the Arakan region (Tahir Ba Tha, 2007). But in the 2015 National Elections, the Union Election Commission (UEC) rejected 88 candidates from contesting the elections without giving any reasons. The Election Commission withdrew their "white cards" to disenfranchise them (ANFREL, 2015). According to another report, more than a third of the Muslims and twenty-eight from Rakhine state were denied tickets to contest the election. Out of them was U Shwe Maung, a sitting Rohingya MP, was denied a chance to contest the election as an independent candidate (Parashar & Alam, 2017).

Citizenship and Nationalism

Citizenship is one of the marker of nationalism. Nationalism employs citizenship to define the nation and embarks on the process of nation-building. The nation-building process is a carefully crafted policy for nation-state formation to "diffuse and strengthen a sense of nationhood". In the process, the state privileges the majority culture through the national system, supporting national media, adopting national symbol and citizenship. In this context, Kymlicka argues that instead of calling it the nation-states one should label it as "nationalising state" (Kymlicka, 2001, p. 229). The state tries to diffuse a common national identity which is an ongoing process. In this context, the question is how the ethno-cultural minorities constitute themselves vis-à-vis the majority nationalism? Will Kymlicka provides three options. The first is the part of the minorities to integrate into the majority culture by renegotiating the terms of the integration process. The second option is to demand for the right of self-government by maintaining own culture with a competing nation-building project. The third option is accepting permanent marginalization. Taking three case studies of national minorities, immigrants and Metics, Kymlicka argues that the three types have different ways of accommodating themselves into the nation-building project of the majority. Within the national minorities, he distinguishes between "stateless nations" and indigenous people. He asserts that what minority nations want is to maintain political autonomy provided they respect the "liberal limitation" of rights of other minorities (Kymlicka, 2001, p. 31).

The critical aspect of Southern Asia is the movement among the dominant religious groups to infuse religion into politics leading to the prevalence of the variety of religious-nationalist models. Rejection of modernity is the common factor among the religious-nationalist groups in Southern Asian states where the trans-mutation of ethnic nationalism into religious nationalism is taking place in a rapid scale. They endorse a religious state with politics of violence against religious minorities. (Yusuf, 2018, pp. 517–518). This is not only true of Myanmar but also true to India, Indonesia, Sri Lanka, Malaysia and the Philippines (Yusuf, 2018, pp. 517–518). Religious nationalism is a process of ideological evolution from "democratic, ethnic, and language based nationalism to religious based nationalism" (Yusuf, 2018, p. 519). It privileges the national religious majority over the rights of religious minorities. It is based on the ideology that the majority have a right to land or territory where the religious minorities are outsiders, a threat to the national solidarity and possess no legitimate citizenship rights. The legitimacy of a "religious nationalist state" flows from the fact that the majority population is legitimately organized by politico-religious principles. In other words, the racial or ethnic-religious identity of the majority population of the country determines the nature of the nationalist state. It does not reject the idea of the nation- state but rather takes the help to imbibe the exclusivist nationalist ideology. It is born out of the globalization process and "marked by conditions of ontological insecurity, existential uncertainty and résistance to the acceptance of human diversity" (Yusuf, 2018, p. 520).

Burma has almost 89.8% of Buddhist followed by 6.3% Christians and Muslims constitute 4% of the total population. The Muslims are not homogenous groups in Burma and fall into several groups with diverse social and political identity. There are Zerbadee Muslims, Indian Muslims, Panthay-Chinese Muslims, Malay or Pashu Muslims and Arakan Muslims. The nation-building process not only destroyed the minority nationalism but also through violation of the political, social, civil and human rights promoted majority nationalism in Burma.

Rohingya crisis is the outcome of this process. The military government in Myanmar after the 1962 coup followed a strong nationalist policy. There were a robust counter-insurgency policy followed through Four Cuts Strategy that forcefully relocated entire ethnic communities. Tatmadaw was the dominant political force that suppressed many protests. It started with the delegitimisation process in 1974 when the new constitution was formulated. The Burmese government mainly followed a unitary assimilation policy except in 1974 when it adopted a sort of ethno-federal structure. It divided the country into different regions based on the ethnic population. There were seven ethnic regions and seven Burmese-dominated provinces. Arakan, Chin, Kachin, Karen, Kayah and Mon were ethnic-dominated areas, and Rangoon, Irrawaddy, Tenasserim, Pegu, Magwe, Mandalay and Sagaing were the Burmese-dominated regions. According to Farzana, these divisions in practice could hardly be called federal. During this time, the military-led government took steps to give recognition to the ethnic groups from different regions in the lower house of parliament known as *Amyotha Hluttaw* or the House of Nationalities. In June 1989, the name Arakan was changed to "Rakhine state", as per the "Adaptation of Expressions Law", and is identified as an exclusively Buddhist state. The ethnic divisions lacked autonomy as well as enjoyed less degree of control over resources (Farzana, 2017, p. 19). In 2012–2013, the Ma Ba Tha or 969 movements led by the radical Buddhist monk Ashin Wirathu was established that pressurized the Thein Sein government to invalidate the White Cards issued to the Rohingyas. The stripping of white cards made the Rohingyas de facto stateless.

Identity, territoriality, bureaucratically organized state and possessing legitimate control over violence, constitutes the crucial core of modern nation state. Since the nation state is "map-driven" and territory control, the governments are stressing on identity formation through various modes of socialization of the population. The indigenous elites and forces of the Western European countries could achieve this form of the state. But in post-colonial Burma, the concept of "indigeny" is often constructed to distinguish the local inhabitants from the "other". It becomes a primary instrument of exclusion which came through various legal means, for instance, through constitutional provisions or other statist institutions or discriminatory practices. In Myanmar, for instance, the indigenous elites had no political authority to form such kind of nation-state. Political identities of elites were in opposition to rather than in support of the political authority of the colonial and post-colonial state. In Burma, ethnicity, and religion independently or in combination, became the pivot of identity formation. Religion has become one of the primary organizing institutions. The complex processes of identity formation in Burma was antithetical to the Barmar nationalism. The post-colonial state in Burma at times ignored and, at other times, politicized other identities leading to the formation of complex identities. In this situation, "not only did the forces of anti-state nationalism need to be turned into pro-state nationalism, but also the colonial state's reification of ethnicity as the salient political characteristic of the country had to be reshaped into an ideology that would support the state, rather than tear it asunder." (Taylor, 2005, P, 267-8) Myanmar's ethnic elites have built nationalism and their political base by combining religion and ethnicity. And local elites are opposing the dominant form of nationalism. In post-colonial countries, the concept of "indigeny" is often constructed to distinguish the local inhabitants from the "other". It becomes a primary instrument of exclusion which may come through various legal means, for instance through constitutional provisions or other statist institutions or discriminatory practices. This provides the basis for the contestation of identity leading to statelessness. In an interesting article Thawnghmung (2016) comparing two competing narratives of the National Democratic Party for Development (NDPD), a political party representing the Muslim population and the Rakhine Nationalities Development Party (RNDP), the Buddhist party reveals how indigeneity as a concept to understanding "positionalities" is connected to indigenous conflicts. She explores how Rohingyas and the Rakhine monks have employed historical narratives within the power dynamics of the state–society relationship to ascertain their claim to indigeneity. She argues, instead, that common ground could be leveraged to foster more pragmatic approaches to deep-seated communal problems.

Thus, the genealogy of citizenship and nationalism, a critique of those dominant ideas and practices that try to "hide the contingency of human life behind formal ahistorical or developmental perspective" (Bevir, 2008, p. 274), reveals that nationalism in Burma is embedded in the question of *taing-yin-tha* or sons of soil or more specifically "national race". It reveals "how political actors' capacity to speak and act authentically as taingyintha is contingent on subjugation to the modes of state practice for the organisation of truth" (Cheesman, 2017, p. 2). Taingyintha had two interpretations in the colonial history, one denoting "single ascription" by pulling various groups together and the other distinguish groups from each other (Cheesman, 2017, p. 4). In February 1964, it became the "paradigm for military-dominated statehood". It got laced with larger political programme of political domination and subjugation. Subsequently, Taingyintha became embedded into the constitution and taxonomic configuration of different groups. The taxonomy of population got translated into "a political idea like national races into a truth regime for differentiation, domination and exclusion of population" (Cheesman, 2017, p. 9). The term "national people" became "the collective people of taingyintha" symbolizing as a "trope for Myanmar's many linguistic and cultural groups pulled together in a state-building enterprise" (Cheesman, 2017, p. 10). The Constitution of 2008 addressed the political community not as citizens but as "national race" in which "national races precede and surpass citizenship" (Cheesman, 2017, p. 13). The foundation of the national race was laid in the 1982 Constitution when it delineated 135 ethnic groups as part of the collective called Taingyintha. As Cheesman remarks, the Rohingya became de facto stateless: excluded juridically and leading precarious life the Rohingyas were desperate to come back into the political community and submit them to the politics of taingyintha. Cheesemen has mistaken the effect for the cause as he fails to explain the reason for Rohingyas exclusion at the first instance, instead emphasises more on the politics of inclusion.

The ensuing genocide has a political-economy dimension. The early 1990s saw major policy changes in Myanmar. The economy was partially liberalized. This resulted in the signing of agreements between the government and the armed rebel groups. The aim was to exploit the abundant natural resources falling in the rebel areas. Companies affiliated to the Tatmadaw could generate significant wealth from many locations. Access to these resources was considered as a means to achieve wider ambitions and controlling of resources became an end in itself (Burke et al., 2017, p. 22). The rioting and burning of Rohingya villages in 2012 and subsequent attacks in 2015 may have to do with the capture of land in this area. The Government Documents reveal that 17,000 acres of rural land was allocated in the national list for "economic development". In 2016, the Aung San Su Kyi's government decided to include 3 million acres of land in the list (Sassen, 2017, p. 1). The military has long been associated with the land grab. But what is new in this was that the Rohingyas, unlike other attacks, have been "radically expulsed" from the area. This is probably to facilitate the Chinese plan to develop a 7.3 billion seaport at Kyaukpyu on the coast of Rakhine and a 3.2 billion industrial park nearby. This would facilitate China's Belt and Road Initiative. Beijing is also a major supporter of the 3.6 billion dollar Myitsone Dam project. China is an important player in Myanmar's timber industry. The expulsion of Rohingyas is to facilitate the Chinese project, it is argued.

To sum up, the historical processes of nation- and state-building projects of the Myanmar government and concomitant erasure of citizenship rights, precarious living conditions, and the subjectivity and identity formation of the Rohingyas within and outside their homeland form the core analysis of the chapters.

Structure of the Book

In the introductory chapter titled **Contextualizing Citizenship, Nationalism, and Refugeehood of Rohingya** Nasreen Chowdhory and Biswajit Mohanty examines historically the changing definition of refugees. The changing definition, according to authors, indicates historically generative conditions, the geographical and political contexts and normative and empirical considerations behind understanding refugee crises and issues. It becomes an interesting epistemological exercise to examine how the changing definition of refugees has overcome "methodological territorialism" inherent in the world system perspectives (Audebert & Dorai, 2010) and to pave way for "methodological nationalism" (Wimmer & Schiller, 2003) for studying refugee issue. The introduction also provides the historical background to understand the Rohingya crises and weaves it with the question of citizenship rights and nationalism not only within Myanmar's political economy but also in Southern Asian states.

Shamna Thacham Poyil in Chap. 2, on **National Identity and Conceptualization of Nationalism Among Rohingya**, examines the discourse on nationalism that establishes contested terrains of identity formation among Rohingyas. The emphasis on the primordial nationalist tendency among Burmese state created alterity among Rohingyas to yearn for a basic set of rights that would instill a "sense of belonging" among them. She explores how the Rohingyas are trying to negotiate and renegotiate, shape and reshape the notion of nationalism in their everyday life.

Chapter 3 on **The Unmaking of Citizenship of Rohingyas in Myanmar by** Meghna Kajla and Nasreen Chowdhory examines the processes and procedures of marking and unmaking of citizens in a post-colonial state. They interestingly argue that the state creates marginal citizens, which is a state between citizens and non-citizens. Marginality, they argue, was achieved by the state by changing Myanmar's Citizenship Act, 1982. Kaveri, in Chap. 4 on The Politics of Marginalization and Statelessness of the Rohingyas in India, interrogates the case study of the Rohingyas refugees settled in Delhi, Mewat, and Jammu. Biswajit Mohanty's Chap. 5 on **Understanding Media Portrayal of Rohingya Refugees** analyses the portrayal of Rohingyas in the visual media in India. Mohanty argues that the media that acquires the power of and control over symbolic resources manufactures consent and consensus within the discourse of "insider" versus "outsider" narrative. It many a time becomes the ventriloquist voice of the state and at other times plays the role of saviour. He concludes that the media, through the interplay of discourse and ideology dialectics, constructed the stereotypical images of Rohingya refugees. Chapter 6 on **Being Stateless and Surviving: The Rohingyas in Camps of Bangladesh**, Sucharita Sengupta, interrogates how forced migration has blurred the boundary between volition and forced migration. Taking the case study of Rohingyas in camps of Bangladesh, she narrates survival strategies among Rohingyas. She argues that the Rohingyas have been using their liminal identity for own benefit in an unfamiliar and hostile environment.

Chapter 7 on **The Assimilation of Stateless Rohingyas in Bangladesh** by Meherun Ahmed, Syeda Nafisa Nawal, Ugyen Samdrup Lhamo and Nhung Tuyet Bui, analyse the socio-economic assimilation processes among Rohingyas in the host country of Bangladesh. Authors with empirical evidence argue that a good number of Rohingyas have been assimilated in Bangladesh by becoming self-employed. Shahana Chowdhury and Ayesha Tasnim Mostafa, in Chap. 8 on **Rohingya Refugees: Risks and Safety in Bangladesh,** describe the risk and safety network among the refugees in an alien country. They highlight the plight and vulnerability of the Rohingya migrants in Bangladesh, especially of girls below the age group of 18 years. They underline the wretched condition of those children who have undergone sexual abuse, trafficking, child labour and child marriage. She illustrates that despite the presence of the United Nations schemes and NGOs' pro-active role children are suffering due to malnourishment in the camps of Cox's Bazar. In Chap. 9, on **Women, Conflict and Conflict Reporting: The Deeply Gendered Discourse on the Rohingya Crisis in the News Websites in India,** Ritambhara Malaviya interrogates the gendered aspect of reporting about the illegal migration and migrants. She, following Galtung, divides the news reporting on Rohingyas into two categories and asserts that how war- or victory-oriented journalism by emphasizing masculinity is degrading the soft journalism, which is considered as a symbol of femininity. Through the nuanced reading of news portals, she unravels the gendered stereotypes and power equation between Rohingyas and their representation in the Indian print media. Mafia Mukta as an experienced freelance jurnalist in Chap. 10, on **Radio in the Lives of Rohingyas in Camps in Bangladesh,** provides an interesting insight into the importance of community radio, Radio Naf, in transforming the life of both Bangladeshi and Rohingya youths by imparting skill through radio programmes. She highlights how by providing space to the Rohingya voices alongside others foreign voices has made things qualitatively different for people to get information regarding availability of aid and disbursement of other benefits in the camp. Nergis Canefe in

Chap. 11, on **New Faces of Statelessness: The Rohingya Exodus and Remapping of Rights,** analyses that the greatest humanitarian crisis in contemporary Asia is the product of the progressive erasure of citizenship of the Rohingyas. Through two central concepts—lawfare and statelessness—she has explored state-induced oppression and segregation of minorities in general and Rohingyas in particular. She concludes that the ongoing cycle of dispossession would continue. In concluding Chap. 12 on **Within a Legal Vacuum, is Repatriation a way forward? Some Theoretical Reflections,** Nasreen Chowdhory and Biswajit Mohanty examine the problems of repatriation.

The Rohingyas are remaining in a continuous state of statelessness in the Southern Asian region. It is a liminal state of existence and consciousness. It embodies the materiality of life-world of a community along with a suspended feeling about the very material existence within a given territory. Belongingness to a place with a disembodied existence and assimilation and assurance from the sovereign with the simultaneous feeling of alienation constitutes liminality. The Rohingyas are placed within a shifting power relationship where once dignified becomes debased and degraded is exalted. Systematic discriminations are sometimes subtly and many a time brazenly practised and normalized. The citizens overpower the state, and the state in connivance with the citizen creates conditions of statelessness.

References

Amin, M. (2018). *'Nobody's Children, Owners of Nothing': Analysing the Indian State's Policy response to the Rohingya refugee crisis*. Delhi: The Hindu Center for Politics and Public Policy.

Amnesty International. (2017). *Caged without a Roof: Apartheid in Myanmar's Rakhine State*. London: Amnesty International.

Anfrel. (2015). Myanmar 2015 General & Local Elections Mission Report https://anfrel.org/wp-content/uploads/2016/08/ANFREL-EOM-2015-Report.pdf.

Arendt, H. (1973). *The origins of totalitarianism*. New York :Harcourt Brace Jovanovic.

Audebert, C., & Dorai, M. K. (2010). International migration in the era of globalization: Recent issues and new concerns for research. In C. Audebert & M. K. Dorai (Eds.), *Migration in a globalised world: New research, issues and prospects*. Amsterdam: Amsterdam University Press.

Balibar, E. (1988). Propositions on citizenship. *Ethics, 98*(4), 723–730. Retrieved January 27, 2020, from www.jstor.org/stable/2380893.

Bellamy, R. (2008). *Citizenship: A very short introduction*. Oxford: Oxford University Press.

Bevir, M. (2008). "What is Genealogy?" *Journal of the Philosophy of History, 2*(3), 263–275.

Benhabib, S. (2004). *The rights of others: Aliens, residents and citizens*. Cambridge: Cambridge University Press.

Bose, S. & Jalal, A. (1998). *Modern South Asia: History, culture, political economy*. London: Routledge.

Bosniak, L. (2000a). Citizenship denationalized (the state of citizenship symposium). *Indiana Journal of Global Legal Studies, 7*(2), 447–508.

Bosniak, L. (2000b). Universal citizenship and the problem of alienage. *Northwestern University Law Review, 94(*3), 963–982.

Bosniak, L. (2002). Constitutional citizenship through the prism of alienage. *Ohio State Law Journal, 63*(1285).

Bosniak, L. (2017). Status non-citizens. In A. Shachar, R. Bauboeck, I. Bloemraad, & M. Vink (Eds.), The Oxford handbook of citizenship. New York: Oxford University Press.

Burke et al. (2017). *The contested areas of Myanmar: Subnational Conflict, aid, and development. The Asia foundation*. https://asiafoundation.org/wp-content/uploads/2017/10/ContestedAreasMyanmarReport.pdf.

Calhoun, C. (2014). Interview with Elliasi Barzoo. Nationalism, cosmopolitanism and statelessness: An interview with Craig Calhoun. *Kurdish Studies, II*(1), 61–74.

Chaudhury, S. B. R., & Samaddar, Ranabir. (2015). *Rohingyas: The emergence of a stateless community*. Kolkata: Calcutta Research Group.

Chaudhury, S. B. R., & Samaddar, R. (2018). *The Rohingya in South Asia*. London: Routledge.

Cheesman, N. (2017). How in Myanmar "National Races" came to surpass citizenship and exclude Rohingya. *Journal of Contemporary Asia*, 1–23.

Chimni, B. (Ed.). (2000). *International refugee law: A reader*. New Delhi: Sage.

Chowdhory, N. (2018). *Refugees, citizenship and belonging in South Asia contested terrains*. Singapore: Springer Nature Singapore.

Chowdhory, N. (2019). Citizenship and membership: Placing refugees in India. In: N. Uddin, & N. Chowdhory (Eds.), *Deterritorialised Identity and Transborder Movement in South Asia*. Springer, Singapore. https://doi.org/10.1007/978-981-13-2778-0_3.

Chung, E. A. (2017). Citizenship in non-western contexts. In A. Shachar, R. Baubock, I. Blomemraad, & M. Vink (Eds.), *The Oxford Handbook of Citizenship*. Oxford: Oxford University Press.

Coles, G. (1985). Voluntary repatriation: A background study. *Paper prepared for the round table on voluntary repatriation*. San Remo, Italy: International Institute of Humanitarian Law/UNHCR.

Crouch, M. (2015). Constructing religion by law in Myanmar. *The Review of Faith & International Affairs, 13*(4), 1–11. https://doi.org/10.1080/15570274.2015.1104961.

Crouch, M. (2018). Dictators, democrats, and constitutional dialogue: Myanmar's constitutional tribunal. *International Journal of Constitutional Law, 16*(2), 421–446, https://doi.org/10.1093/icon/moy056.

Craig, E. (2016). "Who are the minorities? The role of the right to self-identify within the European minority rights framework". *Journal on Ethnopolitics and Minority Issues in Europe, 15*(2), 6–30.

Dahrendorf, R. (1974). Citizenship and beyond: The social dynamics of an idea. *Social Research, 41*(4), 673–701.

De Genova, N. P. (2002). Migrant "Illegality" and deportability in everyday life. **Annual Review of Anthropology, 31**, 419–447. Retrieved January 27, 2020, from www.jstor.org/stable/4132887.

Farrelly, N. (2013). Nodes of control in a South (east) Asian borderland. In D. N. Gellner (Ed.), *Borderland lives in Northern South Asia* (pp. 194–213). Durham and London: Duke University Press.

Farzana, K. F. (2016). Voices of the Burmese Rohingya refugees: Everyday politics of survival in refugee camps in Bangladesh. *Journal of Social Science and Humanities, 24*(1), 131–150. Retrieved from http://repo.uum.edu.my/22199/.

Farzana, K. F. (2017). *Memories of Burmese Rohingya refugees: Contested identity and belonging*. New York: Palgrave MacMillan.

Forchhammer, E. (1891). Arakan, Rangoon, Superintendent Government Printing. https://archive.org/stream/Arakan-Forchhammer-1891/Arakan-Forchhammer-1891_djvu.txt. Accessed June 1, 2019.

Furnivall, J. S. (1948). *Colonial policy and practice: A comparative study of Burma and Netherlands India*. Cambridge: Cambridge University Press.

Galache, C. S. (n.d.). The Rohingya and national identities in Burma. https://www.academia.edu/8424230/The_Rohingya_and_National_Identities_in_Burma. June 1, 2019.

Gellner, D. N. (2013). *Borderland lives in Northern South Asia*. Durham and London: Duke University Press.

Hartling. (1979). 129, *Text of the Statute: Annex to the UN doc*. A/Res/428 (V) (1950)

Hathaway, J. (1991). Reconceiving Refugee Law as Human Rights Protection, *Journal of Refugee Studies, 4*(2), 113–131. https://doi.org/10.1093/jrs/4.2.113.
Htin, K. M. (2007). Historical geography and urbanization in ancient Arakan: The archaeological landscape of the old capitals up to 1400 AD. *Aseanie, 20,* 55–73.
Ibrahim, A. (2016). *The Rohingyas: Inside Myanmar's hidden genocide*. London: Hurst and Company.
Imtiyaz, Y. (2017). Nationalist ethnicities as religious identities: Islam, Buddhism, and citizenship in Myanmar. *American Journal of Islamic Social Science 34*, 101–119.
Inter-Section Coordination Group. (2019). Situation Report Rohingya Refugee Crisis, Cox Bazar. https://www.humanitarianresponse.info/sites/www.humanitarianresponse.info/files/documents/files/sitrep_march_2019.pdf.
Internally Displaced Persons. https://www.unhcr.org/4444afce0.pdf. Accessed May 26, 2019.
Joint Response Plan For Rohingya Human Crisis. (2019, January–December). http://reporting.unhcr.org/sites/default/files/2019%20JRP%20for%20Rohingya%20Humanitarian%20Crisis%20%28February%202019%29.comp_.pdf Accessed 5 May 2019.
Jillani, A. F. K. (2007). *A Short History of Rohingya and Kamans of Burma, Myanmar, Kaladan News & Network*. http://www.burmalibrary.org/docs21. Accessed May 7, 2019.
Kabeer, N. (2005). *Inclusive citizenship: Meanings of expressions*. New Delhi: Zubaan.
Kibreab, G. (1987). *Refugees and development in Africa: The case of Eritrea*. Trenton: The Red Sea Press.
Kyaw, N. N. (2015). Alienation, discrimination, and securitization: Legal personhood and cultural personhood of Muslims in Myanmar. *The Review of Faith & International Affairs, 13*(4), 50–59.
Kymlicka, W. (1995). *Multicultural citizenship: A liberal theory of minority rights*. New York: Oxford University Press.
Kymlicka, W. (2001). *Politics in the vernacular: Nationalism, multiculturalism, and citizenship*. Oxford: Oxford University Press.
Leider, J. (2018). Rohingyas: The history of a Muslim identity in Myanmar. *Oxford Research Encyclopedia of Asian History*, An on-line Journal. https://doi.org/10.1093/acrefore/9780190277727.013.115. https://oxfordre.com/asianhistory/view/10.1093/acrefore/9780190277727.001.0001/acrefore-9780190277727-e-115?print=pdf. Accessed May 7, 2019.
Leider, J. P. (2014). Rohingyas: The Name, The movement, the quest for identity. http://www.networkmyanmar.org/ESW/Files/Leider-Rohingya.pdf. Accessed May 6, 2019.
Marshall, T. (1950). *Citizenship and social class and other essays*. Cambridge: Cambridge University Press.
Nandy, A. (2005). The idea of South Asia: a personal note on post-Bandung blues. *Inter-Asia Cultural Studies, 6*(4), 541–545. https://doi.org/10.1080/14649370500316828.
Parashar, A., & Alam, J. (2019). The national laws of Myanmar: Making of statelessness for the Rohingya. *International Migration, 57*(1), 94–108.
OAU (1974). Convention governing the specific aspects of refugee problems in Africa. https://www.unhcr.org/about-us/background/45dc1a682/oau-convention-governing-specific-aspects-refugee-problems-africa-adopted.htm.
Raffoul, F. (2010). *The origins of responsibility*. Bloomington & Indianapolis: Indiana University Press.
Reed-Danahay, D., & Brettell, C. (Eds.). (2008). *Citizenship, political engagement, and belonging: Immigrants in Europe and the United States*. New Brunswick, New Jersey; London: Rutgers University Press. Retrieved January 27, 2020, from www.jstor.org/stable/j.ctt5hj33r.
Samaddar, R. (1999). *The marginal nation: Transborder migration from Bangladesh to West Bengal*. New Delhi: Sage.
Sassen, S. (1999a). *Guest and aliens*. New York: The New Press.
Sassen, S. (1999b). *Globalization and its discontents: Essays on the new mobility of people and money*. New York: New Press.

Sassen, S. (2017). The Assault on the Rohingya is not only about religion—It's Also About Land. *Huffington Post*. https://www.huffpost.com/entry/rohingya-land-grab-military_b_59b96400e4b02da0e13e79f4?section=us_theworldpost. Accessed July 10, 2019.

van Schendel, W. (2013). Making the most of 'Sensitive' Borders. In David N. Gellner (Ed.), *Borderland lives in Northern South Asia* (pp. 266–275). Durham and London: Duke University Press.

Scholte, J. A. (2005). *Globalisation: A critical introduction*. Palgrave.

Soguk, N. (1999). *States and strangers: Refugees and displacements of statecraft*. Minnesota:University of Minnesota Press.

Somers, M. (2008). *Genealogies of Citizenship: Markets, statelessness, and the right to have rights*. Cambridge, UK: Cambridge University Press.

Soysal, Y. N. (2000). Citizenship and identity in post war Europe. *Ethnic and Racial Studies, 23*(1), 1–15.

Stewart (2008). *Horizontal inequalities and conflict: Under-standing group violence in multiethnic societies*. Hampshire: Palgrave Macmillan

Tahir Ba Tha, M. A. (2007). A short history of Rohingyas and Kamans of Burma (A. F. K. Jillani, Trans.). http://www.burmalibrary.org/docs21/Ba_Tha-Kaladan-News&Network-Myanmar-2007-09-13-A_Short_History_of_Rohingya_and_Kamans_of_Burma-en.pdf. Accessed May 7, 2019.

Taylor, R. H. (2005). Do states make nations? The politics of identity in Myanmar revisited. *South East Asia Research, 13*(3), 261–286.

Tilly, C. (1996). *Citizenship, identity and social history*. Cambridge: Cambridge University Press.

Thawnghmung, A. M. (2016). The politics of indigeneity in Myanmar: competing narratives in Rakhine state. *Asian Ethnicity, 17*(4), 527–547. https://doi.org/10.1080/14631369.2016.1179096.

The Constitution of Burma, 1947. https://www.ilo.org/dyn/natlex/docs/ELECTRONIC/79573/85699/F1436085708/MMR79573.pdf. Accessed June 9, 2018.

Tonkin, D. (2014). The Rohingyan identity-further thoughts. http://www.networkmyanmar.org/ESW/Files/Rohingya-Identity-II.pdf.

Uddin, N. (2019). The State, Vulnerability, and Transborder Movements: The Rohingya People in Myanmar and Bangladesh. In: Uddin N., & Chowdhory N. (Eds.) *Deterritorialised Identity and Transborder Movement in South Asia*. Springer, Singapore.

Uddin, N., & Chowdhory, N. (Eds.). (2019). *Deterritorialised identity and transborder movement in South Asia*. Singapore: Springer.

UN News. (2019). UNHCR: Future of Rohingya refugees in Bangladesh 'hangs in the balance'—UNHCR chief. https://news.un.org/en/story/2019/04/1037421. Accessed May 4, 2019.

UNHCR. *IDP definition emergency handbook*. https://emergency.unhcr.org/entry/250553/idp-definition. Accessed May 26, 2019.

UNHCR. Internally displaced persons. Chapter 7 (pp. 153–200). https://www.unhcr.org/publications/sowr/4444afce0/state-worlds-refugees-2006-human-displacement-new-millennium-chapter-7.html. Accessed May 27, 2019.

UNHCR. (1996). *Handbook: Voluntary repatriation international protection*. Geneva.

UNHCR (2010). Convention and Protocol relating to the Status of Refugees. https://www.unhcr.org/3b66c2aa10.

United Nations High Commissioner for Refugees. (2017). Global Trend: Forced Displacement in 2017, UNHCR. https://www.unhcr.org/5b27be547.pdf. Accessed May 5, 2017.

UN High Commissioner for Refugees (UNHCR). Information note on UNHCR's activities for refugee law promotion, dissemination and training, 11 September 1995, EC/SCP/91, available at: https://www.refworld.org/docid/3ae68cbe8.html [accessed 27 January 2020].

Wade, F. (2017). *Myanmar's enemy within Buddhist violence and the making of a Muslim 'other'*. London: Zed Books.

Walzer, M. (1995). Education, democratic citizenship and multiculturalism. *Journal of Philosophy of Education, 29*(2), 181–189.

Wimmer, A., & Schiller, N. G. (2003). Methodological nationalism, the social sciences, and the study of migration: An essay in historical epistemology. *International Migration Review, 37*(3), 576–610. (Transnational Migration: International Perspectives).

Yusuf, I. (2018). Three faces of Rohingya Crisis: Religious Nationalism, Asian Islamophobia, and Delegitimising Citizenship, Islamika. *25*(3), 517–518).

Zieck, M. (1999). *UNHCR and voluntary repatriation of refugees: A legal analysis*. The Hague:Martinus Nijhoff.

Chapter 2
National Identity and Conceptualization of Nationalism Among Rohingya

Shamna Thacham Poyil

Abstract The discourse on nationalism is a highly contested terrain for Rohingyas, especially to those denied of their Burmese citizenship. The denial of citizenship not only expels them from "state-nation-territory" as argued by Agamben (Homo Sacer. Stanford University Press, Stanford, 1998) but prevents access to basic set of rights that instils a sense of belonging in them. The overt emphasis on primordial nationalist tendency of the Burmese state warrants an introspection on how the Rohingya refugees' conceptualize nationhood and belonging. How do they conceptualize nation? The chapter intends to introspect the theoretical assertions to emphasize on the state-centric discourse of nationalism and focus on the abstraction of nationalism among the very individuals that comprise the nation state. Such an analysis necessitates a deeper understanding on the formation of national identity and the constitution of "self" with respect to nation. The Rohingyas are conveniently an outcast from the nation state that relegates them to physical, territorial and symbolic margins of Burmese nation by deliberately othering them as the "enemy of the state". A bottom-up approach on the conceptualization of nationalism among Rohingya refugees will enable us to understand how the symbols, practices and ideas of shared history, ethnicity and culture that shapes, re-shapes and propagates the notion of nationalism is constantly negotiated in their everyday struggle for survival as a stateless refugee.

Keywords Nationalism · National identity · Burmese Buddhist nationalism · Deterritorialization · Rohingya Muslim

Nation and Nationalism

Nationalism is an elusive concept, drawing from a multiple strands of political thought. "Modernists" such as Gellner, Anderson and Hobsbawn considers nation and

---

S. Thacham Poyil (✉)
Department of Political Science, University of Delhi, New Delhi, India

N. Chowdhory and B. Mohanty (eds.), *Citizenship, Nationalism and Refugeehood of Rohingyas in Southern Asia*,
https://doi.org/10.1007/978-981-15-2168-3_2

nationalism as a consequence of the political, economic or historical context.[1] Gellner and Breuilly (2006) attributes the rise of nationalism to industrialization, while Hobsbawm and Ranger (2006) considers it to be a by-product of French Revolution and Deutsch (1966) finds it as inevitable consequence of revolutionary transformations in social communication.[2] Primordialist nationalists such as Grosby consider nation to be an organic entity and argue that "territoriality" as a primitive and sublime supplement of nation. Ethnosymbolists such as Anthony Smith constitute a midway between modernist and primordial approach. He considers nations to be perennial (Smith, 2009, p. 3) as well as a self-perpetuating ideal that reflect a common "myth of origin, ethno-historical memories of 'golden ages' and national ceremonies" of the past (Smith, 2009, p. 104). Our analysis though does not completely subscribe to any of the above strands tries to deconstruct nationalism towards an understanding of national self. The next few paragraphs will try to comprehend how imperative it is to be recognized by a nation to constitute a national identity.

Nationalism is a manifestation of the human tendency to form territorially distinctive collective groups by distinguishing "us" versus "them" (Grosby, 2005). The constant differentiation of one group from other by explicit separations and the occasional hostility is something that is visible from the time of Plato where he differentiates between "Hellenes" and "Barbarians", and it still extends to the conflicts in the twenty-first century as between Kurds and Turks or Slovaks and Czechs. The formation of nations brought about "nationalism" as an attribute that mandated undisputable loyalty and allegiance to the nation by the constituting individuals. Compared to nationalism, a nation signifies a "territorial community of nativity" which develops a collective memory of a distinctive past that is perpetuated through a shared history (Grosby, 2005, p. 5). According to Grosby (2005), every nation has its own "temporal depth" where present is inevitably conditioned by an understanding of the past. The memories of an individual are the aggregate of the recollection of his development as a person in the society. The everyday conduct and interaction with other fellow beings within the framework of customs and traditions of the nation cause them to identify commonalities such as similar language of speech, observance of similar rituals or even adherence to same laws (Grosby, 2005, p. 9). Thus, the social interaction of the various individuals due to their partaking traditions generates a shared self-cognizance; as it evolves in relation to others. Over time, it plays a significant role in shaping a characteristic culture for the nation. This culture as it develops becomes more distinct by simultaneously evolving margins that differentiate "self" from "other". The nation is then a "social relation of collective self- consciousness" (Grosby, 2005, p. 10).

According to Anderson (1986, p. 133) the primary commonality that precipitated the conception of nation was language and not blood' thereby refutes the significance of ethnic affiliations as the reason for formation of nation. While Anderson acknowledges the role played by communication in cultivating solidarity, scholars

[1] See Gellner and Breuilly (2006), *Nations and Nationalism*; Anderson (1986), *Imagined Communities*; Hobsbawm and Ranger (2006) *Invention of Tradition*.

[2] The observation was comprehended by Gorski in (2000), p. 1428.

like Weber (1978, p. 922) assert that just the language was not sufficient to build solidarity among people to nurture the nationalist sentiments. As much as language could have been a cohesive factor, the widespread usage through both verbal and printed mass media have emphasized the differences between people rather than their constituent commonalities. Weber (1978, p. 923) considers this feeling of "solidarity" among people is to be associated with "memories of a common political destiny".

Just as much as the temporal factor, collective memories of the past are also a function of the spatial factor. The people who co-inhabit a space also trace their commonalities to shared location. This transforms a mere geographical space to the "territory" of the nation that one physically belonged to. Examples of such territorially formed people of a nation that concurrently denoted both territory and its populace can be seen in most of Europe i.e. England, France, Germany etc., indicating the hyphenation between land and its people (Grosby, 2005, p. 11). Various scholars agree to the above-mentioned notion of temporal and spatial commonality observed within the land and its people as a precursor to the nation. Anderson's (1986) approach to consider nation as an "imagined community" of the people who constitute it, Bhabha (2013) to depict nation as a "narration" of the actually lived cultural and social life of individuals, or Deutsch (1966) to portray nation as the assimilation of multiple social mobilization made possible by "social communication" are all exemplifying the significance of people who constitute the territory in forming the nation rather than the territory of sovereign state itself in establishing a nation. This leads us to analyse how the discourse of nationalism assumes significance for any nation state.

Nationalism provided a certain degree of legitimacy to the sovereign power of nation state. Marx (2005) denotes how the cohesion among people facilitated the consolidation of state power. "Forging a complimentary popular allegiance" supplanted the states' effort to strengthen and preserve itself through means other than the employment of force reducing any centralizing tendency that would incite defiance from the natives (Marx, 2005, p. 4). State building sometimes precedes the advent of loyalty and commitment among the territorial people and eventually develops as entities that reciprocally strengthen each other. In this context, Marx (2005, p. 6) defines nationalism as that "collective sentiment or identity, bounding and binding together those individuals who share a sense of large-scale political solidarity aimed at creating, legitimating, or challenging states". For such shared popular sentimentality to transcend to a "historical force", it is necessary to involve state as a potential stakeholder in the evolution of discourse on nationalism (Marx, 2005, p. 6). Nationalism can often precipitate the conversion of the pre-existent popular solidarity to formation of a new state; it can legitimize the existing state power or even confront it in a bid to reconfigure the same state. Whether to validate the state power or to challenge it, nationalism entails in itself the essence of a "nation-state" in which "mass allegiance and institutional power coincide" (Marx, 2005, p. 7). But how does then nationalism impact those who have been excluded from the matrix of "state-nation-territory"? (Agamben, 1998).

their spatial context. Using an agency-based approach, Lluch (2009, p. 2) proposes three types of political alignments exhibited as a part of nationalist assertions generally: independentists-who strive for complete political sovereignty, autonomist-who pursues to obtain self-government/self-administration for their constituent territorial unit by repudiating options of complete independence and federalist—who seeks equality within a larger federal framework of states. The predicament of a stateless nationalist is that they have to opt one of the above three, any of which he cannot subscribe owing to not having a state in the first place. Lluch (2009, p. 2) opines that nationalism generated among the stateless people often creates "concentric political identities" that simultaneously reflects both their commonality in having a sense of national identity and belonging and also the digressing ideas of constitutional politics for the prospect of their community. The precarious context of the stateless people causes them to develop a nationalistic approach that tries to poise a balance between various political, economic and sociocultural aspects of their everyday life of plight. Brubaker (2009, p. 5) has emphasized the significance of political and cultural geography in creating small inconsistencies in the nature of "national self-understanding" in his demonstration of patterns of nationhood. Yet findings show a predominance of political factors in determining the contours of their nationalism even in a nation state framework that is reluctant to accommodate them (Lluch, 2009, p. 16). Apart from the statelessness, the consequent displacement and crossing of borders further obscure the standing of their national identity.

Displacement, Exile and Identity Flux

Migration whether forced or voluntary and consequent deterritorialization has rather become usual order of things in the present times. Though we are largely aware of the various ramifications of such movements across the border, its impact on national identity needs to be analysed. Voluntary migrations are mostly sanctioned within the legal framework of nations constantly monitored under the process of immigration and emigration. The plights of refugees while they cross the borders or their daily hardships once they make into the camps have been etched to the popular memory through images such as that of drowned bodies of Aylan Kurdi and Angie Valeria.[3] Movement across borders often involves more than mere physical translocation of individual bodies, it also resonates the existence of misplaced identities as well. Much of the socially constructed identities disassociates and realigns themselves in

[3]Two-year-old Aylan Kurdi along with his mother and brother drowned to death when the boat that carries the migrants from Turkey to Greece capsized at Turkish coastline. See https://www.nytimes.com/2015/09/04/world/europe/syria-boy-drowning.html.

Oscar Alberto Martinez and his one-year-old daughter Angie Valeria from El Salvador drowned to death during their attempt to cross Rio Grande to bypass US-Mexico border. See https://edition.cnn.com/2019/06/26/politics/mexico-father-daughter-dead-rio-grande-wednesday/index.html. Both these images catalysed public attention on the issue of misery of migrants who try to cross the borders for a better life.

their newly possessed territorial realm. A new collective history emerges from the narratives of not just who moved across the border, but also from those who hosted them. These narratives often challenge each other and, in the process, often shape and reshape the identities they carry. According to scholars like Malkki (1995, p. 11), "interstitial position of refugees in the system of nation-states" often necessitates and enables "the anthropological rethinking of nationness, of statelessness and of the interconnections between historical memory and national consciousness".

The indispensability of territory for the constitution of identity is emphasized by scholars like Wolff (2001), who opines that an individual's identity is rendered incomplete on losing the spatial component. Malkki (1995) similarly describes identity as a construct that is "historical essence rooted in a particular place". A similar perspective is mirrored in the works of scholars like Uddin (2019, p. 13) considers deterritorialization as a concept that signifies the mobility of people across territorial borders "as part of globalisation process through mediatisation, transnational connection and everyday cultural practices". Though speaking on the context of education, scholars like Robertson, Bonal, and Dale (2002) postulate that the shift on a spatial scale creates hyphenated practices of deterritorialization and reterritorialization. When someone transcends the spatial boundary of a state, they simultaneously leave one territory and enter the other (Uddin, 2019, p. 17).

The spatial fixation of identity is theorized as "place identity" by scholars like Proshansky, Fabian, and Kaminoff (1983) who points out the interaction of self with physical social world signifying the spillover effects on spaces and places in which one is found. Such perspectives on identity strengthen the view that on crossing borders, their habits, culture and identity is tampered with (Stein, 1981). The notion of refugee as a "naked unaccommodated man" (Turner, 1967) or a stateless who has "the abstract nakedness of being nothing" (Arendt, 1973, p. 300) is equally about the loss of his identity as much as his other vulnerabilities. The deterritorialized refugees are those who undergo the "rite of passage" (Gennep, Vizedom, Caffee, & Kertzer, 1960) by being separated from their place of origin until they get assimilated in the host society or repatriated to the state of origin. Though earlier formulated by Van Gennep, Turner (1967, p. 95) further elaborates the notion of "rites of passage" to suggest that the temporal phase in the process as a "liminal period" that constitutes "structural invisibility" which renders the refugees "structurally invisible, if not physically". This structural invisibility that they acquire on crossing of borders can be simultaneously aligned to the forfeiture of culture and identity.

People cross the borders and transcend their territorial rootedness not as a voluntary action, but rather as an act induced by the vulnerable conditions created by the state (Turner, 1967, p. 83). The distinct categories perpetuate the exclusion by the state, often prompting these hapless individuals to undertake a "forced migration" necessarily making them "refugees" or illegal immigrants determined by the spaces they land in for protection. Based on an empirical study, Uddin (2019, p. 73) describes the ways in which statelessness creates the conditions that make people vulnerable and how this vulnerability in turn forces them to undertake transborder movement. By asserting that their vulnerability was "state-created", he compares the gravity of the "vulnerability" of Rohingyas as akin to "bare life" of Agamben, "state of insecurity" suggested by Isabell Lorey and "precarious life" put forth by Judith Butler (Uddin, 2019, p. 75). Nasir Uddin (2019, p. 75) differentiates deterritorialization from deterritorialized identity in that it is a identity that loses its spatial or geographic component due to the crossing of border. MacLean (2018) similarly depicts the deterritorialization as "progressive erasure of home" of Rohingyas. She has used two concepts of lawfare and spacio-cide to explain how there is "progressive erasure of citizenship" that mutually reinforces the "progressive erasure of home" for Rohingyas (MacLean, 2018, p. 85). Here MacLean (2018) elaborates on the various tactics and strategies such as denial of citizenship, used by state of Myanmar to render them deterritorialized. These people have to daily live and relive the trauma of having to function or rather merely survive in a space surrounded by perpetual hostility. It is a continuum for stateless people for whom the plight of being the "unwanted" in the place one has sought for refuge is just an extension of being alien in the place they belonged to. While immigrants try to renegotiate the asymmetry in the subjection of rights, refugees grapple with the ambit of protection that they receive in the host state. The stateless people on the other hand have their very existence denied with no state to acknowledge their origin, no state to protect them and no state to advocate for them. The territorial rootedness of identity and its sedentary bias is even more problematic for stateless like Rohingyas, as even in crossing the borders, and taking refuge their condition of unterritoriality remains the same. That is to say, they were neither to claim the part of the territory from which they crossed the border, nor could they expect to be a part of the territory that they crossed over to. Their statelessness puts them into a continuous state of suspended animation. Hence, it is vital to understand the ambit of Rohingyan identity within the context of Burmese nationalism even before they crossed the border to comprehend how it has been altered later.

Nationalism and Construction of Burmese Identity in Post-colonial Burma

The discourse of nationalism in Myanmar both among the Rohingyas and majority Buddhists should be analysed in an historical continuum. The administrative policies of British in Burma as well as the later marginalizing policies brought about by military junta should be introspected with respect to the historical context in post-colonial Burma. There is a need to deconstruct the multi-layered narrative of nationalism of both the stakeholders and locate the emergence of ethno-religious nationalism in Myanmar. Origin of the ethno-religious nationalism and consequent violent conflict in Myanmar consist of two conflicting narratives of Buddhists and Rohingyas. Kipgen (2013) believes Rohingyas to be descendants of the Muslim Turks, Arabs and Persians who were settled in pre-colonial Burma as soldiers and trading communities. According to Ullah (2011), as of 1784, Rohingyas essentially belong to Muslim Kingdom of Arakan and have been assimilated to Buddhist Burma and a segment of these Rohingyans migrated then to Coxs Bazar region of Bangladesh. Whereas Coates (2014) explains Burmese Buddhist belief that existence of Rohingyas as an after-effect of colonial administration that increased the influx of migrants into Burma, such an influx combined with the porous borders caused the movement of a significant number of Muslims in Bengal to cross to Rakhine state in Myanmar that borders current Bangladesh. Coates (2014) also signifies the tension caused by the resource scarcity such as an abrupt increase in race for land caused by influx of wealthy Indian Chettiar communities in Burma who controlled British economic administration in Burma. The change in demography of the region combined with the economic distress caused the non-affluent Buddhists to be gradually ousted from their homes. So the Buddhist narrative traces the enstrangement and hostility against the "outsider Bengali Muslims" to British administrative policies. The military regime in post-colonial Burma wanted to instigate a pride in their ancient past and integrate this historical memory in constructing Burmese nationalism (Blackburn, 2010). Even though Myanmar was subjected to military rule in the later years, Buddhist monks wielded an undue influence in shaping Burmese nationalism by linking it to Buddhist religious identity (Ullah, 2011). Scholars like Alam (2017) have a given broad classification of nationalism as a civic and ethnic in which civic nationalism entails conceptualization of nation as an unbiased and political entity whereas ethnic nationalism provides an understanding of nation as a characteristically cultural entity. It can be established from the following section that the trajectory of nationalism in Myanmar fits to that of ethnic nationalism that tries to cultivate an ethnically homogenous population.

Eriksen (1993) opines that certain conditions such as fluidity across borders, consequent alterations from the usual, potential risk on boundaries and rivalries for the acquisition of resources—all of these furthers the consolidation of nationalist tendencies based on ethnic identities. He further substantiates the evident parallels between nationalist theories and ethnicity-oriented anthropological research to affirm the perspective of "nationalism as a metaphoric kinship" (Eriksen, 1993, p. 108). By extrapolating the basic tenets of kinship to nation, the members forge a bond of social cohesion to an otherwise nonfigurative group. Most of the dominant nationalisms are those that have successfully linked the "ethnic ideology with functional state apparatus" (Eriksen, 1993, p. 109). Buddhist-Burmese nationalism in Myanmar as it exists today has exemplified this in the manner in which "*taing-yin-tha*" *(national race)* is conceptualized by combining ethnic and religious identities (Haacke, 2016). *Taing-yin-tha* largely should be understood as a group identity-based categorization rather than individual identity-oriented. This is so because an individual despite having documentation to prove his residence in Burma even before 1823, they could not consider as Taing-yin-tha if his ethnic group was not included. Identity serves as a marker for exclusion for most of the marginalized throughout the world. Yet, the same identity offers the basis for constituting their "self" among others and claiming the rights.

Addressing them as "illegal Bengali-Muslim immigrants" rather than Rohingya symbolizes their simultaneous ethnic and religious differentiation from the accepted Buddhist-Burmese national. The Buddhist religious component of nationalism in

Myanmar denotes the criticality of religion in the conceptualization of nation (Barker, 2009). It would be wrong to assume that the marginalization of Rohingya is based only on the aspect of religion as there other non-Rohingya Muslims such as Pahu Muslims, Panthay, Zerbadees and Kamans who have been provided with the citizenship of the state (Kyaw, 2015). Hence, it can be stated that it is the confluence of both ethnic and religious identity that has been used by the state to discriminate against the Rohingyas. The prevalence of religious nationalism is a clear deviation from the Western notion of constructing state by separating religion from public sphere and relegating it to private sphere (Friedland, 2001). Religious affiliation has often found its match in pairing with ethnicity in forming a social order in many ethnic communities as in the case of Buddhist-Sinhalese in Sri Lanka. Often religions like Buddhism and Islam have blurred demarcation of the private and the public causing certain oriental cultures to perceive both the personal life and social life as regulated by guiding principles of the religion (Friedland, 2001). In this context, it is apt to consider Juergensmeyer's (2010, p. 265) observation that the present times showcase the prospects for an amalgamation between religion and nationalism, "making them not only rivals but also allies for social order". The association between religion and nationalism can be substantiated by both of their necessity to preserve their identity by inculcating a public mandate that permits to wield authority (Friedland, 2001). Both find "othering" where the differentiation and segregation of those who do not belong as central to constitution of their identity. They also find a commonality that both religion and nation eventually create institutionalized structures like groupings and organization that subtly instils a sense of fraternity in them (Kinnvall, 2004). Eventually, the features that signify religious values transform to symbolic representations of nationalism generating a mutually reinforcing identity (Kinnvall, 2004).

The uncertainty and political instability in Myanmar offered a platform for Buddhism to forge a "new national consensus and new kind of leadership" (Juergensmeyer, 2010, p. 268). Surfacing of movements such as "969" in 2012 and "MaBaTha" in 2014 saw the bolstering of Buddhist nationalism in Myanmar. "969" movement spearheaded by decentralized Buddhist monks aimed at building a counter-narrative to the usage of "786" as symbolic representation among Muslims. They started popularizing the numerological representation of "969" which signified the nine noble virtues of Buddha, six attributes of "dhamma" and nine for the "sangha" which was formerly used in the Ashokan pillar edicts (Arai, 2013). Similarly, "MaBa Tha" indicated the congruence of Burmese national, religious and ethnic identity with Buddhist constructs. "MaBaTha" was epitomized such that: "*-myo* is a variant on *lu-myo*, which is alter- nately understood as ethnicity or race; *batha,* in this case, refers to religion; and *thathana* is the Burmese rendering of *sasan*a, the Pali word for the Buddhist tradition as a whole" (Walton and Hayward, 2014, p. 27). Many such major and minor instances of mobilization among the Buddhist monks such as those led by U Wirathu also called as the "militant monk" was a testimony towards explicit "othering" of Rohingyas and perpetuating a national rhetoric that portrayed Rohingyas as foreigners (Mahtani, 2013).

Articulation of Rohingya as "Rakhine Muslim"

The multidimensionality associated with the construct of identity, mostly renders ambivalent identities for the vulnerable like refugees and the stateless. According to Ross Bond (2006) rules, customs and traditions within a specific territory determine the various aspects of identity of an individual and this could in turn validate their legality within the same borders. The national identity of Rohingya has been created and contested over time by the pre-colonial Burma, colonial administration of British Burma and post-colonial nation building of Myanmar. Provision of citizenship though is a vital aspect for their integration, denial of the same will not be sufficient to decipher the structurally embedded patterns of cultural, socioeconomic and political marginalization prevalent in Myanmar. Hence, it is necessary to analyse the formation of Rohingya identity and its present perpetuation both in a historical perspective as much as in the current scenario.

As mentioned before the lineage of Rohingyas could be traced back to the presence of Arab and Persian traders who settled in the Arakan region owing to the contiguity with coastal belt that gave them access to Bay of Bengal which was facilitative for their trading enterprise (Yegar, 1972). Proximity to Indian Ocean resulted in the expanding trade relations among Malabar of South India, Malacca, Burma, Sri Lanka and Bengal for these traders (Khan, 1936).[4] The predominance of Muslims in the Arakan region and their restricted interaction with interior Burma owing to the physical parting by Arakan Yoma mountain provided these Muslim inhabitants with a characteristic "spatial identity" and aided the "sociological formation of a different unified entity" (CK & CS, 2018, p. 86). The gradual alliance between Muslim Sultans of Bengal with Mrauk-U Buddhist kingdom of Arakan (Bhattacharya, 1927) resulted in the increasing influence of Islam among the latter, which was evident in their adoption of Muslim names (Jilani, 1999). Scholars like Blackburn (2000) establish the peaceful co-existence of various religions like Buddhism, Hinduism and Islam in seventeenth century till the conquest and annexation of Arakan Kingdom by Burmese ruler Bodawpaya in 1784 (CK & CS, 2018). The Arakanese were subjected to massacre and oppression forcing them to migrate to Bengal region of British India towards the end of the seventeenth century (Harvey, 1967).

Colonial British administration further facilitated the hostility between Burmese and the Arakanese by designating Arakan region as the buffer zone of British Empire and following an instrumentalist policy of constructing categorical identities by forming artificial fault lines between various ethno-religious groups (CK & CS, 2018). Scholars such as Taylor (2015) and Steinberg (2006) shows the ways in which British colonial administration undertook the census activities in Burma and categorized people based on the language they spoke rather than racial attributes or ancestry (Kyaw, 2015). This in retrospective facilitated the divide between Bengali-speaking population of Arakan and the Burmese speaking majority Bamar population in colonial Burma. Consequently, this also added a linguistic component to the formation of

[4]Khan (1936), as seen in The Muslim of Burma: A Study of Minority Groups as seen in Yegar (1972).

Rohingyan identity apart from the existing spatial affiliations of their identity with the geographical regions of Arakan and British Bengal. Malkki (1992) refers to such associations between people and places where specific boundaries are often hyphenated with the individual's identity as "sedentarist metaphysics" denoting the need to analytically look beyond such essentialist construct of identities.

The independence of Burma from British in 1948 led to the well-calibrated manufacturing of Myanmar as a nation state based on a homogenous ethno-religious group was undertaken by the various governments of post-colonial Burma. This has caused the ousting of those who do not fit into the predetermined contours of idyllic nation state. Despite the integration projects and the liberal policies initiated by leadership such as U Nu and Aung San, marginalization of Rohingyas to the peripheries had been set to motion by pitching Bamar Burmese Buddhists as "us" against Rohingyas as "them". The multiple political measures undertaken by government of Myanmar posed a systematic trajectory to deprive them of their rights and to exclude them. In Myanmar, the identity of Rohingya is that of a Muslim minority where the state has used biased and unjust categorization to demarcate the religious minorities and the national law supports this marginalization by providing them with an ambiguous judicial status (Alam, 2017). But what sanctions their exclusion as stateless is their ethnic identity as Rohingya rather than their religious minority Muslim identity alone. It is here than we can parallel the emergence of Rohingya identity as a "resistance identity" that was being reciprocally developed to counter the "legitimizing identity" of Bamar Buddhists (Castells, 2010, p. 8). Castells (2010, p. 8) conceptualizes "legitimizing identity" as deeply embedded in the established power relations of the specific society and introduced by the prevailing group "to extend and rationalize their domination vis à vis social actors". "Resistance identities" on the other hand are instituted by the repressed group so as to offset the subjugation inflicted on them by the dominant actors thereby "building trenches of resistance and survival on the basis of principles different from, or opposed to, those permeating the institutions of society" (Castells, 2010, p. 9). The identity exclusions by nation state mediated by majoritarian Bamar Buddhists caused Rohingyas to undergo a systematic "space deterioration process" rendering them incomplete citizens in any societal framework (CK & CS, 2018, p. 84). This systemic exclusion reached its climax in the promulgation of 1982 citizenship law, by legally sanctioning the exclusion through the mandate that only those who belonged to a national race (taing-yin-tha) could be a citizen. Notwithstanding the substantial existence of Rohingyas within Myanmar for centuries, the government refuses to identify Rohingya as a *taingyintha*, leaving them nationless and consequently a stateless refugee.

Unlike many other ethno-religious conflicts that aim to establish an autonomous region or sovereign territory, the struggle of the Rohingyas is largely one of equal recognition. For a group that is not even acknowledged by the government among the 135 different indigenous ethnic groups of Myanmar, demand for an autonomous region is nevertheless a far cry. Let alone territorial autonomy, in order to claim any bundle of basic rights, primarily their existence within the territorial borders of Myanmar ought to be recognized by the state. The demands drawn up by the refugees of Kutupalong refugee camp who also represented 40 villages from Rakhine conflict area which was submitted to Ms. Yanghee Lee[5] (the UN special rapporteur on the human rights situation in Myanmar) on January 2018 was indicative of their above-mentioned struggle for equal recognition. Their demands included "citizenship and equal rights to Rohingyas"[6] apart from providing them with a "nationality card" before undertaking repatriation and that their original property and earlier inhabited land in Arakan region of Myanmar be returned to them.[7] If at all one can perceive any mite of nationalism in their aforementioned demands or even in their daily struggles of existence—it is only their desire to reclaim the right to be part of the very nation they belong to—Myanmar.

Cresa Pugh through the ethnographic study that she undertook in Kutupalong and Teknaf refugee camp in Bangladesh tried to analyse how Rohingyas understood the "concepts that seem to undermine their very existence".[8] Some of them even understood that the contestations in their identity emanated from the categorical divisions fabricated by colonial administrations of Burma (Pugh, 2019). She postulates that their comprehension of the Rohingyan ethno-cultural identity is based on the larger ethno-political context in Myanmar that caused their conflict. This is reflected in statements from interviewees such as Ko Myo who said "Where we are from, race and religion are the same" (quoted in Pugh, 2019). They also acknowledge the ethno-religious nationalism in Myanmar by conceding that the conjunction between religion and ethnicity has been instrumental in their systematic exclusion from Myanmar (Pugh, 2019). When asked how they would identify themselves, most of them responded as "Rohingya Muslim/Myanmar Islam/Rohingya Myanmar/Islam, Muslim" (quoted in Pugh, 2019). Their experiences had caused them to understand that one ought to be a member of an indigenous race or religion of the land to effectively be a national of any country. This also demonstrates the success of the primordial identity-based nation building undertook by the ruling elites of Myanmar such that it has been internalized and perpetuated not just by those who are included, but even by those who were excluded.

As evident from the multiple interviews and case studies, Rohingyas remember most of the discriminations they underwent—restrictions on movement, forced labour, heavy taxes on marriage, false accusations, confiscation of land and property, destruction of religious settlements, eviction from land and villages, forced relocation to specific areas, physical torture[9]—all emanating from the deprivation of citizenship making them less than equal to others (Farzana, 2017, p. 105). These individual memories of various refugees constitute the "social memory of Rohingyas" (Farzana, 2017) as all of them are equally positioned in their past and shapes their collective

---

[5]As per the news article in Reuters https://in.reuters.com/article/myanmar-rohingya-petition/exclusive-rohingya-refugee-leaders-draw-up-demands-ahead-of-repatriation-idINKBN1F80SH. Accessed July 14, 2019.

[6]Arab News http://www.arabnews.com/node/1405901/world. Accessed July 14, 2019.

[7]E-International Relations https://www.e-ir.info/2018/04/05/nationalism-persecution-and-repatriation-of-the-rohingya/. Accessed July 16, 2019.

[8]Pugh (2019).

[9]These factors were elaborated in detail by Kazi Fahmida Farzana in *Memories of Burmese Rohingya refugees-Contested Identity and Belonging,* Palgrave Macmillan (2017) from page 91–105.

memory. Durkheim's (2013) conceptualization of "collective memory" was further expounded in the works of Halbwachs, and it attempts to explain the ways in which communities and societies construct and perpetuate memories (Coser, 1992). The collective memory of the past in Rohingyas conditions their identity in the present. According to Dickinson (1997, p. 21), the function of memory is not limited to an abstract emotive process, rather it is also a spatial and corporal process that situates both the person and the territory inside a "stabilizing past". Collective memories of the shared past and the aspirations for a secure future incessantly demolish, assemble and reassemble the boundaries in the realm of identity construction. Despite the uncertainty in their lives of exile and refuge, their identity as a "rohingya refugee" was embedded in their narratives of the past. Some of them explicitly express their desire to return "home" to Myanmar once the violence subsides and such a desire is despite the knowledge that they would not be able to retrieve what they had lost in Rakhine. As quoted by Farzana (2017), refugees such as Hamza Mohammed say: "*I miss my home. If I close my eyes, I can vividly see my town just the other side of the River Naff. I can see my home, but I cannot go there*". Their connection to "home" is a poignant subject which is now restricted to their memory from past and their yearning for a secure future. Their desire for homeland is blurred by the vicious cycle of exclusion, exile and refuge they undergo on a daily basis.

Farzana (2017) "Taranas"/poems sung by the Rohingya refugees in her attempt to record "music and art as symbols of their identity and everyday resistance". Such casual aspects of daily life like songs and art forms become the alternative ways in which grief and plight are articulated among the vulnerable themselves. As Scott (1985, p. 33) observes, covert informal resistance becomes the routine space of struggle for the disadvantaged who have been ousted from the ambit of overt institutionalized politics. These unconventional means of resistance become a part of narrative through which they register their defiance. The narratives that are thus developed when they often get enacted and re-enacted through art forms like music, plays a significant role in shaping the collective identity. A textual analysis of the "taranas" provides insights on rudiments of the nature of national identity cherished by Rohingyas.

O fellow Rohingya lend me your ears,
Come to a mission O dear

Let's fight with the Mogs of Burma
And let's build our golden Arakan.
—Ismail Hossain (Farzana, 2017, 193).

In the land where we are born,
My native Arakan take my thousands salutes
O o o … we are sons of mother Arakan

For the hatred of our step-brother, strangers we became
Didn't get peace in mother's lap even we are her sons
—Molla Kamal from Nayapara camp (Farzana, 2017, 198).

Apart from their desire to return to the homeland, these couplets also reflect the conceptualization of an Arakan identity that they nurture. These lines also mirror their anguish towards the majority for alienating them in their own motherland. As suggested by Brodsky (1992, p. 221), such art forms not only challenge the imperfection of the given reality, but also offer an opportunity to form an alternative reality. It can be inferred that their affirmation of identity as an "Arakan Muslim" is also an effort to create an alternative reality by responding to the estrangement that they had to undergo due to the assertion of Buddhist nationalism. Othering the rest of the Burmese as "step-brother" is also a component of differentiation and segregation, which is central to any identity formation. Dichotomy of domination by the powerful and subjugation of the vulnerable is also a recurrent theme in most of the music and art produced by Rohingyas in various campsites (Brodsky, 1992, p. 224).

Leider (2018) opines that until twenty years back, Muslims from the Rakhine region were only occasionally or rather less frequently referred to as "Rohingyas". The non-refutable acceptance of the term "Rohingya" among the international fora, humanitarian agencies, media and public at large, reflects the "informal recognition of the right of self-determination" of an assemblage of hapless individuals who have been imperilled through constant persecution instituted by the state (Leider, 2018, p. 17). Incorporation of Buddhist fundamentalism with the immediate partisan politics of the state of Myanmar has led to the emergence of Burmese Buddhist nationalism that has been used to provide legitimacy to their rule. Houtman (1999) explains how the post-colonial "Burma" transitioned to the state of "Myanmar" by adopting constructs such as *taing-yin-tha* in a process he refers to as "Myanmafication". But this process should be seen as an attempt to connote the Burmese Buddhists as the predominant ethno-religious and linguistic group of Myanmar. As Cheesman (2017, p. 467) observes that for one to belong to Myanmar, one had to "to speak and read the language of the Burman, to be civilised and cultured like a Burman was nothing other than to belong to Myanmar, which is to say, to be *taingyintha*". This attempts to forge a "mythic unity" at the cost of confuting the ethnic and cultural diversity of Myanmar is mirrored in the way the Constitution of Myanmar uses the term "the collective people of taingyintha" instead of addressing them as "people of the nation" (Holliday, 2014, p. 410). Cheesman (2017, p. 470) hence rightly observes that by instituting a tangible and concrete rapport between national race and citizenship, the constitution lets the abstract notion of national race transcend the construct of citizenship and thereby become the "gold standard for membership in the political community of Myanmar". Consequently, groups like Rohingyas who were not designated as *taingyintha* were denied citizenship, making them stateless. Their exclusion from the above-mentioned "state-nation- territory" matrix (Agamben, 1998) obliges them to determine their way to reclaim the membership of the nation state by constructing and perpetuating their collective identity as "Rohingya".

Scholars such as Clifford (1988, p. 270) conceptualize identity in two ways—that is individual and collective. While individual identity corresponds to a person's understanding of himself, collective identity refers to the way in which he similar to others in a group. The historical narrative of Rohingyas is vital in their establishment of "Muslim political self-affirmation" along with the gradual development of their collective identity (Leider, 2018, p. 17). In *National Identity and the Role of the "other" in Existential Conflicts*, Kelman (2005, p. 5) stresses the continued significance of "integrity of collective identity" for the assertion of national identity of any group. He opines that the "integrity of national identity is an end in itself" as the unanimity, permanence and feeling of "belongingness" for the members of any group are based on this identity (Kelman, 2005, p. 5). Apart from the claim for ownership and use of resources, the motive for developing and nurturing the distinctive attributes of one's own group without being assimilated is also based on the acceptance of one's national identity. Hence, recognizing and accepting the identity of the "other" and their associated narrative become equivalent to denying the existence of one's specific group (Kelman, 1999). Such a denial of the narrative as seen in contrasting Israeli or Palestine narratives for the claim of territory and its resources is not seen in the case of Rohingyas (Kelman, 2001). Denial of Rakhine Buddhists or majoritarian Burmese Buddhists does not seem to be integral to Rohingyas to assert their narrative of collective identity. This perception of potential threat and denial of other's narrative of identity is often bolstered by the presence of religious differences in addition to ethnic differences (Kelman, 2001). Kelman (1997, p. 329) postulates that such identities are based on concurrent negation of the other showcases "an exclusivist and monolithic character where all dimensions of the group's identity-such as ethnicity, religion and language tend to be highly correlated". Such a construction of national identity that is monolithic and exclusive fits the description of Burmese Buddhist identity rather than Rohingyas as it focuses on negating the existence of the Rohingyas from Myanmar and denying them any claims to the fair share in land or any resources of the state where as Rohingyas base their identity on co-existence and equal recognition through the acquisition of citizenship. According to Malkki (1995, p. 4), displacement and consequent deterritorialization result in two possible scenarios—the vulnerable groups like refugees in camps attempt to "fit" into the predominant national scheme of things, by aspiring to another "nation", or on the other hand there might be a "subversion of identification" where they rebuff any attempt to be categorized as any one national identity. Rohingyan refugee identity does not categorically belong to either of these two scenarios completely; they seem to ascertain their "Rohingya Muslim" identity without aspiring to be a separate nation.

Conclusion

Identities are constructed and often become responsive when they are co-opted or even contradicted by societal and collective dynamics for a variety of reasons (Castells, 2010). Rohingyan identity that had developed through self-construction in pre-colonial and colonial period was metamorphosized as a "resistive identity" in response to the exclusion subjected on them as a part of homogenized state building in post-colonial Burma. Reiterating my earlier observation, they yearn for equal recognition as a Burmese national whose individuality as a Rohingyan Muslim would be acknowledged by the state of Myanmar. Rather than challenging, the narrative of Rohingya identity and its claim to be a part of the Myanmar only seems to reassert the construct of "national race" or *taingyintha.* The actual national identity of stateless individuals has its basis in the collective memory of the community anchored by their sense of belonging and further shaped by their social interactions. Often going beyond the tangible and intangible boundaries created by nation states, the evolution of Rohingyan national identity mirrors their everyday life of resistance against the exclusion imposed on them by Myanmar. Yet, unlike the many minorities who resist the majoritarian nationalist repression by detaching themselves from their original nationality and developing a separate strand of nationalism that counters the majoritarian narrative,[10] Rohingyas strive to carve a niche "rohingyan muslim" identity within the Burmese nationality.

References

Agamben, G. (1998). *Homo Sacer*. Stanford, Calif.: Stanford University Press.

Alam, J. (2017). The Rohingya of Myanmar: Theoretical significance of the minority status. *Asian Ethnicity, 19*(2), 180–210. https://doi.org/10.1080/14631369.2017.1407236.

Anderson, B. (1986). *Imagined communities*. London: Verso.

Arab News. (2018). *Rohingya leaders to visit Myanmar.* http://www.arabnews.com/node/1405901/world. Accessed July 14, 2019.

Arai, T. (2013). Toward a Buddhist theory of structural peace: A case study of Myanmar. In *Asia Pacific Peace Research Association Conference*. Bangkok, Thailand.

Arendt, H. (1973). *The origins of totalitarianism*. Harcourt Inc: New York.

Barker, P. (2009). *Religious nationalism in modern Europe: If god be for us* (pp. 12–45). New York: Routledge.

Beissinger, M. (2002). *Nationalist mobilization and the collapse of the Soviet state*. Cambridge: Cambridge University Press.

Bhabha, H. (2013). *Nation and narration*. New York: Routledge.

Bhattacharya, B. (1927). Bengali influence in Arakan, Bengal past and present. *Journal of the Calcutta Historical Society, 33*(65–66), 139–144.

Blackburn, K. (2010). War memory and nation-building in South East Asia. *South East Asia Research, 18*(1), 5–31. https://doi.org/10.5367/000000010790959857.

Blackburn, T. (2000). *The British humiliation of Burma* (p. 17). Bangkok: Orchid Press.

Bond, R. (2006). Belonging and becoming: National identity and exclusion. *Sociology, 40*(4), 609–626. https://doi.org/10.1177/0038038506065149.

Breuilly, J. (1993). *Nationalism and the state*. Manchester: Manchester University Press.

Brodsky, J. (1992). Poetry as a form of resistance to reality. *PMLA, 107*(2), 220. https://doi.org/10.2307/462635.

Brubaker, R. (2009). *Citizenship and nationhood in France and Germany*. Cambridge: Harvard University Press.

Castells, M. (2010). *The power of identity* (pp. 8–11). Chichester: Wiley-Blackwell.

Cheesman, N. (2017). How in Myanmar "National Races" came to surpass citizenship and exclude Rohingya. *Journal of Contemporary Asia, 47*(3), 461–483. https://doi.org/10.1080/00472336.2017.1297476.

[10]Kurd nationalism can be an example where they elevate their subnational identity to develop a nationalist discourse that validates their effort to create a new nation altogether—Kurdistan.

CK, A., & CS, R. (2018). Institutional strategies of identity constructions and exclusions: Exploring the state of Rohingya Muslims in Myanmar. *Otoritas: Jurnal Ilmu Pemerintahan, 8*(2), 82. https://doi.org/10.26618/ojip.v8i2.1231.
Clifford, J. (1988). *Identity in Mashpee*. Cambridge, MA.: Harvard University Press.
Coates, E. (2014). Sectarian violence involving Rohingya in Myanmar: Historical roots and modern triggers, Centre of Excellence for National Security (RSIS) – Singapore.
Coser, L. (Ed.). (1992). *Maurice Halbwachs: On collective memory*. Chicago, IL: University of Chicago Press.
Deutsch, K. (1966). *Nationalism and social communication: An inquiry into the foundations of nationality* (2nd ed.). Cambridge, (MA), London: M.I.T. Press.
Dickinson, G. (1997). Memories for sale: Nostalgia and the construction of identity in Old Pasadena. *Quarterly Journal of Speech, 83*(1), 1–27. https://doi.org/10.1080/00335639709384169.
Durkheim, E. (2013). *The elementary forms of the religious life—The original classic edition*. Newstead: Emereo Pty Ltd.
E-International Relations. (2018). *Nationalism, persecution and repatriation of the Rohingya*. https://www.e-ir.info/2018/04/05/nationalism-persecution-and-repatriation-of-the-rohingya/. Accessed 16th July 2019.
Eriksen, A., & Sigurdsson, J. (2010). *Negotiating pasts in the Nordic Countries*. Chicago: Nordic Academic Press.
Eriksen, T. (1993). *Ethnicity and nationalism: Anthropological perspectives*. London: Pluto Press.
Farzana, K. (2017). *Memories of Burmese Rohingya refugees—Contested identity and belonging*. [S.l.]: Palgrave Macmillan.
Friedland, R. (2001). Religious nationalism and the problem of collective representation. *Annual Review of Sociology, 27*(1), 125–152. https://doi.org/10.1146/annurev.soc.27.1.125.
Gellner, E., & Breuilly, J. (2006). *Nations and nationalism*. Malden, MA: Blackwell Publishing.
Gennep, A., Vizedom, M., Caffee, G., & Kertzer, D. (1960). *The rites of passage*. London: Routledge.
Gilroy, P. (1990). Nationalism, history and ethnic absolutism. *History Workshop Journal, 30*(1), 114–120. https://doi.org/10.1093/hwj/30.1.114.
Gorski, P. (2000). The Mosaic moment: An early modernist critique of modernist theories of nationalism. *American Journal of Sociology, 105*(5), 1428–1468. https://doi.org/10.1086/210435.
Grosby, S. (2005). *Nationalism*. Oxford: Oxford University Press.
Guibernau, M. (2004). Anthony D. Smith on nations and national identity: A critical assessment. *Nations and Nationalism, 10*(1–2), 125–141. https://doi.org/10.1111/j.1354-5078.2004.00159.x.
Haacke, J. (2016). Myanmar. In B. Alex J & D. Tim, *The Oxford handbook of the responsibility to protect*. Oxford, U.K.: Oxford University Press.
Habermas, J., Cronin, C., & De Greiff, P. (1998). *Inclusion of the other: Studies in political theory*. Cambridge, MA: MIT Press.
Harvey, G. (1967). *History of Burma: From the earliest times to 10 March 1824 the beginning of the English conquest* (pp. 44–45). London: Frank Cass and Co., Ltd.
Hobsbawm, E., & Ranger, T. (2006). *The invention of tradition*. Cambridge: Cambridge University Press.
Holliday, I. (2014). Addressing Myanmar's citizenship crisis. *Journal of Contemporary Asia, 44*(3), 404–421. https://doi.org/10.1080/00472336.2013.877957.
Houtman, G. (1999). *Mental culture in Burmese crisis politics*. Tokyo: Institute for the Study of Languages and Cultures of Asia and Africa (ILCAA), Tokyo University of Foreign Studies.
Huddy, L., & Khatib, N. (2007). American patriotism, national identity, and political involvement. *American Journal of Political Science, 51*(1), 63–77. https://doi.org/10.1111/j.1540-5907.2007.00237.x.
Jilani, A. (1999). *The Rohingyas of Arakan: Their quest for justice* (pp. 32–33). Dhaka: The University Press Limited.
Juergensmeyer, M. (2010). The global rise of religious nationalism. *Australian Journal of International Affairs, 64*(3), 262–273. https://doi.org/10.1080/10357711003736436.
Khan, M. S. (1936). Muslims intercourse with Burma. *Islamic Culture, 10*(3), 409–427.

Kelman, H. (1997). Negotiating national identity and self-determination in ethnic conflicts: The choice between pluralism and ethnic cleansing. *Negotiation Journal, 13*(4), 327–340.

Kelman, H. (1999). The interdependence of Israeli and Palestinian national identities: The role of the other in existential conflicts. *Journal of Social Issues, 55*(3), 581–600. https://doi.org/10.1111/0022-4537.00134.

Kelman, H. (2001). The role of national identity in conflict resolution: Experiences from Israeli-Palestinian problem-solving workshops. In R. D. Ashmore, L. Jussim, & D. Wilder (Eds.), *Social identity, intergroup conflict, and conflict reduction*, pp. 187–212. Oxford and New York: Oxford University Press.

Kelman, H. (2005). National identity and the role of the "other" in existential conflicts: Israeli-Palestinian case. In *Conference on transformation of international conflicts*. Amsterdam. Retrieved from http://citeseerx.ist.psu.edu/viewdoc/summary?doi=10.1.1.561.565.

Kinnvall, C. (2004). Globalization and religious nationalism: Self, identity, and the search for ontological security. *Political Psychology, 25*(5), 741–767. https://doi.org/10.1111/j.1467-9221.2004.00396.x.

Kipgen, N. (2013). Conflict in Rakhine state in Myanmar: Rohingya Muslims' conundrum. *Journal of Muslim Minority Affairs, 33*(2), 298–310. https://doi.org/10.1080/13602004.2013.810117.

Kyaw, N. (2015). Alienation, discrimination, and securitization: Legal personhood and cultural personhood of Muslims in Myanmar. *The Review of Faith & International Affairs, 13*(4), 50–59. https://doi.org/10.1080/15570274.2015.1104971.

Leider, J. (2018). Rohingya: The name and its living archive. *ASEAN Focus ISEAS, 2*, 17–19.

Lluch, J. (2009). *National identity and political identity: Resolving the stateless nationalists' dilemma*. Florence: European University Institute.

MacLean, K. (2018). The Rohingya crisis and the practices of erasure. *Journal of Genocide Research, 21*(1), 83–95. https://doi.org/10.1080/14623528.2018.1506628.

Mahtani, S. (2013). Myanmar plan to curb interfaith marriage gains support. *Wall Street Journal*. Retrieved from http://online.wsj.com/news/articles/SB10001424127887323829104578619462267929512.

Malkki, L. (1992). National geographic: The rooting of peoples and the territorialization of national identity among scholars and refugees. *Cultural Anthropology, 7*(1), 24–44. https://doi.org/10.1525/can.1992.7.1.02a00030.

Malkki, L. (1995). *Purity and exile: Violence, memory and national cosmology among Hutu Refugees in Tanzania*. Chicago: Univ. of Chicago Press.

Marx, A. (2005). *Faith in nation: Exclusionary origins of nationalism*. New York: Oxford University Press.

Proshansky, H., Fabian, A., & Kaminoff, R. (1983). Place-identity: Physical world socialization of the self. *Journal of Environmental Psychology, 3*(1), 57–83. https://doi.org/10.1016/s0272-4944(83)80021-8.

Pugh, C. (2019). How do Rohingya explain concepts that undermine their existence? *The Globe Post*. https://theglobepost.com/2019/04/09/rohingya-social-identity/. Accessed 15 July 2019.

Robertson, Bonal, & Dale, (2002). GATS and the education service industry: The politics of scale and global reterritorialization. *Comparative Education Review, 46*(4), 472. https://doi.org/10.2307/3542181.

Rosenberg, S., & Beattie, P. (2018). The cognitive structuring of national identity: Individual differences in identifying as American. *Nations and Nationalism, 25*(1), 361–384. https://doi.org/10.1111/nana.12416.

Scott, J. (1985). *Weapons of the weak* (p. 33). Haven and London: Yale University Press.

Smith, A. (1991). *National identity*. London: Penguin Books.

Smith, A. (2009). *Ethno-symbolism and nationalism: A cultural approach*. London: Routledge.

Stein, B. (1981). The refugee experience: Defining the parameters of a field of study. *International Migration Review, 15*(1/2), 320. https://doi.org/10.2307/2545346.

Steinberg, D. (2006). *Turmoil in Burma: Contested Legitimacies in Myanmar*. East Bridge: Norwalk.

Taylor, R. H. (2015). *Refighting old battles, compounding misconceptions: The politics of ethnicity in Myanmar today*. ISEAS Perspective, December 15. Singapore: Institute of Southeast Asian Studies.

Turner, V. (1967). Betwixt and between: The liminal period in rites of passage. In V. Turner (Ed.), *The forests of symbols: Aspects of Ndembu Ritual*. Ithaca: Cornell University Press.

Uddin, N. (2019). The state, transborder movements, and deterritorialised identity in South Asia in Nasir Uddin. In N. Uddin & N. Chowdhory, *Deterritorialised identity and transborder movement in South Asia*. Springer.

Ullah, A. (2011). Rohingya refugees to Bangladesh: Historical exclusions and contemporary marginalization. *Journal of Immigrant & Refugee Studies, 9*(2), 139–161. https://doi.org/10.1080/15562948.2011.567149.

Walton, M., & Hayward, S. (2014). *Contesting Buddhist narratives* (p. 27). Honolulu: East West Center.

Weber, M. (1978). *Economy and society*. Berkeley, CA: University of California Press.

Wolff, S. (2001). German expellee organizations between 'homeland' and 'at home': A case study of the politics of belonging. *Refuge, 20,* 52–65.

Yegar, M. (1972). *The muslim of Burma: A study of minority groups* (pp. 37–39). Jerusalem: Hebrew University Press.

Chapter 3
The Unmaking of Citizenship of Rohingyas in Myanmar

Meghna Kajla and Nasreen Chowdhory

Abstract The chapter examines the unmaking of citizens of Rohingyas in Myanmar as a result of nation building. The concept of citizenship is contested, and based on particularity of marking identities—language, religion and sex, and on the other hand, the universal notion of citizenship provides equality to all. But the prevalence of ascribed identity constitutes the basis of exclusion that includes and excludes (Chowdhory in Refugees, citizenship and belonging in South Asia contested terrains. Springer Nature Singapore, Singapore, pp. 43–69, 2018). The central idea is to unravel the religious identity vis-à-vis citizenship discourse, wherein the state marginalizes citizens on the basis of religion, by committing violence against minority communities. The minorities are carved as marginal citizens living on the periphery between the citizens and the non-citizens. In Myanmar, the process was enacted by the changing laws of Citizenship Act of 1982. The chapter interrogates the citizenship discourse of Rohingyas and what constitutes the narrative of marginalisation in Burmese society.

Keywords Citizenship · Identity · Stateless · Minorities · Nation state

Introduction

The idea of unmaking citizens and making citizens stateless has been the key issue of the twentieth century around the globe. The nation states are devising certain norms and criteria to exclude its citizens from seeking rights in their own country. There is a careful precision that state undertakes by involving various arguments of nation building in the true sense of the form, which traces the lineage, in order to establish a state led by majoritarian politics. In the context of South Asian states, Sri Lanka and East Pakistan's[1] experiences of state formation adopted models of cultural homogenization with centralized and strong unitary states. This approach contributed to persistent tensions between political structures and the aspirations

[1]In 1971, the state of Bangladesh was created after East Pakistan seceded from West Pakistan.

M. Kajla (✉) · N. Chowdhory
Department of Political Science, University of Delhi, New Delhi, India

N. Chowdhory and B. Mohanty (eds.), *Citizenship, Nationalism and Refugeehood of Rohingyas in Southern Asia*,
https://doi.org/10.1007/978-981-15-2168-3_3

of some minority groups that often resulted in separatist struggles fuelled by state repression and violence.[2] Sri Lanka developed a "demotic state"—instead of an "independent multi-ethnic polity"—that imposed a discriminatory constitution[3] that did not adequately address the question of minorities in the political system.[4] Subsequently, this constitution provided opportunities to "persecute minorities" when a given problem could have been resolved with effective devolution and power-sharing mechanisms between the provinces and the federal structure.[5] These constitutional shortcomings in protecting minority interests in Sri Lanka were manifested through policies of marginalization against Tamil minorities in Sri Lanka. Consequently, this led to struggle between the Tamil rebel groups and Sri Lankan army resulting in

[2]Chowdhory (2018).

[3]The 1948 Constitution of Sri Lanka provided adequate provisions to counterbalance any attempt of the dominant group (Sinhalese) to seize power. However, the protective mechanisms were gradually diluted in the subsequent Constitutions of 1972 and 1978, which consolidated the dominance of the majority group, as well concentrating executive power in the hands of the President.

[4]In Sri Lanka, the unitary state attempted to create a unified Sinhala identity by imposing the Sinhala language as the national language and Buddhism as the national religion. Thus, overt majoritarianism became apparent when the government in Sri Lanka institutionalized the "Sinhala Only" policy, which predates constitutional change.

[5]The Ceylon Tamils enjoyed certain traditional rights under the communal method of representation provided for in pre-1931 colonial legislature. Moreover, universal adult suffrage granted under Britain in 1931 provided a partial self-governing system of constitutional reforms. However, under the Donoughmore Constitution of 1931, the communal means of representation was changed to territorial. This change did not affect the Ceylon Tamils because they were safeguarded by constitutional protection that prevented any discriminatory legislation, and also the governor had a reserve of powers, including the right of disallowance. Later, the Soulbury Constitution of 1947 completed the process of vesting complete autonomy to conservative leadership. The Reform Commission provided a compromise on the distribution of seats among the Sinhala majority and the ethnic minority; the Ceylon Tamils demanded a 50–50 representative split of seats between the Sinhala and the combined ethnic minorities. In 1957, the Bandaranaike–Chelvanayakam Pact (B-C) was an agreement between Sri Lankan Prime Minister S.W.R.D. Bandaranaike (SLFP) and the leader of the Tamil Federal Party (FP), S. Chelvanayakam, who made several important proposals on devolution and the Tamil language question. Provisions were put forward for the formation of directly elected Regional Councils, which would have jurisdiction over such areas as colonization, agriculture, land and education. Also, Tamils were promised that due recognition would be given to the Tamil language. Bandaranaike tried to offset the rigour of the "Sinhala Only" policy with concessions such as the Tamil Language (Special Provisions) Act, which was enacted in 1958. The B-C pact fell short of any demand for a federal constitution or regional autonomy, or to abrogate the "Sinhala Only" option. Moreover, the B-C pact was largely unimplemented. The Pact of March 1965 between Senanayake and Chelvanayakam essentially reproduced the earlier 1957 pact, with some modifications. This Pact promised to take action under the Tamil Language Special Provisions Act to make Tamil the language of administration and of record in the northern and eastern provinces. Another landmark was the provision on amending the Land Development Ordinance in

steady inflow of refugees to India.[6] In Bangladesh the state pledged to be secular and to uphold the basic rights of its various ethnic minorities, adopted two paths—first, the universal model of state building based on forced assimilation, leading to the expulsion or exclusion of one or more minority groups; and second, the particularistic model of state building that did not emphasize the majoritarian discourse.[7] Citizenship has a prominent role in determining the idea of the majority and minority and subsequent unmaking of citizens. It is this very theoretical debate that has been outlined by scholars like Brubaker (1996) and Wimmer (2002) on ethnic conflicts and nation formation that hold significance. Especially in the context of post-colonial states, it follows a historical trajectory of colonial state and nation building with bringing the social aspects of cultural homogeneity along with the religious majoritarian foundations of nations. While deriving the notion of citizenship that has three fundamental sections of rights, a key in exercising one's citizenship—a state begins to deny civil rights like owning land and property-related issues (Ibrahim, 2018) and then subsequently takes away the social rights like education, ration, health, etc. In the end, it takes away political rights or activities related to political representation which stands as the central to the idea of citizenship. Citizenship rights that a state chooses to give, under the legal, political and social rights, often discriminate between citizens while giving those rights; as each right carries entitlement, accountability, assurance of security and other legal procedures. Therefore, there is a hierarchy of rights; legal and civil rights are the basis of all the other rights that a citizen could access (Janoksi and Gran, 2002). And then there are differentiated rights on the basis of power ideology, Ariely (2011) brings out that rights with low power potential are given to the outsiders, while with high potential power could be given to a citizen. It may be argued that the social rights are on the low point because they cannot be ensured by the state and are mostly provided to minorities in a state. Similarly, legal and political rights that hold state institutions accountable formulate a principle of high potential power rights that may form the basic exclusion of minorities in a state. Benhabib (2004) argues that there are certain rights that form the basis of exclusion for minorities even after a substantiated citizenship. This procedure of taking away rights through precision is the key to unmake citizens.

The chapter is divided into four sections: the first section of the chapter develops on the key debates in the nation formation as foundation for exclusion of minorities and how does a state mark certain minorities to be excluded. The second section develops the idea of political majority and ethnic exclusion of minorities, by empirically interrogating the Rohingyas as an example, and the third section develops on the hierarchy of rights debate and examines how the state finds legal methods to outlaw its citizens. The fourth section brings the Rohingya hypotheses to the centre of the chapter. It brings narratives of the exclusion of Rohingyas and develops an argument

---

order to allot land to the Ceylon Tamils. Also, provisions were made to make land in the north and eastern provinces available to landless persons in the district.

[6]See Chowdhory (2018) for details.

[7]See Footnote 6.

on the citizenship rights that have procedurally been denied to the ethnic minority community. Followed by conclusion with bringing the central argument that careful plan and execution done by nation state, by taking unlawful and lawful actions against minorities, a state can unmake its citizens.

Citizenship—A Form of Exclusion

Citizenship is accomplished by utilizing all the categories of rights[8] that are made available and attained by a citizen. It is accessing of these rights that form the key parameter in measuring the inclusion and exclusion of citizens. Epistemologically, the process of exclusion and inclusion has conditioned citizenship, and states have followed the norms of *Jus Sanguinis* or *Jus Soli* process in terms of its acquisition for citizens within a political community.[9] When states choose between the two forms, it is conditioned by various dynamics pertaining to its history of having adopted one of them along with the idea of hierarchy of rights[10] accessed by a citizen. Specifically, in the context of post-colonial states, state building and majority and minority consensus played a significant role in determining who is to be considered citizen by developing various categories. As noted, it is this practice of exclusion that intertwines with the idea of nationality[11] for the Western context and in post-colonial context with creating minorities and excluding them while the process of state building begins.[12] The idea that the minorities in the land of Myanmar have been differentiated and treated unequally since the formation of the constitution is because of the interplay

[8]Marshall states, "I propose to divide citizenship into three parts. I shall call these three parts, or elements, civil, political and social" and it is these composed of various rights (Marshall, 1950, p. 10). However, there are critiques of the social rights but the foundations of citizenship lies embedded on the articulation of rights.

[9]The literature on the two Jus Soli and Jus Sanguinis is applied by the states variously across the globe to mark a citizen and an outsider on the basis of their history of nation building or how the states have come to exist. Jus Soli gives a person the right to be a citizen of a state on the basis of being born on its land, and Jus Sanguinis comes into existence on the basis of "blood ties". And there are some states have followed the mixture of these two concepts. See Safran (1997).

[10]The literature on hierarchy of rights brings the notion of giving more weightage to civil on which the rest of the rights lie. This notion will be later discussed in the chapter and forms the basis of central argument in the unmaking of citizens. However, theory of multiculturalism in the liberal democracies provides substantive arguments on giving equal treatment to all the citizens irrespective of cultural, ethnic, racial and religious connotations. See Castles (2005), Janoski and Gran (2002: 13–52) and Gutmann (1994).

[11]See Brubaker (1996).

[12]See Chowdhory (2018, p. 44).

of the religion[13] and state building[14] in the country. It is the idea of hierarchy of rights, where certain sections of rights are not accessed by citizens and make him/her on the marginality of citizenship.

The process of attaining citizenship has various historical and political complexities, and to address the notion of unmaking citizens, both these variables are held significant. Egin and Turner (2002) have genealogically, and Turner historically has noted the ideas of inclusion and exclusion to citizenship that are distinctly exercised by nation states (2002, p. 3). The problem of exclusion lies in the very foundations of citizenship as something that includes must as well exclude (Turner & Engin, 2002, p. 5; Stevenson, 2001), in a different context, relating the idea of universalism and particularism within citizenship (Kabeer, 2005, p. 10; Roy, 2016) and in terms of refugees (Chowdhory, 2018, p. 44, 2019, p. 43). To attain membership or in order to become a citizen, some categories of individuals are excluded as the history of citizenship starts with cities (Egin, 2002; Turner, 2002; Barbalet, 2010).[15] This is an ontological problem of the conception of citizenship, but the ideal form of citizenship has been argued to include all the citizens with the categories of rights as civil, political, economic and social propagated by Marshall.[16] On the other hand, as argued by Arendt that every citizen by virtue of being part of a political community and state is the only legitimate authority that can dispense citizenship rights. [17] Now, these two ideas of excluding some citizens and including others do not find a validity in terms of arguments given that a man belongs to some political community, it is rather the idea of to what extent a man may belong bestows on the kinds of rights accessed by him that makes him on the marginality of citizenship.[18] Some citizens are excluded from a nation state and find defined as refugees, stateless, and outsiders. The idea of the chapter is to step back and analyse contextually and specifically locating certain citizens who are excluded and how this exclusion process takes place.

---

[13]In a perspective analysed form the orientalist understanding about various religions. Morrison argued "While orientalist narratives of citizenship construct subjects and practices associated with Islam as anti-political, those associated with Buddhism appear as apolitical—as turning away from the political or a rejection of politics rather than a potential agent of religious contamination of the political" (2014, p. 326). It has often been considered about the Buddhist religion that it was apolitical and was very peaceful, but in a recent works by Morrison (2014), the argument has been constructed as to how the Buddhist monks have played a significant role in the politics of states like Burma, etc.

[14]See Gungwu (2005) for State building in the Southeast Asian countries.

[15]See Barbalet (2010) carves out an understanding of citizenship from the writings of Weber and specifically brings the notion of cities.

[16]To note the central argument of Marshall (1950) that citizenship is a process, always evolving and changing in order to include all the members of the society. It also comes with the critiques from the social rights perspective elaborated by Fraser and Gordon (1994, pp. 90–107), and specifically argued form the perspective of post-colonial citizenship.

[17]Baehr (2002). And see Kajla (2019) on argument nation states being the only authority to dispense rights and at the same time curtail them, and this creates statelessness.

[18]See Arendt (2017) on the idea of nation states.

Citizenship in Post-colonial Societies

The contestation on citizenship in post-colonial countries follows a legacy of colonialism bringing the conception of hierarchy between subjects,[19] considerations about the plight of the creation of boundaries with the administrative and local governance,[20] historical and cultural complexities of the diverse ethnic communities and their practices together form the annotations and complexities underlined.[21] Kapur states that within post-colonial India, citizenship has been marked by the very feature of exclusion that has characterized its colonial incarnations (Kapur, 2007).[22] The idea of citizenship within the post-colonial societies existed on the notion of governance, where citizen would become the simultaneous subject of rights and securities (Samaddar, 2012). Samaddar notes that history of citizenship should be noted with history of rights and specifically meant peasantry rights that later separated as voting rights, minority rights and language rights.[23] Particularly, citizenship can be understood as the bundle of rights[24] given to citizens, wherein there exists notion of hierarchy of rights.[25] So, in order to argue that the rights are given or attained by a citizen ascertain, there exist kinds of rights exercised by a particular section, which in other words, not all the rights are exercised by all the citizens. To argue further, these rights that are not accessed by a community or section of people make them marginal or on the margins of citizenship. Sadiq (2017) argues, experiences of post-colonial states indicate that such rights were separated from the top, in which equal status (civil and political rights) had no bearing on the ability to engage in social rights at bottom. These rights have remained bifurcated for the citizens of the post-colonial states.

Understanding the post-colonial societies in terms of the discrimination on the basis of inability to access rights is the first step towards making people marginal. Chatterji argues that post-colonial citizenship was different than the West and can be analysed in terms of the creation of "minority citizens", neither citizen nor alien, but a hybrid subject of new national regimes of identification and law.[26] It is centrally this idea of minority citizens being analysed in the chapter that leads to unmaking of citizens and creating statelessness. This has not only created a hierarchy, but Kabeer

[19]In context of Burma, the differences created on the mainland Burma and ethnic communities geographically located on the borderlands as elaborated by Myint-U (2004).

[20]Taylor (2007) argues that the British had ethnic yardstick to carve the territories of Burma and within the contemporary political issues.

[21]See Roy (2016), Kapur (2007), Taylor (1982) and Silverstein (1990) for Burma.

[22]Taking the idea from the context of borders and migration that created exclusion and outsider in the post-colonial context, Kapur (2007) essentializes Murayama (2006). See Ibid Thomson (1995).

[23]See Samaddar (2012).

[24]Chowdhory (2018) developing on various categories of how citizenship is conceptualized and one of them is through rights.

[25]This hierarchy of right is formed on the basis of ascriptive identities of a citizen that delimits them to access certain rights.

[26]Here Chatterji (2012) argues from the perspective of partition of India and Pakistan, but the context that is manifested lies within the post-colonial states.

argues that persisting colonial hierarchies were actively strengthened and reified… through defining powers of a modern state apparatus and a codified system of law (as cited in Sadiq, 2017). And in Myanmar, the creation of insider and outsider by the British through the administrative and military distinctions plays a contentious role in contemporary times as well (Taylor, 2007, p. 76). Mamdani argues that when a post-colonial state identities citizenship on the basis of some as indigenous and non-indigenous, it certainly claims colonial state as its true parent (2001, p. 30). So, in a way the practices of the post-colonial state in differentiating between citizens by claiming as outsiders, minorities and strangers are to uphold the differentiation manifested by the colonial state. Now, it is these differences during the nation building or state formation that have acted as lynch pin in marking out minorities. As Chowdhory opines, the state-building processes in post-colonial societies were responsible for constructing a particular trajectory of accommodation for minority rights in South Asia (2018, p. 44). In the post-colonial societies, the idea of citizenship comes parallel with nation building, as the state was all readily build by colonizers and the nation had to be built by "the people", wherein the West, the idea of citizenship comes with fraternity and solidarity, through culturally homogenous nations. If it may be argued from the above outlined notion of nation building, where the Buddhist majority controlled both the institutional structures after the independence of Burma in 1947, it was their agenda to homogenously construct a nation based on religion. To this, Pugh (2013) argues that the pushing out of Rohingyas from Burma is to homogenously construct a nation. These then could be outlined as two major theoretical links of creating the differentiated citizenship in Burma by restricting the idea of giving equal status to religious ethnic minorities. It is then along with nation building and citizenship in Burma that laws enunciated on the first citizenship law of Burma define Rohingya Muslims as nationality and other Buddhist Burmese as citizens.[27] The contestation within citizenship of post-colonial countries follows a legacy of colonialism bringing the conception of hierarchy between subjects and British. This has not only created a hierarchy but some scholar posits that these have also created new forms of hierarchy and made the earlier ones more rigid.

Nation Formation as Foundation for Exclusion

While considering the context of South Asia and Southeast Asia, the historical trajectory of colonial state and nation building by bringing the social aspects of cultural homogeneity along with the religious majoritarian foundations is predominant. Tarling states that the Southeast Asian states focused on regime[28] building rather than state building (Tarling, 2004, p. 13). Similarly, Gungwu points out that the immediate task for the Southeast Asian states after independence was to make nationals out of citizens (as cited in Blackburn, 2010), whereas Chowdhory argues that the

[27] See Ibrahim (2018, pp. 1–17).

[28] Here when Tarling (2004, p. 12) uses the term regime, he specifically means form of government.

state formation had an impact on state building and policies of accommodation that were dominated by policies of homogenization.[29] The debates on nation building have been analysed from the perspective of industrialized,[30] imagined[31] and territorial[32] categorizations. However, it may be argued that theoretical debates on nation building have been dominated by West but an emphasis on building a nation and the national movements across the Southeast Asian states brings different social and political trajectory. Anderson brings out that the nationalism and nation formation in the colonial countries were led due to three factors: industrial capitalism, russification and education, where both provided by colonial state and private institutions (Anderson, 1991, p. 116). And he further argues that intelligentsia was responsible for nationalism because of its bilingual and literacy[33] and forms the idea of nation.[34] These states have tried to adopt a distinctive feature of nation building by keeping diverse ethnicities, religions or the social fabric. And it is these indicators that can lead to the comparison between the states.[35]

However, Smith argues that the polyethnic post-colonial states have been dominated by the religious homogeneity for nation building after the colonial state builds the institutional structure of state, which led to the exclusion of Muslims and Sikhs in India (Smith, 1986, p. 36). Nation building in most of the post-colonial states in such a manner postulates the exclusion of religious minorities. Smith states, "In Asia and Africa, religion was drawn into the service of ethnic nationalism, wherever (as often the case) the customs and vernaculars were embedded in a traditional ethnic religion (Indian Hinduism, Burmese Buddhism, Arab Sunni Islam) which had so long served to identify communities and their cultures" (Smith, 1986, p. 146). In this sense, Smith argues that the majority of religions in the states have created nation building, which led to the exclusion of some. Elaborating further, he somewhere argues that nation formation as a process that has not been achieved by post-colonial nations, which leads to an ongoing process of culturally homogenous creation of nations at large. In other words, it may be argued that the nation formation is still an ongoing process. It so far makes a claim that the process of nation building led to exclusion of minorities with the rise of bilingual intelligentsia for Anderson and for Smith, the creation of cultural religious homogeneity. Anderson states, "a nation is an imagined political community and imagined as both inherently limited and sovereign" (Anderson, 1991, p. 6). It may be argued that the people connected through the imagination may realise that after all whose imagination was it? To which Partha Chatterjee calls

[29]In here, Chowdhory (2018, pp. 44–46) makes a distinction between nation formation and state formation by bringing the argument from the state formation perspective of the South Asian states by highlighting the weak state and strong societal tendencies.

[30]Gellner (2006).

[31]Anderson (1991).

[32]Smith (1986).

[33]Smith (1986, p. 116).

[34]Anderson's (1991) idea of formation of nations comes from a sociologist perspective, which is imagined territorially and collectively irrespective of the ethnic, vernacular and religious differences; not all the people will know each other but are connected through horizontal comradeship.

[35]See Cheah (2003).

no one imagines more than the intelligentsia (Chatterjee, 1986, p. 22). On the other hand, Smith presents a political analysis of nation. Smith further claims that in order to develop a culturally homogenous nation like West, the post-colonial states tried to follow a similar trajectory of territorial and ethnic common lineage. Since British administrative governance defined territorial boundaries, the other aspect could only be developed that is common ethnic culture. In order to find common historical lineages, the construct was given by Buddhist religious majority, who had strong hold on the institutions of state (Ibrahim, 2018; Lewa, 2004).

How is that religion became the centre for exclusion of the minorities in Burma? A brief history outlining the annexation of Burma by the British where the institutional changes like the Western education, administrative jobs and replacement of monarchy was fractured that controlled the Sangha and other affairs of the society. In transition of British left Burma, there was a constitutional and state-building set-up required. It is during the nationalist movement that the popular Buddhists in the mainland Burma felt neglected and wanted to gain the control over the Sangha and society.[36] The Buddhist started to feel defamed after the abolition of monarchy, which led to displacement of Buddhism as the religion of the state (Taylor, 2007, p. 79). It has been argued that in Myanmar, the evolution of nationalist organizations (Young Men's Buddhist Association) based their claims that the British has degenerated the Myanmar Buddhist customs (Taylor, 2007, p. 81).

Political Institutions and Religious Majority Dominance

The political institutional structure is dominated by elites and majoritarian politics in the post-colonial states. Smith argues that the larger tensions are apparent due to the nation formation process, which is influenced by the western idea of culturally homogeneous nation.[37] This can also be located in the context of Asia, where states are found, but nations are still in process of marking homogenous formations religiously. However, the examples of South Asia vary with Pakistan; the social and political complexities of the nation led to change secular nation to Islamic in 1962; with Bangladesh, it was after the military rule in 1980s though not constitutionally but socially it found an Islamic nation.[38] As in the context of Burma, the constitution changes and institutions influenced by the Burmese Buddhist majority bring the other ethnic and religious minority clashes. The promises are made to the other ethnics that they could find autonomy in the state after the set-up of the first constitution.[39]

Brubaker (1996) and Wimmer (2002) believe that the whole problem is embedded in the institutional apparatus of the modern state in creating ethnic mobilization and

[36] See Tarling (2004), and Gungwu (2005).

[37] See Smith (1986).

[38] See Jalal (1995).

[39] See Taylor (1982) and Silverstein (1990).

exclusion of others. An inference could be drawn from the debates developed from standpoints of nation building and the creation of state structure that supports one community at large. In both the cases, majority has strong hold in deciding who is to be included and who is excluded. However, religious majority played a significant role in outlining the context of religious minorities. The nation formation could have been heterogenous and not homogenous. Some argue that nation states could have survived in an ethnically heterogenous nation (Brubaker, 1996).[40] To this, Smith would argue that "the reality of states without nation in Asia and Africa, makes it inevitable that political elites in the new states look for alternative models of the nation, and different modes of national integration" (Smith, 1986, p. 144). As remarked, the national elites of Burma who had availed the opportunity to study form the institutional structure of British in the Lowland Burma were Burmese intellectuals (Safman, 2007, p. 54). The diverse religious ethnic groups find their shared territorial trajectory to be institutionally assimilated into one nation state, with having ethno-nationalism within the the ethnic community and larger solidarity of citizenship with the nation-state.[41]

Wimmers (2002) variant of how politicization of ethnic conflicts takes place stresses on how the modern state becomes related to specific ethno-national groups. And in this variant, the state elites start acting in the name of a national majority. This would require denouncing of the illegitimate representation of "the people" within the state administration and would lead to conflict; otherwise without this, there would be no question of ethnic representation (Wimmer, 2002, p. 95). This underlines the larger discourse of institutions playing a significant role in representation and marking out of ethnic minorities, which is largely seen in the sense of citizenship that is often differentiated not only on the basis of rights but also as a status. Brubaker states, "the single most important development is the fact that the new state's bureaucracy is not representative of the whole population of the country, but takes on ethnic hues" (Brubaker, 1996, p. 92). In this manner, the institutional structure developed by weak states, depending on social resources, tends to create differences within the society on the ethnic basis. Having articulated the control of the institutions and political majority dominance of the Buddhist Burmans in devising the policies for nation building, it is they who formulated the exclusion through constitution.[42]

[40]The pre-given notion of the account that heterogeneities could not exist in the nation has been presumed by the scholars to have existed, and this should be taken as an account for nationhood and nationality. See Brubaker (1996) and Young (1976) as and when they use the data given by Walker Connor in 1972, only twelve of the world's (then) 132 states were essentially homogenous from an ethnic viewpoint.

[41]Brubaker (1996).

[42]Taylor (1979).

Citizenship Rights: The Unmaking of Citizens

Locating the debate in domain of citizenship ensures rights accessed by individuals as citizens, which is ensured on the basis of equality. Some scholars argue that citizenship is an act of closure that marks out some people, where this idea is driven from the concept of nationhood (Brubaker, 1996). It is mostly done on the basis of religion and gender as they are regarded as culturally foreign (Taylor, 1979, p. 35). Smith (2002) would like to call modern citizenship by finding the difference between nationality and citizenship, where a citizen enjoys full rights, but to all those whom nationality has been given, they lack certain rights.[43] The idea of modern citizenship bases its claim on nationhood and citizenship, and it has blended republican and liberal form of citizenship for marking ethnic, gender and other identities (Smith, 2002, p. 109). He further elaborates that such bar for citizenship has been removed over the period of time,[44] but as we note in the case of Rohingyas, it still exists. However, the debate on nationality and citizenship is not the concern of the chapter, but the idea is to understand how the minorities are created in a nation on the basis of legal rights and civil rights with procedural loss of citizenship even after the struggle for establishment of democracy. An unpacking of statelessness of Rohingyas[45] has been done by Kyaw (2017) by locating the argument that the problem of the Rohingyas has been held categorically under microscope after the 1980s new citizenship law. The international community also recognizes the 1980s citizenship law to be amended in context of Rohingyas (Kyaw, 2017). However, the problem as enunciated started right after the independence of Burma and the first citizenship act.[46]

Having outlined the idea of citizenship in the first section where the debate on the origins of citizenship focused the ontological idea of exclusion embedded in the concept. As articulated above, nation building and creation of majority and minority consensus some citizens have been excluded from being citizens. There are various examples where an ethnic community is not given political right because it is not considered necessary for them to participate or women are not considered as eligible for political rights.[47] On the other hand, immigrants and migrants also have limited rights,[48] although the proposition and cases of the two are quite different. Citizenship rights that a state chooses to give are often discriminated on the basis of categories of citizens as each right carries entitlement, accountability, assurance of security and other legal procedures. There is hierarchy of rights; Janoksi and Gran (2002) argue

[43]Smith (2002).

[44]Smith (2002).

[45]The centre of Kyaw (2017) argument as to how Muslim Rohingyas are made stateless through the legal policies and active stance of delays in implementation of citizenship laws.

[46]See Taylor (1979) and Gungwu (2005).

[47]This lineage can be followed on the basis of the demands made by women of Western countries for equal rights along with men; rather in post-colonial countries, they were given at once to all the subjects but by creation of minority citizens. It has been critically analysed in the section on post-colonial citizenship of this chapter.

[48]See Benhabib (2004), Chowdhory (2019).

that legal and civil rights are the basis of all the other rights that a citizen could access.[49] The hierarchy with respect to rights is created due to various reasons; for Janoski and Gran (2002), civil and legal rights are the procedural rights on which rest of the rights can be ensured.

However, an Israeli scholar has differentiated rights on the basis of power ideology; he brings out that rights with low power potential are given to the outsiders and with high potential power could be given to a citizen (Ariely, 2011). Now, according to him power potential of rights is in the sense of involvement with the state, as in the rights that are unaccountable or those rights states cannot ensure, fall on the low potential and can be given to an outsider.[50] It may be argued that the social rights are on the low point because they cannot be ensured by the state and are mostly provided to minorities in a state. Similarly, legal and political rights that hold state institutions accountable formulate a principle of high potential power rights that may form the basic exclusion of minorities in a state. Even Benhabib argues that there are certain rights that form the basis of exclusion for minorities even after a substantiated citizenship (Ariely, 2011). It can be acknowledged that there is differentiation between the rights accessed by minorities with or without a formal status of citizenship. It can be argued that states do not decide in an instance that minorities need to be targeted for exclusion from the state, rather there is a procedure followed and governed in finally declaring minorities as stateless. This procedure is followed constitutionally through the hierarchy of rights and discriminating between the citizens, and some are also enhanced with the power of violence. Now, having underlined this difference by stating that Rohingyas are nationals along with other ethnic communities excluded on the basis of outsiders to Burma.[51] Can we locate the difference between nationality and citizenship, which was first law that marked Rohingyas to be unable to access some rights. In the next section by tracing the historical trajectory of exclusion of Rohingyas and making them stateless, it will be argued that the minorities in the post-colonial countries are discriminated on the basis of their ascriptive identities and in the procedure to build a strong nation. Kyaw (2017) states that Rohingyas have been questioned on the basis of their legal and cultural belonging of Muslims and of the Rohingyas in particular, have been raised by nationalist Buddhist monks led by Ma Ba Tha (organization for the protection of race and religion) and by wider Myanmar society as well.

Rohingyas and Their Hypothesis

The conceptions and research on Rohingyas bring different analyses of their contemporary situation as refugees to the bordering countries (India and Bangladesh).

[49] Janoksi and Gran (2002, p. 15).

[50] See Ariely (2011).

[51] See Ariely (2011).

Who are the Rohingyas[52]? What is their identity? Where do they come from[53]? All these questions have been well debated and defined in numerous articles and books. The question of whether the Rohingyas should be understood from the vantage point of ethnic identity or their religious identity since they are one of the ethnic communities geographically located in the borderland (North Arakan region) of Myanmar. Scholars significantly working on ethnicity have pointed out a different picture of Burma by highlighting the context of British and the way they are geographically and culturally located communities were categorized under various ethnics (Taylor, 1982). Although Taylor (2005) denies the existence of religion for the society and politics of Burma as it happened in the context of Sri Lanka, but argues that ethnicity and religion have been intermingled. However, Taylor further argues that policies pursued by the British reified ethnic identity and made religion an issue of politics (Taylor, 2005). However, the intricate problem lies in the way the stateless Rohingyas have been conceptualized and their relationship with state of Myanmar. This can be noted both from the constitution of the state[54] and the violence[55] and atrocities disposed on them.

Understanding the sensitivity of the Rohingyas, various scholars have signified to one or various issues that brought the situation of Rohingyas as outsiders. The historical lineage of British annexation of Burma in 1885 of the Buddhist Kingdom, where other religious ethnic communities supported British, and the Buddhist king had close allies with Japan (Myint-U, 2004). The ethnic communities that supported British were Kachin, Karen and Chin (Farzana, 2017, p. 17), this leaves out the people of Arakan. Just before British India annexed the territory of Burma, the King had the powers of the state along with the religious order (Taylor, 2007, p. 74). However, the monarchy in the ministerial Burma was abolished in 1889, but the ethnic minorities settled at the frontiers were still ruled by the traditional headmen. In 1930, when democracy was established in Burma, it did not give equal representation to communities due to the British administrative division of Burma (Smith, 1997, p. 102). Taylor remarks that the British never had a policy towards Burma rather through multiple accidents (Taylor, 2007, p. 70); it came to be situated as it was. Later, with the development seen in Myanmar, the migrants from neighbouring states were allocated and the Muslims in the Arakan region were treated of the Indian origin.[56] As noted there was massive immigration of labour from India during the British rule, when this population surpassed the one million mark, the Thakin movement

---

[52]See Pugh (2013), their disputed identity whether they should be called as Rohingyas or people of Rakhine state or citizens of Myanmar. However, for the claims made in the chapter they are understood as citizens of Myanmar. And as Kyaw (2017) argues that staking claims on their ethnicity would further complicate the matter.

[53]The focus has been on the geographical location of Rohingyas living in the upper Arakan region and to notify the hill region of Burma. Now, the difference is analysed form the perspective of diverse ethnicities, living in the lowland areas and uphill areas during the British conquest of Burma in 1844.

[54]See Kyaw (2017) states that the problem of statelessness of the Rohingyas is analysed through the legal policy texts and is supported by analyses of events.

[55]See Kyaw (2017).

[56]See Footnote 55.

and Young Nationalist of Burma Independent army chased them out (Smith, p. 101). Rohingyas having migrated to Burma from Bengal has led them to pose lesser claims on citizenship, which is largely extended to other ethnic communities and as it is this context of being outsider marks the claim of exclusion (Ibrahim, 2018). Inhabitants considered to be of Indian ethnic origin, especially Muslims in the Rakhine state, remain one of the most discriminated against groups in Burmese society, a situation which reached new heights during the post-1988 period (Smith, 1997, p. 101). This does not explain the intricate relationship of why selected ethnic communities[57] were denied citizenship after Burma was an independent nation and cannot be substantiated as the ground for exclusion of religious and ethnic minorities today. The hypothesis of military rule targets minorities, and this became the basis of domination by the Buddhist majority (Ibrahim, 2018) and the state building in Myanmar supported military form of government (Beehner, 2018). The military rule of 1970s started with the agenda of alienating and forcing the Rohingya Muslims to flee. This hypothesis stands inadequate, as there have been series of attacks on the Rohingya Muslims since first citizenship law was enforced.[58] There has been shifting debates on when did Rohingyas come to Burma either before 1846 or after? Which is the basis of the 2008 citizenship? Why would this debate of an outsider be constructed in recent times? It has been argued earlier in the chapter that the exclusion and statelessness of Rohingyas are the problem of post-colonial state policies and of the process of nation building.

Rohingyas—A Denial of Citizenship

Interrogating historically, the denial of citizenship rights to Rohingyas has been a contested issue for both scholars working on the question of ethnicity[59] and their identity, and on those working on Modern Burma.[60] The literature on Rohingyas while bringing the discourse of citizenship has been limited to analysing the debate from Kymlicka's idea of multiculturalism and so the denial of the rights of their political identity[61] and as refugees their citizenship cannot be addressed (Farzana, 2017, p. 21). However, along with universal notion of citizenship based on equality,

[57]A long duree and relationship initiated by Aung San for arguing that once the ethnic minorities come together they can later be given autonomy.

[58]See http://www.ibiblio.org/obl/docs/UNION_CITIZENSHIP_ACT-1948.htm. Accessed July 10, 2019. See Arriaza and Vonk (2017). Report on Citizenship law: Myanmar http://cadmus.eui.eu/bitstream/handle/1814/48284/RSCAS_GLOBALCIT_CR_2017_14.pdf?sequence=1. Accessed July 11, 2019.

[59]Taylor (1982), Smith (1997).

[60]As elaborated in Myint-U (2004).

[61]See Taylor (1982) and Mamdani (2001) on the creation of political identity in the colonized countries.

there is an underlying dimension of Indigenism or indigenous status[62] for the people of the soil. As Suryadinata argues that the all the indigenous people get the status of citizenship automatically of the country concerned.[63] But the empirics provided by Burma government states a very different perspective on its minority indigenous groups even after the ethnicities being the people of the land they have not been treated at par on equal citizens. Within the Southeast Asian nations, the conception of citizenship has been undertaken as a legal foundation or in terms of law. As stated, citizenship law is therefore a law, which stipulates the status of the population, the rights that the citizens enjoyed and obligations that the citizens have to the state (Suryadinata, 2015, p. 55).

It has been argued that the problem of national unity in Burma has been attempted to solve through constitutional provisions (Taylor, 1979). The critical aspect of the denial of rights is also noted under the conception of democracy that has been a struggle in Myanmar since independence. The history of establishing a democracy in 1948 was seen positive by Aun San, until the scenario changed with U Nu's idea of democratic socialism (Maung, 1961, p. 90). However, democracy became wobbly after the assassination of Aun San in the hands of U Nu and later with the military coup of 1962 by General Ne Win. U Nu promised various reforms with the introduction of Buddhism as the state religion, giving state autonomy to Mons and Arakanese and free political participation (Maung, 1961, p. 216). The 1948 citizenship law of Burma encrypts the conception of indigenous groups or ethnic groups, and binds the idea of *Jus Sanguinis* along with *Jus Soli*.[64] However, as Kyaw (2017) argues that approximately 22,000 citizens were accorded citizenship until 1960 and rest were without citizenship. There was also the conception of national registration certificates in 1951 which were given to Rohingyas that stated only about the residence and did not mean citizenship rights. This procedure started with a basic differentiation in law, while formulating citizenship laws, which basically meant that they could reside with full legal and political rights in the country but are not citizens in the sense their rights can be repealed within the power of state as noted in the next citizenship law of 1984. The citizenship law of 1984 amended to the 1948 act of the ethnic communities as nationals also stated "the council may decide whether any ethnic group is national or not".[65] This gives the state power to make a decision on the validity of a citizen by first making him a national and then recognizing him as a citizen. In the later section, we note the time lapse between the first citizenship act and the citizenship law of 1984, the military targets Rohingyas and they flee to the neighbouring states. The 1948 citizenship act constitution formally

---

[62] Indigenous status refers to the local population that has a homeland within the territories of the country concerned. See Suryadinata (2015, p. 55). And legal conception found in the first citizenship act of 1948, see http://www.ibiblio.org/obl/docs/UNION_CITIZENSHIP_ACT-1948.htm. Accessed July 10, 2019.

[63] See Suryadinata (2015, p. 55).

[64] The Union Citizenship Act 1948 http://www.ibiblio.org/obl/docs/UNION_CITIZENSHIP_ACT-1948.htm. Accessed July 10, 2019.

[65] Burma Citizenship Law https://www.refworld.org/docid/3ae6b4f71b.html. Accessed July 11, 2019.

acknowledged that all ethnic groups in Burma were immigrants and differential treatment of Rohingyas would be subsequently addressed (Ibrahim, 2018).[66] Stating Rohingyas as nationals without any citizenship certificate and since then there have been series of loss of rights both constitutionally and with violence enforced by the state (Kyaw, 2017). This difference between nationals and citizens can be highlighted that their status as citizenship is not confirmed and at the provision of the law they can still live. With the changes in the political scenario of Burma following the military coup, demolishing the military structure led to the further violence against Rohingyas. In 1960s, the land belonging to Rohingyas was taken from them and the Buddhists were made to resettle. This is one of the civil rights, taking of land for resettlement, the marriages between the Rohingya Muslims and Buddhist men were strictly restricted. These were the major changes that took place during the military rule, and there was no accountability in loss of civil rights of Rohingyas with emerging violence against them. This denial of citizenship led to restrictions on movements, land holding, education, health and employment in civil services. Rohingya children are allowed to attend primary school but secondary is reserved for citizens only (Lewa, 2004). This was a denial of social rights along with legally changing the status of Rohingyas in Myanmar. So, the balancing of the depreciating social rights along with the legal definition of their status as nationals and then outsiders has made them not incapable of demanding rights. However, the political rights were ensured with some Rohingyas continued to support Burmese road to serfdom by political participation in 1970. In 1974, the constitution of the Socialist Republic of the Union of Burma defined citizenship in (Article 145); all persons born of parents both of whom are citizens of the socialist republic are citizens of the union. Now, when in the first citizenship law, the Rohingyas were not given citizenship; then, under the new law, they cannot claim. This further changed the law with the Emergency Immigration Act imposed ethnicity-based identity cards (white, blue, etc.),[67] with Rohingyas only being eligible for the foreign registration card (Pugh, 2013; Kyaw, 2017). It was during this period that the Buddhist ideology took part with the military to bring popular support for monasteries and monks. It was after the legal changes in 1974, there was widespread increase in the violence against Rohingyas and this led them to flee (Ibrahim, 2018; Kyaw, 2015). This forced most of the Rohingyas to flee to the neighbouring countries for shelter and survival (Uddin, 2019). The 1982 citizenship law was based on the residents in Burma before 1824, and this finally denied any citizenship right to Rohingya (Kyaw, 2017). The history of Rohingya Muslims and their residence in Burma has been 1780s with the Burmese Kings, and during the first annexation of British, Rohingya Muslims resided in the South region of Rakhine state and later when the military started taking their land, they shifted to the Northern region (Ibrahim, 2018). The 2008

[66]Citizenship would be granted on the basis of having lived in the territory of Burma for at least eight out of previous 10 years. As a result, Article II (iv) of the constitution awarded the Rohingyas national registration certificates with full legal and voting rights. They were asked not to apply for citizenship, as you are not one of the indigenous races of the Union of Burma.

[67]See Kyaw (2017) for detailed study.

Constitution strengthened 1982 citizenship law and mass persecution of Rohingyas emerged with episodes of mass genocide. The anti-Muslim campaign started by Buddhist nationalist of 969 ideologically on the basis of religion in 2012 (Kyaw, 2015). However, Rohingyas were allowed to contest elections until 2015, and this government denied their political rights. On this front, some scholars argue that the strife of Myanmar to establish democracy could not be achieved till today. It has been argued by Huang (2017) that Myanmar could not establish a democracy rather a democratic military regime has been in power even during the 2015 elections.

Conclusion

The law and violence are used as central tools by the state for marking out minorities and creating them as marginal citizens with the framework of exclusion that has specifically and systematically targeted Rohingyas to create them stateless. The argument of the chapter marks that the processes of nation building and keeping the institutional set-up in control of the majority (Buddhist Burmese) have excluded minorities (religious) in representation and status of citizenship. The unleashing of independent country Myanmar into the hands of majority from the British and the consequent formation of constitution led to the discrimination of the ethnic and religious minorities The precarious situation of Rohingyas is the result of the changes in the citizenship law that understood in the chapter through the conception of hierarchy of rights and the power potential of rights that makes minorities at the rock bottom to demand their rights. The Rohingyas have a precarious state due to the changes in citizenship laws and the procedural loss of rights from civil and finally political. In the first section, debate on nation formation marked that in post-colonial countries, nationalism has been the tool of elite intelligentsia, and how religious majority was an alternative foundation for nationalism in polyethnic states. This was accompanied with the arguments developed of politics of ethnicization in a modern state with the help of institutions and representation. This makes a case that Rohingyas have been targeted as a minority group since the inception of Burma with Buddhist religious majority and institutional structure plays a significant role in their exclusion. The idea of citizenship in this chapter is identified with the notion of bundle of rights that a citizen is ensured. The debate on rights brings an argument that along with the legal changes in the constitution, the social rights were taken away by the authorities and by other dominant organizations. The changes with the due process of taking away rights one by one and finally making them stateless accompanied with the strategies of violence are noted in the chapter.

References

Anderson, B. (1991). *Imagined communities reflections on the origins and spread of nationalism*. New York: Verso.

Arendt, H. (2017). The decline of the nation-state and the end of the rights of man. *The origins of totalitarianism* (pp. 349–396). St Ives: Penguin Classics.

Ariely, G. (2011). Exploring citizenship spheres of inclusion/exclusion: Right as potential for power. *Patterns of Prejudice, 45*(3), 241–259. https://doi.org/10.1080/0031322x.2011.585020. Accessed July, 2018.

Arriaza, J. M., & Vonk, O. (2017). *Report on citizenship law: Myanmar*. http://cadmus.eui.eu/bitstream/handle/1814/48284/RSCAS_GLOBALCIT_CR_2017_14.pdf?sequence=1. Accessed July 11, 2019.

Baehr, P. (2002). The public and the private realm. In *The portable Hannah Arendt* (pp. 182–230). Ontario: Penguin Books Ltd.

Barbalet, J. (2010). Citizenship in Max Weber. *Journal of Classical Sociology, 10*(3), 201–216. https://doi.org/10.1177/1468795x10371717. Accessed May 10, 2019.

Beehner, L. (2018). State-building, military modernization and cross-ethnic violence in Myanmar. *Journal of Asian Security and International Affairs, 5*(3), 1–20. https://doi.org/10.1177/2347797017748464.

Benhabib, S. (2004). *The rights of others: Aliens, residents, and citizens*. Cambridge: Cambridge University Press.

Blackburn, K. (2010). War memory and nation-building in South East Asia. *South East Asia Research, 18*(1), 5–31. https://doi.org/10.5367/000000010790959857.

Brubaker, R. (1996). Nationhood and the national question in the Soviet Union and its successor states: an institutionalist account. *Nationalism reframed: Nationhood and the national question in the new Europe* (pp. 23–54). Cambridge: Cambridge University Press.

Burma Citizenship Law. https://www.refworld.org/docid/3ae6b4f71b.html. Accessed July 11, 2019.

Castles, S. (2005). Hierarchical citizenship in a world of unequal nation-states. *American Political Science Association, 38*(4), 689–692. https://doi.org/10.1017/S1049096505050353.

Chatterjee, P. (1986). *Nationalist thought and the colonial world: A derivative discourse*. Tokyo: Zed Books.

Chatterji, J. (2012). South Asian histories of citizenship 1946–1970. *The Historical Journal, 55*(4), 1049–1071. https://doi.org/10.1017/s0018246x12000428. Published online November 15, 2012. Accessed February, 2019.

Cheah, P. (2003). Grounds of comparison. In J. Culler & P. Cheah (Eds.), *Grounds of comparison around the work of Benedict Anderson* (pp. 1–20). New York: Routledge.

Chowdhory, N. (2018). State formation, marginality and belonging: Contextualising rights of refugees in India, Bangladesh and Sri Lanka. *Refugees, citizenship and belonging in South Asia contested terrains* (pp. 43–69). Singapore: Springer Nature Singapore.

Chowdhory, N. (2019). Citizenship and membership: Placing refugees. In N. Uddin & N. Chowdhory (Eds.), *Deterritorialised identity and transborder movement in South Asia* (pp. 37–54). Singapore: Springer.

Egin, I. F. (2002). *Being political: Genealogies of citizenship*. London: University of Minnesota Press.

Egin, I. F., & Bryan, T. (2002). Citizenship studies: An introduction. In I. F. Egin & B. S. Turner (Eds.), *Handbook on citizenship studies* (pp. 1–10). London: Sage Publication.

Fraser, N., & Gordon, L. (1994). Civil citizenship against social citizenship? On the ideology of contract-versus-charity. In B. V. Steenbergen (Ed.), *The condition of citizenship* (pp. 90–107). London: Sage Publications.

Frazana, K. F. (2017). *Memories of Burmese Rohingya Refugees: The Contested Identity and Belonging*. New York: Palgrave Macmillan.

Gellner, E. (2006). *Nations and nationalism*. Oxford: Blackwell.

Gungwu, W. (2005). Contemporary and national history: A double challenge. In W. Gungwu (Ed.), *Nation-building: Five Southeast Asian histories* (pp. 1–20). Singapore: Institute of Southeast Asian Studies.

Gutmann, A. (1994). Introduction. In A. Gutmann (Ed.), *Multiculturalism: Examining the politics of recognition* (pp. 3–24). Princeton, NJ: Princeton University Press.

Huang, R. L. (2017). Myanmar's way to democracy and the limits of the 2015 elections. *Asian Journal of Political Science, 25*(1), 25–44. https://doi.org/10.1080/02185377.2016.1245154.

Ibrahim, A. (2018). *The Rohingyas: Inside Myanmar's hidden genocide*. New Delhi: Speaking Tiger Publishing Ltd.

Jalal, A. (1995). *Democracy and authoritarianism in South Asia: A comparative and historical perspective*. Cambridge: Cambridge University Press.

Janoksi, T., & Gran, B. (2002). Political citizenship: Foundations of rights. In I. F. Egin & B. S. Turner (Eds.), *Handbook on citizenship studies* (pp. 13–52). London: Sage Publications.

Kabeer, N. (2005). Introduction. In N. Kabeer (Ed.), *Inclusive citizenship: Meanings of expressions* (pp. 1–27). New Delhi: Zubaan.

Kajla, M. (2019). Nation-state and its production of statelessness: A study of Chin refugees. In N. Uddin & N. Chowdhory (Eds.), *Deterritorialised identity and transborder movement in South Asia* (pp. 91–109). Singapore: Springer.

Kapur, R. (2007). The citizens and the migrant: Postcolonial anxieties, law, and the politics of exclusion/inclusion. *Theoretical Inquiries in Law, 8*(2), 537–569. Retrieved July 12, 2019 from https://www7.tau.ac.il/ojs/index.php/til/article/view/645/606.

Kyaw, N. N. (2015). Alienation, discrimination, and securitisation: Legal personhood and cultural personhood of Muslims in Myanmar. *The Review of Faith & International Affairs, 13*(4), 50–59. https://doi.org/10.1080/15570274.2015.1104971.

Kyaw, N. N. (2017). Unpacking the presumed statelessness of Rohingyas. *Journal of Immigrant & Refugee Studies, 15*(3), 269–286. https://doi.org/10.1080/15562948.2017.1330981.

Lewa, C. (2004). The Rohingyas forced migration and statelessness. In O. Mishra (Ed.), *Forced migration in the South Asian region: Displacement, human rights and conflict resolution* (pp. 325–339). Delhi: Manak Publication.

Mamdani, M. (2001). *When victims become killers: Colonialism, nativism, and the genocide in Rwanda*. Princeton, NJ: Princeton University Press.

Marshall, T. H. (1950). The development of citizenship to the end of the nineteenth century. *Citizenship and social class and other essays* (pp. 10–26). London: Cambridge University Press.

Maung, M. (1961). *Burma's constitution*. The Hague: Martinus Nijhoff.

Morrison, I. A. (2014). Orientalism and the construction of the apolitical Buddhist subject. In I. F. Engin & P. Nyers (Eds.), *Routledge handbook of global citizenship studies* (pp. 325–334). New York: Routledge.

Murayama, M. (2006). Borders, migration and sub-regional cooperation in Eastern South Asia. *Economic and Political Weekly, 41*(14), 1351–1359. http://www.jstor.org/stable/4418058.

Myint-U, T. (2004). *The making of modern Burma*. Cambridge: Cambridge University Press.

Pugh, C. L. (2013). *Is citizenship the answer? Constructions of belonging and exclusion for the stateless Rohingya of Burma*. Working Paper No. 76. https://www.compas.ox.ac.uk/wp-content/uploads/WP-2013-107-Pugh_Stateless_Rohingya_Burma.pdf.

Roy, A. (2016). *Citizenship in India*. New Delhi: Oxford University Press.

Sadiq, K. (2017). Postcolonial citizenship. In A. Shachar, R. Bauböck, I. Bloemraad, and M. Vink (Eds.), *Oxford handbook of citizenship*. https://doi.org/10.1093/oxfordhb/9780198805854.013.8. Accessed February, 2019.

Safman, R. M. (2007). Minorities and state-building in mainland Southeast Asia. In N. Ganesan & H. Y. Kyaw (Eds.), *Myanmar state, society and ethnicity* (pp. 30–69). Singapore: Institute of Southeast Asian Studies.

Safran, W. (1997). Citizenship and nationality in democratic systems: Approaches to defining and acquiring membership in the political community. *International Political Science Review, 18*(3), 313–335. https://doi.org/10.1177/019251297018003006.

Samaddar, R. (2012). The heterogeneous world of the citizen. *Citizenship Studies, 16*(5–6), 839–849. https://doi.org/10.1080/13621025.2012.698514.
Silverstein, J. (1990). Civil war and rebellion in Burma. *Journal of Southeast Asian Studies, 21*(1), 114–134. https://doi.org/10.1017/S0022463400001983.
Smith, A. D. (1986). The formation of nations. *The ethnic origins of nations*. Oxford: Basil Blackwell Ltd.
Smith, M. (1997). Burma's ethnic minorities: A central or peripheral problem in the regional context? In P. Carey (Ed.), *Burma: The challenge of change in a divided society* (pp. 97–128). New York: Palgrave Macmillan.
Smith, R. M. (2002). Modern citizenship. In E. F. Isin & B. S. Turner (Eds.), *Handbook on citizenship studies* (pp. 105–116). London: Sage Publications.
Stevenson, N. (2001). Culture and citizenship: An introduction. In N. Stevenson (Ed.), *Culture and citizenship* (pp. 1–11). London: Sage Publications.
Suryadinata, L. (2015). *The making of Southeast Asian Nations: State, ethnicity, indigenism and citizenship*. Singapore: World Scientific Publishing.
Tarling, N. (2004). *Nationalism in Southeast Asia: If the people are with us*. New York: Routledge.
Taylor, R. H. (1979). Burma's national unity problem and the 1974 constitution. *Contemporary Southeast Asia, 1*(3), 232–248. http://www.jstor.org/stable/25797574.
Taylor, R. H. (1982). Perceptions of ethnicity in the politics of Burma. *Southeast Asian Journal of Social Science, 10*(1), 7–22. Retrieved from http://www.jstor.org/stable/24490906.
Taylor, R. H. (2005). Do states make nations? The politics of identity in Myanmar revisited. *South East Asia Research, 13*(3), 261–286. https://doi.org/10.5367/000000005775179676.
Taylor, R. H. (2007). British policy towards Myanmar and the creation of the Burma problem. In N. Ganesan & K. Y. Hlaing (Eds.), *Myanmar state, society and ethnicity* (pp. 70–95). Singapore: Institute of Southeast Asian Studies.
The Union Citizenship Act 1948. http://www.ibiblio.org/obl/docs/UNION_CITIZENSHIP_ACT-1948.htm. Accessed July 10, 2019.
Thomson, C. (1995). Political stability and minority groups in Burma. *Geographical Review, 85*(3), 269–285. https://doi.org/10.2307/215273. Accessed May 9, 2014.
Turner, B. S. (2002). Religion and politics: The elementary forms of citizenship. In I. F. Egin & B. S. Turner (Eds.), *Handbook on citizenship studies* (pp. 259–276). London: Sage Publication.
Uddin, N. (2019). The state, vulnerability, and transborder movements: The Rohingya people in Myanmar and Bangladesh. In N. Uddin & N. Chowdhory (Eds.), *Deterritorialised identity and transborder movement in South Asia* (pp. 73–90). Singapore: Springer.
Wimmer, A. (2002). Who owns the state? Ethnic conflicts after the end of empires. *Nationalist exclusion and ethnic conflict* (pp. 85–113). Cambridge: Cambridge University Press.
Young, C. (1976). The arena: State, nation and nationalism. *The politics of cultural pluralism* (pp. 66–97). Wisconsin: The University of Wisconsin Press.

Chapter 4
The Politics of Marginalization and Statelessness of the Rohingyas in India

Kaveri

Abstract The Rohingyas from Myanmar are the world's most persecuted minority without citizenship. For over five decades, they have faced continuous waves of communal violence, extrajudicial killings and discrimination. Especially, after the global denunciation of the military crackdown in August 2017 and United Nations accusing the country of "ethnic cleansing and genocide", it is currently estimated that approximately 1.9 million ethnic Rohingyas are refused nationality/citizenship and its foreseen rights, while more than 723,000 Rohingyas have fled Myanmar. The recent deportation of seven Rohingyas by India and Bangladesh, and UNHCR signing an agreement with Myanmar on the return of Rohingya Muslims but without any guarantee of citizenship further tarnishes their identity between the man and the citizen, dumping them into a socio-legal limbo. Thereby, this raises debate over democracy, nationality/citizenship, human rights humanitarian assistance and protection regime for victims of forced migration and denationalization within the nation state paradigm. Based on the ethnographic inquiry conducted among stateless Rohingya refugees living in Delhi, Mewat and Jammu, the chapter looks into the historical and political dimension of the Rohingya crisis, while exploring their refracted and displaced realities and complexities of "everyday life" in asylum. It even contests the dominant discourse of the state and statehood while bringing the focus back to the "illegal-immigrant" transcending the South and Southeast Asian borders and beyond as stateless, refugees, cross-border migrants or simply as displaced persons.

Keywords Refugees · Statelessness · Cross-border migrants · Rohingya · Myanmar

Introduction

Exclusion, disenfranchisement and exile have been an intrinsic part of the exercise of political power in human history. The recent version of the history of exclusion and

---

Kaveri (✉)
Tata Institute of Social Sciences, Mumbai, India
e-mail: kaveri.urmilesh2014@tiss.edu

N. Chowdhory and B. Mohanty (eds.), *Citizenship, Nationalism and Refugeehood of Rohingyas in Southern Asia*,
https://doi.org/10.1007/978-981-15-2168-3_4

statelessness emerged from the post-Westphalia model of the nation state. The end of two World Wars and the subsequent Cold War period have witnessed a large number of political upheavals around international order. Reasons for such a large-scale disturbances range from simple sociopolitical tensions, regional conflicts within the country, rise of modern nation states, armed conflicts, ethnic issues, creation of new territorial boundaries, unequal distribution of natural resources and not to forget the developmental and environmental hazards which has out-streamed the minority from the majority population and further forces them to leave their land or simple persecution (Chakraborty, 1998; Muni & Baral, 1996; Samaddar, 2003). However, the emergence of modern nation states, demarcated legal boundaries built on the premises of *jus sanguinis* (right of blood) or *jus soli* (right of soil), has added to the complexities of citizenship or nationality, giving birth to statelessness. Perhaps, what is more, problematizing is the state-centric idea of citizenship based on the notion of nationality, assuming nationality as manifestation of a country's sovereignty and identity[1] based on historical and territorial understanding that imprints the idea of ethno-religious nationals. Making it benchmark for inclusion and exclusion since they both comply with the link between the individual and state (Goldston, 2006), wherein, the sphere of inclusion and exclusion is determined by the state (Chowdhory, 2018). Thus, such approaches to citizenship are based on cultural and ethnic terms leads to practical problems of non-incorporation of minorities (cultural, linguistic and religious), thereby inevitably being responsible for the much ethnic division and conflict. Considering, both nationality and citizenship represent the two sides of the same coin i.e. state membership but analytically are distinct concepts; belonging to a different sphere of meaning and activity precisely because all citizens may possess the nationality of a given state but not all nationals of a given state are citizens. The possession of citizenship is usually linked with the right to work, live and engage in a country's civil-political exercises, whereas the "nationality" is a cultural concept that can be understood as an informal and subjective relationship between an individual and state based on racial and ethnic grounds and connected with international law (Rubenstein & Adler, 2000). The idea of nationality connotes relationship between the state and individual, irrespective of one's legal citizenship status. A nation and national identity can be described as a group of people representing and recognizing some kind of shared identity through a distinctive culture, tradition, a history of association and language, etc., unlike, the status of a citizens denotes connection between state and individual dictated through a political structure within defined territorial boundaries that may incorporate more than one nation. As explained by Anderson (1996) in form of "imagined community", citizenship is a legal and political concept inferring from people's relationship with the state. In simple terms, state-ness and nation-ness are increasingly not aligned, but if it does, it gives rise to tension and violence on both territorial and ethnic grounds. Hence, the question of citizenship and nationality is exceedingly problematic and contentious particularly when nationality-based citizenship rights draw its legitimacy from the territorial boundaries of state,

[1]Nationality and Statelessness: A Handbook for Parliamentarians https://www.un.org/ruleoflaw/files/Nationality%20and%20Statelessness.pdf. Accessed May, 2018.

which by default excludes non-nationals (Chowdhory, 2018). This result in creating a notion of citizenship based on majoritarian perspective—"We as the citizens" and the "other". This widespread continuity and incongruity fail to appreciate multiculturalism and pluralism in the sociopolitical processes of the state and is prone to violence, destruction, forced migration and displacement (Parivelan cited in Banerjee, 2013, ed). Wherein the category of citizens is celebrated with legitimacy of rights, a sense of belonging and identity is recognized by and within the territorial jurisdiction of the nation state, without which people are vulnerable to exploitation and countless injustices as deprives an individual from all sociopolitical and legal claims or rights and a place in today's nation state ordered world.

Such absolutism of state sovereignty, i.e. the right of states to determine and recognize citizens and non-citizens along with policy of homogenization, is responsible for the generation and the very existence of stateless people. The statelessness across the globe is regarded as a human dilemma trapped in legal complexities, which is equally regarded as a condition of rightlessness, hence statelessness can be regarded as both a product and cause of other human rights violations. This is particularly true in the case of Myanmar (formerly known as Burma) where the process of assimilation was based on the principle of Buddhist identity, with little scope to retain the distinctiveness of minorities, especially the Muslim Rohingya community. Thus, the various ethnic minorities resisted the imposition of a "Buddhist-Burman" identity through a sustained mass movement that gradually led to armed struggle for greater autonomy and independence.

Despite the global adherence to the Universal Declaration of Human Rights (Article 15), ensures everyone has the right to a nationality and no one shall be arbitrarily deprived to his nationality yet, there is a rapid increase in new cases of statelessness since its silent on citizenship which gives legal recognition between a state and individual thereby granting specific rights and responsibilities. Moreover, with the growing concerns of civil wars, violent intra- and inter-state or inter-group conflicts and gaps in legal apparatus wherein, such population becomes absent from the event of census or are denied special status determination process, as "unknown citizenship/nationality".

There are no clear estimates of the stateless population around the globe. The United Nations High Commissioner for Refugees estimates 10 million stateless globally (UNHCR Global Trends, Forced Displacement in 2018).[2] But this number is very fluid and has remained unchanged from previous years' statistical reporting. Of this number, at the end of 2017, only 3.9 million stateless people were "captured" in the data published by UNHCR, pushed into a web of poverty, isolation, abysmal disenfranchisement and deprivation for generations largely due to "state-centric conflicts" (Farzana, 2017). This tarnishes their identity between the man and the citizen, dumping them into a socio-legal limbo. Sen (2001) has argued that citizenship is integral for the enhancement of human capabilities; therefore, ensuring citizenship removes some of the "unfreedoms" that restrict personal and social development. Also, compatible with Sustainable Development Goal 16 which focuses on building

[2]UNHCR, Figures at Glance, https://www.unhcr.org/figures-at-a-glance.html.

just, peaceful and inclusive society which will help prevent and reduce statelessness in itself.

Interestingly, if we read the global scenario, the six biggest economies in the world—the USA, UK, Germany, France, China and Japan with 56.6% of global wealth—barely host less than 9% of the world's refugees. While Jordan, Turkey, the Palestinian Territories, Lebanon, Pakistan and South Africa—with 1.9% of cumulative global GDP—are shouldering the bulk of the responsibility by housing 50.02% of global refugees (Oxfam, 2016), inequality could not be clearer. The unwillingness to provide asylum to refugees and stateless population is reflected in the highly securitized political response by most nation states. Even, the path-breaking commitment made through "*The New York Declaration for Refugees and Migrants 2016*" called the world leaders for "more equitable sharing of the burden and responsibility" in hosting and supporting the refugees/migrants in the post-conflict situation, sustaining peace and increasing opportunities at home. The declaration seems to be committed to promoting diversity, sustainable development, deepening cooperation and demanding a more pluralistic society while advancing inclusion. It lays significant need on a comprehensive approach to the issues involved; however, it has overlooked one of the major rising issues of statelessness at the global level.

This chapter is based on the ethnographic inquiry conducted among stateless Rohingya refugees living in three major locations of India: Delhi, Mewat and Jammu. The study used both primary and secondary sources of data, based on both structured and semi-structured interview schedules to gather data about their journey, documentation, everyday life, employment and other issues. Interviews with women largely employ the semi-structured method. Since, they remain a passive group within the community, due to religious and cultural norms dictating their relationships and the role in their society and outside, which is often restricted with little or no engagement. While the method of observations also helped to understand the general impact of statelessness and refugeehood, it helped to understand the views, attitudes and behaviour as well as their interactions within the community, the way they support each other, culture and social functions. The study also draws from my engagement with different stakeholders, organizations and individuals who have been engaged with issues of forced migration, refugees and statelessness and particularly with the Rohingyas in India.

From Citizenship to Statelessness: A Historical Overview

It was only until 2009, when the haunting pictures of wandering Rohingyas in the rickety boats in the sea, often said to be the world's most persecuted ethnic Muslim minority from Myanmar, with traffickers making their lives more vulnerable and precarious, has vehemently hit the news headlines. Especially, after 2012 riots and the military crackdown on 9 October 2016, the border posts of Northern Rakhine state in Myanmar was never at rest rather continues to witness the killing of hundreds of Rohingyas and many thousands displaced. August 2017 again witnesses ferocious counter-insurgency campaigns which made no difference between the civilians and insurgents. Rohingya villages were pillaged and burned; women and girls were gang-raped and fleeing civilians executed by military soldiers.[3] Thus, between August 2017 and January 2018 approximated more than 656,000 Rohingyas fled from Myanmar into Bangladesh alone.[4] This evokes an uncanny resemblance with the unprecedented forced displacement and migration as of Vietnamese boat people in 1970s. Notably, the case of "Ethnic Rohingya Muslims" is far more discrete and revolves around the state induced-violence based on ethno-religious lines, since Myanmar's independence in 1948. Consequently, 1974 Constitution and enactment of 1982 Citizenship Act which barred them as a "national race", or citizenship/nationality under conservative nationalist ideology based on the exclusivity of Myanmar language, culture and the religion of the majority—Buddhism (International Crisis Group [ICG], 2000), unless they prove their ancestors lived in Myanmar before 1823. Most failed, rendering Rohingyas as *de jure stateless*[5] in the world of nation states. Since, it is the ethnic recognition that provides primordial constitutional legitimacy for citizenship. Contrasting the historical records, Muslims have lived in the Arakan region (now Rakhine) for centuries when it was an independent kingdom and not part of Myanmar; it can be traced as Arab traders who came in the region as far back as the eighth century (Bhaumik, 2013). Even the colonial records testify that the community, which embraced Islam, has been part and parcel of Burmese society.

While the situation was not always similar, under U Nu government in the 1950s the Rohingyas were accepted as an indigenous ethnic group and were active in the country's politics and governance. There were Rohingya MP's serving in Myanmar's Parliament and held at various other administrative positions. In 1951 election, five Rohingyas and six MPs got elected during 1956 election. While during 1990 general election, Rohingyas led National Democratic Party for Human Rights (also known as The Democracy and Human Rights Party) won four seats in Myanmar's Parliament. But later after putting Aung San Suu Kyi under house arrest, the party was banned by the military and their leaders were arrested and subsequently jailed. Yet, as latest as 2010–2012, the Rohingyas participated in the local municipal elections and were allowed to vote. But the community has steadily lost their political and constitutional identity with the oppressive military regime of General Ne Win[6] and the subsequent junta. There have been various instances when Rohingyas and pro-Rohingyas politicians were imprisoned to debar from contesting elections. In 2005, Shamsul Anwarul

[3]Rohingya Refugees "Stand on Precipice of More Tragedy" One Year After Brutal Breakdown, August 24, 2018 http://time.com/5374143/myanmar-rohingya-august-25-crackdown/.

[4]UNICEF, Bangladesh, Humanitarian Situation Report 17 (Rohingya Influx), January 7, 2018. https://www.unicef.org/appeals/files/UNICEF_Bangladesh_Humanitarian_SitRep_7_Jan_2018.pdf.

[5]Under the Article 1 of 1954 Convention relating to the Status of Stateless Persons, de jure statelessness refers to "a person not considered as a national by any State under the operation of its law".

[6]ARAKAN Monthly, September, 2009, http://www.burmalibrary.org/docs08/mag_arakan01-09.pdf.

Huq (also known as Kyaw Min) was arrested and sentenced to 47 years of imprisonment under the 1982 Citizenship Act. In 2015 again, Shwe Maung, a Union Solidarity and Development Party's MP, was barred from contesting election indicting that his parents are not citizens beneath the same controversial Citizenship Act.[7] He was among the few who speaks for the Rohingyas. Today, Rohingyas have no voting rights.

Many believe that the anxiety dates back to the 1942 Japanese invasion in Burma, the Rohingyas stayed loyal to the British while the majority Buddhist supported the Japanese that sparked conflict with the Rakhine and the Buddhists (Ibrahim, 2017; Smith, 1993). This also led to radicalize the independence movement against Muslims and foreigners, i.e. the British. Post-independence the animosity between the two communities grew and continues to destabilize the relationship. With the failure and exclusionary approach of Panglong conference[8] which envisaged "full autonomy to the frontier regions" under the union of Burma included only three major ethnic communities—the Chins, Shans and Kachins excluding other ethnic minorities—Wa, Mon, Karen, Kerenni and Arakanese including Rohingyas (Walton, 2008) under the state's policy of exclusion and ethnicization that has resulted in segregation and the creation of new identities for ethnic minorities (Farzana, 2015). However, there was a lot of opposition to the Panglong agreement demanding the creation of single "MahaBama" or greater Burman nationality. Thus, following the Aung San's assassination, the agreement was abandoned that further manifested the mistrust, hatred and violence. While the key policy shift took place shortly after general Ne Win launched the "Burmese way to Socialism (BWS)" through his Burma Socialist Programme Party (BSPP) that seized the control of the country in 1962 with the idea to strengthening economic development, reduce the influence of outside world and increasing the role of military, the problem for Rohingyas aggravated and began to be deprived of the basic rights on the pretext of being foreigners through the policy of "othering"; they dismantled Rohingya sociopolitical organizations. It is the Myanmar military's outlook towards the Rohingyas that has disrupted their equation in the society. They have always been suspicious of the Rohingya community and have viewed them as a demographic extension of Bangladesh—the Chittagong region. And, the policy also sought to reorient the dichotomous understanding of Burmese society aimed at creating an exclusive Burmese national identity based on the essentialist notion of nation-building through the exclusion of the ethnic "other" who were considered by-product of British colonial rule (Maung, 1963) leading to introducing the 1974 emergency Immigration Act that stripped Burmese (Myanmar) nationality from the Rohingyas which later got solidify with 1982 citizenship law and its 1983 procedures. Thus, in the name of "identifying and screen" foreigners, massive military operations like—"*Operation Naga Min*" (Dragon King) in 1977

[7]Irrawaddy (2015) https://www.irrawaddy.com/news/burma/rohingya-mp-and-mandalay-doctor-barred-from-contesting-november-election.html.

[8]A meeting on the dawn of Independence in 1947 between General Aung San and representatives of ethnic minorities at Panglong to discuss their status and demand for autonomy in a independent Burma. An agreement was signed which is known as "Panglong Agreement".

and prior to a national census "*Operation Pyi Thaya*" (Clean and Beautiful Nation) in 1991—were basically an effort to cleanse the providence of Rohingyas resulted into rise of nationalist groups and armed rebels like Rohingya Patriotic Front (RPF), Rohingya Solidarity Organisation (RSO) which came out of RPF in 1982 and RPF became Arakan Rohingya National Organisation (ARNO). There was a demand to join the then East Pakistan now Bangladesh and later for an independent Muslim state within the Union, but both these demands failed to mark any political impact (Bhaumik, 2013; Farzana, 2017; Lintner, 1999) rather the Myanmar government classified the groups as secessionist and terrorist organizations. Under the 1982 citizenship law, the government introduced colour coded Citizens Scrutiny Cards (CSC) in 1989—pink cards for full citizens, blue for associate citizens and green for naturalized citizens while the Rohingyas were not issued with any cards rejecting their claim to citizenship. However in 1995 after an aggressive campaign by UNHCR, the Rohingyas were issued with Temporary Registration Card (TRC), i.e. white card but the card does not hold any legal validity because it does not specify the nationality, place of birth as well as cannot be used to claim citizenship (Lewa, 2008; Ullah, 2015).

Currently, more than 800,000 ethnic Rohingyas are refused nationality/citizenship and its foreseen rights within Myanmar (UNHCR, A special report, Ending Statelessness with 10 years, 2015). But in 2013, Khin Yi, Minister for Immigration and Population, Myanmar put their numbers at 1.33 million in the country; 1.08 million are in Rakhine state. And, only 40,000 Rohingyas with citizenship in the country.[9] They were largely disenfranchised from census and election conducted in 2014 and 2015, respectively. And, continue to remain the "unwanted and most persecuted minority community" with repeated dismissal of the human rights that includes destruction of mosques, summary executions, confinement within the three major towns of Rakhine region (Buthidaung, Maungdaw and Rathedaung), travel, extortion, detention, enforced disappearances, arbitrary arrests, forced labour by the army on economic and infrastructural projects with zero pay and often under harsh conditions, sexual violence, land confiscated and other humiliating laws on marriage, procreation (forbidden from having more than two children), birth registration, no right to dignified funerals and death certificates as well as strict regulation on religious exercise and religious conversions[10] have pushed over 909,774 Rohingyas into displaced person camps (UNHCR factsheet, Bangladesh, 2019). Many others have sought refuge in the neighbouring Association of Southeast Asian Nations (ASEAN) and South Asian Association Regional Cooperation (SAARC) countries and beyond as the "boat people". Thus, they are forced to languish into ghetto-like conditions that lack access to healthcare, livelihood opportunities and education. When few attempted returning home, military and government rejected the returnees by classifying them as foreigners or illegal immigrant, all-encompassing in limbo. And, till now no human rights agencies, global observers, media, independent researchers

[9]Szep and Marshall (2013).

[10]Through personal in-depth interviews with the Rohingyas living in Delhi, Mewat and Jammu.

except the United Nations (with executive limitations) are allowed to travel and work in Rakhine region without permission.

The democratic transition that began in 2011 had galvanized hopes for the minorities and many human rights advocates from around the world expected ethnic reconciliation and peace in Myanmar. However, the faulted silence maintained by Aung San Suu Kyi exposes the dark underbelly of the emerging state wherein, the pervading sense of insecurity and discrimination against minorities is rampant, but acutely against Muslim Rohingyas. Clearly explains how much we misinterpreted Aung San Suu Kyi as a full spectrum democrat; she has proved to be a true politician who is an elected leader and is answerable to her own electorate, i.e. ethnically Barman community who is dominantly Anti-Rohingya. In fact, Suu Kyi's pragmatic approach was quite apparent while choosing the candidates for the 2015 elections; there was not a single Muslim stood as a candidate for the National League for Democracy (NLD) which did pay her off. Thus, the growing fundamentalism, i.e. the extreme nationalist vision of Buddhist Myanmar (Project Burmanization), is contributing to serious unrest and heightened securitization in the region. This systematic extermination of a large section of minority religions or ethnic identities is a state apparatus and is typically a modern phenomenon dedicated to realizing the ideal of ethnonational homogeneity by means of force, violence and institutionalizing exclusion (Mann, 2005). Furthermore, it is an effort in order to get advantages for the Buddhist Burmans majority population (Knuters, 2018).

Apparently, in a fragile state like—Myanmar where for more than five decades of military rule and continuous civil unrest resulted in a hostile culture—conflict resolution is a mammoth task. And, one should also not forget that irrespective of the election result and Aung San Suu Kyi's National League for Democracy party's victory, her administration has no control over the military (Tatmadaw), as they continue to hold a very secure position as per the provisions of 2008 Constitution of Myanmar. The military holds 25% of the reserved legislative seats (both union and state) in the parliament. Hence, they have the power to legally block any Constitutional amendments. It requires more than 75% votes to amend the Constitution. Similarly, they continue to hold key cabinet positions like interiors, defence and border security. It is a fact that in the state of emergency, the military has the power to control the country (Bhatia, 2015; Pradhan, 2015; The Constitution of Myanmar, 2008), and it is the army who define what is an emergency; it also controls large parts of the national economy. With such important portfolios, the military would always remain in a strong position in the country's governance and the overall functioning of the administration. In such a highly institutionalized military climate, Myanmar's democratic transition is facing many hurdles, and Rohingya crisis is one of them. Thus, it is a messianic wait for an unprecedented future.

Some of the grievances shared by the Rohingyas interviewed explains their frustration and ambiguous future back in Myanmar, one of them, named Mhd. Shajjad (name changed) at Mewat, Haryana said;

> Since childhood, we have been hearing 'democracy and peace would come back to Myanmar' but nothing happened till now. We were forced to leave our homeland. We expected a lot

> from Aung San Suu Kyi but it's only after she has come to power, things have gone worst. She has done nothing for us…She is with the army.

The above testimony clearly highlights how the country has stepped back into the dark past or could say a dystopian reality especially for the Rohingyas, who were positive and dreaming for change and peace with the victory of pro-democratic civilian leader—Aung San Suu Kyi but the way she defended the military, the generals and government and continues to reject the allegations of the crimes committed against Rohingyas rather said fighting with Rohingya militants and terrorism and denies targeting civilians. However, the accelerated violence and mass displacement speak a different story. Thus, she is now widely seen as an enabler of ethnic cleansing and genocide.

Statelessness Beyond Boundaries: Rohingyas in India

> We would have been killed in Burma; therefore, I with family decided to flee. We first sneaked into Bangladesh…, later, entered India in 2012, in the hope to have a better life. We paid Rs 10000 for each person to a broker (Dalal) at Cox Bazaar to cross the Bangladesh-India border…,it took 3 days to cross the border by walking at night…I was very scared of the security forces as I knew if got caught would have been jailed. Later, after reaching to Kolkata … and, we again paid Rs 3000 each to reach Delhi via train. But unfortunately, living conditions here are bad. There are no proper toilets or drinking water facilities. No one is willing to give a job. Surviving has become challenging. We don't know where to go or what to do? Don't we have any right to live? I feel being born as a Rohingya Muslim in Burma is like punishment… and has left us to nowhere…

—Rushaal, (name changed), New Delhi

As narrated above, experiences of brutal violence, the lack of recognition and citizenship in a land they have traditionally called home and being forced to flee leaving all their possessions and belongings behind is humiliating in the very least. The desperation to gain protection, security and hope for life has forced the innocent Rohingyas with children to embark on perilous sea voyages and long odyssey across lands, mountains and paddy fields through the economy of human traffickers and smugglers, without proper food, water or medical support. Although many international and national agencies are allegedly aware of these smuggling rackets involving transnational syndicates, yet nothing much has been done since no one wants to take the responsibility of unwanted burden. Henceforth, the plight of the Rohingyas seems irreconcilable and interminable due to inadequacy, inconsistency and incongruity between the international, regional and national law/policies on humanitarian care and protection, asylum and hospitality towards forced migration and refugee/stateless population movement. It has failed to respond to the crisis. The attrition is now telling on them. Following the same, there is also a real politik angle for India's negligence and long maintained silence wherein India's "Act East policy" which currently focusing on building economic and strategic relations along enhancing connectivity through Kaladan multi-modal transit project at its north-western frontier with Myanmar, Sittwe port, Shwe Natural Gas Extraction Project besides other investments in Tamu-Kalea and Moreh-Kalewa-Yargi corridor as well as overwhelming presence of China in the country sets outs a depressing picture to the Rohingya crisis. Hence, India is extremely wary, considering it as an internal matter of Myanmar. Notably, Myanmar and the rising crisis in the country hold much significance from India's point, not just because it is an adjacent country, but also because their borders are sensitive, porous and militancy prone. And, the country shares its borders with two prominent countries, i.e. India and China holding geopolitical importance (Bhatia, 2015; Quraishi, 2015). Nevertheless, India's larger interest lies in restricting China from entering the Bay of Bengal could also be a key motive why India wants to build goodwill with Myanmar, further providing a good reason to stay away from the Rohingya issue. In short, India's response is a cold cost-benefit calculation based on bilateral relations concerning trade, security, securing cooperation on counter-insurgency operations in its northeast and maintaining leverage vis-à-vis China. Besides, the Hindutva politics of the current dispensation is clearly evident through the Citizenship (Amendment) Act, 2019. It considers all non-Muslim refugees or illegal migrants from Bangladesh, Pakistan and Afghanistan eligible for Citizenship. Thus, with the growing religious majoritarianism in India, Rohingya Muslims are facing the brunt.

India is neither signatory to the UN Convention related statelessness[11] and refugees[12] nor has any specific domestic law governing the treatment of such a population. Assuming these conventions will affect India's security and domestic laws (Nair, 2007); India is largely governed by ad hoc and ambivalent approach grounded on the morality, humanitarianism and political and administrative willingness (Ananthachari, 2001; Dhanvan, 2004). Legally, like any other foreign nationals, refugees and stateless persons are governed under the jurisdiction of Foreigners Act 1946 and Passport Act 1955 (Banerjee, Chaudhury, & Ghosh, 2015). Thereby, does not hold accountable for neglecting or criminalizing any legit case of asylum on the grounds of national security or travelling without valid documents and are liable to detention and deportation. Further marginalizes a group of already stigmatized and vulnerable individuals and a grim reminder of serious humanitarian crises in the legal apparatus of the country.

It is difficult to enumerate the Rohingyas living in India, given the presence of a large number of unregistered refugees and stateless persons in the Indian sea of humanity thus, there are many estimates. The Government of India estimates, there are 40,000 Rohingyas as of 2017. However, the United Nations High Commissioner for Refugees (UNHCR), India registered records, as of 2019; there are approximately 18,000 stateless Rohingya refugees. The Indian government had given Long Term Visas to 500 Rohingyas but none got renewed after 2016. And, the majority continues

[11]Till now, there are only 70 countries who are party to 1961 Convention on the Reduction of Statelessness and 89 countries to the 1954 convention relating to the Status of Stateless Persons and 1961 Convention on the Reduction of Statelessness.

[12]1951 UN Convention on Refugees and 1967 Protocol Relating to the Status of Refugees.

to live under deplorable conditions in makeshift camps of unauthorized colonies of semi-urban slums spread over different parts of the country—Jammu and Kashmir, Delhi, Haryana, Uttar Pradesh, Rajasthan, West Bengal, Andhra Pradesh, Tamil Nadu and Andaman and Nicobar Islands.

The timeline of their arrival in India is quite unknown until 2012. It is only when they were in news through their protest outside the UNHCR's office in New Delhi, demanding for lawful aid and protection that there was a notice of them. Most of the stateless refugees whom I interviewed for the purpose of my research have lived in Bangladesh either for a significant or a short period before coming to India. And, the decision was made on the premises of the then harsh conditions and scare opportunity in Bangladesh as well as what their fellow Rohingyas has described India. The majority is very well connected through mobile phones and other informal communication channels. One such experience shared was by Akram (name changed), from Kanchan Kunj, New Delhi, he said

> …After the death of my father, my mother was unable to take care of us (brother and sisters), we didn't even have enough to eat, we couldn't even go out of the camp to work and earn thus she asked me to go to my uncle in India, who can at least feed me.

New Delhi, being the national capital and the seat to UNHCR's head office, makes it an obvious destination. But initially, most stateless Rohingya refugees followed the path of Bangladeshi's economic immigrants to places like Jammu. They believe that living around a substantial Muslim population will be much safer and has also proved to be welcoming and supportive. However, it has also been observed that there is a clear divide between them (Indian Muslims and Rohingya Muslims). Although they both practice Islam yet, they believe that their ways and culture is different. The Indian Muslims do not like the fact that Rohingyas can use the same burial ground for themselves, hence, have extended a separate land. Even the Rohingyas feel likewise. One of the Rohingya, named Mhd. Ropik (name changed) to whom I interviewed in Mewat's Chandeni village, said—"*Indian Muslims are different. Their practices and beliefs are different from us…*". Thus, it is apparent that the feelings are mutual and the "Muslim Brotherhood" does not work in this case.

> After coming to India, I got to understand what it is like sleep in peace at night but now the situation is changing here too, I fear they might send us back just as what they did to 7 Rohingyas recently, the police is also enlisting us, they come regularly…we do not want to go back till the situation improves, it's horrible there, we will die…even the UNHCR is doing nothing about it, we don't know what is going to happen tomorrow, we just want to have a peaceful living…

—Shaffi (name changed, from Bhatindi, Jammu)

Such testimonies clearly explain that following the deportation of seven stateless Rohingyas in October last year (2018) and later a family of five members in January this year (2019) on grounds of national security or public disorder as are "*illegal immigrants*" became a nightmare for the marginal community. Even though, this stands against India's long-term commitment towards the principle of non-refoulement[13]

[13]The right to seek and enjoy asylum is a customary principle in international law, under UDHR, Article 14.

as well as against fundamental rights guaranteed under Article 14 and 21 and is inconsistent with the spirit of 51(C) of Indian Constitution. Mostly, refugees fleeing persecution cross borders without any prior planning and documentation. Thus, often blur the difference between victim and illegal immigrant. Surprisingly, India has not raised any question on the 14,300 refugees from other ethnic communities of Myanmar, who has also sought refuge/asylum in the country like—the Chin, Kachin, Falam, Tedim, Matu, etc. The point here is that why one particular religious community have been tagged as having terrorist linkages? It is clear that with the Hindu nationalist agenda dictating the current state policy has further fed into the global Islamophobic industry by using the "Islamic" identity of the stateless Rohingyas refugees as "terrorist". Thus, India is gearing up to expel them. However, India should move beyond its insecure discursive milieu and act maturely.

Extreme bureaucratic measures including extensive surveillance, border control and biometrics of Rohingyas have intensified the prevailing fear and anxiety among the community. I have personally encountered many Rohingyas who were unwilling to speak. While few who agreed shared that they are very unsure of their situation in India, they fear that the biometrics will be used to send them back to Myanmar. They mentioned that the form is been directed by the Ministry of Home Affairs in confidence with Embassy of Myanmar but before filling seven pages long detailed biometrics form, they contacted UNHCR to understand the consequences and to clear their apprehensions. Apparently, they did not have any other option except to cooperate with the authorities and to fill the forms. Such incidences have led many Rohingyas from Delhi, Mewat and Jammu[14] to flee back to Bangladesh or other countries fearing forced deportation to Myanmar which may cost their lives. Specifically, in Jammu, the animosity between the local and Rohingyas has grown over the years fearing their linkages with terrorist organizations and bringing change in the demography by marrying locals. However, fear of marrying the locals actually holds true as there are fewer cases in both Delhi and Jammu, wherein Rohingya women have married the locals.[15] While various Hindutva ideological political parties or groups and even the Jammu Chamber of Commerce have openly called for the Rohingya to be driven out, in fact mysterious incidences of fire in Rohingya settlements truly speaks for the propaganda and triggers "sabotage" theory said by Anuradha Bhasin during the personal interview.[16] She even shared that most of the Rohingyas have been living in Jammu since 2005. And, it was 2008, during the Amarnath land agitation when campaigns against Rohingya started. In 2017, several billboards were put-up with messages such as "Wake up Jammu, Rohingyas and Bangladeshis quit Jammu" and "Threats of Rohingyas looms large over the heads

[14]According to the NGO—Save the Children (Jammu), 130 Rohingyas have gone back to Bangladesh in 2018 alone.

[15]Through personal interview with Ms. Rena Senyal, senior project coordinator, DAJI, Jammu, February 2019.

[16]Through personal interview with Anuradha Bhasin, executive editor of Kashmir Times, February 2019.

of peace loving Jammuites, let's all unite to save Jammu", has fanned the xenophobic discourse.[17] Thus, due to this mounting animosity, there was an attempt in late 2017 to shift Rohingyas from Jammu to Hyderabad. Approximately, 300 families were shifted. The process was initiated by UNHCR with its implementing partners Development Justice Initiative (DAJI) and Save the Children (Jammu) to provide safe zones to Rohingya families facing threats from right-wing political parties in Jammu. However, the process phased out by April 2018 as all safe zones were filled up and increasing attacks on minorities in other states as said by Rena Senyal, DAJI (Jammu) during the interview. Interestingly, when I interviewed Ravi Nair, executive director, South Asia Human Rights Documentation Centre (SAHRDC), who is closely working on the Rohingya issue in India, said

> Government of India does not want to recognize the refugees/stateless population especially under the given political scenario of increasing Hindu fundamentalism and nationalist policies whereas as far as UNHCR Delhi is concerned, they are incompetent and have not fulfilled any of their protection duty. They lack the political will to push for protection issues in whole of South Asia. They have failed to tackle the issue of arrested Rohingyas at the border or in jail as well as on the deportation issue. Even the partner NGO's want to play save and doesn't want to take any strong position which may jeopardize their position with UNHCR or Government of India as that may affect their funding or FCRA.

Again, as shared by Rena Senyal and Ravi Nair, it highlights the UNHCR's project based top-down approach wherein local NGO's treated as subcontractors rather than partners. Moreover, staggering fund-based commitment of most NGO's is also problematic. Thus, has failed to tackle the issue.

Apparently, under the 1951 Convention on the Status of Refugees, the onus is on the individuals seeking refugee status in India to prove "the fear of persecution" at the time of seeking asylum thereby making their life a living hell, denoting them as illegal immigrant during the period of undefined status or on rejection of asylum application. Perhaps what is more damaging is that Indian Government does not acknowledge the UNHCR issued documents as legitimate and jeopardizing their living and access to services at the host country. Additionally, unlike the other refugee mandate, in its India operation, UNHCR seems to club the "stateless" and "refugee" categories together. Since Rohingyas in India are not recognized as "stateless" but as "refugees", although in registering their legal status is marked "stateless".[18] Thus, contradicts with the UN definition of refugee (a person who is forced to flee his/her country, i.e. country of nationality/citizenship due to a well-founded fear of persecution. A refugee not only has a nationality/citizenship but also when this fear is gone, he/she may return). And, there is a clear overlap of stateless and refugee identity in case of Rohingyas which may further create operational complexities since they are not only stateless but with crossing the international borders are refugees too.

---

[17] See Footnote 16.

[18] Though personal interview with Ipshita Sengupta, UNHCR, India, Delhi, March 2019.

Nature of Refuge in India

Delhi,[19] Mewat[20] and Jammu[21] show remarkable similarity in the living conditions since none of these settlements is officially designated by Government of India or UNHCR rather are "self-settled". The majority lives in slum-like settlements on privately owned lands except for the Kanchan Kunj near Madanpur Khadar, Delhi as earlier were living on land owned and provided by a non-governmental organization (NGO), Zakat Foundation but after the April 2018 fire incident, they have shifted to nearby government-owned land. These habitations are crudely built temporary shelters propped up by bamboo, plywood, cardboard and covered with tarp sheets wherein rooms are small, unsteady or asymmetrical and very dingy, with no proper sunlight and an unhealthy atmosphere. Such materials do not provide sufficient resistance from extreme climatic conditions and usually lack facilities like sanitation especially no toilet facility, water, sewage and electricity. Mostly, the electricity connection which they access in all these settlements is illegal. Similar is the condition of water availability as mostly, they call for water tankers and store the water in the water tanks which they have collectively bought. At Saran Vihar in Shaheen Bagh, Delhi, they have installed hand pumps, while the electrical connection they have been using is through their landlord to whom they pay additionally with the land rent.[22] In fact, both in Saran Vihar and in Kanchan Kunj, Rohingya settlements coexist with other migrants from Bihar and Nepal. In Jammu again, mostly all settlements are built on private land for which they pay rent individually depending on the size of land or hut acquired, usually it ranges from Rs. 800 to Rs. 1800 per month with additional Rs. 200 to Rs. 400 for electricity.[23] While in Mewat, the Rohingyas pay an annual rent of Rs. 60,000, Rs. 40,000 and Rs. 35,000, respectively, for the three plots where they are living in Chandeni village.[24] The fear of eviction and fire continues to haunt these stateless Rohingya refugees at all the three locations;

[19]There is around 800 Rohingyas living in Delhi. Rohingyas are scattered in Delhi. They live in slum-like settlements such as in Kanchan Kunj near Madanpur Khadar, Saran Vihar in Shaheen Bagh near Jasola metrostation and Khajuri Khas in northeast Delhi where they are living in rented houses as well as few scattered families living in the unauthorized colonies of Vikaspuri and Uttam Nagar near Don Bosco's field Office.

[20]There are 1300 families of Stateless Rohingya refugees are living in Mewat, Haryana. Three plots in Chandeni village and two plots in Nagli and Punananear the Nuh's District Bus Depot, Nuh District of Mewat, Haryana.

[21]According to DAJI and save the children (Jammu), there were 8000 Rohingyas in Jammu till October 2018. But now it is estimated that approx. 5000–6000 Rohingyas in Jammu across nine major clusters. The two major settlements in Jammu are Narwal and Bhatindi with around 80% of the total population in Jammu. While other are—Sunjuwan, Malik Market, Channi Rama, Channi Himmat, Trikutu Nagar, Pananma Chowk, Bagh-e-Bahu, Bhagwati Nagar, GolPuri, Durga Nagar, Paloti, Paloda, Toph and Bari Brahmana. And, there are approximately 20–30 Rohingya families in Srinagar district near Dargah Hazratbal of Kashmir. There are few in Qazigund Anantnag, but they remain in a regular movement to Jammu to Srinagar and vice versa.

[22]Through personal interview—Noor Yunus, January 2019.

[23]Through personal interview—Mhd. Shafi, February 2019.

[24]Through personal interview—Jaffarulla, January 2019.

incidences of snake bite have been repeatedly reported. Due to the absence of legal documents and illiteracy, the Rohingyas are usually employed in the informal sector as daily wage labourer's—construction or factory workers, rag pickers, meat-shops, rickshaw pullers or fewer have opened small groceries shops or tea stalls in their vicinity. Mostly, Rohingya women are not encouraged to work, rather, confined in the veil "Pardah" since the accepted cultural and religious perception is that women are the weaker sex. Therefore are better off inside the house, looking after home, children, and husband is their principal job. There is no need for them to go out and access public spheres. In fact, most of the women are neither much educated nor able to adopt the local language, except for few, further restricting their mobility and is another attack on their agency, liberty and dignity. "*…Eating out of woman's salary is forbidden 'haram' for us*". As said by Mhd. Roopik (name changed) living in Mewat during the interview. Life is much harsh for single, divorced and widow women. Recently in Jammu, many women have started to take up work of walnut cracking which they do from home and earn around Rs. 100 to Rs. 150 per day.[25] While I remember meeting Sancita (name changed) at the Madanpur Khadar Rohingya settlement in New Delhi, India, she came to India in 2012 and is working as an interpreter at Don Bosco's Refugee Programme. She has been separated from her husband, who is presently in Kolkata jail as got arrested while illegally crossing the border. She shared; *"I have not seen my husband since last four years. I was helpless and being a woman alone in a foreign land, it wasn't easy…I was hesitant and scared but was forced to work for survival…though in our community, a woman working outside is not considered good"*.

She even shared that has requested and filled many applications to UNHCR and Don Bosco to help her to bring her husband out of jail but unfortunately, there is no success yet. Moreover, the struggle for stateless Rohingya refugees gets further convoluted when language becomes a barrier. This cumbers their daily functioning. In May 2018, Supreme Court of India gave a landmark judgement on the writ petition filled in 2013 by two Rohingyas wherein, Rohingyas living in India are entitled to the basic human rights and services.[26] Yet, they still find it difficult to access basic healthcare services, clean drinking water, hygienic living condition, basic education facility or access to livelihood opportunities etc. bringing a significant decline in the living standards, often run on low rations.

Highlighting similar experiences, one of the participants, Rehman (name changed) shared that,

> When I came to India in 2011, surviving here was very difficult. I knew no one, neither the language. I had to sleep on footpaths and couldn't even buy food for myself since I didn't even know how to ask though had some money. Occasionally was able to buy through gestures and signs but few days had slept empty stomach too. Infact when I went to look for jobs, no one was ready to hire me, people rejected me saying, I cannot talk to them in the local language, so how will I be able to work? But now, things are quite better since I have learned the language…

[25]Through personal interview—ShabukManhar, February 2019.

[26]Writ Petition (Civil) No 859/2013- Jaffar Ullah and Anr versus Union of India and Ors.

While another related her experiences, Noorjahan (name changed), a Rohingya women who came to India with her family (husband and four children) in 2012 from Bangladesh and presently living in Kanchan Kunj near Madanpur Khadar, South Delhi recounts that

> Most employers ask for Aadhaar card but how come my husband show that since we don't have one. In fact, when my husband showed his UNHCR's Refugee card, they would laugh and ask what was it? Now, you only tell me? How will we survive without job and money, how will we buy food. Thankfully, nowadays my husband has got some work as daily wage labourer at the metro construction site but still, we don't know whether tomorrow he will get work or not…

The above testimonies encapsulate the human stories that lie behind their continuous struggle for existence that has been inevitably nebulous and shrouded in uncertainty wherein it acutely affects their daily struggle to earn their livelihood and welfare. Moreover, the oxymoron state's laws and policies beleaguered flotsam of endemic discrimination, exploitation and harassment that continues to haunts them even at the host country; targeting their very existence, according to the "targeted delivery of financial and other subsidies, benefits and services Act, 2016", i.e. Aadhaar, every "resident" of India except Jammu and Kashmir (J&K) shall be entitled to obtain unique identification number by submitting his demographic and biometric information. The Act further states—a "resident" is an individual who has resided in India for a period or periods amounting in all to one hundred and eighty-two days or more in the twelve months immediately preceding the date of application for enrolment[27] yet, many Rohingyas living in India were criminalized for acquiring Aadhaar cards and forced to return. While its absence has estranged them from acquiring jobs as it has become a pre-requirement to seek for a job, most employers ask for the same.

Mhd. Iqbal (name changed) at Kanchan Kunj near Madanpur Khadar, South Delhi, who was fortunate enough to acquire decent job as night security guard at Dyal Singh College of Delhi University with remuneration of 13,000 (INR) but soon got fired, when a police officer patrolling came to college one night and coincidentally found that he was a Rohingya Muslim from Myanmar, who later arrested and investigated him, suspecting him a Bangladeshi, enquiring the reasons for coming to India, when Iqbal showed his UNHCR refugee card. Officer discarded its authenticity. After much questioning and persuasion by local NGO, he was left to go. But, the very next morning, he was summoned by the college authorities, where he was questioned again about his identity. Later, he simply got sacked saying the post demanded an Indian national. I can still recall him saying

> what was my crime that I am a Rohingya Muslim from Myanmar and not an Indian? I was just doing my duty; don't I have any right to live peacefully. I also want a good life. Want to get out of this hut and shift in a proper house. I want to educate my daughter like the other kids at the college but now since I don't have a job. I don't know how I will sustain my family…

---

[27] Aadhaar Act (2016) https://uidai.gov.in/images/targeted_delivery_of_financial_and_other_subsidies_benefits_and_services_13072016.pdf.

Listening to the experiences and learning about their manifold difficulties make one thing clear that the feeling of non-belonging and construction of "other/othering", designed through governmentality which in this context argues through a universal and preconceived paradigm, falling back upon creation of binaries—"the citizens and the aliens/other", signifies that the notion of one language, culture or religion is so embedded that it excludes all others and becomes exclusive, believing "the others (i.e. non-citizens including migrants/refugees/stateless)" as "threat", reflecting the superiority and inferiority or exclusionary relations among different groups wherein nation as a unity is based on people with single culture or religion. Generating national feeling is the central reason behind the sociopolitical bedlam and subsequent refugee generation and inflow in the region (Shils, 1995). Making citizenship document as the most important document for recognition, i.e. the identity to an individual to avail any socio-legal and political rights and services like—employment, opening a bank account, property, rent, marriage, vote or even the right to dissent or to appeal against, etc., through which people form daily routine. In short, it acts as an integrative function that promotes shared identity among various social groups within the state as well as with the state. While, if it is denied or the absence drops one's identity as the faceless mass affecting their overall functioning and protracted exclusion for generations resulting in an intractable state of limbo.

Emerging agnostic milieu wherein, not just ethnic violence and denationalization but also the discrimination, denigration, and isolation has become a part of their everyday lives irrespective of the place of habitat (i.e. country of origin or at host country), leading to a profound impact on their collective imagination through a constant sense of fear of uncertainty. And, often become the victims of mistaken identity as "Bangladeshi i.e. economic illegal immigrant". Thus, criminalization, suspicion and mistaken identity as well as facing repulsion and repercussion are the reality for the Rohingyas living in India leaving them dismantled. As Arendt portended and explained, "The stateless person, without the right to residence and without the right to work, had of course constantly to transgress the law. He was liable to jail sentence without ever committing the crime…" ensuring a pervasive sense of limbo and emptiness, a sense of being stuck and not knowing when things would change further burden the individuals who are already vulnerable and outcasted. This narrates the jarring truth about the relationship between state and refugees/stateless persons as highly hostile, conflictual and lopsided. It is the states, who have all the executive powers to decide and control the movements of such a population. In the "state of exception", Agamben (2005) asserted that refugees/stateless persons are politically insignificant and unwanted, and thereby are anticipated to maintain a passive life so to remain entitled to receive support and stay permissions within the territorial jurisdiction. Concurrently, they ought to be prepared for forced deportation at any moment's notice. Thus, their relationship with the host states is marked by intense distrust, suspicion and dissatisfaction, and they remain the permanently exempted from citizenship wherein the state acts as a monolith and totalitarian in nature.

However, in last few years, there are many organizations that came forward in collaboration with UNHCR or independently to work for the Rohingyas and their concerns. Mostly, the interventions made are in areas of healthcare accessibility, education and personal hygiene and protection. Organization like Don Bosco and Zakkat foundation has helped the Rohingya children to access Government Schools and healthcare in Delhi while, Jamaat-e-Islami Hind, an Islamic charitable organization allows the Rohingyas to receive free treatment at Al Shifa hospital near Jamia Nagar in Delhi.[28] However, usually all the Rohingyas prefer to visit private hospitals or clinics for their treatment to avoid long queue and follow-up visits; they also believe that private hospitals provide more attention and better treatment.[29] Development and Justice Initiative (DAJI) in Mewat and Save the Children in Jammu as the implementing partners of UNHCR are mandated to create awareness on education among the community. DAJI is also working independently in Jammu. Sakhawat centre is another NGO working with Rohingya in Jammu, since 2012 on education, medical camps and distribution of ration to some families. Association for Social Media Professionals (ASMP) a voluntary organization is working on digital livelihood opportunity for the Rohingyas living in the Saran Vihar settlement in New Delhi. Another UNHCR mandated organization, Fair Trade Forum India (FTF-I) is working around Delhi and Mewat on building self-reliance through skills training and employment opportunities under which loans have been provided to few Rohingyas to open small shops/business in their vicinity. The Socio-Legal Information Centre (SLIC) is part of the Human Rights Law Network (HRLN) and South Asian Human Rights Documentation Centre (SAHRDC) provides free legal assistance to refugees and asylum seekers and liaises with the local authorities. However, these organizations continue to face excessive inquiries, monitoring and objections from the government authorities; one of the organization's representatives on condition of anonymity shared,

> "our organization was working with Rohingyas in Delhi and Mewat in partnership with UNHCR, we were receiving regular enquiry phone calls from Home Ministry and local authorities to know about our involvement with the Rohingyas…they even suggested to opt-out of the project as already a case of their deportation is in court". He further added, "We didn't want to get into any unnecessary trouble with the government authorities, hence were forced to drop our work with the Rohingyas."

Few recurring issues highlighted by most of the Rohingyas were that they do not receive the subsistence allowance from UNHCR which all other refugee groups in India receive. In Delhi, most of the Rohingyas pointed out that they have not been receiving any support from UNHCR in terms of livelihood, the last time any small business loan provided was in 2016 and there have been no life skill training programmes in 2018. Most of the stateless Rohingya refugees whom I interviewed mentioned that they expect to receive more support from UNHCR hence are disheartened. Additionally, since UNHCR's Refugee Status Determination is done on the case to case basis hence, every time to get a new card or renew their refugee card, they have to travel with the whole family which again cost them a lot and difficult

---

[28]Through the personal interview with Mohammad Nayyar, production manager, MMI Publishers, 2015.

[29]Through the personal interaction with the stateless Rohingya Refugees in all three locations (Delhi, Mewat and Jammu).

to manage because most live from hand to mouth. One such similar grievances were shared by Shambur (name changed), one of the Rohingya women living in Bhatindi, Jammu, she came to India in 2012 along with her husband, she mentioned

> We do not get any assistance or services from the government, its only UNHCR that has provided one UNHCR refugee card, which has no meaning and no use as neither can provide a job or admission to our children in school, we can't even get a sim card from this refugee card. The only thing UNHCR sometimes gives us in 7-8 months is some soaps, mosquito net, sanitary pads. Even S.A. (Subsistence Allowance) is not provided to us, which other refugees get. UNHCR officials do not understand our issues, neither listen to us.

It is the stopgap approach of UNHCR and other agencies which is problematic as it continues to focus on care and maintenance with their limited funds and waning donor commitment. Thus, it turns to be recurring expense rather comprehensive durable solutions for the future. Interestingly, Rohingyas themselves have begun to assert their agency through their collective efforts and formation of NGO's or committees like—Rohingya Human Rights Initiative (ROHRInga) in Delhi and Rohingya refugee committee in Jammu. But, in amidst, of all positive development, there are few prevalent issues within the community like-its usual for Rohingya girls dropping-out school as soon they hit puberty, child-marriage, polygamy (multiple marriages by Rohingya men), domestic violence and abuse and use illicit drugs—mostly cannabis (ganja) or using thinners. Thus, Rohingya woman and children especially girl child continues to face humiliations from within, as a result of the socio-religious context of their community. Additionally, finding themselves within the larger ambit of the stateless population faces multiple humiliations of their own. This constant cycle of humiliations and abuse from multiple spheres is characteristic of the lived experience of the Rohingya woman and children, where they are devoid of autonomy and agency.

Politics of Humanitarian Issues and the Debate of Neutrality

Engaging in a rights-based humanitarian approach has long been highly political and precarious. Moreover, keeping impartial and equitable functioning is becoming a far more complex and challenging task. Especially in today's globalized era of market economy wherein, there is a sudden boom of humanitarian organizations and aid workers/actors around the globe, all concerned with war, armed conflict, wanton violent extremism and growing inequalities. Yet, refugees and stateless are mere objects of assistance and in the very process of aid disbursement are deliberately pushed to the margins (Indra, 1999).

Most of the national and international humanitarian organizations/actors and peacekeepers working for protection and assistance for victims of war and other situations of violence, promoting respect for international humanitarian law and the implementation in national law claims to be autonomous, neutral and impartial, are actually depended on major powers for funds to run their operations. Also, the need of permission from governments and various other authorities to function in a particular war zone/region or community has raised the question of funding and their autonomy which often gets conflated with protection regime. Since usually these funds directly or indirectly come from voluntary contributions through supranational organizations (like the European Commission and other major states), public and private donors including corporate houses concerned or driven by increasing human rights violations which might affect their business and protection of their own people. This has brought questions of accountability to the fore. The question such as—are they accountable to the funding agencies or to the people? And, what about decision-making, who has the power to decide? This explains how protection regime is inconsistent, inadequate and also politically driven as then why do certain groups/communities receive international/national protection, while other equally needy do not? This has also a lot to do with what kind of bilateral (political and economic) relations the countries share (the host country and country of origin of the disadvanced community seeking refuge), which is clearly visible in case of Tibetan refugees in India. They are the most fortunate population living within India territory, running a government in exile and receive a great deal of assistance and services from India and other governments from all around the World. Even the case of Sri Lankan Tamil Refugees, the Government of India runs official refugee camps. However other asylum seekers, refugees and stateless population such as Chakmas, CHT, Afghanis, Rohingyas, Sudanese and Lotshampas from Nepal and Bhutan—to name few examples do not receive the same kind of support. At times, it is also been observed that the international organizations/actors have to withdraw their operations or cut short their programmes in the conflict region or community in need due to the sudden lack of funds or security reasons, especially when funding agency/country itself is a part of conflicting parties. Additionally, channelling aid to the conflict regions or states in the emergency is also a strategy by most of the developed nations to restrict such population from migrating and entering their borders. And, no human emergency becomes an emergency until it hits the European borders. While for a few others aid assistance is just a way to fulfil their participation in global politics and get away from the real issue, it has become part of their foreign policy. Similarly, in case of Rohingyas, India came forward with humanitarian assistance and relief-*operation Insaniyat* in Bangladesh but at the same time, remained mute on the crisis rather the decision can be seen as de-incentivizing Rohingyas entering into India. Interestingly, juxtaposing humanitarian and political aspects the Ministry of External Affair's in the first press release on "*Operation Insaniyat*" avoided the term Rohingya rather referred refugees in Bangladesh,[30] while the same population in India is considered as illegal immigrants and continues not to receive any kind of assistance from the government.

Even the principle of neutrality, i.e. not to take sides in hostilities or engaging in controversies of a political, religious, racial or ideological nature is again seen as a matter of contention in the humanitarian approach of the International and national peacekeeping agencies/actors. How can we separate justice and peace from human

---

[30]Government of India, Minister of External Affairs, Press Release September 14, 2017. https://mea.gov.in/press-releases.htm?dtl/28944/Operation_Insaniyat__Humanitarian_assistance_to_Bangladesh_on_account_of_influx_of_refugees.

right, humanity and humanitarian work or approach? It could be regular encounter or confrontation with the state, governments or armed actors asserting the rights of people during conflict especially when the greatest perpetrator of mass violence and discrimination is the "State" itself. In such a situation keeping oneself aloof or staying neutral questions the credibility of such humanitarian organizations. Thereby, no one questions or challenges the authority of a violent and oppressive state/government. As the saying goes, not objecting or opposing a crime or criminal, facilitates feeder to the crime. Keeping a focused approach to relief work rather on eradication or prevention maintains a sheer balance between crime/violence and relief or aid work as parallels, i.e. Band aid humanitarianism. Henceforth, their work not just remains on the superficial level; rather, they also become a predator of democracy and humanity because the pillars of democracy stand on dissent against exploitation, violence and inequality. Humanitarian actors and aid organizations and countries are expected to act and stand against injustice and violence. India's so-called strategic decision to remain salient on the gross human rights violations by Myanmar, refraining to use the word Rohingya or talk about the crisis even during Prime Minister Modi's visit to Myanmar in September 2017 speaks for itself. India has refused to pressurize Myanmar instead choose a middle path of strategic neutrality in order to maintain a cordial relationship with both countries and continued to support both Myanmar and Bangladesh with humanitarian aid, who is facing the blunt of the crisis and hosting nearly one million stateless Rohingya refugees, thus, trying to balance its ties with both the countries. Moreover, India's recent abstention from voting on the "UN Human Rights Council Draft resolution on the situation of Human Rights in Myanmar" explains India's passivity on this humanitarian crisis.

Conclusion

The issue of statelessness revolves around the fault lines of modern nation state built along the ethno-religious lines. Moreover, the rising intolerance, ultranationalist sentiments, extremisms and the highly limited and uneven humanitarian protection regime both on geographical and political terms makes it even more precarious and protracted. This is particularly true in case of ethnic Rohingya Muslims, who have been discriminated, denationalized and persecuted for decades.

Former U.N. High Commissioner for Human Rights Zeid bin Ra'ad al-Hussein calling it a "textbook example of ethnic cleansing". Later, the UN Fact-Finding Mission on Myanmar report that came in September 2018 presented damning evidence of the military's crimes and atrocities committed against Rohingyas. Thereby, many scholars, human rights activists and observers categorized it as "genocide" and compared with past tragedies of Rwanda, Bosnia and Darfur did shock the world. Still, the Rohingya crisis remains worrying and shrouded in silence maintained by most nations and international agencies including UN. The lack of democratic culture in Myanmar, legal impunity, piecemeal approach of the neighbouring countries and the limited and uncoordinated international humanitarian response has contributed to the collective failure in addressing the crisis. With the mounting international condemnation and scrutiny, Myanmar was forced to buckle and allowed Rohingyas to repatriate under a formal agreement signed with Bangladesh and United Nations in January and June, respectively. However, not even a single Rohingya refugee has returned. Despite being voluntary in nature, the agreement is problematic at various ends. It has deliberately avoided the use of the term "*Rohingya*" and also lacks the plan to repatriate, resettle and reintegrate the returnees while, ensuring their rights, safety and security. The agreement neither guarantees citizenship/nationality rights to the Rohingyas and will be placed and confined within authorized displaced camps. Thus, the problem remains intact; they are and will be stateless and homeless even after they return to their "homeland", belonging "nowhere", living a life of nomads with no right to human rights and protection. Despite Myanmar's ongoing political transition, there is no quick fix solution to this long-drawn crisis. Therefore, necessitates for a careful rethinking and scrutiny of the concepts like citizenship, rights, security, peace and protection and justice within the nation state paradigm through collaborative and constructive international and regional cooperations like UN, EU, ASEAN and SAARC is imperative in resolving this crisis.

Moreover, India being the immediate neighbour, member of UNHCR's governing Executive Committee (ExCom) and the emerging leader must break its long-standing silence by coming out of mere economic and direct geopolitical implications or interests. Accept the moral responsibility to make meaningful transformations, replacing arbitrary decision-making on the case to case basis and act towards ending "humanitarian tragedy" through improved and institutionalized delivery of humanitarian assistance and refugee protection making it inclusive and secular.

To ensure accountability and to address the root problem of political exclusion and citizenship, Indian government must mediate and support a critical engagement through diplomatic channels focusing on long-term humanitarian intervention strategies to deal with the crisis is required. Since the most efficacious way to establish ethnic-religious peace involves structural changes in the political and constitutional set-up. Given the fact, the state is the basic unit for conferring nationality/citizenship that not only ensures the sense of identity/belongingness but more importantly, it enables them to exercise a wide range of rights to construct their life with dignity. Thus, putting Kofi Annan commission at place is important and a way forward towards developing comprehensive and inclusive state policies ensuring greater participation of ethno-religious minority communities in the country's governance by giving them the status of stakeholders. It focuses on four major points—(1) investment and development of Rakhine, (2) lifting all restriction on Rohingyas, (3) reviewing Citizenship Act 1982 and (4) lastly instigates a calibrated approach to security along holding perpetrators of human rights violations accountable. Otherwise, the culture and a cycle of refugeehood and statelessness will continue to exist and would remain permanent exception to citizenship and inclusion.

References

Aadhaar Act. (2016). https://uidai.gov.in/images/targeted_delivery_of_financial_and_other_subsidies_benefits_and_services_13072016.pdf.

Agamben, G. (2005). *State of exception*. Kevin Attell Trans, Chicago: University of Chicago Press.

Amnesty International Report. (2014). *What we do people on the move*. https://www.amnesty.org/en/what-we-do/people-on-the-move/. Accessed on February 20, 2015.

Anderson, B. (1996). *Imagined communities: Reflections on the origin and spread of nationalism*. London: Verso (revised edition).

Ananthachari, T. (2001). Refugees in India: Legal framework, law enforcement, and security. *ISIL Yearbook of International Humanitarian and Refugee Law, 1,* 118–143.

Arendt, H. (1985). Decline of the nation–state: End of the rights of man. In *The origins of totalitarianism*. New York: Harcourt.

ARAKAN Monthly (2009, September). http://www.burmalibrary.org/docs08/mag_arakan01-09.pdf.

Banerjee, P., Chaudhury, A., & Ghosh, A. (2015). *The state of being stateless: An account of South Asia*. New Delhi: Orient Blackswan Pvt. Ltd.

Baorren, M. (2008). *Towards an Arendtian politics of in/visibility on stateless refugees and undocumented aliens*. http://www.ethicalperspectives.be/viewpic.php?LAN=E&TABLE=EP&ID=1108.

Biopage, Lionel. (2017, October 5). Myanmar: A good example for politics of polarization. *Colombo Telegraph*. https://www.colombotelegraph.com/index.php/myanmar-a-good-example-for-politics-of-polarisation/.

Bhatia, R. (2015). *India-Myanmar relations: Changing contours*. India: Routledge India.

Bhaumik, S. (2013). The East Bengali muslims in Assam and Rohingyas of Myanmar: Comparative perspectives of migration, exclusion, statelessness. *Refugee Watch, 41,* 30–46.

Chakarborty, M. (2001). *Human rights and refugees: Problems, laws, and practices*. Delhi: Deep and Deep Pub. Ltd.

Chimmi, B. S. (2000). *International refugee law: A reader*. New Delhi: Sage.

Chowdhory, N. (2018). *Refugees, citizenship and belonging in South Asia: Contested Terrains*. Berlin: Springer.

Constitution of Burma. (2008). https://www.wipo.int/edocs/lexdocs/laws/en/mm/mm009en.pdf.

Dhanvan, R. (2004). *Refugee law and policy in India*. New Delhi: PILSARC.

Ernest, G. (2008). *Nations and nationalism*. New York: Cornell University Press.

Espenilla, J. J. F. (2010). Injustice ignored: A case study of the irregular sea migration of the Rohingya Boat People. *Asia Europe Journal, 8,* 45–59.

Farzana, F. K. (2017). *Memories of Burmese Rohingya refugees: Contested identity and belonging*. Berlin: Springer.

Ferris, Elizabeth G. (2011). *The politics of protection: The limits of humanitarian actions*. Washington, DC: Brookings Institution Press.

Giddens, A. (1985). *The nation-state and violence*. Cambridge Polity Press.

Goldston, J. A. (2006). Holes in the rights framework: Racial discrimination, citizenship, and the rights of noncitizens. *Ethnics and International Affairs, 20*(3), 321–347.

Government of India, Minister of External Affairs, Press Release. (2017, September 14). https://mea.gov.in/press-releases.htm?dtl/28944/Operation_Insaniyat__Humanitarian_assistance_to_Bangladesh_on_account_of_influx_of_refugees.

Human Rights Watch. (2000, July 1). Living in Limbo: Burmese Rohingyas in Malaysia. *The Human Rights Watch, 12*(4). http://www.refworld.org/docid/3ae6a8743.html.

Ibrahim, A. (2016). *The Rohingyas: Inside Myanmar's hidden genocide*. London: C Hurst & Co Publishers Ltd.

International Crisis Group. (2000, May 7). *Myanmar backgrounder: Ethnic minority politics*. ICG Asia Report N° 52, Bangkok/Brussels.

Chapter 5
Understanding Media Portrayal of Rohingya Refugees

Biswajit Mohanty

Abstract The chapter examines the media representation of Rohingya refugees in India. Media is playing a significant role in building consensus and shaping people's perception of modern nation-states. The ability to control the symbolic resources enable mass media to build consensus and shapes people's perception to manufacture consent. The representation of minority ethnic refugee communities by the mass media is an appropriate illustration of manufacturing consent. Media, is instrumental in providing platform to a particular ideology of nationalism through the dynamics of interplay of discourse and ideology to constructs image of refugees, and migrants as the "other" within the nation state. At times it disproportionately amplifies refugee issues to construct public discourse against them. This paper studies Rohingyas, an ethnic minority group of Myanmar facing execution from the dominant Buddhist community, to analyse the construction of public imagery in visual media in India. The paper argues visual media facilitates the construction of negative image of Rohingyas and shape public imagination around narratives of nationalism.

Keywords Media · Mediatization · Public sphere · Trust · Stateless · Ontological security

Introduction

The image of the floating body of Aylan Kurdi, a three-year Syrian boy clad with bright red T-shirt, lying face down on sand not far off from Turkey's resort town of Bodrum became an icon image. The image went viral with a hash tag of "humanity washed ashore." The image made global headlines and was circulated extensively across the world. Following this image, there was a shift in the discourse on the refugee crisis in the media throughout Europe (Bozdag & Smets, 2017). The images

B. Mohanty (✉)
Department of Political Science, Deshbandhu College, University of Delhi, New Delhi, India

N. Chowdhory and B. Mohanty (eds.), *Citizenship, Nationalism and Refugeehood of Rohingyas in Southern Asia*,
https://doi.org/10.1007/978-981-15-2168-3_5

are visual "quotation" (Sontag, 2003, p. 22) that provides the window to understand the mass media, and media representation of refugees in contemporary world that is becoming more mediated and mediatized. In the era of mediated politics, what matters is the role of mass media, irrespective of its form, as a trusted source of information and communication between people and the political actors. Television news and reporting have become preeminent source of information and knowledge not only of things happening within a country but also of the world outside.

It is a global phenomenon that people trust visual media for information. According to the Edelman Trust Barometer Global Report 2019, 49% of the global population trusts the "owned" media and 65% of the population trusts the traditional media for the news and general information. There are only 43% of the global population who trust the social media for news and general information (Edelman Report, 2019, p. 50). The CSDS- Lokniti had conducted a pan-India National Election Study in 2019, where it had interviewed respondents from the various social and economic backgrounds. The survey found that 51% of respondents trust television news; 52 % of respondents stated they trust the print media, and only 37% trust social media like WhatsApp and Facebook.

Print media, an important source of information and knowledge before the invention of the television readership, was restricted to a handful of educated persons. Anderson (2006) argued that the sense of a national community developed among people through the development of a common language. It was possible because of the printing press and the presence of a large number of readers who used mutually understood language to communicate with each other. The question is when the readership among the community is restricted to a limited few then how a shared feeling of national community did emerge? The contemporary mass media, and especially the electronics media, bridged the hierarchy between the readers and non-readers of the print media by reducing everyone into viewers/audience.

Words have authority over imagination in the print media. In the visual era, the power of visual representation of an event, along with narrative, allows images to enjoy "authority over imagination" (Moeller, 1999, p. 47). The media orchestrates participation of viewers, who could not be part of the event organized out "there". By abrogating distance and framing events into one narrative, it democratizes participation and creates a community of television viewers. It produces a sense of oneness through "mediatization of modern culture". It enables millions of people by "virtue of their participation in a mediated culture, a common experience and a collective memory" (Tsaliki, 1998, p. 347). Thus, the collective memory constructed and reconstructed through symbols, images and meanings could bring the disparate groups together to achieve nationhood. The mass media, including the electronic media, has become an important means of the construction of an "imagined community".

Edward Said argued that the knowledgeable community of writers, novelists, theorists, economists and administrators also constructed the image of the "other", the "oriental", both ontologically and epistemologically (Said, 1979, p. 3). The "other" is constructed through cultural differences. The "othering" is a process of domination and subjugation of a community or peoples in an asymmetric power relationship through cultural hegemony. The asymmetric power does not correspond to the "raw power" directly. It rather interacts with "power political", "power intellectual", "power cultural" and "power moral" in an "uneven exchange" relationship (Said, 1979, p. 12). Domination is achieved by retaining "flexible positional superiority" (Said, 1979, p. 7). The in-group can become the out-group, but the reverse does not hold true. The "other" is differentiated through categorization and discriminatory practices of the dominant groups. The differentiating markers are constructed through several stereotypes and stigmas, finally, relegating them to the "margins of humanity". In broader sense, it can be labelled as "orientalism in discourse": a cultural mindset that manipulates, manufactures and masters the "other" and structures segregation through the construction of binaries of "us" versus "them", "insider" versus "outsider", "we" versus "they", "white" versus "black" and the list goes on. It differentiates the essentialized orient from the essential Occident (Said, 1979, p. 3).

In the contemporary world, a lot of new people are included in the list of "the category of a lesser being" (Said, 1989, p. 207). There are new entrants to the list of the colonized and depraved: minority communities living within the state, refugees, stateless persons, migrants and internally displaced persons. The phenomenon of stateless though, occurs locally; the ramifications are felt and perceived globally. The departure from the country of origin and arrival into a new juridical space contains and dispossesses the stateless. The spectral people—disenfranchised, unpaid, miserable, dispossessed and disempowered—are "produced" as stateless, and they are "jettisoned from juridical modes of belonging". The state binds and unbinds them through the nation by invoking sorted belonging (Butler & Spivak, 2007, pp. 18 and 4). The isomorphism of the nation conflates "citizenry, sovereign and solidary group" within it and "entail a congruence of the corresponding boundaries" (Wimmer & Schiller, 2003, p. 583). Migrants become "antinomies" in the host country as they are extrinsic to society—who would destroy the "shared loyalty" to nation and "shared rights" guaranteed by the government—and become a blotch on the social fabric, who would be detrimental to the nation-building project (Wimmer & Schiller, 2003, pp. 584–85). Cultural differences are highlighted for measured steps to be taken for assimilation and/or non-assimilation into the national society.

In this context, the pertinent questions are: Do the media by creating a community of television viewers also create the "other"? Are citizens and non-citizens, nationals and non-nationals represented equally without any biases? Are refugees, the immigrants and stateless persons within the given territory provided equal space in the media to voice their concerns? Does the media construct internal orientalism within the orient?

The chapter tries to grapple with the idea of the refugee as constructed by the Indian visual media with the case study of the Republic TV. There are two reasons for undertaking the current work: first reason, it is an under-researched topic and very few theoretical and empirical studies have been undertaken in India on electronic media on refugees. It is especially true of the stateless Rohingyas. In India, the first-ever study that I traced on media portrayal of Rohingyas was conducted by Madhura Chakraborty in an extensive report prepared by Mahanirban Calcutta Research Group compiled by Chaudhury and Samaddar (2015). Chakraborty in a chapter edited by Chaudhury and Samaddar (2018) used the print media reporting, editorials and articles to examine portrayal of Rohingyas in the national dailies (Chakraborty, 2015, 2018). In both the essays, she has elaborated Samaddar's idea of "calculated hospitality". She concludes:

> the absence of the national security issue when the focus was on other countries, made it possible to sympathetically portray the Muslim 'others' who once within the borders represented a threat to sovereign integrity" and "this dichotomy in reportage is a manifestation of the "calculated hospitality" that Samaddar talked about" (Chakraborty, 2018, p. 123).

Between both the MCRG's report of 2015 and Chaudhury and Samaddar's 2018 publications another report from the Hindu group of public policy was published by Amin (2018). The findings on the media reportage of Rohingyas in this article is in line with Chakraborty's argument. Amin examines the newspaper write-ups, reports, the manifesto of the Bharatiya Janata Party of 2014 elections and the Rajya Sabha questions to conclude that unlike "calculated hospitality" shown to the other refugees, for instance, to Tibetans and Chakmas, the Rohingyas are facing hostilities from all the quarters.

Both the authors have not analysed the nature of the Indian visual media from the perspective of the Rohingya refugees. In the present chapter, I have made a modest attempt to grapple with the issue of media representation of the stateless Rohingyas in the Indian television news channels.

vanDijk was first to theorize the relation between news and the portrayal of refugees. He analysed news paper articles and editorials written on Tamil refugees in the Dutch press to understand the nature of the Dutch media. He, in the study, has examined how the Dutch print media became the medium for successfully constructing, propagating and, finally, reproducing racism in Dutch society. Many studies have been undertaken, subsequently, on the media discourse on refugees. Take, for instance, Lynn and Lea have examined the letters written to the British print media by people and conclude that the newspapers' "elite" discourse is employing the idea of citizenship, identity and nationhood to socially construct the image of the asylum seekers and contributing to the transmission of idea of "new apartheid" (Lynn & Lea, 2003). Similarly, Kaleda (2014), in an essay, compares the grassroots newspaper published by refugees in Kenya and the Western media to infer that the Western newspaper trivialize what is important for the grassroots newspaper. Bleiker, Campbell, Hutchison, and Nicholson (2013) have examined the role of print media in dehumanizing the refugees in Australia and influencing the state policies. The Brookings Institute of Governance in its report *A Report on the Media and the Immigration Debate: democracy in the age of new media* examines the impact of the television reporting on immigration and its impact on immigration policy in America in 2007

(Suro, Rosenstiel, Kaplan, Dionne, & Akdenizli, n.d). In the Southern Asian context, there is hardly any literature on television portrayal of refugees in general and Rohingyas in particular: hence the essay in the book.

A set of guidelines has been published by the UNHCR, the National Union of Journalists in Ireland and the Irish Refugee Council for the Journalists reporting the migration and asylum issues. It highlights, first, the significance of truthful reporting to avoid harming refugees. The guideline issued emphasises the importance of the best practices of interviewing the refugees. The report should be bereft of bias to maintain the accuracy of reporting. Second, the journalist must be aware of the national and international laws to provide correct definition to the concepts that they are using to report conditions of refugees and stateless persons in any country. Third, it is pertinent to "show humanity" by reporting individual and collective stories with sensitive background information regarding the reasons for mass migration and their entry into the destination country. Fourth, the reporters should not speak for the refugees rather should "talk to" them to provide a platform and an opportunity to "speak for themselves". Finally, the guidelines specifically advise journalists to "challenge hate" to avoid conflict of interest and potential conditions of violence committed on refugees and migrants. The second reason to study media reporting is to find out: the best practices of ethical journalism followed in television channels while discussing stateless persons in India? The chapter in the process would address a deeper issue of exploring the politics of news reporting and visual images of Rohingyas in the news channels. For this purpose, I have studied one "owned" channel, the Republic TV, as a case study to analyse the refugee portrayal in the news channel.

Media and Trust

The vast expanse of the media has enabled people to see, hear and remember events of their choices. It is an integral part of everyday life because of its emotional, cognitive, "spatial and temporal significance" and "political significance" (Silverstone, 2003, p. 3). The mass media mediates the content of everyday life experience, cognitive processes within individuals and communities, and national and political identity building (Stevenson, 2002, p. 1). The media is increasingly structuring our daily life through what Luhmann calls "transcendental illusion" or "doubling of reality" (Luhmann, 2000, p. 4) manifested at the level of observation: at the level of "self-reference" and at the level of "other reference". Thus, the question arises: Could we trust the media that operates at both the levels for the construction of reality?

There are several theories those explain the growing trust on media. Discussion on the issue of trust is beyond the scope of the essay. A brief summary is presented to give a theoretical dimension to the issue of why is it that the public trust media for news and information?

Trust has a major role to play in modern society because it "increases the 'tolerance of uncertainty" of the future" (Luhmann, 1979, p. 15). It is because of its capacity to manage "indeterminate complexity" that there are enhanced possibilities for experiences and actions, augmentation of social complexities and possibilities of reconciliation within the structure (Luhmann, 1979, p. 8). Complexities and specialization make people rely on the system and public authorities. He further states that trust "is to behave as though the future were certain…through trust time is superseded" (Luhmann, 1979, p. 10).

Anthony Giddens subsequently builds on the conception of uncertainty and risk that the globalized society faces. He structures his argument in the following way. He first theorizes "ontological security" to understand life in the modern world. He explains it through the concept of the "abstract systems" consisting first "of face-work commitments", that is, trust activity in "circumstances of copresence" and second, of "faceless commitments", which is trust in "symbolic tokens or expert systems" (Giddens, 1990, p. 80). Day-to-day civil interaction in modern society is characterized by "civil inattention", which is "carefully restrained and controlled social rhythms". Trustworthiness is not always established in face-to-face interaction. For Giddens, "disembedded mechanisms" can also be trusted. From this basic background, he argues that "*the nature of modern institutions is deeply bound up with the mechanisms of trust in abstract system*" (Giddens, 1990, p. 83 italics original). He further relates mechanisms of trust with ontological security, which is to do with the "being-in-the-world", "rooted in the unconscious" and emotional world (Giddens, 1990, p. 92).

He further argues that not everyone is located within a high ontological insecurity state. It is because they have received "dosages of trust" in early life, and have been "emotionally inoculated" (Giddens, 1990, p. 94). To explain this point, he borrows ideas from Erik Erikson and D. W. Winnicott. Quoting Winnicott, he states that the trust between individual begins at the infant stage where the child and the caregiver develop "potential space" between them (Giddens, 1990, p. 96). Crucial to the development of trust for a child is the absence of the mother. The feeling of reliability is predicated on the premise that the absence of the mother does not mean withdrawal of love. Giddens thus concludes that a sense of trust and psychological security is firmly bound up with routines of day-to-day life. The continuity of secure routine life is possible with the constant vigil of the parties involved, that is, through face-work engagement: "chronic monitoring of the gaze, bodily posture, and gesture, and the conventions of orthodox conversation" (Giddens, 1990, p. 99).

Modern society is characterized as a risk society, and abstract system transforms intimacy through different means. The face-to-face interaction has been attenuated. There is decreasing reliance on kinship relations for support. In the absence of this in modern times, people have become more reliant on "relational networks and mechanisms" mediated by abstract tokens or the expertise of others, whose presence cannot be part of immediacy of the routine life. Giddens concludes that we trust the symbolic authority from a distance. Media becomes the part of the distance authority, and trusting media hence becomes important to secure our ontological insecurity.

Silverstone, drawing extensively from Winnicott's idea of "transitional object" and sequencing, has argued about the reposition of trust on the media. Silverstone argues that the sequencing happens through the following stages. First, the transitional object is identified and related to having ontological security. In the second phase, the attempt is made by the subject to destroy the transitional object through "constant flow and switching off" (Silverstone, 2003, p. 15). Despite its attempts, it cannot be destroyed, leading to the situation of "invulnerability and its dependability", making television a primary level of acceptance and trustworthiness. This can happen to any technology. The difference between technologies and television is that the attachment to television is "over-determined" by its "schedules, genres and narratives" (Silverstone, 2003, p. 15). The news as a genre is the prime example of articulation of anxiety and security along with the creation of the trust. It is this characteristic of televised news that television becomes a transitional object and is trusted from a distance.

How does trust in the individual sphere transforms into the trust of the public? The relationship between media, state and people can be established within the public sphere. Habermas' (1986) account of the public sphere has been widely used as a yardstick of measuring a democratic society. According to Habermas, the bourgeois public sphere developed from the yoke of a feudal system to rationally and critically discuss the matters of public interest. The public sphere is the critical intermediary domain between the state and the civil society (Habermas, Lennox, & Lennox, 1974, p. 50), where a critical and rational reflection on the public and the practices of the state is encouraged. The participants of the public sphere were though small, but it brought into the public domain the importance of universality of reasonable argument. The public sphere, through its principle of publicity, established the importance of public use of reason. It provided the cultural ground for critique where better argumentative reason could establish authority over the status quo and less articulated argument (Silverstone, 2003, p. 49). Since the best communication can occur without coercion, the public sphere becomes the ideal site for free and critical analysis of the state and the public. The citizens, when are given freedom of expression of opinion, behave as a "public body". In the public body, like the modern nation- state, the mass media acquires critical importance to transmitting information and influencing those who receive it. Television becomes one of that medium of transmission in the public sphere (Habermas et al., 1974, p. 49). Media becomes an independent forum for citizens for public debate, discussion and engagement with fellow citizens and the state authorities. The independence of media becomes the reason for trust in the public sphere (Bakir & Barlow,2007, p. 19). To become a full citizen, the members of the political community should have free access to the media to form an informed opinion and political choices on the state and its policies.

There are major critiques of Habermasian conception of the public sphere. For our purpose, I would pick two. The first critique is against his distinct division between the public, consisting of the politically structured systemic world and its attendant bureaucratic regulations and, on the other, the life-world, consisting of "horizon" where citizens would realize their projected goals. According to Baker and Blaagaard, the public sphere and the life-world are not two distinct spheres mediated by the media to discuss and debate, rather it is an organic whole where "both the public and systemic discourses intermingle and interact". Hence, public sphere is a discursive sphere (Baker & Blaagaard, 2016, p. 04). Secondly, though Habermas laments that the forces that brought the public sphere into prominence became the very agents of its decline and destruction (Silverstone, 2003, p. 50), he rarely discusses the role of media, especially the televised news and its relation in dealing with the issue of non-citizens in the public sphere.

The major question is, when the non-citizens like refugees and immigrants have become a reality in many Asian, European, African and American countries, then how do we link the public sphere, media and non-citizens? There are several related questions as well. Like citizens, can non-citizens become part of the public sphere in expressing their ideas? Do media give them adequate space to express their views? Whether the media speak for them, or are they given adequate space in the television channel to speak for themselves? How do media, especially visual media, deal with the non-citizens in Southern Asian countries where religious nationalism is at its height? Can non-citizens trust media in depicting their condition, their history and the true story of the context of refugees?

News and Representation of the Rohingyas in India

Before delving into the discourse on the construction of the Rohingya identity by the Indian television, the moot question is when and why did the news channels start articulating the Rohingya issue aggressively? The Rohingyas have been trickling into India through the porous border of Bangladesh and Myanmar since the 1970s. According to the UNHCR's October 2018 report, there are about 18,000 Rohingya refugees in India. But the informal sources claim it to be roughly around 40,000. Of them, about two-thirds are residing in the cities of Hyderabad and Jammu, a large portion of Muslim communities reside here. In Jammu, the Rohingya shelter has been declared as an official camp where the concentration of Rohingyas could be noticed. The Live Mint newspaper reports that in Jammu, according to the state government of Jammu and Kashmere report, about 5,700 Rohingya Muslims are taken refuge here. But, the central government claims that there could be 10,000–11,000 Rohingyas living in Jammu (The Live Mint, 2017). The rest are scattered in Haryana, Delhi, Uttar Pradesh in the North and Rajasthan in the West, and Karnataka, Tamil Nadu, Kerala and Andaman Nicobar islands in the South. They have taken shelter in the north-eastern states as well. They were staying in Assam, but fearing prosecution they fled to the other north-eastern states. They have been supported materially and financially by many NGOs, like "Shikawat", "Daji" and Zakat Foundation, from time to time.

Demanding recognition of refugee status, home, better life and Long Term Visa (LTV) from the Indian government in April 2012, about 3000–4000 thousand Rohingyas had held a demonstration in front of the UNHCR Indian office. This demonstration was also supported by Indians sympathetic to their cause. They mainly had come from Rajasthan, Jammu, and various parts of Uttar Pradesh. The event was reported in the print media and some in visual media. Sumitra Mahajan, a BJP MP, raised the issue of Rohingyas in the Parliament by labeling them as "illegal migrants", who are a "security threat" to the Indian state (Basavapatna, 2015, p. 32).

The timing of the protest coincided with a series of attacks on Rohingyas in Myanmar. Since then, the Rohingyas gained public attention and have become part of the politics of media debate in India. After the Bharatiya Janata Party came to power in 2014, the Rohingya issues figured conspicuously in debates and discussion on the pages of the national and local newspapers and prominent news channels.

The year 2017 was momentous for Rohingyas for two reasons. First, a Public Interest Litigation was filed in Jammu to identify the Rohingyas and Bangladeshis and deport them to their respective countries. The Tibetan and Afghan refugees have been residing in India; however, the Rohingyas have become the targets in recent times. The causes may be because of their Muslim identity, public confusion over the mistaken identity of Rohingyas with Bangladeshis and the prevalence of divisive anti-Muslim sentiment in the country. Second, there was a case filed by two registered Rohingya immigrants, Mohammed Salimullah and Mohammad Shaqir, pleading before the Supreme Court against refoulement. The plea was that India may not be a signatory to the 1951 Convention on Refugees, but has been the signatory to many other conventions that protect the rights of the refugees and are against deportation. To that effect, the Central Government filed a counter affidavit in the Supreme Court, citing unverified reports of link with the Pakistani terror groups. The newspaper and news channels picked this point, and the overjealous media spin started for repatriation of Rohingyas in the country, especially in the Times Now and the Republic TV. Other Hindi channels toed the same line. But, the current study is based on the analysis of the Republic TV's reporting and news-hour discussions. The limitation of the article is that a comparative study of the television channels could not be conducted for two reasons. First, it is a tremendous task to gain full access to the news items on Rohingyas of all the television channels over the Internet to do the content analysis and subsequent theorization. Secondly, given the limited space, an extensive study would become impossible—a project has been left for the future.

The Republic TV News and Portrayal of Rohingya Refugees

In the lead statement in the episode Debate with Arnab Goswami in the Republic TV on 18 September 2017, the anchor Arnab Goswami pronounces "Why People Fighting for Rohingyas and not for Assamese? India is for Indians. Those philosophically inclined and those pseudos who insist that India is for Myanmarese and India is for Bangladeshis, I want a poll carried out among the Indians to ask if the idea of *Atithi Devo Bhava* (Guest is God) means that the armed Bangladeshis can attack the state of Assam. Atithi Devo Bhava means that Rohingyas can threaten Indian security and we still say they have equal rights as us? The fact is that they don't have equal rights as us. India is for the Indians first. Amnesty International should ask Donald Trump to accommodate Rohingyas in Texas. The Amnesty international should ask Theresa May to take one lakh Bangladeshis since they have so many, forget Brexit and settle them down in East London. This is such hypocrisy. I want to ask if there is a greater International design behind this".

He further states, "as part of our campaign that you must join, as # tag tonight appeals me, and all of you, that we have taken this rubbish prolong enough to and we need to hit back. The # tag is India for Indians and I have posted many questions on my twitter. Here are few questions: why did the Rohingyas come via Bangladesh, an Islam dominated state where the Muslims are happy, and choose to settle in Hindu dominated Jammu in India, where according to the pseudo brigade Indians are unsafe. That is my first question to the pseudos. It makes no sense to me".

"The second question is why don't the people, who are fighting for the Rohingyas, fight for Assamese who are run over by Bangladeshis violent infiltrators, who have run away from their own soil"?

"Third, are we the only dumping ground of the world? Why don't the Rohingyas go to Norway, Sweden, Switzerland, which are self-professed peaceful state, which are much safer for them? Are we the moral dumping ground for waste?"

"Fourth, why do you pay taxes viewers? Do you pay taxes to subsidize Rohingyas who will come into our India and threaten our own security?"

"Fifth, are Rohingyas our problem or Myanmar's problem? My view is that the problem is for Aung San Syu Kyi to sort out not for Narendra Modi to sort out. What do you think: Do you agree with me?"

"You get the exclusive report on the state of Assam. You would be shocked to know that what is happening in Assam, which is India. Don't let your brother and sisters of Assam suffer any more".

The channel announces "The government files a tough affidavit on the Rohingyas in the Supreme Court". The stand is very clear. India is for Indians; there is no compromise. He further states,

"40,000 Rohingyas are here. Why do political parties want India to be the refugee dumping ground"? The clip shows the stealth movement of people and scrolling caption reads Rohingyas part of Inter-Services Intelligence of Pakistan's design. A headline scrolls which reads "Pandits thrown out, Rohingyas throng in". Another caption reads, "Identity of the Assamese is under threat".

The channel shows two interviews of Asaduddin Owaisi the leader of All India Majslis-e-Ittehadul Muslemeen, a political party based in Hyderabad, Telengana and Kiran Rijjuju, the union minister in the ruling Bharatiya Janata Party. The subtitles of the interview show that Owasi is speaking in favour of Rohingyas in terms of humanitarian issue and Kiren Rijuju is justifying the draft of refoulment based on the ground data.

The Republic TV in a visual clip shows that people are crossing the border surreptitiously. Arnab Goswami announces "the people of state of Assam have been run over by illegal infiltrators from Bangladesh". He further states "the government and some politicians are trying to hide secret documents that say that 15 of 33 districts of Assam have been dominated by the Bangladeshi infiltrators". Then, the debate continues.

For Ignatief, the news is like stories. It is a "genre" where they have the structure and content, and involve the expectations of the audience of what they want from the news "stories". The news thus involves a kind of standardization of narrative and pattern of presenting according to the demands of the audience, what they like to listen, and like to watch. As an "imagined community", the viewers through news construct their national or international collective identity. It constructs "we" versus "them" narrative through the "ventriloquist" newsreader. Through the circuitous route, it becomes the authority (Ignatief, 1998, p. 71).

News is not a genre of stories. It is a process about production, marketing as well as consumption. It is an "*institutional discourse*" that feed into and form generic structure. The institutional discourse is manifested through cognitive practices and textual conversations (van Dijk, 1988a). Discourse involves a micro- and a macro-processes. The micro-process is about the structure of the sentence that the news anchor or reporter utters on the television set (van Dijk, 1988b, p. 81). Discourse, in its micro-process form, also involves the role of the lexical order of words. The use of words to describe the event in the frame of "rhetorical strategies" is an important element of comprehension processes of the audiences. Since media is dependent on socially shared knowledge and beliefs, the script is organized around the social—psychological dimension of persuasion. The rhetoric of terror attack and security threat to the nation constitutes the rhetoric of political script. News reporting is shared knowledge that indicates the socio-political ideology at play in the production houses. The political scripts have evaluative and normative beliefs of social groups; the news script is qualified as a social attitude (van Dijk, 1988a, p. 13). Thus, news events or reports are shared knowledge scripts that would indicate the socio-political ideology at play in media production houses. Ideologies, according to Althusser (1971), have the material basis in the form of Ideological State Apparatus which albeit others include communications. But it is not limited to it alone. It includes the system of meanings: the connecting link between the real world and the imaginary relations in which people live. Ideology is thus a "tangible 'lived experience' rather than an 'intellectual' one, rooted in social mechanisms and practices" (Lynn & Lea, 2003, p. 426). The news becomes a practice: a discourse where the social reality is not empirically depicted; rather, social reality is constructed (Fowler, 1991, p. 2). Meanings are part of the "ideological sphere" and discourse, which is one of the ideology's specific forms, can be viewed as "knowledge in the service of power" (Burr, quoted in Lynn & Lea, 2003, p. 427).

The ideology of the Republic TV could be discerned within the framework. It is an "ideological consensus"; a nationalist ideology where India is meant only for Indians. The anchor conflates the Hindu with Indian and Indian nationalism with Hindu identity. Bangladesh is a Muslim state and Jammu is dominant Hindu area that clearly manifests the Hindu nationalist ideology. By addressing any contrarian voice as "pseudos", the Republic TV has labeled them as the enemy within. The presence of the "pseudo" and their support to the Muslims are, therefore, disruptive and the threat to the nation. Both become anti-nationals, should be closely monitored and reprimanded in the public.

Vocabulary is integral to the image depiction. Images without words become polyphonic and polysemic. Images are indispensable for televised news, but the depiction of acceptable and unacceptable, favourable and non-favourable, friends and foes is done through chosen vocabulary. Categorization is part of the discourse. The identity markers of the community are provided through words or vocabulary. Vocabulary, which is taxonomically organized, provides the "sense relation among words" and becomes the ideology of the community and "instrument of handling discrimination" (Fowler, 1991, p. 91). Republic TV's language categorized event in the vocabulary of war: a "structure of feeling" that depicted a "general sense of crisis" engulfing India. It "refracted" the events and bent it to suit popular image of the Muslim. It construed them as infiltrators and terrorists. By categorizing the Rohingyas as terrorists he particularized them. The Republic TV through reiterated vocabulary of discrimination assigned a particular status and image to the Rohingya community. It constructed the image of the "Other" as terrorists and their supporters as harbingers. It "locked" the identities in the cycle of stereotypes. The construction of the "other" precluded the "group" to be part of the larger political community. The Republic TV when announced that Rohingyas are part of the larger design appealed to citizens and the ruling power not to allow Rohingyas to be assimilated and/integrated into the Indian polity. The anchor did not speak to the power; rather, he spoke "against the emollient assurances of the powerful."

The Republic TV, instead of examining the complexity of differences, created a simple binary of legal citizens versus the illegal refugees. It successfully constructed the image of the Muslims whose image is generalized by the public as a potential threat to "our" national security as they are effortlessly shown to have connections with Islamic State of Iraq and Syria/Inter-Services Intelligence or Al Qaeda. Thus, all Muslims are homogenized as the harbingers of terrorism, hence should not be allowed to enter into the country. The language in which the refugees are represented through the media has a critical impact on their identity to the general public. Since subject is not able to represent themselves and also lack power to voice their concerns, the Republic TV as the dominant power has taken representation in its own hands where "the culture of power remained within the culture of representation". Portraying Rohingyas as terrorists and criminals made them undesirable elements, thereby distorting the image of real condition of Rohingyas. By reporting a xenophobic rhetoric, it tried to fuel a negative stereotypical and prejudiced image of them by showing this one-sided picture of the Rohingyas; it created a "moral panic" and spread a message of crisis.

Through the creation of positive in-group versus negative out-group dichotomy, the Republic TV created a process of the "othering". It tried to create a strong differentiation between host country citizens and impoverished image of immigrants who are a drain on and competitors for resources. It by doing so dehumanized the Rohingyas in particular and the minority community in general.

The TV channel also tried to emulate the "CNN Effect", where the underlying assumption is that the news can make and change policies. It tried to influence domestic and the foreign policy of the government: a hawkish foreign policy where the government should start a war against terrorism, terrorists and the countries sheltering the terrorists.

It is evident that the Republic TV apart from trying to affect the CNN effect also tried to manufacture consent. Two implicit versions of the manufacturing consent paradigm can be discerned in relation to the Republic TV's portrayal of Rohingya imagery. First, the executive version: this insists that news media reports conform to what might loosely be called the official agenda (White, 2000). The second, elite version of the manufacturing consent paradigm claims that news media coverage conforms to the interests of political elites, where elites are defined broadly as members of the executive, legislative or any other politically powerful group (van Dijk, 1988a). The Republic TV, it seems, has committed to both the versions of manufacturing consent as is quite evident from the above episode. In its totalizing version, the channels, it seems, are operating on the basis of a set of ideological premises, depending heavily and uncritically on elite information sources and participating in propaganda campaigns helpful to elite interests. It rarely produced coverage in the deviant sphere, rather reflected the elite consensus. In this sense, the channel has been trying to paraphrase van Dijk, to establish Elite Communalism. It played a crucial role in reproducing the communal politics symbolically through the reproduction of negative image of the Rohingya Muslims.

Conclusion

The refugee problems are extremely political. Refugees are not just a mixed category of people sharing a certain legal status: they represent a culture; they are identities and are thus part of a community. Refugees confront several arrays of responses when they travel across the boundaries of nations. As fugitives, they remain under the constant gaze of the state surveillance systems, they are sometimes cared for and at other times identified as threat to social fabric and denigrated as enemies of the nation. In the mediatized and mediated world, media plays an important role in constructing the image of the refugees. Rohingyas have been depicted as potential terrorists. By doing this, the Republic TV did not play a responsible role. The ethics of journalism was not followed by the Republic TV. The channel created not only binaries but constructed a negative image of the Rohingyas by depicting them as terrorist, threat to nation and potential destabilizing forces. It brings in the question of identitarian politics and resource constraint argument tried to set the communal political agenda of the elites. The TV lacked the basic journalistic ethics of protecting human rights of refugees by not reporting sensibly and truthfully about their living conditions. Thus, the objective depiction of issue got reduced to conflict of interest that had the potential for commencement of violence against the Rohingyas. It tried to construct a negative image of refugees and appealed to the citizens to treat the refugees as the "other" and tried to influence the government to repatriate them as they would become a burden on nation's scarce resources. It is evident that the construction of image was shaped by the religious nationalist ideology of the host nation, and channel's role was restricted to the ideological mouthpiece of the party in power. It did not provide the platform for the "other" voice to speak for them. This had a deep and lasting impact on refugees. As seven Rohingyas have been deported to Myanmar, the future of the refugees has remained very uncertain and thus precarious.

References

Althusser, L. (1971). Ideology and ideological state apparatuses: Notes towards an investigation. In *Lenin and philosophy and other essays*. Monthly Review Press. http://www.csun.edu/~snk1966/Lous%20Althusser%20Ideology%20and%20Ideological%20State%20Apparatuses.pdf.

Amin, M. (2018). *'Nobody's children, owners of nothing': Analysing the Indian state's policy response to the Rohingya refugee crisis*. Chennai: The Hindu Center for Politics and Public Policy.

Anderson, B. (2006). *Imagined community: Reflections on the origin and spread of nationalism*. London and New York: Verso.

Baker, M., & Blaagaard, B. B. (2016). *Citizen media and public spaces diverse expressions of citizenship and dissent*. New York: Routledge.

Bakir, V., & David, M. B. (2007). *Communication in the age of suspicion trust and the media*. New York: Palgrave Macmillan.

Basavapatna, S. (2015). Where do #ibelong? The stateless Rohingyas in India. In S. Basu, R. Chaudhury, & R. Samaddar (Eds.), *Rohingyas, the emergence of a stateless community: A report by Calcutta Research Group* (pp. 30–45). MCRG: Kolkata.

Bauman, Z. (1998). *Globalisation: The human consequences*. Cambridge: Polity Press.

Bleiker, R., Campbell, D., Hutchison, E., & Nicholson, X. (2013). The visual dehumanisation of refugees. *Australian Journal of Political Science, 48*(4), 398–416.

Bozdag, C., & Smets, K. (2017). Understanding the images of Alan Kurdi with "small data": A qualitative, comparative analysis of tweets about refugees in Turkey and Flanders (Belgium). *International Journal of Communication, 11,* 4046–4069.

Brenner, Y. (2019). *Rohingya migration to India: Patterns, drivers and experiences*. New Delhi: Mixed Migration Studies.

Butler, J., & Spivak, G. C. (2007). *Who sings nations states? Language, politics, belonging*. Calcutta: Seagull Books.

Chakraborty, M. (2015). The limits of belonging: Rohingyas in Bangladesh and India. In R. Chaudhury, S. Basu, R. Samaddar (Eds.), *Rohingyas: The emergence of a stateless community. A report by Calcutta Research Group* (pp. 70–86). Kolkata: MCRG.

Chakraborty, M. (2018). Rohingya in Bangladesh and India and the media planet. In R. Chaudhury, S. Basu, & R. Samaddar (Eds.), *The Rohingyas in South Asia: People without state* (pp. 109–133). Oxon and New York: Routledge.

Chaudhury, R., Basu, S., & Samaddar, R. (Eds.). (2015). *Rohingyas: The emergence of a stateless community. A report by Calcutta Research Group*. Kolkata: MCRG.

Chaudhury, R., Basu, S., & Samaddar, R. (Eds.). (2018). *The Rohingyas in South Asia: People without state*. Oxon and New York: Routledge.

Edelman Trust Barometer. (2019). https://www.edelman.com/sites/g/files/aatuss191/files/2019-02/2019_Edelman_Trust_Barometer_Global_Report_2.pdf. Accessed 25.06.19.

Fowler, R. (1991). *Language in the news discourse and ideology in the press*. London and New York: Routledge.

Giddens, A. (1990). *The consequences of modernity*. Stanford: Polity Press.

Habermas, J. (1986). *The theory of communicative action. Vol. 1: Reason and rationalisation*. UK: Polity Press.

Habermas, J., Lennox, S., & Lennox, F. (1974). The public sphere: An encyclopedia article (1964). *New German Critique, 3*(Autumn), 49–55.

Hall, S. (Ed.). (1997). *Representation: Cultural representations and signifying practices*. Delhi: Sage Publications.

Ignatief, M. (1998). Is nothing sacred? The ethics of television. *The Moving Image* (Fall, 1985), *114*(4), 57–78.

Kaleda, C. (2014). Media perceptions: Mainstream and grassroots media coverage of refugees in Kenya and the effects of global refugee policy. *Refugee Survey Quarterly, 33*(1), 94–111.

Luhmann, N. (1979). *Trust and power: Two works by Niklas Luhmann*. New York and Toronto: Wiley.
Luhmann, N. (2000). *The reality of the mass media* (K. Cross, Trans.). California: Stanford University Press.
Lynn & Lea. (2003). A phantom menace and the new apartheid': The social construction of asylum-seekers in the United Kingdom. *Discourse & Society, 14*(4), 425–452.
Moeller, S. D. (1999). *Compassion fatigue: How the media sell disease, famine, war and death*. London: Routledge.
Said, E. W. (1979). *Orientalism*. New York: Vintage Book.
Said, E. W. (1989). Representing the colonized: Anthropology's interlocutors. *Critical Inquiry, 15*(2), 205–225.
Schiller, D. (1981). *Objectivity and the news—The public and the rise of commercial journalism*. Philadelphia: University of Pennsylvania Press.
Silverstone, R. (2003). *Television and everyday life*. London and New York: Routledge.
Sontag, S. (2003). *Regarding the pain of others*. New York: Straus and Giroux.
Stevenson, N. (2002). *Understanding media cultures* (2nd ed.). London: Sage.
Suro, R., Rosenstiel, T., Kaplan, M., Dionne, E. J., Jr., & Akdenizli, B. (n.d). A report on the media and the immigration debate: Democracy in the age of new media. media%20and%20immigration%20study%20imp.pdf.
The Live Mint. (2017). Government exploring ways to deport 10,000 Rohingya Muslims from Jammu, 4 April.
Tsaliki, L. (1998). The media construction of an 'imagined community': The role of media events on Greek television. *European Journal of Communication, 10*(3), 345–370.
United Nations High Commission on Refugees. (2017). Global trends: Forced displacement in 2017. https://www.unhcr.org/5b27be547.pdf.
van Dijk, T. A. (1988a). *News as Discourse*. New Jersey: Lawrence Erlbaum Associates Publishers.
van Dijk, T. A. (1988b). *News analysis: Case studies of international and national news in the press*. New Jersey: Lawrence Erlbaum Associate.
White, P. R. R. (2000). Media objectivity and the rhetoric of news story structure. In E. Venetola (Ed.), *Discourse and community: Doing functional linguistics* (pp. 379–390). Tubengen: Gunter Narr Verlag.
Wimmer, A., & Schiller, N. G. (2003). Methodological nationalism, the social sciences, and the study of migration: An essay in historical epistemology. *International Migration Review, 37*(3), 576–610 (Transnational Migration: International Perspectives).
Wright, T. (2002). Moving images: The media representation of refugees. *Visual Studies, 17*(1), 53–66.

Chapter 6
Being Stateless and Surviving: The Rohingyas in Camps of Bangladesh

Sucharita Sengupta

Abstract Forced migration across the borders in South Asia is often conflated with "economic migration", thereby blurring the distinction between "forced" and "volition". A migrant in need of asylum often gets branded as an "economic migrant" or "illegal immigrant". In a similar context, this research would unveil the exclusion, counter-resistance and self-resilience of stateless Rohingya refugees fleeing persecution in Myanmar, that emanated as a post-colonial fallout spanned between the murky borders of Myanmar–Bangladesh–India, but is now a widely discussed global and transnational phenomenon. The chapter will focus on the experiences of the Rohingyas in camps of Bangladesh and explore their survival strategies, economic activities, and how they are using transforming their identities and changing them with time and context as a means to survive. I aim to look into predicaments of life in dire vulnerabilities, a statelessness, yet a life, that is resilient and looking beyond the victimization of the Rohingyas as refugees, which remains a poignant truth. In this chapter, I have referred to two periods of my field work, the first in 2015 and the second, in 2019. A massive change in the stance of the Bangladesh government on the issue of the Rohingyas has changed within these two periods. While following a massive influx of Rohingyas in Bangladesh from August 2017, the government was welcoming, and it supported almost 1 million Rohingya refugees; however, patience appears to be wearing thin. Bilateral talks with Myanmar to repatriate the Rohingyas have failed attempts to look into their agency from invisibility to being audible globally and desperate bid to survive against all odds and addresses the following questions: Way forward for the Rohingyas? How do the Rohingyas perceive themselves? Do they consider themselves as stateless? Is there a way forward?

Keywords Rohingya · Bangladesh · Refugee camps · Kutupalong · Ukhiya · Refugee agency

---

S. Sengupta (✉)
Graduate Institute of International and Development Studies, Geneva, Switzerland

N. Chowdhory and B. Mohanty (eds.), *Citizenship, Nationalism and Refugeehood of Rohingyas in Southern Asia*,
https://doi.org/10.1007/978-981-15-2168-3_6

Prelude

"Where is Toba Tek Singh? He asked.

Where? Why, it is where it has always been.

In India or in Pakistan?

In India… no, in Pakistan.

There, behind barbed wire, on one side lay India and behind more barbed wire, on the other side, lay Pakistan. In between, on a bit of earth which had no name, lay Toba Tek Singh"—a story by Saadat Hasan Manto.[1]

The event that gave birth to this story during the decade of forties still has profound significance in how nation states have been conceived in South Asia. Questions surrounding nationality, citizenship, religion and identity are recurrent themes between the countries once united but separates nation states now. The state has a sovereign power to include at times and excludes many times population groups, pushing them to the margins or outside its borders. The chapter narrates one such story of exclusion and counter-resilience, which although had emanated as a post-colonial fallout spanned between the murky borders of Myanmar–Bangladesh–India but is now a widely discussed a global and transnational phenomenon.

The quote above, is indicative of people who are stranded in-between boundaries, who do not belong or are excluded but trigger concerns that result in new frontiers. The entire history of nation-making in South Asia bears testimony to this. How does one live in a vacuum, between or beyond boundaries of nation states? What does statelessness or being non-citizens mean? What is, if at all, significance in the daily lives of the people enduring it? Is there a difference between the existential experiences of stateless people vis-à-vis refugees living in protracted refugeehood? Is it an important point of discussion in international politics and what is the role of modern state or governance vis-a-vis refugees? Last but not least, is how the people inhabiting and surviving the condition of statelessness perceive themselves, i.e. do the Rohingyas consider themselves too as non-citizens and if so, then how do they accept or rebel against it? This chapter thus raises these questions in its attempt of studying predicaments of life under situations of threat, like that of "statelessness". It does go through the study of stateless Rohingya refugees from Myanmar, in the camps of Bangladesh, after being forced into fleeing Myanmar under compelling situations. The chapter focused on field work conducted in camps, life experiences and survival mechanisms of the Rohingyas in Bangladesh. Presently the camps in Bangladesh are the biggest operational refugee camps worldwide. Not undermining the inherent pathos that the Rohingyas are subjected to and the haplessness of their extreme precarious plights for livelihood, the chapter nonetheless attempts to go beyond the narratives of victimization, and unearth their stories of resilience, survival, coping up mechanism, strategies of visibility and agentive capabilities. This chapter is divided into two broad sections: first, a background to the Rohingya crisis of the

[1]This introductory part of the chapter and some portions in the literature review section on Statelessness was written by me for my Ph.D. proposal defence and was presented in a workshop on forced migration organised by the Calcutta Research Group in December 2018. It is unpublished otherwise and has not been used anywhere.

legal definition of statelessness and implications thereby and second, a glimpse of my fieldwork in Bangladesh in the first half of 2019.

Nascent Borders and the Birth of the Rohingya Crisis Across the Indo-Bangladesh Myanmar Borders

As is widely known, the long-pending independence of the Indian subcontinent, giving rise to new nation states of India, Pakistan and Myanmar in 1947 and 48, had come with a heavy price, laced with the gruesome event of partition dividing homes and hearts. The history of these new and naïvely decided borders had severe geopolitical implications in the foreign relations of states even in the decades to follow. The independent nation states had sprung to life with turbulent and vague borderlines, never distinctly disconnected and linked forever with each other through shared history, culture, tradition and customs. Lord Curzon, the governor general of India, had once commented that frontiers (or borders) "are the razor's edge on which hang modern issues of war and peace" (Banerjee, 2010, p. xiii). It is since then that the politics of borders keep on surfacing in so far as the relations between India–Bangladesh–Myanmar are concerned. Post-colonial societies worldwide are entangled into the messy knots woven by politics at the margins shaping the internal politics of a nation state. Strict security measures and inclusion or exclusion of population groups are often results of the insecurity with which the borders have sprung to life. The entire histography of the subcontinent before 1947 in a way gets blurred as the year was the threshold after which distinct nation states, controlling the movement of people and new definitions of "citizenship" emerged (Zamindar, 2007, 1; Banerjee, p. xii). The process of nation building legitimizes national identity by linking territory to culture, history and memory. Discourses of these national identities "are created by privileging certain spatial units, such as the borders" which make us reflect upon the relation between territory, political community and democracy. The significance of a place is often conceived not as "locations in space" but as related to individual subjects. National identity therefore enforces territorial inclusion and exclusion on various spatial scales. The space delineating states is one such site of exclusion (Banerjee, p. xii). It has to be borne in mind here that borders are not static, non-negotiable lines that form a state but are vibrant lands inhabited by life, economy and mobility. They are fluid spaces, social and cultural systems of power, sovereignty, subversions, negotiations, endurance and existence (Banerjee, p. xvi). National security necessitates borders to be markers of control, leading to control of bodies not only at the margins but within the power and sovereign control of states. The borders that divide India–Bangladesh and Myanmar continue to remain as spaces that produce "spectacles of 'illegal' passage", and as Joseph Navins defines, "landscapes of death", "as well as zones of rape, mutilation, disappearance and protracted irremediable trauma" (De Genova, 2013, p. 1182). The term "Border" used in this exercise does not only imply merely border checkpoints like airports or land and sea frontiers, but as the author points out, it also encompasses "a much more variegated spectrum of spaces" (De Genova, 2013, p. 1183). As van Schendel states in his seminal work on borders, how borderland studies can tell us much about states, because borders form a clear link between geography and politics (van Schendel, 2004, p. 3).

Statelessness or lack of the state, or citizenship is an interesting nodal point to understand international relations. This debate on the meaning and implications of statelessness is crucial to understand the modes of governance of the modern state and international relations, raising important questions *like how a social life is organized within and by a state when it is complex*. It empowers the state to select its own citizens. As it is, we inhabit a "paradoxical time" as often the unpopular policies adopted by the state is claimed to be shaped by the market or global capital. In contemporary times, there is also ambiguity as to the role of the state, "which is conceived of as both central and marginal". With the advent of globalization, the external and internal sovereignty of the state seems to have reduced (Randeria, 2007). Thus, the citizenship literature permits two conclusions: one, decreasing importance of the state in wake of globalization and second, "with the emergence of deterritorialized citizenship, identity need not be tied to specific national residency, ethnicity, language or other allegiance" (Chowdhory, 2018, p. 19). However, it remains indispensable through the policies it frames. Thus, even in a discussion on statelessness, the state becomes an indispensable actor.

Studying both the roles of India and Bangladesh in this discussion of statelessness is crucial in order to unveil the intricacies of power relations that are dominantly shaping the politics of inclusion and exclusion in the subcontinent. Citizenship is the basic mechanism through which the state can exercise its power of inclusion/exclusion. It is the state that determines the characteristics of belonging within a geographically determined area (Chowdhory, 2018, p. 17). There are two approaches of how scholars working on citizenship address the question of a lack of it. One side is dominated by the "geopolitical and conceptual borders of citizenship's exclusionary lines of demarcation" by scholars working on immigration, globalization, transnational citizenship and so on. The other is the "inside/interior" one that dwells on the meaning and legalities of citizenship (Somers, 2008, p. 21). This research will engage with the binary between citizenship rights—what Hannah Arendt contends as the *right to have rights* (1979) and human rights. While citizenship rights are inclusionary in nature and relational, human rights are believed to be possessed by all humans for simply being human (Somers, 2008, p. 7). Human rights are therefore universal in nature and my approach to the subject of statelessness stems from this humanitarian lens. This research perceives a stateless life here, irrespective of being citizen or not, as a human foremost entitled to the basic rights of shelter and protection.

Elucidating the above contention further below, I will discuss the next sections from two vantage points. One, through reference to scholarly works on statelessness to understand the importance of state in steering domestic and international politics that shape population and subsequent effects that flows, and the second through contextualizing the case of Rohingyas against this literature, throwing light on existing international legal mechanisms, and introspect on whether a durable solution to the Rohingya crisis is possible.

Statelessness and the Importance of Life in a State or/and State in a Life?

> "If one is not a human being, what is one?"—Achille Mbembe.

The meaning and implications of statelessness in this chapter are approached through refugee studies. As often, but not always, statelessness leads to forced migration or situations of protracted refugeehood, rendering one the status of a "refugee". The difference between the two categories is crucial to mention because it indicates the life of a stateless person who is also a refugee. One of the most crucial problems a modern nation state can face is that of statelessness as it challenges the citizen–state relationship of the contemporary state model. It becomes even more complex if statelessness is followed by forced eviction and migration, as in the case of the Rohingyas forcefully evicted from their homeland Myanmar. Statelessness has not been studied adequately within academia and has remained confined mostly to policy studies.

To put simply, statelessness is an existence when people are without a formal citizenship status. It means living without having a nationality or the protection of a state one is entitled to, for being a citizen. A concern with stateless population was prevalent during the decade of the twenties, following the First World War when many people were rendered stateless in the wake of the international passport system in 1920.[2] In the post-First World War in 1920, the "civil wars in Russia and genocide in the Ottoman Empire" had rendered million people stateless. The Nansen passport was created then which had not granted citizenship status to the families, but it had allowed movement across borders.[3]

---

[2]For details, see UNHCR's document, https://www.google.ch/url?sa=t&rct=j&q=&esrc=s&source=web&cd=5&cad=rja&uact=8&ved=0ahUKEwiDn9738ZXYAhWBnBQKHYyNBYMQFghOMAQ&url=http%3A%2F%2Fwww.unhcr.org%2Fevents%2Fnansen%2F4aae50086%2Fnansen-man-action-vision.html&usg=AOvVaw0QsmcJKwvp7X1A2EiiWrqX.

[3]The Little Known Passport that Protected 450,000 Refugees, https://www.atlasobscura.com/articles/nansen-passport-refugees.

While the Convention relating to the Status of Refugees was drafted in 1951, the one relating to the stateless people was drafted on 28 September 1954 that came into force on 6 June 1960. It defines a stateless person as someone "who is not considered as a national by any state under operation of its law".[4] This was drafted in order to provide minimum protection to stateless people. The Convention also provides important minimum standards of treatment to the stateless people so that they have the same rights as citizens with respect to freedom of religion and education of their children. In order to help overcome the vulnerabilities associated with statelessness, the Convention also provides for rights of association, employment and housing. Although the Convention clearly mentions that these protective measures are not substituted for citizenship, it still "requires that states facilitate the assimilation and naturalization of stateless persons", if they have not committed grave crimes against peace, war crime or crime against humanity. The office of the United High Commissioner for Refugees has been officially mandated to help "stateless refugees" since its establishment on 1 January 1951. The 1954 and later 1961 Conventions on the other hand have provided for a number of resolutions that empower the United Nations High Commissioner for Refugees (UNHCR) to assist the non-refugee stateless people (Conventions Relating to Status of Stateless Persons, 3). This line is important here as we can see a clear distinction has been made within the provision itself between stateless people and stateless refugees. While the vulnerability in both these cases is of equal and paramount significance, the precarity of the stateless refugees like the Rohingyas is undeniable. Things get even worse for them as they have sought refuge mostly from countries who are not parties to these Conventions, as is the case with most countries in South Asia.

According to the International Law Commission, the definition of stateless persons contained in Article 1(1) of the 1954 Convention relating to the Status of Stateless Persons now forms part of customary international law. The article defines "stateless persons" as those who are not recognized as nationals by any state under the operation of its law. They therefore have no nationality or citizenship and are unprotected by national legislation and left in the arc of vulnerability. The 1954 International Refugee Convention deals specifically with defining the Status of Stateless Persons and 1961 refugee Convention with the Reduction of Statelessness. In legal terms, there are two forms of statelessness *de jure* and *de facto*. *De jure* is when a person is not considered as a national by any state under the operation of its law, and *de facto* is when people have been described broadly as those who are effectively without a nationality because they are unable to avail themselves of the protection of the state. Recent years have seen debates over the validity of *de facto* statelessness (Parsons & Lawreniuk, 2017, p. 1). One instance of *de facto* stateless people in the contemporary world is the ethnically Vietnamese communities in Cambodia, and many of whom have never crossed a border (Parsons & Lawreniuk, 2017). The Rohingyas are *de jure*, deracinated and scattered through their mobility across international borders in South and Southeast Asia.

[4]Convention Relating to Status of Stateless Persons, UNHCR, http://www.unhcr.org/ibelong/wp-content/uploads/1954-Convention-relating-to-the-Status-of-Stateless-Persons_ENG.pdf.

The UNHCR aiming to eradicate statelessness by 2024 mentions the importance of the 1954 Convention as millions of people are still stateless, yet few are signatories to these Conventions. Stateless people pose more threat to sovereign states as they cannot be repatriated to their place of origin, a right that refugees have. That renders them much more vulnerable. What do we do with stateless people thus remains a puzzle? However, they tell us much about sovereign states, international relations and about the way the world is arranged and the way they fit (or do not fit) within those boundaries. Laura Van Waas writes, for many years, since the Conventions have been made, existing cases of statelessness remain unresolved and new cases have emerged (Waas, 2008, p. 17). She contends the failure to resolve statelessness in most cases lies in the fact that states do not adopt or implement the standards outlined in the Conventions (Waas, 2008, p. 17). It is only since the decade of the 1990s, "states, international organisations like the UNHCR and human rights institutions began to pay greater attention to nationality matters and statelessness in their activities and reports" (Waas, 2008, p. 19). Taking the concept of statelessness as an analytical category, Kelly Staples argues, that it is a situation of exclusion and vulnerability on the one hand and "has interesting implications for theorizing world politics" (Staples, 2012, p. 3). The existence of statelessness proves valorization of state sovereignty at the expense of human rights and dignity (Staples, 2012, p. 3). Engaging with the works of Hannah Arendt in "The Decline of the Nation-State and the End of the Rights of Man" (1973) and Giorgio Agamben on his "bare life", "in which power is confronted only by pure life without any means of mediation", the author argues that "there is theoretical and practical potential for a more guardedly optimistic political response to statelessness". Although the transnational population flow/migration/forced migration/asylum seekers/stateless people as categories are distinct, the difference in their meaning often gets blurred in practice. They can neither be branded as fixed or watertight categories nor situations of exception or banality. Images of a toddler Aylan Kurdi's lifeless body evoked mass sympathy, and these flows in the wake of globalization have made us wonder about the worth of various categories of displaced population groups that we use in terms of analysis and policy responses.[5]

Article 15 of the Universal Declaration of Human Rights says, "everyone has a nationality. No one shall be arbitrarily deprived of his nationality or the right to change his nationality"—this bears two implications: "one cannot have the option of remaining stateless" and secondly deprivation of nationality is possible, given it is not arbitrary.[6] In the international agreement on Global Compact on Refugees and the Global Compact for safe, orderly and regular migration mandated by the New York Declaration for Refugees and Migrants, 2016, both the categories of migration and forced migration have been used synonymously which reinforces conflation of categories and defies existing ones. Not only does the declaration acknowledges that the two has deep interlinked relations, but also "the limits and unwillingness

[5]This has been fleshed out in a Report that I was a part of writing, http://www.mcrg.ac.in/WC_2015/Final_Report_on_Interrogating_Forced_Migration.pdf.

[6]Module D, Statelessness in South Asia, http://www.mcrg.ac.in/Statelessness/ModuleD.pdf.

of states to carry primary responsibility of refugees and migrants and hence opened up the possibility to include the 'whole of society', which is to say the 'whole of globe' covering various stakeholders including business and commercial segments" (Samaddar, 2018, p. 1). In the same meeting, it was also highlighted how the existing Refugee Conventions are increasingly becoming inadequate to render protection to refugees and stateless people seeking refuge. It also shows how in the wake of global migration crisis like that of the Syrian Refugees and European Migration crisis, categories such as who is a refugee, or economic migrant or asylum seeker are getting blurred increasingly.

This can be witnessed in case of the Rohingya too. For instance, in India, they have been often linked to terror activities and incarcerated as "illegal immigrants" without sufficient proof. Religion has also played a marker here. However, can UNHCR recognized refugees, and in this context, also stateless people, be held responsible for crossing borders without sufficient "documents"? This indicates a lacuna in the way international legal system functions and shapes the course of borders and politics.

Modern states and governance are thus about population flows and managing them (Samaddar, 2018). "Population movements as a matter of governance acquired global importance because the movements became mixed and could not be categorized anymore" (Samaddar, CRG Module Note, 2018). This has produced not only a paradox but crisis too, of that of a migration and refugee regime, that wants to impose restrictions on migratory flows, but population movements are little concerned with migration regime, resulting in contradictions. Territories, borders and floating population thus have become crucial to understand state systems in this century, more than ever. Aradhana Sharma and Akhil Gupta talk about how the chief problem within the study of state has remained confined to the theorization of state as a cultural artefact. Cultural framing not only gives importance to everyday practices of the state but also imagines the state as a nation. However, some emergent studies on the state have a transnational approach, which is different from the traditional approaches. This transitional analytical frame of the state necessitates the need to go beyond conceptualizing the state as a nation. They argue that the study of the state needs to be "disentangled from the territoriality of the nation state. The present era of globalization has been often termed by state theorists as "neoliberal governmentality" (Gupta & Ferguson, 2002, pp. 276–278). There has been a predominance of the political and economic approaches to understanding modern state systems but the authors in this text argue that an "ethnographic examination of the state" (Gupta & Ferguson, 2002, p. 278) can broaden the horizon, and cultural and transnational approaches to the state add something valuable to the discourse.

This transnational approach is obviously interwoven with the concept of mobility. Therefore, migration or mobility[7] is natural and historically inevitable and is not one moment in history but lived experiences of a people beyond time and space. It did not start with modern borders, that is to say, borders did not presuppose migration, but it is the other way round; migration is a way of life. A state without borders thus is a myth as concepts like international security; nation formation and nationalism are

[7]Here, I have used two words interchangeably not as concepts, but to indicate movement.

intricately enmeshed with the making of international borders and state formation. A historical analysis of population flows across borders in the nineteenth and twentieth centuries thus can provide a "genealogical perspective on current discussions and debates" within migration studies in relation to state structures and governance of population flows. Governing the mobile and messy flow of population, determining the legality of it and separating the alien[8] from the citizen thus have enticed a number of scholarly works in the recent decade (Samaddar, 1999).

Our time can be thus called as the age of life, or "biopolitics"—that is politics organized within the state to control life and regulate *life*, which is regularized and controlled by governmental policy and free market (Murray, 2006, p. 192). The query what is life, and living it, therefore "is an arrogant one" (Arif, 2016, p. 1). How can the questions of a damaged life, "in all its incessant living and dying, be posed as a query of the social?" (Arif, 2016, p. 1). This articulation of life as it lives or dies, through its decay, "inscribes an emerging, dynamic, fluid, ever-changing explosion of relationalities on the cognizable realm called society" (Arif, 2016, p. 1) that exists within the state. Scholars like Giorgio Agamben and Mitchel Foucault, both of whom talked on how "management of life becomes an affair of the state, thus inaugurating the biopolitical state" (Das, 2007, p. 15). The biopolitical form of sovereignty as envisaged by Foucault, the power to "make" live and "let" die, is aimed to produce and regulate and "make efficient use of life" (Edkins &Vaughan-Williams, 2012, pp. 8, 26).

Visualizing from the perspective of Agamben, it can be stated that a biopolitical state strips a life to its naked or bare form, producing thereby bodies "that are killable with impunity" (Das, 2007, p. 16). Graeber (2015) terming state as a "problem" states that modern state is based on a principle of popular sovereignty which although is said to be derived from people, is a farce, and that it exercises power through bureaucratic structures. Sovereignty of course, he writes, is one of the three principles along with administration and politics that constitute the current notion of the "state". In daily practice, sovereignty has come to mean the right of the government to act according to its wishes within its borders. Sovereignty is synonymous to "independence" or "autonomy" in practices of the state (Graeber, 2015). We see this through physical manifestations of violence when the state decides who stays or not stays within its borders. It could be said therefore that state machinery is inherently subjugating and exclusionary. The way the balance of power between the stateless and the state is manoeuvred shows the omnipresence of the state. This power of nation states as "the standard and nearly exclusive unit of sovereignty" has proven immensely detrimental to non-state people (Scott, 2009, pp. 10–11) Most nation states have tried to drive away "disloyal" populations outside its territory or relegate them to the periphery. However, there is the realization that the once seemingly useless territories inhabited by stateless people at the margins are of great economic value, for instance, Rakhine in Myanmar, the homeland of the Rohingya, is an economic attraction to the great global powers for its natural resources. They might be rich in mineral resources or be apt for logistical expansions and trading with the big power blocks, contributing to

[8]Here, I have used the word to denote someone who is termed or viewed by a state as an 'outsider.'

the state revenue. Hence, "all the more reason to project state power" to these once ungoverned, out of reach lands, and bring their inhabitants either under firm control or drive them away completely (Scott, 2009, p. 11). Have not we witnessed the exact replica of this in the case of the Rohingya?

Sovereign power exercised by the state is however not only about controlling territories but bodies too (Das & Poole, 2004, p. 10). In fact, producing the biopolitical body is the result of the sovereign power of the state. Many anthropologists have used this notion of biopower to understand how power is exercised in the social. Yet as the authors write, the interesting question at this juncture is how "politics becomes the domain in which life is put in question" (Das & Poole, 2004, p. 10). Here, margin through its exclusion provides an important locus of studying the state as "strategies of citizenship, technological imaginaries and new regions of language" through an analysis of the state and its margins (Das & Poole, 2004, p. 10).

Malkki (1995a cited in Hoffstaedter 2014, p. 876) talks about the agency of refugees. Refugees exhibit agency in reshaping and creating new spaces, to give them a sense of belonging through their lived experiences in the new place. Malkki looks at the lives of refugees as not only "bare lives", stripped of rights, but rather stresses on their agentive capabilities, resistance and resilience. The important question that arises here is whether as Hannah Arendt critics, refugees have no rights to have rights.

My fieldworks in Bangladesh camps, that I illustrate more in the next section, only prove that whether rights are given to them or not, Rohingya refugees are trying to negotiate their existences and manoeuvring lives in order to articulate their rights. Bangladesh has been housing the Rohingya for almost three decades now, since the 70 s. However, fresh violence that had erupted in August 2017, after some "Rohingya militants attacked border police" ushered in the darkest era in the history of Rohingya persecution. Fights between the military and militants had erupted around Rathedaung Township, where according to media reports, there was a build-up of Myanmar troops following the attack by the Rohingya militants.[9] Since then, Rohingya refugees fleeing the escalating violence in Rakhine state have only doubled the figure of refugees in Bangladesh. More than 70,000 refugees have sought shelter in Bangladesh, and around 52% among them are women, constituting an even more vulnerable section among the marginalized. There are now nearly 1 million Rohingya refugees in areas of Cox's Bazar and Ukhiya, Kutupalong. Needless to say, the camps are overcrowded and the needs for resources are immense, despite tremendous efforts from humanitarian agencies in Bangladesh to tackle the crisis (Pictures 1 and 2).[10]

[9]Dozens Killed in Fighting Between Myanmar Army and Rohingya Militants, The Guardian. https://www.theguardian.com/world/2017/aug/25/rohingya-militants-blamed-as-attack-on-myanmar-border-kills-12. Accessed July 15, 2019.

[10]http://www.unwomen.org/-/media/headquarters/images/sections/news/stories/2018/8/bangladesh_dignitykitdistro_rohingyarefugees_actionaid_dec2017_img_4864_1_960x640.jpg?h=640&w=960&la=en&vs=2317. Accessed July 15, 2019.

Picture 1 Lambassia, extension 4 of Kutupalong Refugee camps, where views of both newly settled Rohingya refugees and old settlers could be found. Picture has been clicked by the author. A similar but different picture clicked by her was submitted for a recently published media piece (Sengupta, 2019)

After the outbreak of refugee crisis in 2017, in particular after 25 August 2017, now known as Genocide Day (The Quint, 2019), when thousands sought shelter in Bangladesh, the first basic needs were food and shelter. A sort of a stability in tackling the initial crisis has been attained in sectors such as food, shelter, basic medical facilities, wash and hygiene through efforts from local and international humanitarian agencies.[11] However, discontent is now spreading wide mainly due to the lack of education and employment opportunities leading to frustration and depression among the youths, in particular adolescent orphan youths.[12] In my recent fieldwork, I noticed desperation among the youths to make at least small changes in their lives to make a fundamental difference. There is also a significant difference in their attitude of how they perceive themselves as refugees, between the old Rohingyas living in Bangladesh for years now and the current influx that started from 2016 and

[11]My first-hand experience in 2019 and 'We Must Prevent a Lost Generation', PRIO Paper 2019. https://www.prio.org/utility/DownloadFile.ashx?id=1836&type=publicationfile&fbclid=IwAR3ZZ8-ZZvHy_SLyDIM6BhCvgwfiEA_lr-PgP79GBsXxBAlCANL_fGwBqAk.

[12]I have written about this more in https://www.thequint.com/voices/opinion/rohingya-crisis-life-in-bangladesh-refugee-camps-as-seen-by-field-researcher?fbclid=IwAR36RhL65Yhpwu5puIf7_BaqkCpXoGC-3mXy8h3p2vxsjU8wk3Eaw4_YuLQ.

Picture 2 One of the many camps in Cox's Bazar, Bangladesh. For lack of adequate space, some houses are built extremely close to each other lacking amenities like fire protection. As a result, in case of a disaster like an outbreak of fire, there is a chance of a rapid spread risking the life of thousands. Picture has been clicked by the author

increased from August 2017. While the old settlers were mainly silent on their needs and lived a life of "invisibility", the new refugees are more vocal and aware of their rights as refugees, despite Bangladesh being a non-signatory to all Refugee Conventions. The youths, for instance, whoever I have interacted with from Ahmed Hussain of camp number 13 to Mohammad Zubair of Camp number 8 and Aziz of Camp 7, between the age group of 15–20 said, as refugees they are entitled to basic rights like education and work. Education was singularly pointed out to be the most important right that the youths in Bangladesh camps demand after the right to food and shelter. They agree to the fact that lack of education among the Rohingyas has resulted in frustration, depression, angst and a lack of unity of mistrust. In their bid to change their lives, these young refugees were waiting for that one opportunity to get enrolled in universities in Bangladesh. They are even ready to leave the country and get admitted wherever they get an opportunity; be it in India or Malaysia, the countries where a substantial number of Rohingya refugees could be found. The will to break free is so utmost and urgent that making false national identity cards of Bangladesh, the ones who could afford paying a hefty sum to local agents, is on a rise.[13] There is also a clamour for attention to acquire educational aid from local and international

[13]Notes from the field, March 2019.

agencies which further result into a fragmented, disunited community, and lack of representation, although there are prominent voices now from within the community across in Europe and elsewhere. Zubair, from Camp 8, for instance shared his angst for lack of education. He is a bright boy with undying zeal for education. On our first day of an hour-long interaction, he kept on stressing on it as the most fundamental basic right that they as humans are entitled to. "I was in class X when we had to flee Myanmar, so I could not pass the entrance examination of standard X, but I was a good student and really miss my classes. We had a nice life in Rakhine, barring the military interventions in our lives that have unsettled and uprooted us. Otherwise, I could have also become like you, isn't it? Pursuing education in a reputed place and getting established in life are these too much to ask for? Why can't we have this basic opportunity? I do not want money or any other favour from you, but if possible, could you please help me to get enrolled in a registered university in Chittagong or India where I can complete my education?"—he asked me. On politely reminding him about my limitations and restrictions and that the refugees are not allowed to move out of the camp area he said, "I and all of us have the deepest respect to the government of Bangladesh. The prime minister is like our mother, what she has done for us has made all of us indebted to her and this country for life. We are safe and feel protected here unlike our own country; however, we need education in these camps and work, in order to avoid a lazy mind that breeds frustration and petty crimes. Education will not harm anyone. I would really hope and urge you all and the Bangladesh government to help and allow us to go to schools. If we get established, it will help everyone".[14] Zubair himself was teaching in a temporary school set by a local non-governmental organization (NGO) inside his camp. At the time of this interview, however, he had left this job and was working with Building Resources Across Communities (BRAC), another NGO in Bangladesh. Amidst a lot of negativities that mark the lives of these people in the camps, it is also note and praiseworthy that many of the youths, mostly the ones who have received basic education or were working in Myanmar, in the 30 plus camps, are attached to several local NGOs or UNCR and International Organization of Migration (IOM). There is also a necessity to take cognizance of the class divide among the refugees. For instance, Zubair belongs to a wealthy family. His maternal grandfather was the owner of a famous industry in Myanmar. His family never had any direct confrontation too with the Myanmar government. They had to flee nonetheless because the situation was getting worse since 2012 and escalated in 2016–17. This, however, is not the story of all refugees.

The ones who lacked money and establishment in Myanmar are the lot living in the most deplorable conditions as they are depending solely on the ration provided by the World Food Programme, in collaboration with the Bangladesh Government. Mohammad Aziz, whom I met in a child-friendly space by a local NGO, also stressed on education. Child-friendly spaces are run by local NGOs where children are provided with basic education. However, people like Zubair argued that most of these child-friendly spaces lack merit as unskilled students teach here. Rohingya teachers

[14]Personal interview in Camp 8, at Zubair's house.

like Aziz can teach in Rohingya language which will help the children to learn their mother tongue. But the "Bengali" teachers (meaning recruitments of Bangladeshi citizens in these schools according to Zubair or Aziz does not help much as they neither can teach in their language, or Burmese or English—that is in anyway not allowed inside the camps. Basically, formal education is not allowed by the Bangladeshi government in camps so as to restrict them in the job market. Aziz was lamenting about the differential treatment meted out to refugee's vis-a-vis the locals in terms of the jobs they were doing inside camps. "We get 7-8000 while the Bangladeshis for the same work get 12-15,000. We are grateful that we are still getting some work opportunities within the camps, but the disparities in every field are visible, even in how many NGO workers behave with us. It feels as if we are criminals".[15]

Some of the Majhi's (Majhis are Rohingya leaders working under the CIC in his camp) that I met in the 34 camps of Bangladesh, although, expressed huge gratitude to the government of Bangladesh, but they also argued that it has created job opportunities for many nationals of Bangladesh, at times even when some of them have hardly completed their basic education. Hence, there is gratitude for the aids that the refugees are receiving, but the massive changes in the infrastructure of Bangladesh creating new jobs for people have given the Rohingyas' right to be not mere silent, vulnerable recipients of the humanitarian aids, but powerful right seekers of the same. This change in attitude, however, often does not go well with the locals, who were sympathetic when the new influx had started, but their patience now is wearing thin, going by the countless testimonials I collected during my field on the same.

Existing literature on Rohingyas till recently was scarce. However, since the last two years, and especially after renewed violence in 2016–17 in Myanmar triggering massive flight, there have been a mushrooming of scholars or activists working on the issue. Scholars working on the issue have mostly studied it through the lens of politics and security, for instance, Meghna Guha Thakurata has written on Rohingyas living in Bangladesh, exploring the issue through analysing the relationship between democracy and citizenship. Guhathakurta (2017) defines participatory democracy or what she also calls as Participatory Governance and argues that refugees seeking asylum in any host country might not get rights that a citizen is liable to receive but might still have claims to basic rights like food and shelter, basing on humanitarian values of Participatory democracy that includes both state and non-state actors. Amal de Chickera in his article, "Stateless in Burma: Rohingya Word Wars" has been cited by Guha Thakurata, as they have similar terrains of arguments where both of them look at violence as a space that has been structurally embedded in the existence of the Rohingyas.

Through an exploration of social exile and collective memory in Hutu camps of Burundi in her monograph, Malkki delves into an analysis of categories of refugees, displaced and stateless persons as defined by international laws, questioning their ability to explain many contemporary drives. With brilliant eloquence she asks, "what is the state of not being a refugee-like, and how is it denoted"? (1995a, p. 13). These questions, she says are theoretically linked to notions such as citizenship, nationality,

[15]Interview with Aziz in a child-friendly space run by a local NGO in Camp number 7.

origins, nativeness, nationalism, racism and to concepts of identity, ethnicity and culture. She explores categories and critics relating to the making of a citizen, of being a refugee and not being one, and traces the journey of the metamorphosis of a "refugee" to an "immigrant" when they move from camps to towns (Malkki, 1995a, pp. 204–207). Referring to these concepts, she argues, discussions on migration studies should not be centred on purity the of belonging which essentially views displacement and emplacement as problems, but rather movement across borders and diasporas should be seen as not an aberration but as natural as belongingness. Therefore, the reason why migration most often appears as an anomaly is because for many, societies and cultures are rooted within the geographical territory of one land. It "is also anomalous in relation to the political organization of the world, divided as it is into a multiplicity of nation-states" (Malkki, 1995a, p. 19). Concepts such as nationality and citizenship that distinguish between a citizen and foreigner' often used interchangeably are important words in this context, that denote the relationship an individual share with the state he/she belongs to. Thus, as already mentioned above, within this discourse of migration and forced migration studies, refugees who do not belong to any state, or lack nationality or citizenship rights from a state, falling under the category of "statelessness" constitutes an even more complex phenomenon.

Gaining Visibility: Narratives of Rohingya from Camps in Bangladesh

"Can you please call my daughter once you are back in India and tell her about us? Can you put us in touch with her? It has been quite a while since we last spoke to each other". It was one afternoon in 2015. I was in one of the makeshift camps in Cox's Bazar, Bangladesh, and was in conversation with Abdul Mafatlat.[16] He hails from Maungdaw Village of Myanmar and has been living in the camps of Cox's Bazar for thirteen years. His daughter was in India at the time of this interview, and they had not met in years. Mafatlal just knows she was in Jammu, India, at the time of the interview. My Indian citizenship prodded the request from his end as he gave me her number. Mafatlal is the informal head or representative of their settlement area. I was told that he will lead the conversation with the Rohingyas in this particular makeshift camp. There have been various phases of violence towards the Rohingyas in Myanmar which have led them to flee in huge numbers. The last one was in 2017, but before that, even in 2012, there was mass exodus in Myanmar following which many had crossed over Naf to reach Bangladesh. Mafatlal and most residents of this particular settlement I visited came after the 2012 violence, following which a large number of Rohingyas had fled to settle in Bangladesh.

[16]Interview, June 2015 at Cox's Bazar. An elaboration of my experiences then in the camps, of stories of Mafatlal and many others have been published in a chapter 'Rohingyas at Sea' in 'Rohingyas in South Asia', Routledge, 2018.

A very similar experience ensued coincidentally in 2019. I was talking to a group of five in the house of Ahamad Hussain[17] in Camp number 13, called Thengkhali. Md. Shoufique, 16 years told me, "M'am I have heard my father was arrested and is in a prison in Goalpara of Assam, India. He had left the country in 2003 and first came to Bangladesh for work and then went to Saudi Arabia for work. However, in recent years there have been the deportation of Rohingyas from Saudi and we lost track of my father too. There was no news of him and now we have heard this".[18] Shoufique was studying in tenth standard when violence in his village compelled him to flee with his mother and younger brother to the camps. They left their Village Kadur Para of Dabin Sara in Buthedaung, Rakhine state. What struck me was his indomitable spirit to learn English and get educated. Like Zubair, he also came across a very disappointed youth, in the absence of proper education in the camps. At the time of this interview, he was working as a volunteer in UNHCR, like Ahamad and all the others I was chatting within his house. They get a salary of 8000 Bangladeshi Taka (BDT). The main work of Soufique is to work on victims of sexual violence (SGBV), to look into their needs and provide psychological assistance.

Ahamad is 25 years old and the brother of a Majhi (block leader) of his block—C—of Camp 13. Incidentally, camp number 13 houses most direct victims of the violence of 2017 as most of the people in block C of Thengkhali Camp 13 are from Rathedaung Township, that was the worst hit during the violence. He gave me a list of 358 dead's in his village alone, in Rathedaung. There were barely any survivors. Ahamad story of escaping death was spine chilling. He along with other survivors of his village remained hidden under water for almost three days, and finally when the military left the region, they fled. Ahamad was a chairman of his locality in his village, and hence, he had taken a major role in their escape to the Bangladeshi camps. They arrived at the camps on 10 October 2017. His father and brother have been killed in the violence. He now works as a volunteer in the UNHCR and said that despite adequate rationing, the resources were still scarce to feed the teeming population. They are hence sensitizing the camp dwellers on reproductive health and the need to have small families. In Camp 13, there are three main blocks—A-30, B-28 and C-30. Block A has 15,740 total number of populations, Block B—14,715 and C—16,421.[19] Camp 13 is one of the largest camps, but its location on the hills makes it very difficult for the people to fetch water or other relief products. In particularly during monsoon, the situation worsens as communication becomes difficult and landslides result in casualties.

None of them like staying in these overcrowded camps amidst such dire difficulties. A guarantee of citizenship right in Myanmar and security would suffice them to go back. However, without such a guarantee they do not want to go back. In fact, the greatest fear that the refugees in these camps have is that they might become victims once again to a renewed wave of violence, if they are repatriated back to

[17]I have sought his permission, and all other interviewees' permission to quote them or refer to them in this chapter.

[18]Interview was taken in Ahamad Hussain's House in Camp 13, Thengkhali.

[19]This data was shared by Ahamad and the volunteers I interacted with in his block.

Myanmar. Hence, the repatriation process in November 2018 between Bangladesh and Myanmar has failed. Bangladesh has officially admitted that the process of voluntary repatriation was difficult to implement because there was no willing Rohingya to go back, "though efforts to 'motivate' people to leave will continue". It was also said that most people mentioned in the list had gone into hiding on the day the repatriation was supposed to take place in November 2018. More than 2000 Rohingya refugees from the camp were in the list[20] but none of them were available to go. Although the Bangladesh government has acted in a much more humane manner after the October violence in 2017, a departure from their previous policies towards the Rohingya, yet, patience among members of the government appears to be wearing thin. Many of them are publicly complaining that Bangladesh does not have the resources to bear such a large number of refugees. The country has also signed a repatriation agreement with Myanmar in November 2017, the vague terms of which has triggered fear among the refugees that they will be pushed again to a life of unsafe precarity (Wire, 2017, pp. 12–13) The point being made here is that bilateral negotiations such as these or initiatives between states should take into account the people, unless which there will be no real change or durable solution.

During my visits to the Rohingya camps in Bangladesh in 2015, and later in 2019, I have visited several camps. In 2015, I had first visited the camps in Teknaf, and Kutupalong and makeshift settlements in Ukhiya, the scenario then was completely different than what it is now. It was not a spectacle drawing massive international attention. The entire economy in Cox's Bazar District of Bangladesh has undergone a sea change surrounding the new influxes of Rohingya refugees in 2016–17. Since August 2017, more than 745,000 Rohingyas have come to Bangladesh from Myanmar. Currently, till May 2019, the official number of total Rohingyas in the 34 camps of Bangladesh is 902,000.[21] There are still now two registered camps, directly under the management of UNHCR—the camps of Kutupalong in Ukhiya and Nayapara in Teknaf. The rest, although are under government supervision, are managed by different NGOs, headed by the IOM. Since Bangladesh has not officially declared the Rohingya as refugees, except the old settlers in the two registered camps; hence, they are not under the direct supervision of UNHCR. Each camp has one camp in charge (CIC) who is the main government official responsible for the overall jurisdiction of the camp. Under him, there are subgroups of Rohingya volunteers headed by NGO workers from Bangladesh. The roads leading to the two registered and makeshift camps before the present influxes in 2018 have been changed and made into properly constructed roads. Previously these were all kaccha roads. Presently there are new restaurants, tea shops, five-star hotels and housing complexes for NGO workers that have been built both in Cox's Bazar and Ukhiya, places surrounding the camps. However, despite all these developments, security issues and fear of the Rohingyas surpassing Bangladeshis in Cox's Bazar has strained the relation between the two communities. Prime Minister of Bangladesh, Sheikh Hasina, pointed out that

---

[20]Same as Footnote 2.

[21]UNHCR document, https://www.humanitarianresponse.info/sites/www.humanitarianresponse.info/files/documents/files/2019_jrp_at_a_glance_-_snapshot.pdf. Accessed June 2019.

Bangladesh's security and stability may be hampered if the Rohingya Refugees cannot be repatriated to Myanmar soon. She said the Rohingyas are dissatisfied with their current state of deprivation and camp lives, which might lead to security issues and lawlessness in Bangladesh. There have been incidents of violence too in the camps. She also strongly criticized the role of Myanmar in delaying the repatriation process citing number of excuses. The repatriation deal was signed between the two countries in November 2017. The same media report also suggest the arrest of Rohingyas for sneaking out of camps to various parts of the country. Often there were people from the camps being caught for travelling on the basis of false identity cards, pretending to be citizens of Bangladesh. However, given their current state of living, this is not something that is very unusual. A life that is unlawfully stripped off rights of a citizen could probably defy the same by not abiding by laws conforming to nation states. It is also interesting that on the repatriation question, the stance on the older generation of Rohingyas and younger ones is very different. For instance, Abdul Monsur of Camp 9, Balukhali, said he is still now keen to go back to Myanmar and that he never had shared a bad relationship with the government. It is because of extremist groups rebelling the government of Myanmar that they are enduring the current persecution. He was not supportive of the militant attach that triggered the exodus in 2017. Monsur (61), belongs to a respected family of Rohingyas, is wealthy and educated. The reason why he could not go back on the day of the repatriation is because his name was spelt wrongly in the list. There was a hint of sabotage in his voice that indicated the Majhi's of his block did not deliberately make a correct list of people who were willing to go back because most Rohingyas do not want to go back and if one does, it somehow weakens their position in ten international scene. There was also hint that several stakeholders like national NGOs and so on actually want the Rohingya camps to sustain in Bangladesh because as many as 130 local NGOs are now working in the camps.[22]

There was minimal international media attention to the Rohingya crisis in 2015, and the situation was not looked upon as a global humanitarian "crisis" or even "genocide", as being increasingly termed by international humanitarian organizations. At that point, my research inquiry was geared around mixed migration flows by both Rohingya and Bangladeshis in their boat journeys—it was intriguing for me to witness, how the idea of citizenship was manifested through conflated categories like refugee or stateless or asylum seekers because Bangladeshis found in the same boats were none of these and were only economic migrants looking for work in countries like Malaysia or Thailand. Incidentally as I have found out that, Malaysia being a desired location for the Rohingya was also due to the interaction that the Rohingya in Bangladesh had with the locals there because labour migration between Bangladesh and Malaysia was formally agreed upon around 2008 and also religion did play a key factor here. The informal labour migration in this case too was going on for a while but when more and more people started going there, the government of Malaysia in May 2016 refused to accept them and the then home minister in no

[22]Personal interview with Abdul Monsoor conducted in March 2019 in his house in Camp 9, Balukhali.

uncertain terms said, "we have to send the right message that they are not welcome here". I say here this to project that it is not clear whether the status of refugeehood on the Rohingya at all mattered to these countries because for them, and also India, they were no different from the illegal Bangladeshi economic migrants.

While Myanmar harps on the point that the Rohingyas never originally belonged to Myanmar, and hence, they lose the rightful claim to live there, the argument of the Rohingyas is exactly opposite. The official statement maintained by Rohingya activists and the people is that according to the 1948 citizenship law of Myanmar, they were considered as "citizens" of Myanmar.[23] It was much later, that a new law was framed for which they lost their citizenship status and became stateless. So, the Rohingya do not perceive themselves as stateless or homeless, rather they emphatically point out that they have a state in Myanmar, and that was forcefully taken away from them. However, it is important to understand this dynamics, war of words, and various interpretations of history, to gauge the flight of the Rohingyas from Myanmar and the genesis of the contemporary situation. The most crucial aspect of their existence or precarity is the aspect of statelessness (Staples, 2012, p. 140).

While speaking on this issue on 21 August 2018, the President of Myanmar Aung San Suu Kyi said, "Terrorism remains a threat in Myanmar's Rakhine state and could have grave consequences for the region". Mentioning the crisis there, she further added "Unless this security challenge is addressed the risk of inter-communal violence will remain. It is a threat that could have grave consequences, not just for Myanmar but also for other countries in our region and beyond".[24] The Noble Laurette for piece, once heralded by the world as the face of democracy restoration in Myanmar through this statement in a way acknowledges the humanitarian crisis that has unfolded in Myanmar and increased since the last year. Despite over 70,000 Rohingyas' fleeing to neighbouring countries since August 2017, Myanmar has rejected accusations of ethnic cleansing by UNHCR, counter-blaming the Rohingyas as terrorists (Reuters, 21 August 2018).

It is interesting that owing to international pressure and activism, more and more Rohingya activists are being vocal in public or through social media platforms outside Myanmar. In India too, there are people willing to talk without concealing identity. However, most activists who are connected globally are based in Europe. I had the opportunity to have a long discussion recently, in August 2018, with the secretary of the *European Rohingya Council*, based on Ireland. He is a young activist who was enrolled in medicines and whose father, also an activist, was exiled to sentence by the Myanmar military. Presently, his father is living in the camps of Bangladesh. A fearless proud activist, he was ready to share his identity and true name. His life is an ode to survival. Although it is true that Haikal Mansor belonged to a privileged section of the society, they were landlords in the Rakhine state and propertied class which perhaps has been the most important reasons for his successful assimilation in

[23]Taken from the personal web site of a Rohingya activist who is also a medical practitioner based in Ireland. He holds a number of offices too in Europe www.haikalmansor.com.

[24]Reuters, August 21, 2018. https://www.reuters.com/article/us-singapore-myanmar-suukyi/myanmar-leader-suu-kyi-says-terrorism-in-rakhine-state-a-threat-to-region-idUSKCN1L60OP.

the new place. It was interesting to talk to him as it embodies the kind of narrative or words that the Rohingya activists are using to put forth their claim. It also shows how they visualize them or how they are exercising their claim by using the history. The most interesting part of the interview is the fact that Haikal does not consider them as stateless. He emphasizes that they had a state which was snatched away from them and that no one can be born stateless. This, I have found as the most interesting in the entire conversation as this says a lot about their political agenda, claim-making and portray them as powerful actors of resistance. It conveys a message to the world that they are demanding citizenship status because they have the right to ask for it. It was their once and the state has wrongfully taken it away from them. This also shows their acceptance and faith in the state system; the problem is their exclusion from it. It means that they do not perhaps resist or question how exclusionary the way nation states are structured, what they rather question is their being excluded from it.

The UN has emerged as a very strong platform for Rohingya activists to claim recognition globally and until recently they have been incarcerated in countries like Bangladesh and India where they had sought refuge as "illegal" interlopers. From earlier terming, it as "ethnic cleansing"; till recently, the UN has termed the persecution of Rohingyas by Myanmar as "genocide".[25] Religion often plays a pivotal role in this policy of exclusion. Religion, according to many academics and activists commenting on the Rohingya crisis, has been cited as one of the foremost primary causes for the violence against Rohingyas in Myanmar. Although it is undeniable that there prevails a general animosity against Muslims in the Buddhist state, the reasons for deterritorializing and persecuting the Rohingyas from Myanmar are much graver.

Conclusion

It is ironical that despite stringent international protection regime, there exist stateless people subjected to gross human rights violations. Despite various rounds of dialogues and multilateral meetings between the countries of South and Southeast Asia, till now no resolution of the Rohingya issue is in sight. Growing "Islamophobia" makes the Rohingya even more vulnerable as they often get branded as "terrorists" (Ray Chaudhury & Samaddar, 2018, p. 188). Both Bangladesh and India have been keen to send them back to Myanmar, but without an assurance of citizenship, nothing is likely to change in Myanmar. India is a signatory to several international Conventions including the New York Declaration for Refugees and Migrants (2016) that not only recognized the rights of refugees to asylum but also affirmed the principle of non-refoulement. The UN General Assembly has clearly opined that everyone has the right to seek asylum in other countries from persecution and accordingly forced repatriation violates this core of international law (Ray Chaudhury & Samaddar,

[25]'Myanmar: UN fact-finding mission releases its full account of massive violations by the military in Rakhine, Kachin and Shan states, Geneva, September 18, 2018. https://www.ohchr.org/EN/NewsEvents/Pages/DisplayNews.aspx?NewsID=23575&LangID=E.

2018, p. 190). Without this wider view of responsibility sharing and "in order to explore connections between moral and legal responsibility, and between global and national responsibilities", global or regional initiatives will fail in South Asia (Ray Chaudhury & Samaddar, 2018, p. 191).

As the Rakhine state and its coast have become strategically important for Myanmar in establishing logistical connectivity with China and India, the Rohingya have turned into a completely unwelcome population there (Ray Chaudhury & Samaddar, 2018, p. 194). The Kofi Annan Commission has suggested that the government of Myanmar should have a clear strategy and timeline for the citizenship verification process. It also says that the government should review its citizenship law and clarify the status of those whose citizenship application is not accepted. However, as soon as this report was made public, it created more angst and chaos in Myanmar than mitigating it (Ray Chaudhury & Samaddar, 2018, p. 195). Hence, a potent solution for the Rohingyas that can start by addressing the question of "citizenship" is still nowhere in sight. They have been also denied basic human rights in countries of asylum like India, as deportation as a measure is extremely violative for the people in the current context and scenario. Thus, the Rohingyas remain stateless despite the existence of International Conventions on Statelessness—1954 and 61. Questions with which I started the piece remains—is the current migration regime capable of addressing the issue of de facto statelessness? In order to understand this, we have to take into account the unequal nature of power, influence and responsibility in the global protection regime (Ray Chaudhury & Samaddar, 2018, p. 185). One can suggest that the Rohingyas' reflect an extreme case of haplessness. For the Rohingyas, the only demand to a dignified life could start with the demand of citizenship and hence a possible way out. Whether that happens in the near future or in otherwise what will be strategies of the Rohingya activities or whether at all a durable solution could be attained by the states concerned are yet to be seen.

References

Arif, Y. (2016). *Life, emergent: The social in the afterlives of violence*. London: University of Minnesota.

Banerjee, P. (2010). *Borders, histories, existences: Gender and beyond*. New Delhi: Sage.

Chowdhory, N. (2018). *Refugees, citizenship and belonging in South Asia*. New Delhi: Springer.

Das, V. (2007). *Life and words: Violence and the descent into the ordinary*. United States: University of California Press.

Das, V., & Poole, D. (2004). *Anthropology in the margins of the state*. New Delhi: Oxford University Press.

De Genova, N. (2013). Spectacles of migrant 'illegality': the scene of exclusion, the obscene of inclusion. *Ethnic and Racial Studies*, *36*(7), 1180–1198.

Dozens Killed in Fighting Between Myanmar Army and Rohingya Militants. *The Guardian*. https://www.theguardian.com/world/2017/aug/25/rohingya-militants-blamed-as-attack-on-myanmar-border-kills-12. Accessed July 15, 2019.

Edkins, J., & Vaughan-Williams, N. (2012). *Beyond biopolitics: Theory, violence, and horror in world politics*. New York: Routledge.

Geddie, J., & Ungku, F. (2018, August 21). Myanmar's Suu Kyi says relations with military 'not that bad'. *Reuters*. https://www.reuters.com/article/us-singapore-myanmar-suukyi/myanmar-leader-suu-kyi-says-terrorism-in-rakhine-state-a-threat-to-region-idUSKCN1L60OP.

Graeber, D. (2015). *The utopia of rules: On technology, stupidity, and the secret joys of bureaucracy*. Brooklyn: Melville.

Guhathakurta, M. (2017). Understanding violence, strategising protection: perspectives from Rohingya refugees in Bangladesh. *Asian Journal of Social Science, 45*(6), 639–665.

Gupta, A., & Ferguson, J. (2002). Spatializing states: Toward an ethnography of neoliberal governmentality. *American Ethnologist, 29*(4), 981–1002.

Hoffstaedter, G. (2014). Place-making: Chin refugees, citizenship and the state in Malaysia. *Citizenship Studies, 18*(8), 871–884.

Malkki, L. H. (1995a). *Purity and exile: Violence, memory, and national cosmology among Hutu refugees in Tanzania*. Chicago: University of Chicago Press.

Malkki, L. H. (1995b). Refugees and exile: From 'refugees studies' to the national order of things. *Annual Review of Anthropology, 24*, 495–523.

Module D Statelessness in South Asia, MCRG. http://www.mcrg.ac.in/Statelessness/ModuleD.pdf.

Murray, S. (2006). Thanatopolitics: On the use of death for mobilising political life. *Polygraph, 18*.

Parsons, L., & Lawreniuk, S. (2017). *Seeing like the stateless: Documentation and the mobilities of liminal citizenship in Cambodia*. Department of Geography, Royal Holloway, University of London, UK.

Randeria, S. (2007). The state of globalisation, Legal plurality, overlapping sovereignties and ambiguous alliances between civil society and the cunning state in India. *Theory, Culture and Society, 24*(1).

Ray Chaudhury, B., & Samaddar, R. (2018). *The Rohingya in South Asia*. New York: Routledge.

Samaddar, R. (1999). *The spectre facing the nation in the marginal nation: Transborder migration from Bangladesh to West Bengal* (p. 44). New Delhi: Sage.

Samaddar, R. (2018). Histories of the late nineteenth to early twentieth century immigration of our time. *Current Sociology Monograph, 66*(2).

Scott, J. C. (2009). *The art of not being governed: An anarchist history of upland Southeast Asia*. New Haven: Yale University Press.

Sengupta, S. (2019, July 15). Rape, malnutrition, depression: Life in Bangladesh Rohingya Camps. *The Quint*. https://www.thequint.com/voices/opinion/rohingya-crisis-life-in-bangladesh-refugee-camps-as-seen-by-field-researcher?fbclid=IwAR36RhL65Yhpwu5pulf7_BaqkCpXoGC-3mXy8h3p2vxsjU8wk3Eaw4_YuLQ.

Somers, M. (2008). *Genealogies of citizenship: Markets, statelessness, and the right to have rights*. New York: Cambridge University Press.

Staples, K. (2012). *Retheorising statelessness: A background theory of membership in world politics*. Edinburgh: Edinburgh University Press.

UNHCR Document. https://www.google.ch/url?sa=t&rct=j&q=&esrc=s&source=web&cd=5&cad=rja&uact=8&ved=0ahUKEwiDn9738ZXYAhWBnBQKHYyNBYMQFghOMAQ&url=http%3A%2F%2Fwww.unhcr.org%2Fevents%2Fnansen%2F4aae50086%2Fnansen-man-action-vision.html&usg=AOvVaw0QsmcJKwvp7X1A2EiiWrqX.

UNHR. (2018, September 18). Myanmar: UN fact finding mission releases its full account of massive violations by military in Rakhine, Kachin and Shan states, Geneva. https://www.ohchr.org/EN/NewsEvents/Pages/DisplayNews.aspx?NewsID=23575&LangID=E.

Van Waas, L. (2008). *Nationality matters: Statelessness under international law*. Intersentia.

van Schendel, W. (2004). *The Bengal Borderland and Beyond State and Nation in South Asia*. London: Anthem Press.

We Must Prevent a Lost Generation, Community-Led Education in Rohingya Refugee Camps, PRIO Paper 2019. https://www.prio.org/utility/DownloadFile.ashx?id=1836&type=publicationfile&fbclid=IwAR3ZZ8-ZZvHy_SLyDIM6BhCvgwfiEA_lr-PgP79GBsXxBAICANL_fGwBqAk.
Wire. (2017). *Bangladesh-Myanmar Rohingya deal raises more questions than it clarifies*. https://thewire.in/external-affairs/bangladesh-myanmar-rohingya-repatriation-deal-pressbrief-raises-questions-clarifies, Accessed November 26, 2017.
Zamindar, V. (2007). *The long partition and the making of modern South Asia*. New York: Columbia University Press.

Chapter 7
The Assimilation of Stateless Rohingyas in Bangladesh

Meherun Ahmed, Syeda Nafisa Nawal, Ugyen Samdrup Lhamo and Nhung Tuyet Bui

Abstract Since 1972, waves of Rohingya refugees have entered Bangladesh fleeing the military-backed human rights violations in their native Myanmar. Despite attempts of repatriation and the government's consistent refusal to integrate the Rohingyas, an indefinite number has assimilated in mainland Bangladesh. Considering the daunting challenges to quantify the size and nature of this population, we use a small sample of 167 participants to identify how these refugees have assimilated in local communities. Most of them, who arrived approximately 16 years earlier as children or adolescents, have now been absorbed into the informal labour market earning an average monthly household income of BDT 10,270 (roughly USD 120). Unsurprisingly, participants have also adapted to the language and earned some level of education. As the Rohingya crisis remains protracted with the mass influx of 2017, this chapter aims to inform the primary features of past unassisted assimilation, in order to pave the way for further research and for long-run policy formulation.

Keywords Rohingya · Integration · Assimilation · Local communities' identity

Introduction

Over the last five years, armed conflict, violence and persecution have led to the continuation of several protracted forced displacement crises as well as the emergence of substantial new ones. By the end of 2017, the global aggregate of people displaced

M. Ahmed (✉) · U. S. Lhamo · N. T. Bui
Asian University for Women, Chittagong, Bangladesh
e-mail: meherun.ahmed@auw.edu.bd

U. S. Lhamo
e-mail: ugyen.lhamo@post.auw.edu.bd

N. T. Bui
e-mail: nhung.bui@post.auw.edu.bd

S. N. Nawal
North South University, Dhaka, Bangladesh

N. Chowdhory and B. Mohanty (eds.), *Citizenship, Nationalism and Refugeehood of Rohingyas in Southern Asia*,
https://doi.org/10.1007/978-981-15-2168-3_7

forcibly within and beyond borders had reached 68.5 million (UNHCR, 2018). The onus of the consequent humanitarian action fell largely on developing countries; 85% of all refugees within the operational purview of United Nations High Commissioner for Refugees (UNHCR) were being hosted in emerging economies (UNHCR, 2018). Six of the top ten refugee-hosting nations are in Asia (Turkey, Jordan, Lebanon, Pakistan, Iran and Bangladesh) with Turkey alone providing shelter to 3.5 million. Bangladesh, a lower-middle-income country yet to graduate from least developed country (LDC) status, is hosting 932,200 refugees (UNHCR, 2018), and almost all of whom are ethnic Rohingya forcibly displaced from neighbouring Myanmar.

An ethnic Muslim minority group residing in the north-western part of Rakhine state in Western Myanmar, the Rohingya "have been subjected to decades of state-sponsored discrimination and persecution, which have been extensively documented by Amnesty International and other human rights groups" (Amnesty International, 2016). In 2017, a mass exodus of 700,000 Rohingyas fleeing arson, rape and persecution by the Myanmar military arrived at Bangladesh (BBC News, 2018; Al Jazeera, 2018), in addition to the approximately 200,000 who had been residing in camps and host communities from past inflows (Human Rights Watch, 2018). UNHCR estimates that more than 900,000 Rohingyas have been housed in the three refugee camps in the tiny coastal town of Cox's Bazar under Chittagong district of Bangladesh (UNHCR, 2018). Bordering Rakhine state, Cox's Bazar has become the epicentre of the fastest growing humanitarian crisis in the world (Alam, 2018; Image 7.1).

The Emergency Coordinator for the World Food Programme in Cox's Bazar mentioned,

> We're still at the front end of what is about to become the largest refugee response in recent memory. The Bangladeshi government possibly didn't know what they were signing up for, but thank God they did (Solomon, 2017).

This influx may have been the most extensive recorded till date, but this is not a recent phenomenon. In fact, Rohingya exodus to Bangladesh dates back to the 1970s, with roots in the complex post-colonial politics of Myanmar (Human Rights Watch, 2002). As observed in any protracted crisis, refugees who have been stranded for years or generations often assimilate into the local communities, evading the watchful eyes of authorities and security personnel (Jacobsen, 2001). For the persecution of Rohingya, the different approaches adopted by various governments to deal with prolonged refugee crises and the overall well-being of refugees in stranded situations—all have been well documented in contemporary research. Some studies also focus on economic and well-being outcomes for refugees that have integrated over generations, such as Palestinians in Lebanon (Chaaban et al., 2010).

However, the incidence of unassisted assimilated refugees in local communities and the socio-economic aspects of their existence have often been overlooked in economic discourse. But data-driven work on the Rohingyas has not been explored in the past, partly due to hostile situations in their home country and partly due to the lack of international attention towards the issue. Nevertheless, journalistic inquiries over the years have suggested that assimilation of Rohingyas within Bengali communities has been occurring over the years. This chapter aims to corroborate this observation,

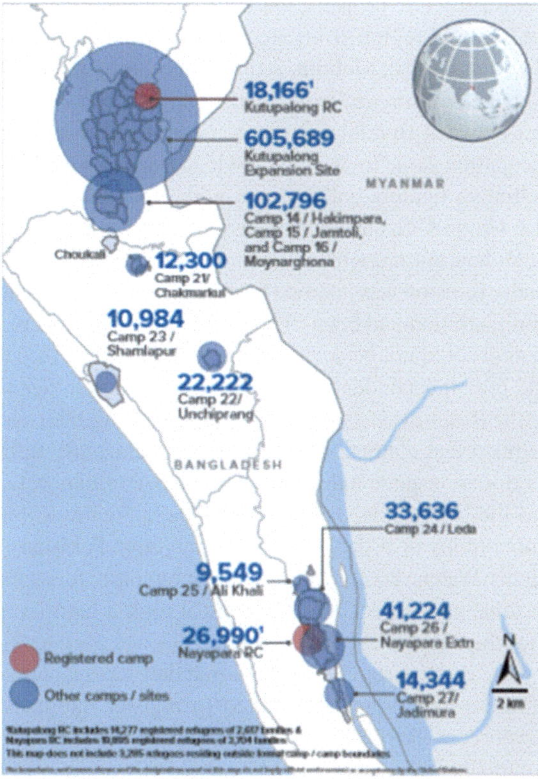

Image 7.1 Refugee camps in Cox's Bazar

using primary data from a sample of 167 participants. Our findings suggest that Rohingyas engage in the informal job market for livelihoods while adapting language and acquiring education to assimilate into local communities.

Literature Review

The term "Rohingya" may have come into public discourse as a collective political identity marker in the 1950s (Albert & Chatzky, 2018; Leider, 2018), but their roots in Myanmar date back centuries as per the accounts of historians and activist groups. Claiming to have descended from Arab traders and various other ethnic groups who have inhabited the region for generations, the Rohingyas are ardent practitioners of Islam with their distinct language and cultural practices (BBC News, 2018), who have lived in the Arakan Kingdom presently known as Rakhine state at least since the fifteenth century if not earlier (Albert & Chatzky, 2018; Al Jazeera, 2018). In the early 1820s, Britain captured Myanmar, then known as Burma, and administered the region as a province of then undivided India. For the purpose of employment in infrastructure projects, the British oversaw significant migration of labourers into the Rakhine region from areas that fall under modern India and Bangladesh (Al-Mahmood, 2016; Mohdin, 2017). This continued until 1942 when the Japanese invasion of Burma drove out the British (Al-Mahmood, 2016) and sowed the seeds of conflict between Buddhist Burmese communities and Muslim communities. Japanese occupation came to an end in 1945, owing to the efforts of Burmese nationalists and Rohingya fighters collaborated with British forces (Human Rights Watch, 2002). The Union Citizenship Act passed during the same year by the Burmese government, had not recognized Rohingyas as one of the country's 135 "national races". Such exclusion was justified based on the argument that mass migration under British administration had been illegal, and the Rohingyas as descendants of Muslims from Bengal could not be acknowledged as a national race (Human Rights Watch, 2002). The post-independence paradigm on Burmese citizenship was essentially accepted by the Rohingyas, as they insisted on proving their identity as a national race based on historical claims, which became increasingly difficult to prove (Leider, 2018). As Burma became independent in 1948, conflicts between the Burmese government and the Rohingyas started to escalate, as many Rohingyas expected Arakan to be autonomous or a part of Muslim majority Pakistan (Al-Mahmood, 2016; Human Rights Watch, 2002). Despite some attempts to establish harmony, the centralized socialist state under military control took a hardline stance against the Rohingyas after the coup of 1962 (Mohdin, 2017).

The earliest reports of state-mandated persecution surfaced in 1978 when the Burmese government attempted to register nationals and weed out foreigners in the process. Rohingyas were brutalized, raped and murdered by the army, which eventually drove approximately 200,000 refugees to pour through the border into Bangladesh. A large proportion of them were repatriated within few months (Human Rights Watch, 2002). By 1982, a new citizenship law enshrining ethnic discrimination had been passed (Albert & Chatzky, 2018; Mohdin, 2017) the law required Rohingyas to prove that their ancestors had settled in the region before independence in 1948, a burden that made it almost impossible for Rohingyas to access citizenship except for a negligible few (Al Jazeera, 2018; Human Rights Watch, 2002). Consequently, Rohingyas were deprived of secondary and tertiary education, healthcare and freedom of movement (Al Jazeera, 2018). Their property would often be seized by the army, and many of them were forced to engage in unpaid physical labour (Human Rights Watch, 2002). As religious persecution persisted, another 250,000 Rohingyas fled into Bangladesh in 1991 and 1992, of which 230,000 were eventually repatriated between 1993 and 1997 amidst widespread controversy (D'Costa, 2012; Human Rights Watch, 2002). Simultaneously, a steady influx of Rohingyas in smaller numbers had continued between 1992 and 1999. Sometimes unbeknownst to authorities and sometimes otherwise, most of them have blended into Bangladeshi communities due to similarities in dialect and appearance (D'Costa, 2012; Human Rights Watch, 2002). In 2012, sectarian violence between Buddhist Rakhine communities and Rohingyas spiralled into widespread hostilities that led to arson, killings and mass internal displacement of Rohingyas. Approximately 30,000 Rohingyas had sought refuge in Bangladesh but were refused entry by the government at the time citing security concerns (Amnesty International, 2016; D'Costa, 2012; Human Rights Watch, 2012). Bouts of sectarian violence and military crackdowns continued well into 2013 (Human Rights Watch, 2013). In late 2016, a militant outfit primarily manned by Rohingyas attacked several border police posts in Rakhine, triggering an unprecedented brute response from the military (Amnesty International, 2016). Bangladesh then received more than 80,000 refugees (Human Rights Watch, 2018). A systematic military campaign of arson, mass murder, rape and torture ensued well until 2017, one that has been dubbed by a top United Nations official as a "textbook example of ethnic cleansing" (BBC News, 2018). It ultimately led to the exodus of more than 700,000 Rohingyas into Bangladesh (Al Jazeera, 2018; BBC News, 2018; Human Rights Watch, 2017), a phenomenon that garnered international attention to this prolonged crisis.

As the Rohingyas have fled the state-mandated persecution in Rakhine, Bangladesh has been the primary destination for an overwhelming number of refugees, though some have managed to escape to Saudi Arabia, UAE, Pakistan, India, Thailand, Malaysia and Indonesia. In fact, the Rohingya population in Bangladesh as of 2017 was almost double that in Myanmar (BBC News, 2018). Over the last four decades, Bangladesh has been grappling with a refugee crisis that has effectively become a protracted one with no immediate solution in sight. Having accounted for multiples exoduses, the official count of the Rohingya population in Bangladesh currently stands at approximately 950,000 (UNHCR, 2018). To assume that the actual count is much higher would not be a far stretch; in 1991, only the number of undocumented Rohingyas were estimated to be around 150,000 (Human Rights Watch, 2002), most of whom had meshed with the local communities in nearby Chittagong, while some had even migrated to the capital Dhaka in search of better economic opportunities (Human Rights Watch, 2002). In 2012, the Refugee Relief and Repatriation Commission (RRRC) estimated around 200,000 Rohingya refugees to be undocumented (D'Costa, 2012). The unknown yet rising numbers of undocumented Rohingyas have also caused resentment among the local communities of the Chittagong Hill Tract areas, where many Rohingyas have informally settled (D'Costa, 2012). The most recent refugee crisis has "changed the demographics" of host areas, where "refugees now outnumber locals 2 to 1" (Alam, 2018). With habits as trivial as wearing pants instead of traditional "longyis", Rohingya men in the camps are already showing attempts to assimilate into Bangladeshi culture (Doshi, 2018). It stands to reason that an undetermined yet substantial number of Rohingyas have assimilated into local communities across Chittagong and Dhaka, albeit causing bitterness among locals, despite formal integration or assimilation never being encouraged by the Bangladeshi government. Starting from the first mass exodus in 1978 till the latest in 2017, the government has consistently and straightforwardly rejected the notion of assisted assimilation or integration for the Rohingya (Alsaafin, 2018; Human Rights Watch, 2002; Reuters, 2018). In accordance with the strategy adopted in the 1970s and 1990s, Bangladesh is still pursuing a solution for "sustainable return" of the Rohingya (Alsaafin, 2018); in other words, repatriation to Myanmar through diplomatic arbitration. The government of Myanmar has shown little to no effort in ensuring that conditions in Rakhine be conducive for voluntary and dignified repatriation (Human Rights Watch, 2018).

The unwillingness of the Bangladeshi government to integrate refugees and that of the Burmese government to create an environment favourable for repatriation are not extraordinary. As demonstrated by multiple cases across Africa, many protracted refugee crises can be characterized by host governments' lingering attempts at ensuring safe repatriation while restricting refugees' mobility within a certain area (Crisp, 2003). Perhaps the situation with most parallels to the Rohingya in Bangladesh is that of the Somalis in Kenya. Somali refugees in Kenya are mostly confined to three designated camp areas with limited rights to movement and work. Most are self-employed or participate in the UNHCR's employment programmes. The presence of a significant Somali ethnic group in Kenya has enabled the refugees to seek employment through networks and to rely on relatives for "social protection", allowing them to assimilate with the Kenyan host community (Betts, Omata, & Streak, 2018). A transition from an aid-based model to a self-reliance model has recently been explored in a designated camp through the joint efforts of the Kenyan government along with the European Union and UNHCR, which has proved to be relatively better for refugees in terms of income, food security and consumption (Betts et al., 2018). Ethiopia has experienced a shift in refugee policy following the implementation of a comprehensive framework, which allows for paid work and assimilation of long-term refugees. Challenges such as ethnic tensions, fall in wages and lack of coordination remain (Abebe, 2018). Uganda is lauded for having the most liberal refugee laws in the world, which allow for rights to work and access to healthcare and education barring only rights to citizenship (World Bank, 2016). Refugee economies are linked with broader economic systems, creating sustainable livelihood opportunities for both refugees and hosts (Betts et al., 2018). A comparison of several refugee crises across Africa asserted that assimilation is to be encouraged wherever possible (Scalabrini Institute for Human Mobility in Africa, 2017). Even in the case of developing economies such as Germany, temporary social and economic integration was viewed as an essential step towards rebuilding refugees' lives and for the economic gains of host communities (Angenendt & Harild, 2017).

Conventional policy approaches to refugee crises are: repatriation, resettlement and integration. As the UNHCR continues to struggle to offer durable solutions through repatriation and resettlement (Cole, 2018), integration as a "forgotten solution" (Jacobsen, 2001) is increasingly being emphasized by experts in migration and refugee studies (Beversluis et al., 2018; Dadush, 2018). When refugee communities preserve their own cultural identities while simultaneously forging relationships with host communities, the process is referred to as integration (Kuhlman, 1991). Integration is more desirable than assimilation, a phenomenon that has been observed in Northern Uganda and Mexico (Jacobsen, 2001). There are important distinctions between "integration" and "assimilation". Assimilation occurs when refugees intrinsically adapt to the host community (Ager & Strang, 2008), or when the refugee group immerses into the dominant society (Kuhlman, 1991). Assimilation is a more likely outcome over the long run as "a culture can only be maintained to the extent that it does not conflict with the dominant one" (Kuhlman, 1991). The case of undocumented Rohingyas residing in Bangladesh is hence one of assimilation. Rohingyas have assimilated within the dominant Bangladeshi community owing to strong similarities in language, appearance and religious practices. However, they are unable to reveal their ethnicities, fearing backlash from locals and punitive measures from authorities. As Kuhlman's idea suggests, the assimilated Rohingya community's culture exists only so far as it does not conflict with the Bengali way of life or identity.

Description of Data and Methodology

Using a structured questionnaire, we undertook a quantitative survey of 167 registered and unregistered refugees residing in four different districts: Bandarban, Chittagong, Cox's Bazar and Teknaf. The survey aimed to identify factors influencing labour market access and employment status of Rohingyas assimilated in Bangladesh. Rohingya inhabitants in unauthorized areas face enormous risks while disclosing their identities. Hence, some participants chose not to disclose their location, and many of those approached refused to participate altogether for fear of being "caught" or identified as Rohingya. Participants were chosen randomly and among the community contacts of the ten Rohingya, research assistants employed for the survey. Participants expressed informed consent and were free to opt out of their interviews anytime. All interviews were conducted in the Rohingya dialect and then translated to Bengali or English. Appropriate research ethics and guidelines by the Institutional Review Board (IRB) committee of the Asian University for Women (AUW) were followed throughout the data collection process.

Given our small sample size we used Analysis of Variance (ANOVA) approach to compare means of different sub categories. We calculated the means of different explanatory variables as different occupation types, different language skills, fluency and competency levels, education levels and experience. We compared these means between the split samples of the above-mentioned categories. The means and the percentages are represented in graphical form for each subgroup for the convenience of comparison.

Findings

Of 167 participants, 36.5% were from Chittagong, 34.7% from Bandarban, 19.7% from Cox's Bazar and 7.1% from Teknaf, whereas 2% chose not to disclose their locations. 76% of participants were male compared to 24% female, likely because most Rohingyas active in the public sphere are male. 78% of respondents were married and all identified as Muslim. The median age of respondents was 34.12 years, with 89% of participants being within the range of 30–60 years. 26% had arrived in Bangladesh between the years 2001 and 2005. 21% migrated between 1996 and 2001, while 20% migrated between 1990 and 1995. 51% of respondents were aged below 18 at the time of their arrival in Bangladesh, and the average length of stay was 16.7 years. The aggregate summary statistics were used in the empirical analysis.

Factors Influencing Labour Market Access and Employment Status

Language Skills

The labour market in Bangladesh requires participants to be fully proficient in Bengali, and in cases of formal high skilled employment, English is also necessary. The informal labour market requires participants to be at least fluent in the local dialect in order to receive and comprehend instructions. As such, refugees' command of the Bengali language is an essential determinant of their ability to access low-skilled employment. We compare the survey respondents' proficiency in Bengali before and after migration, in terms of reading, writing, listening and speaking. Due to the nature of the informal labour market, we put greater emphasis on listening and speaking skills. It is to be noted that proficiency indicators used in this survey are all based on self-reported data and have not been verified independently by a competent testing body.

Before arrival in Bangladesh, most participants did not know any Bengali at all; only about 4% were proficient in Bengali. 72% of those who knew Bengali at the time of arrival were able to secure their first job in Bangladesh within three months. In contrast, 49% of those without the ability to speak Bengali found jobs within three months of arrival. The 23 percentage point gap indicates that language is an important factor in accessing a job in the host community. However, the inability of 28% Bengali speakers to secure a job within three months also hints at other barriers in accessing employment. Over time, as the respondents had assimilated into Bangladesh, their Bengali language skills have improved significantly. While literacy in Bengali is still poor, respondents' overall ability to comprehend and speak has increased, indicating their ability to conduct social communications smoothly. How much of their assimilation can be attributed to their adoption of language skills is difficult to analyse with limited data. Figures 7.1 and 7.2 compare Bengali language skills before and after migration.

Considering that English language skills are a novelty among the low-skilled labour force in the areas surveyed, we checked the English proficiency of our respondents to understand whether Rohingyas were able to access comparatively better jobs than the locals. Figures 7.3 and 7.4 compare English language skills before and after migration, again based on self-reported indicators.

Data indicates that English skills were poor at the time of arrival; it could not have had a significant impact on employment; then, neither did the respondents show any

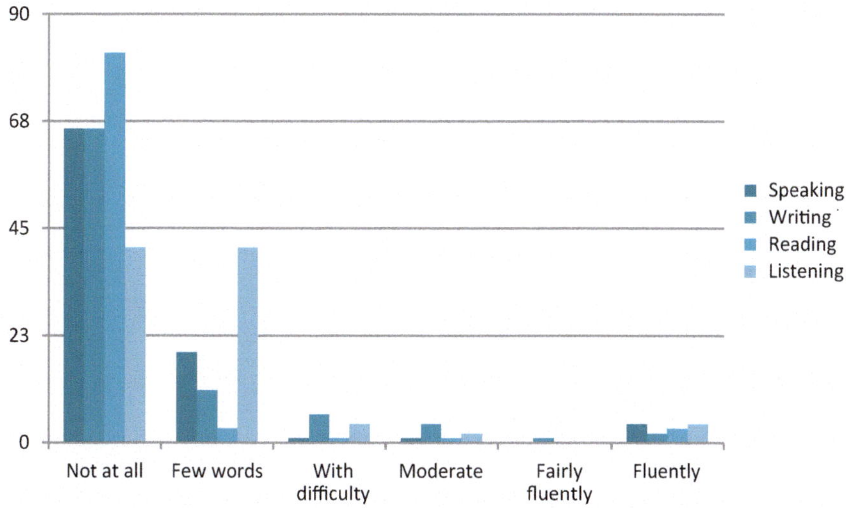

Fig. 7.1 Participants' Bengali language skills before migration (in percentage)

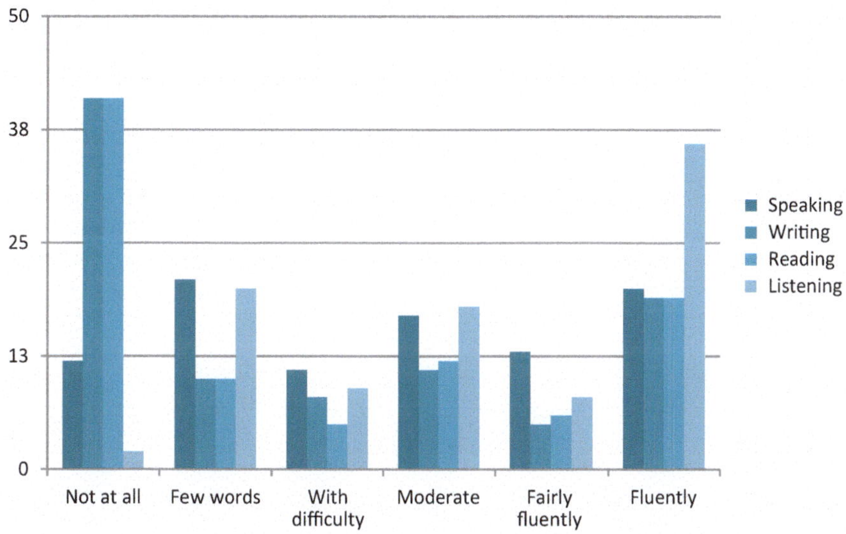

Fig. 7.2 Participants' current Bengali language skills (in percentage)

tendency to improve their skills over time. In fact, the ability to comprehend any English has significantly deteriorated over time, which would mean that any usage of the language for employment purposes would have been impossible. While Bengali language skills proved essential in securing employment, the same cannot be said for English language skills.

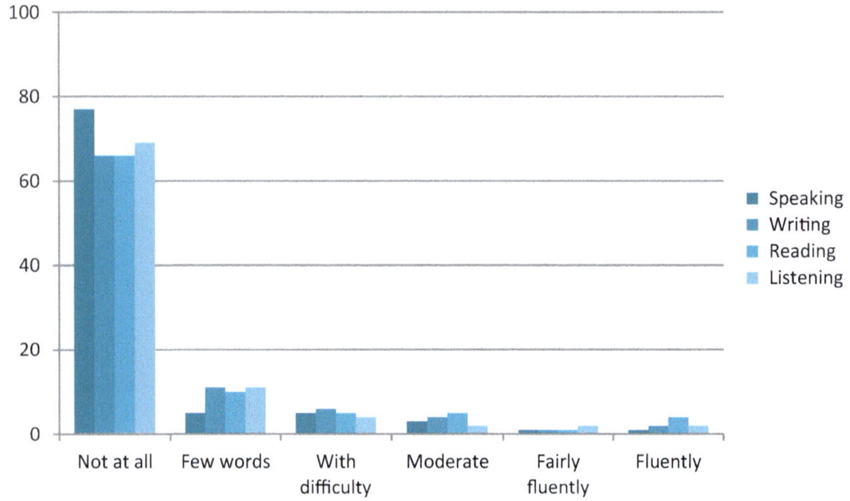

Fig. 7.3 Participants' English language skills before migration (in percentage)

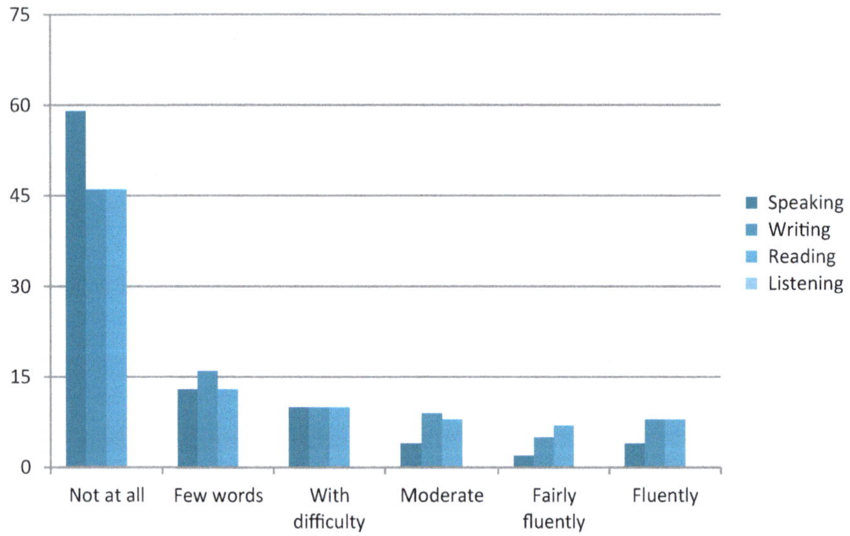

Fig. 7.4 Participants' current English language skills (in percentage)

Education

Education or literacy, at the very least, is an essential criterion to enter the labour market of Bangladesh, even in informal ones. Any level of education is considered

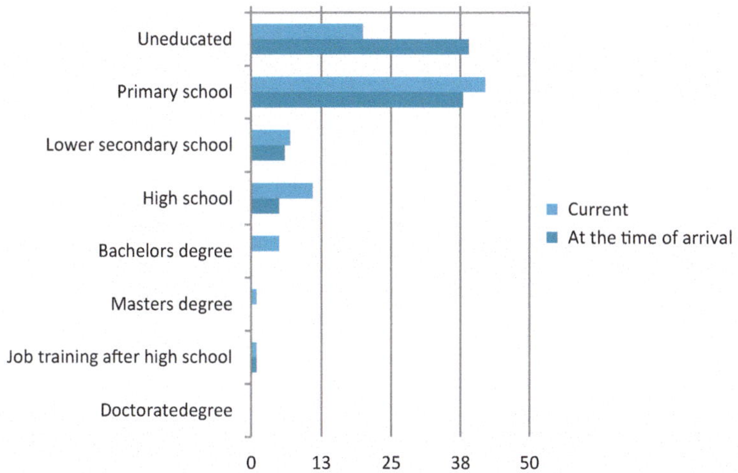

Fig. 7.5 Participants' current education levels and that at the time of arrival (in percentage)

a proxy for skill, or the ability to learn a skill. Undoubtedly, the level of education affected participants' ability to access employment. At the time of arrival, most Rohingyas were uneducated or illiterate, with the highest level of education attained being a high school qualification. Over time though, 27% of respondents sought higher education as they attempted to assimilate, some even striving to attain university degrees. Figure 7.5 shows the comparison between education levels prior to arrival and current ones.

The proportion of those uneducated reduced significantly, while those attending primary school increased. However, the pursuit of formal degrees or job-specific training was still poor; indicating that assimilated Rohingyas would not have the opportunity to progress into higher-skilled jobs.

Prior Job Experience

Among 167 participants, 41% of them were children at the time of arrival, and 42% had prior work experience. Most had worked as farmers on their own farms and supplemented their income from surplus crops. Upon arrival in Bangladesh, 49% of respondents received help from relatives to seek jobs. 22% found jobs on their own, while 29% relied on acquaintances and friends. 25% had secured a job within a month of arrival; 20% needed about 1 or 2 months, and 13% needed up to three months. 37% could not find employment after three months. To understand their prior work experience and how that helped them find work, we divided the employment status of participants into four different types, as shown in Table 7.1.

Table 7.1 Types of jobs

Type	Characteristics	Jobs
1. Self-employed/business	Lesser extent of manual labour	Businessman, shopkeeper, tailor, electrician, etc.
	More freedom	
	Service-oriented	
2. Manual labour	Intensive manual labour	Domestic help, garment worker, rickshaw puller, etc.
3. Office jobs	Requires specific education level and skills	Office/NGO worker, teacher, Imam, doctor, etc.
4. None	N/A	Children, housewives

87% of respondents took upon a different occupation upon arrival in Bangladesh; in most cases, these were jobs of an inferior level compared to their initial jobs in their home countries. Among those who found jobs upon arrival in Bangladesh, 43% took up manual jobs, 34% took up self-employment or research and 13% took up office jobs. Of those who secured employment within three months of arrival, 76% were self-employed or businesspeople in their home country; 60% were office workers and 50% worked in manual jobs. 46% of respondents who arrived as children engaged in child labour within three months of arrival while the remaining engaged eventually. 43% of respondents remained in the first jobs they held since migration; 36% switched between 2 or 3 jobs while very few switched more than that. Figure 7.6 shows the first jobs held by our respondents in Bangladesh compared to their current ones.

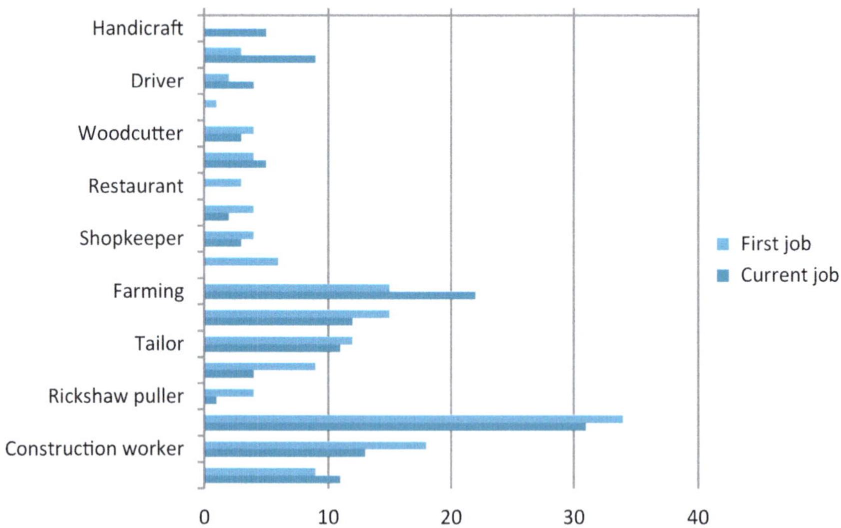

Fig. 7.6 Participants' first jobs and current jobs (in numbers)

69% of our employed respondents work full time; 13% are self-employed, and 12% work part time. 2% have retired or are now housewives. 36% of those who work full time receive salaries compared to 55% of those who work part time. 14% of full-time workers receive daily payments, and 35% receive hourly payments.

Income

The average monthly household income for our sample is Bangladeshi Taka (BDT) 10, 270. Income data has been further analysed for different job types as well as for different education levels, as illustrated in Figs. 7.7 and 7.8.

Income earned from self-employment or business is quite high compared to manual labour, while that from office jobs is highest. However, there is not much gap in income between those self-employed or those engaged in office jobs. In terms of education, higher education does not always translate into higher income, as demonstrated by the case of those with lower secondary education. Those with high school qualifications seem to have the highest returns to education, as their income is quite close to those with university degrees.

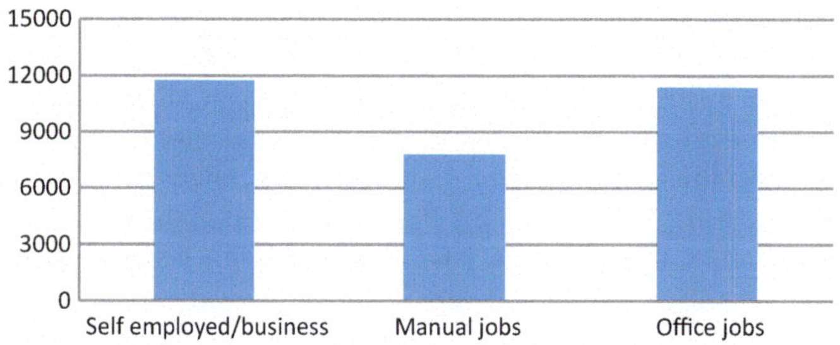

Fig. 7.7 Average monthly household income (for each job type)

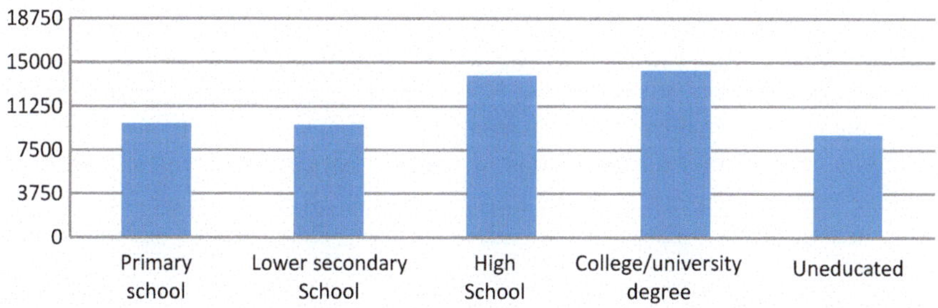

Fig. 7.8 Average monthly household income (for each education level)

Social Aid and Support

72% of our respondents had not received any form of aid from any community or social organization. Of 28% who received were: 15% from relatives, 6% from friends, 3% through awareness programmes and 4% from media organizations. 21% received cash aid, 2% received food and 5% received clothes or shelter.

Discussion

Access to employment is a vital component of every assimilation or integration model, though it may not always be in the benefit of the host community. Turkey granted Syrian refugees the right to access formal work, though structural challenges remain (Carpio, Seker, & Yenern, 2018). The employment of Palestinians and Syrians in Jordan has driven many low-skilled Jordanians out of work, which indicates that assimilation of refugees is impossible without consolidated efforts in skill development of the host population (Stave & Hillesund, 2015). Employment facilitation of refugee populations may transfer vulnerability to low-skilled host populations (Mixed Migration Centre, 2017), an untoward outcome of any integration effort. Despite enabling efforts by governments, integration in the labour market is not straightforward; close social linkages help refugees secure jobs (Shteiwi et al., 2016), as verified by the case of Rohingya refugees who are all economically active to some extent owing to their networks (Nielsen, Jahan, & Canteli, 2012). Any policy encouraging integration or assimilation of refugees must, therefore, take into account the net economic benefits of integrating them as opposed to the trade-offs incurred by local communities, more so in the case of Bangladesh where low-skilled labour is abundant, and underemployment is rife.

Ample research has been conducted regarding the impact of refugees in developed economies, which almost universally indicate that integration yields positive outcomes for the host economy (Dadush, 2018). Adequate research, however, is not available for developing economies. Neo-classical economics may not offer adequate tools to study forced displacement, a gap that has been supplemented by recent developments in game theory and behavioural economics (Verme, 2017). There is a need for additional metrics that can better inform policy-makers on the impacts of hosting refugees (Miller, 2018). Nevertheless, policies such as the Jordan Compact have advocated for the integration of refugees through employment, in lieu of lucrative trade agreements with the European Union (Barbelet, Hagen-Zanker, & Mansour-Ille, 2018). Approaches at better connecting humanitarian assistance and development finance have the potential to ensure both refugees and host populations can benefit from adequate and predictable funding streams directed towards public services, infrastructure and economic opportunities (Luecke & Schneiderheinze, 2017). Whether such policy lessons may be effectively translated into workable action for the Rohingya crisis depends on the nature of ongoing assimilation, the unique aspects of the Bangladeshi labour market as well as a wide range of sociopolitical factors.

Conclusion

While Bangladesh continues to pursue repatriation as the preferred solution to the Rohingya crisis, the government may be well advised to consider the fact that some assimilation will inevitably occur—as demonstrated by our discussion above. Policy analysis targeting this issue needs to strike the delicate balance between upholding human rights and the prevention of more undocumented assimilation. Drafting of asylum laws based on well-accepted precedents should also be considered as part of this process. In addition, it is important to acknowledge the possibility that repatriation efforts may be prolonged or delayed, as is the case with many sensitive bilateral negotiations. As an interim solution, trade and investment agreements similar to the Jordan Compact may be explored, albeit upon adequately ensuring that the labour market access for the local population is not compromised. Future policies addressing the Rohingya crisis needs to account for both short- and long-run implications, accounting for evidence on the impact of assimilation on host communities.

References

Abebe, T. T. (2018). *Ethiopia's refugee response—Focus on socio-economic integration and self-reliance*. Institute for Security Studies. https://issafrica.org/research/east-africa-report/ethiopias-refugee-response-focus-on-socio-economic-integration-and-self-reliance. Accessed March 17, 2019.

Ager, A., & Strang, A. (2008). Understanding integration: A conceptual framework. *Journal of Refugee Studies, 21*(2), 166–191.

Al Jazeera. (2018). *Who are the Rohingya?* https://www.aljazeera.com/indepth/features/2017/08/rohingya-muslims-170831065142812.html. Accessed March 17, 2019.

Alam, M. (2018). How the Rohingya crisis is affecting Bangladesh—And why it matters. *The Washington Post*. https://www.washingtonpost.com/news/monkey-cage/wp/2018/02/12/how-the-rohingya-crisis-is-affecting-bangladesh-and-why-it-matters/?noredirect=on&utm_term=.df5ca0712624. Accessed March 17, 2019.

Albert, E., & Chatzky, A. (2018). *The Rohingya crisis: Backgrounder for the council of foreign relations*. https://www.cfr.org/backgrounder/rohingya-crisis. Accessed March 17, 2019.

Al-Mahmood, Z. (2016). Timeline: A short history of Myanmar's Rohingya minority. *Wall Street Journal*. https://blogs.wsj.com/indiarealtime/2016/12/23/timeline-a-short-history-of-myanmars-rohingya-minority/. Accessed March 17, 2019.

Alsaafin, L. (2018). *Q&A: Bangladesh wants sustainable return for Rohingya*. https://www.aljazeera.com/indepth/features/qa-bangladesh-sustainable-return-rohingya-180815171325334.html. Accessed March 17, 2019.

Amnesty International. (2016). *We are at breaking point—Rohingya: Persecuted in Myanmar, neglected in Bangladesh*. https://www.amnesty.org/en/documents/asa16/5362/2016/en/. Accessed March 17, 2019.

Angenendt, S., & Harild, N. (2017). *Tapping into the economic potential of refugees*. German Institute for International and Security Affairs. https://www.swp-berlin.org/en/publication/tapping-into-the-economic-potential-of-refugees/. Accessed March 17, 2019.

Barbelet, V., Hagen-Zanker J., & Mansour-Ille, D. (2018). *The Jordan compact: Lessons learnt and implications for future refugee compacts*. ODI Briefing Papers. https://www.odi.org/publications/11045-jordan-compact-lessons-learnt-and-implications-future-refugee-compacts. Accessed March 17, 2019.

BBC News. (2018). Myanmar Rohingya: What you need to know about the crisis. https://www.bbc.com/news/world-asia-41566561. Accessed March 17, 2019.

Betts, A., Bloom, L., Kaplan, J., & Omata, N. (2018). *Refugee economies—Rethinking popular assumptions*. https://www.rsc.ox.ac.uk/refugeeeconomies. Accessed March 17, 2019.

Betts, A., Geervliet, R., MacPherson, C., Omata, N., Rodgers, C., & Sterck, O. (2018). *Self-reliance in Kalobeyei? Socio-economic outcomes for refugees in North-West Kenya*. Refugee Studies Center, University of Oxford. https://www.rsc.ox.ac.uk/publications/self-reliance-in-kalobeyei-socio-economic-outcomes-for-refugees-in-north-west-kenya. Accessed March 17, 2019.

Betts, A., Omata, N., & Sterck, O. (2018). Refugee Economies in Kenya. Refugee Studies Center, University of Oxford. https://www.rsc.ox.ac.uk/publications/refugee-economies-in-kenya. Accessed March 17, 2019.

Beversluis, D., Schoeller-Diaz, D., Anderson, M., Anderson, N., Slaughter, A., & Patel, R. B. (2018). *Journal of Refugee Studies, 30*(1), 106–131.

Carpio, X. V., Seker, S. D., & Yenern, A. L. (2018). Integrating refugees into the Turkish labour market. *Forced Migration Review, 58*, 10–13.

Chaaban, J., Ghattas, H., Habi, R. R., Hanafi, S., Sahyoun, N., Salti, N., et al. (2010). Socio-economic survey of Palestinian refugees in Lebanon. https://www.unrwa.org/sites/default/files/content/resources/survey_on_the_economic_status_of_palestine_refugees_in_lebanon_2015.pdf. Accessed March 17, 2019.

Cole, G. (2018). *Questioning the value of 'refugee' status and its primary vanguard: The case of Eritreans in Uganda* (Working Paper Series No. 124). Refugee Studies Center, University of Oxford. https://www.rsc.ox.ac.uk/publications/questioning-the-value-of-refugee-status-and-its-primary-vanguard-the-case-of-eritreans-in-uganda. Accessed March 17, 2019.

Crisp, J. (2003). *No solution in sight: The problem of protracted refugee situations in Africa* (Working Paper No. 68). San Diego: University of California. https://escholarship.org/uc/item/89d8r34q. Accessed March 17, 2019.

D'Costa, B. (2012). Rohingyas and the 'right to have rights. *Forum* (a monthly publication of The Daily Star). http://archive.thedailystar.net/forum/2012/August/rohingyas.htm. Accessed March 17, 2019.

Dadush, U. (2018). *The economic effects of refugee return and policy implications* (Policy Research Working Paper 8497). World Bank Group. https://openknowledge.worldbank.org/handle/10986/29950?locale-attribute=es. Accessed March 17, 2019.

Doshi, V. (2018). Rohingya men in Bangladesh revel in the newfound right to wear pants. *The Washington Post*. https://www.washingtonpost.com/world/asia_pacific/rohingya-men-in-bangladesh-revel-in-the-newfound-right-to-wear-pants/2018/06/17/f6afd5a0-71a0-11e8-b4d8-eaf78d4c544c_story.html?utm_term=.7dfdd7170ed3. Accessed March 17, 2019.

Human Rights Watch. (2002). *Burmese refugees in Bangladesh: Still no durable solution*. https://www.hrw.org/report/2000/05/01/burmese-refugees-bangladesh/still-no-durable-solution. Accessed March 17, 2019.

Human Rights Watch. (2012). *The government could have stopped this—Sectarian violence and ensuing abuses in Burma's Arakan State*. https://www.hrw.org/report/2012/07/31/government-could-have-stopped/sectarian-violence-and-ensuing-abuses-burmas-arakan. Accessed March 17, 2019.

Human Rights Watch. (2013). *All you can do is pray—Crimes against humanity and ethnic cleansing of Rohingya Muslims in Burma's Arakan State*. https://www.hrw.org/report/2013/04/22/all-you-can-do-pray/crimes-against-humanity-and-ethnic-cleansing-rohingya-muslims. Accessed March 17, 2019.

Human Rights Watch. (2017). *All of my body was pain—Sexual violence against Rohingya women and girls in Burma*. https://www.hrw.org/report/2017/11/16/all-my-body-was-pain/sexual-violence-against-rohingya-women-and-girls-burma. Accessed March 17, 2019.

Human Rights Watch. (2018). *Bangladesh is not my country—Stateless Rohingya refugees expelled from Myanmar*. https://www.hrw.org/report/2018/08/05/bangladesh-not-my-country/plight-rohingya-refugees-myanmar. Accessed March 17, 2019.

Jacobsen, K. (2001). *The forgotten solution: Local integration for refugees in developing countries* (Working Paper No. 45). New Issues in Refugee Research, UNHCR. https://www.unhcr.org/research/working/3b7d24059/forgotten-solution-local-integration-refugees-developing-countries-karen.html. Accessed March 17, 2019.

Kuhlman, T. (1991). The economic integration of refugees in developing countries: A research model. *Journal of Refugee Studies, 4*(1), 1–20.

Leider, J. (2018). Rohingya: The history of a Muslim identity in Myanmar. *Oxford Research Encyclopedia of Asian History*. https://doi.org/10.1093/acrefore/9780190277727.013.115.

Luecke, M., & Schneiderheinze, C. (2017). More financial burden-sharing for developing countries that host refugees. *Policy Briefs*, G20-Insights. https://www.g20-insights.org/policy_briefs/financial-burden-sharing-developing-countries-host-refugees/. Accessed March 17, 2019.

Miller, S. D. (2018). *Assessing the impacts of hosting refugees*. World Refugee Council, Centre for International Governance Innovation. https://www.cigionline.org/publications/assessing-impacts-hosting-refugees. Accessed March 17, 2019.

Mixed Migration Centre. (2017). *Decent work for whom? Economic integration of refugees and other foreign nationals in the Middle East* (Briefing Paper No. 09). Mixed Migration Centre, Danish Refugee Council. http://www.mixedmigration.org/wp-content/uploads/2018/08/049_decent-work.pdf. Accessed March 17, 2019.

Mohdin, A. (2017). A brief history of the word Rohingya at the heart of a humanitarian crisis. *Quartz*. https://qz.com/1092313/a-brief-history-of-the-word-rohingya-at-the-heart-of-a-humanitarian-crisis/. Accessed March 17, 2019.

Nielsen, N. S., Jahan, F., & Canteli, C. (2012). *The contribution of food assistance to durable solutions in protracted refugee situations; its impact and role in Bangladesh: A mixed method impact evaluation*. World Food Programme. https://www.wfp.org/content/food-assistance-protracted-refugee-situations-bangladesh-joint-mixed-method-impact-evaluatio. Accessed March 17, 2019.

Reuters. (2018). *Bangladesh says it won't assimilate Rohingya Muslims*. https://www.reuters.com/article/us-wef-vietnam-bangladesh-rohingya/bangladesh-says-it-wont-assimilate-rohingya-muslims-idUSKCN1LS1Z5. Accessed March 17, 2019.

Scalabrini Institute for Human Mobility in Africa. (2017). *Access to socio-economic rights for refugees: A comparison across six African countries*. http://sihma.org.za/wp-content/uploads/2017/03/Access-to-socio-economic-rights_refugees.pdf. Accessed March 17, 2019.

Shteiwi, M., Bayaner, A., Bolani, L., Bölük, G., Fernández, B., Gemi, E., et al. (2016). *Migrants, and refugees: Impact and policies—Case studies of Jordan, Lebanon, Turkey, and Greece*. European Institute of the Mediterranean. https://www.euromesco.net/publication/migrants-and-refugees-impact-and-policies-case-studies-of-jordan-lebanon-turkey-and-greece/. Accessed March 17, 2019.

Solomon, F. (2017). Myanmar's crisis, Bangladesh's burden: Among the Rohingya refugees waiting for a miracle. *Time*. http://time.com/5031342/bangladesh-myanmar-rohingya-refugee-crisis/. Accessed March 17, 2019.

Stave, S. E., & Hillesund, S. (2015). Impact of Syrian refugees on the Jordanian labour market. https://www.ilo.org/beirut/publications/WCMS_364162/lang--en/index.htm. Accessed March 17, 2019.

were allowed to participate neither as candidates, nor as voters—unlike in all previous elections since independence in 1948.[1] The Rohingyas always looked for a safe place to avoid the oppression of Burma. At some stage, the oppressions of Myanmar authorities became so unbearable that a rebel organization called Arakan Rohingya Salvation Army (ARSA) was formed, in the name of protecting the Rohingya Muslims, and on 25 August 2017, they attacked the Myanmar's security forces. Responding to that attack, the Myanmar authorities retaliated with brutal actions, which was termed by the United Nations as "ethnic cleansing". Thousands of Rohingya Muslims were killed, hundreds of Rohingya women were raped, and their villages were burnt. The helpless Rohingyas started fleeing the Rakhine state to save their lives. Many of them crossed the Naf River took shelter in unknown jungles and hills of Cox's Bazar, Bangladesh. As the atrocities and oppression increased, influx of fleeing Rohingyas multiplied in numbers in seeking asylum in Bangladesh. Since 25 August 2017, more than 7,00,000 Rohingyas have fled Myanmar and found refuge in Bangladesh, their closest neighbour, as a safe place to live and joined three hundred thousand Rohingyas living in various camps who had entered earlier.[2]

Looking at the experiences of Rohingyas, the chapter asserts that nationality is a bond among people that provides a sense of identity to citizens, i.e. a legal bond between people and the state. Citizenship provides a wide range of rights to citizens. Thereby, the lack of citizenship would deprive a community of its rights, which appears to be the situation of the Rohingyas in Myanmar. Arendt points out that for a stateless person to become citizen, they should have a "right to have the rights". The state operates as a *janus* face, and it can withhold rights and make the citizen stateless. Thus, the question is if civil, social, economic and cultural rights of the citizens are withdrawn, then do person lose all the rights that they enjoyed as citizens? What does the community do in such circumstances to protect itself from various vulnerabilities and risks?

This dilemma has been overcome by the international statutes and conventions to protect the refugees and stateless from the excesses of the state and vulnerabilities that they face in their everyday existence in the host and native countries. The states are turning to the 1951 Statute of Refugees and the 1954 Convention on the Status of Stateless Persons to protect the refugees from all kinds of violations perpetrated on them. The convention complements provisions of the United Charter for the Universal Declaration of Human Rights. Albeit other rights, Article 3 of the Declaration states that all human beings are entitled to the "right to life, liberty and security".

Interestingly, the International Court of Justice has adjudicated in the South West Africa Case that the Universal Declaration of Human Rights enjoys supremacy over the national legislation. The states cannot eschew their responsibilities in the name of national legislation.[3] Bangladesh has included the direct constitutional reference

[1] ReliefWeb. Inter Sector Coordination Group (2018).

[2] Human Rights Watch (2018).

to the provisions of the Universal Declaration of Human Rights in Article 25 of the constitution. Article 25 states that Bangladesh would have "respect for international law and the principles enunciated in the United Nations Charters and on the basis of those principles shall… c) support oppressed peoples throughout the world waging a just struggle against imperialism, colonialism or racism".[4] In a case of Tayazuddin and another vs Bangladesh, the Supreme Court of Bangladesh[5] invoked Article 3 of the United Declaration of Human Rights. The Court interpreted Article 3 of the UDHR in conjunction with the Fundamental Right to life guaranteed under the constitution. The Supreme Court explained that the right to life, liberty and security of a person "applies as much to a person as to the accused, so that the court could weigh the liberty of the accused against the sense of security of the victims" (Hosain, 2013, p. 1) The Court by upholding universality and importance of Article 3 provided it the status of customary international law.

Right to security can be understood in two broad senses. It may mean the security of the state or the individual. National security may mean the way the state protects its citizens from external threats that include human health and environmental degradation as well. In the Declaration of Human Rights, security basically means the security of individual that is protecting physical integrity of the individual human beings. The bodily integrity includes the "necessities of life, social security, and the protection of health and safety".

Taking the rights-based approach, the chapter has analysed the security concern not only of Rohingyas in camps set up around Cox's Bazar but also the perceived security concerns of Bangladesh citizens. The chapter argues that there is differential perception of risks between the Rohingyas and citizens of Bangladesh leading to growing tension between them.

Security Concerns Among Rohingyas

As of February 2018, the United Nations estimates that almost 1 million Rohingya refugees have fled Burma's violent campaign of ethnic cleansing. Almost universally, they have moved into refugee settlements in Cox's Bazar, Bangladesh. That is straining Bangladesh, which has absorbed a remarkable number of people in just six months, leading to a desperately cramped conditions in the camps. Bangladesh is small, low-lying, under-resourced and overcrowded. The extreme lack of space in the camps cuts through the entire response: health risks from poor hygiene and

[3] South West Africa Case (1966) ICJ; Dissenting opinion of Judge Tanaka. To read the whole opinion, see http://www.icj-cij.org/docket/files/47/4969.pdf, cited in Hosain, Mustafa (2013) Application of UDHR by Supreme Court of Bangladesh: Analysis of Judgements. https://www.clcbd.org/journal/13.html#_ednref10. Accessed 28 July 2019.

[4] The Constitution of the People's Republic of Bangladesh. http://bdlaws.minlaw.gov.bd/pdf_part.php?id=367.

[5] Criminal appeal, 21 BLD (HCD) 2001; ILDC 479 (BD2001) cited in Hosain (2013).

sanitation soar if latrine standards are inadequate. There is not enough room for classrooms, nor for storm shelters or comprehensive evacuation plans for the upcoming cyclone and monsoon season.[6] "Congestion is the recipe for all disaster", said Rezaul Chowdhury, who leads COAST, a local NGO based in Cox's Bazar. The majority of the refugees now live in massive Kutupalong camp, carved out of undulating, flood-prone land. The amount of useable space available per person—less than 10 m^2 in some areas—falls far below minimum international standards for refugee camps.[7]

This severe congestion also adds to the risks faced by women and girls, whose health and protection needs are already "critically underserved" in the camps, according to the Inter-agency Working Group on Reproductive Health in Crises, a coalition of aid organizations.[8] The fact that it is such a crowded camp, women and girls are most affected.[9] They do not have a space and, being from a culture where, not all, but some portion of males, husbands and community leaders, are pressuring them to stay in their homes—we are talking about homes that are actually glorified.

The camps have poor sanitation and are a breeding ground for diseases like diphtheria, measles and cholera, to which newborn babies are particularly vulnerable. This is no place for a child to be born.[10] "The disadvantage these newborn Rohingya babies will face, by virtue of the situation they are born into, is truly heartbreaking. From the very beginning they will battle odds stacked against them, living in an overcrowded environment where everyone is desperate for help".[11]

Currently, Rohingyas are under significant health risks and it has become a challenge to address their health needs. Due to the increasing number of Rohingya refugees and their congested living conditions in camps, there has been an overwhelming increase in their health risks. Refugees and affected community require 9

[6]Human Rights Watch (2018, p. 2).

[7]The Guardian (2017).

[8]Cox's Bazar Zila is comprised of eight upazilas, namely Kutubdia, Pekua, Chakaria, Moheskhali, Cox's.

[9]Bazar Sadar, Ramu, Ukhia and Teknaf have a total local population of around 2.3 million, according to the most recent Population and Housing Census of 2011 http://203.112.218.65:8008/WebTestApplication/userfiles/Image/District%20Statistics/Cox%60s%20Bazar.pdf. Accessed 28 May 2019.

[10]UNDP Human Development Reports (2018).

[11]Inter Sector Coordination Group. ISCG Support to Bangladesh Host Communities in the Rohingya Refugee Response. p. 2, https://reliefweb.int/sites/reliefweb.int/files/resources/2018.03.21_iscg_update_-_support_to_bangladesh_host_communities_in_the_rohingya_refugee_response_0.pdf. Accessed 28 May 2019.

million litres of safe water daily, and water, sanitation and hygiene (WASH) services are reaching only 30% of the Rohingya people in need. Thus, it has left them with no options other than to fetch dirty water from muddy streams.[12] 85% of the refugees still have no access to latrines.[13] All of which in turn increases the risk of communicable disease outbreak.[14] There have been reports of measles outbreak among new arrivals, and the number of cases reported is 419.[15] The largest oral cholera vaccination was held in the refugee camps, and even though it was able to reach 100% of the targeted population, the risks of waterborne and other infectious diseases are still exceptionally high due to their unhygienic living conditions.[16] Diphtheria outbreak has resulted in 38 deaths, and more than 5800 suspected cases of diphtheria have been reported as of February 2018.[17] There have also been reports on respiratory problems and skin diseases among the refugees who have arrived since 25th August with 10,846 and 3422 cases, respectively.[18]

Among the refugees, 720,000 are children.[19] A total of 14,740 orphan Rohingya children have been identified since 20 September 2017 in the settlements in Ukhia and Teknaf.[20] An estimated 250,000 children under the age of 8 require life-saving interventions through community-based activities such as vaccination campaigns, whereas 240,000 children under five years need malnutrition prevention and treatment support through nutritious supplementary food. A total of 16,965 children with severe acute malnutrition (SAM) require inpatient and outpatient treatment. A total of 204,000 adolescent girls need nutritional support and 237,500 children from 6 months to 15 years need to receive measles-rubella (MR) vaccine.[21]

More than 48,000 Rohingya infants are expected to be born in Bangladesh this year and would be exposed to different diseases and malnutrition since birth that might cause untimely death by five, warns Save the Children.[22] According to the Needs and Population Monitoring Report by Save the Children, approximately 4.9% or 42,516 women of the total Rohingya population in Bangladesh (867,673) are pregnant.[23] More than half of the refugees are women and girls. Over half (60%)

---

[12]UNOCHA (2018).

[13]Kiragu et al. (2011).

[14]UNOCHA (2018).

[15]UN General Assembly Resolution 428 (V) of 14 December 1950. Statute of the Office of the United Nations High Commissioner for Refugees. http://www.unhcr.org/4d944e589.pdf. Accessed 28 May 2019.

[16]Currently, only Cambodia, the Philippines and Timor-Leste are signatories to the 1951 Convention related to the Status of Refugees or its 1967 Protocol.

[17]Knowledge, Evidence and Learning for Development (2017, p. 4).

[18]Xchange Foundation. (2018b).

[19]UNOCHA (2018).

[20]Cheung (2011, p. 51).

[21]Siddiqui (2018).

[22]UNHCR The UN Refugee Agency (2018c), International Crisis Group (2017).

[23]ISCG, Humanitarian Response Plan 2017: September 2017–February 2018: Rohingya Refugee Crisis, p. 9, 2017, https://www.humanitarianresponse.info/en/operations/bangladesh. Accessed 28 May 2019.

are children under 18, and around 3% are aged over 60 (Source: UNHCR household survey) There are 120,000 pregnant women and new mothers. Around 36,000 are unaccompanied children.

It is estimated that 15% of them will suffer miscarriage, meaning there will be an estimated 4015 live births per month or 48,184 live births in 2018, Save the Children says.[24] Children make up approximately 58% of the 655,000 Rohingyas, who fled violence in Rakhine of Myanmar to Bangladesh since late August 2017.[25]

"We're expecting about 130 live births per day in 2018. Most babies will likely be born at home in basic tents, in part because of the shortage of quality, 24-h health facilities able to handle and manage basic emergency obstetrics, as well as challenges accessing healthcare", said Rachael Cummings, the aid group's health advisor in Cox's Bazar.[26]

The birth rate among the Rohingya is also much higher than that of Bangladeshis; in 2018 alone, experts expect refugees to give birth to 48,000 babies—who will face severe risks of malnutrition, disease and death.[27] After diphtheria broke out in December, authorities launched a massive vaccination campaign. Although immunization has long been available to Bangladeshis—including in rural areas—public health officials worry that waterborne and other communicable diseases might spread beyond the camps.[28]

Refugees are also at risk of sex, drug and labour trafficking. A local non-governmental organization (NGO) working to prevent trafficking and raise awareness among youth warns that organized crime networks are eager to exploit those displaced by the crisis.[29] An estimated 60% of the refugees are children, many separated from their families and possibly orphaned. They are sick, hungry and traumatized. No law enforcement mechanisms are in place to prevent and address crimes within the camps themselves, including sexual violence and trafficking. Earlier this year, a number of children disappeared from Rohingya camps in Cox's Bazaar, and NGOs working in these camps fear they were abducted and trafficked.[30]

There are more than half a million school-age children and young adults in the camps and surrounding areas, but for the past 18 months, few have been able to access

[24]Inter Sector Coordination. ISCG Support to Bangladesh Host Communities in the Rohingya Refugee Response. *Group*, p. 2, https://www.humanitarianresponse.info/sites/, www.humanitarianresponse.info/files/documents/files/2018.03.21_iscg_update__support_to_bangladesh_host_communities_in_the_rohingya_refugee_response_0.pdf. Accessed 28 May 2019.

[25]UN Women and UNDP (2017, p. 2).

[26]The World Bank (2018).

[27]Burma Citizenship Law (1982).

[28]UNHCR The UN Refugee Agency (2018b).

[29]Cheung (2011, p. 50).

[30]Daily Sun (2018), Knowledge, Evidence and Learning for Development (2017, p. 8).

formal education. It is worried that Rohingya children educated in Bangladesh will integrate into local society and not return home, and Bangladesh's government has placed strict limits on formal education—Rohingya students are not permitted to study using the Bangladeshi curriculum.[31]

Instead, education services are largely limited to informal classrooms run by a range of NGOs and community groups. But aid groups have been slow to finalize an alternative curriculum, and some Rohingya parents have criticized the quality of education on offer. Aid groups say this informal schooling is available to only half of children of 14 years old and younger.[32] At the same time, only primary-level education is allowed, meaning there are few opportunities for Rohingya who are 15 and older. Fewer than 5000 adolescents have any access to schooling or life skill training, out of more than 117,000 who may need it, according to aid groups.[33]

Without formal education, without skills-building, things to do actively and preparing for their futures, a frustrating new generation is developing. Critics say that there has been a lack of long-term planning on education, including coordinated advocacy to convince the government to change its rules.[34]

Authorities want to prevent Rohingya from assimilating into the local population. Camps are educating the Rohingya in English and Burmese, but not in Bengali. New refugees are barred from Bangladeshi citizenship on the basis of either birth or marriage.[35]

Risks and Concerns in the Eyes of the Refugee Children

Children's experiences in Cox's Bazar and the specific vulnerabilities they face are distinct from adults. At the same time, children themselves are best placed to articulate their own needs and desires. Therefore, through this consultation, children from refugee communities—who identify themselves as Rohingya—and children from host communities were engaged in the children's consultation organized by the three participating agencies, Plan International, Save the Children and World Vision International.[36]

The children's consultation took place between 2 December and 5 December 2017, in various refugee camps and host community locations. Teams from all three agencies conducted sessions with children between the ages of 7 and 17 as well

---

[31]As the exact populations for 2018 were not known. Own calculations based on population data from, ISCG Situation Report Rohingya Refugee Crisis, Cox's Bazar, 7 June 2018, https://reliefweb.int/sites/reliefweb.int/files/resources/iscg_situation_report_07_june_2018.pdf. Accessed 28 May 2019.

[32]UNDP Human Development Reports (2018).

[33]The Washington Post (2018).

[34]The Daily Star (2018).

[35]Catholic Relief Services (2017, p. 7).

[36]UNHCR The UN Refugee Agency. Rohingya Emergency. https://www.unhcr.org/rohingya-emergency.html. Accessed 28 May 2019.

Security Concerns Among Local Populace

The massive influxes of refugees—and the aid groups that followed them—have raised tensions among Bangladeshis in Cox's Bazar. Some say they have seen their income plummet as they compete for increasingly scarce resources or services.

Bangladesh's GDP per capita is a meagre $1400. However, in 2016, the national economy grew by 7.1%, and the country has made remarkable progress towards the Millennium Development Goals.[43] While extensive international humanitarian relief has poured into support the refugees, that does not cover all the economic costs to the government or to the border region's Bangladeshi citizens. The influx's full effect may not be apparent for some time.[44] The coastal town and beaches of Cox's Bazar used to be Bangladesh's main tourist destination; now the area is awash with foreign aid workers. The area's hoteliers are prospering, and many Bangladeshis have found jobs with humanitarian organizations. But day labourers and poorer locals have complained about price hikes for basic goods and about losing work to refugees willing to accept far lower wages.[45]

A survey conducted by Ground Truth Solutions, which researches the views of people in crises, pointed to rising tensions among the host communities: "Their attitudes have shifted from the start of the crisis, where they felt much more supportive and welcoming of Rohingya but now are much less so, feeling that Rohingya have 'been here too long'".[46]

Aid groups and the government also warn of a "potential deterioration" of relations between Rohingya and the local communities. The upcoming response plan is expected to place a greater emphasis on building social cohesion and on development projects to improve education and access to water and food in host communities. Some of these projects were started last year, but the UN coordination body said a "severe funding gap" put a limit on this assistance.[47]

The refugees have changed the demographics of Bangladesh's Ukhia and Teknaf areas, where Rohingya now outnumber locals 2 to 1. Of the approximately 900,000 Rohingya, 73% are living in new spontaneous settlements, 13% in makeshift settlements, 9% among host communities and 5% in formal refugee camps. However, Kutupalong camp is the largest and most densely populated refugee settlement in the world.[48]

Bangladesh is highly susceptible to climate change. For years, the country has been grappling with soil erosion, rising sea levels and frequent natural disasters such as cyclones and floods. Landslides are extremely likely; many worry about what will happen to the refugee settlements when the monsoon season arrives next

---

[43] Aljazeera (2018).

[44] Xchange Foundation (2018b).

[45] Strategic Executive Group (2018, p. 4).

[46] Qayum (2017).

[47] Xchange Foundation (2018a).

[48] Human Rights Watch (2018, p. 2), BBC Media Action Translators Without Borders Internews (2018).

month. Groundwater sources are quickly being depleted, and freshwater streams have become contaminated. Air pollution in Ukhia and Teknaf has increased because of smoke from firewood burned by refugees and exhaust from thousands of trucks, jeeps and cars bringing people and goods into the camps.[49] Therefore, the dramatic environmental consequences of this massive migration will last for years, affecting people who live inland in Bangladesh and beyond.[50]

The environmental impact of 1 million refugees is difficult to overstate. The UN Development Programme (UNDP) recently released an environmental assessment, identifying 28 risk factors threatening biodiversity and human security.[51] At the peak of the violence, each week some 100,000 Rohingya—mainly women and children—were crossing into Bangladesh. Where they settled, thousands of acres of national forests were cleared.[52] Areas previously inhabited by wild elephants are now barren. The lush, green, hilly landscape has rapidly transformed into flattened stretches of red earth covered in tarp tents as far as the eye can see.[53]

The Arakan Rohingya Salvation Army (ARSA) militant group, whose attacks on Burmese security posts last year triggered the army's indiscriminate "clearance operations", has pledged to continue its insurgent campaign against what it calls "Burmese state-sponsored terrorism". The Bangladeshi security establishment is concerned both that ARSA will try to recruit within camps and that it will use the camps as a base for cross-border fighting.[54]

Planning for the Future

The upcoming appeal—north of $900 million—represents one of the largest humanitarian appeals for a crisis this year.[55] But the 2018 Rohingya appeal went underfunded through much of the year, which aid groups said had a direct impact on the quality of services available. The aid community continues to concentrate on short-term goals, without planning for a future when funding will wane. Local NGOs and aid workers have effectively been left out of planning, while international aid groups have done little to build skills among the local organizations that call Bangladesh home.

Of the 700,000 people who have arrived in Bangladesh since last August, almost 30,000 have been pregnant women. An entire generation has already been born in the world's largest refugee camp. We have hired and deployed almost 100 trained midwives to make sure both mothers and babies would not just survive but thrive. To date,

[49]Rozario (2018), Bangladesh Court Upholds Myanmar Rohingya Marriage Ban (2018).

[50]Stephan Uttom & Tock Ronald Rozario (2018).

[51]Human Rights Watch (2000).

[52]Human Rights Watch (2000, 2013).

[53]Cheung (2011, p. 52).

[54]UNHCR The UN Refugee Agency (2018a).

[55]Oxfam. https://www.oxfam.org.uk/what-we-do/emergency-response/rohingya-crisis. Accessed 28 May 2019.

almost 4000 babies have been born in UNFPA-supported clean, safe, private facilities.[56] Their midwives are frontline workers are supported by doctors, obstetricians and gynaecologists who perform emergency caesareans and advise on complicated cases. They brought in pharmacists as well, to manage the huge volume of medicines that are needed.

UNFPA has provided all pregnant women with a Clean Delivery Kit, so that if they are unable to get to a clinic or otherwise decide to give birth at home, they will have clean sheets, towels and even a sterilized blade to cut the umbilical cord. When new babies arrive, mothers are given a Mama Kit, which includes cotton baby clothes, a blanket, nappies and hygiene products for the mother. We want the arrival of a new baby to be a celebration and not a financial burden.[57]

Choice, Not Chance

UNFPA community volunteers, health workers and psychosocial experts work with men as well to overcome long-held patriarchal attitudes that prevent their wives and daughters from exercising their rights. UNFPA is a rights-based agency, and informed choice is at the centre of all that we do. They offer a full range of contraception options to women in the camps as well as in the host community, including for new mothers. Each month more and more women are choosing to take contraceptive measures, and more and more men are supporting them in their choice.[58]

UNFPA has taken on leadership roles in sexual and reproductive health and gender-based violence within the UN. Their determined response was only possible because donor governments and other supporters put trust in us. They recognize that reproductive health and gender-based violence programmes are sensitive, and the results are sometimes less immediate or tangible than other programmes that their funders could have chosen to support, especially in the initial phase.

[56] World Vision (2019).

[57] World Vision (2019); UNICEF Rohingya Crises. https://www.unicef.org/emergencies/bangladesh_100945.html. Accessed 28 May 2019.

[58] UNICEF (2019).

Conclusion

The World Health Organization has reported outbreaks of measles, diphtheria, diarrhoea and respiratory infections among children under age five. Malnutrition is another area that young refugees seem very prone too. Malnutrition among refugee children is at dangerous levels with fewer than 10% of children between 6 and 23 months old eating four of the seven food groups and three or more meals per day. A Bangladesh government and UN study reported that 37% of children aged 6–59 months suffer from chronic malnutrition or stunting. "Stunting means that children are under height for the age and may never catch up", says Colleen Emary, a World Vision health and nutrition advisor. "Those who are acutely severely malnourished are also nearly 12% more likely to die than a healthy child if they catch an infection or disease".

Girls are vulnerable to violence, especially as refugees from Myanmar have no legal status in Bangladesh. Many suffer from neglect, abuse, exploitation or sexual violence and resort to negative methods of coping, including child labour and child marriage. Refugees are not allowed to enrol in local education facilities. Child labourers, children with disabilities, girls and children in women-headed households also face barriers to attending educational programmes for refugees. About 98% of refugee children and adolescents aged 15–24 years are not accessing education.

Ultimately, this is a protracted crisis—it will require a consistent, long-term response in partnership with other agencies, the Government of Bangladesh and donors. The Rohingya refugee crisis is of such a magnitude, the suffering so immense and intense, that it requires our shared humanity to ensure we can reach out to fellow human beings and alleviate at least some of this suffering in the spirit of the 2030 Sustainable Development Agenda whose overarching pledge is to leave no one behind.

References

Alam, M. (2018, February 12). How the Rohingya crisis is affecting Bangladesh and why it matters. *The Washington Post*. https://www.washingtonpost.com/news/monkey-cage/wp/2018/02/12/how-the-rohingya-crisis-is-affecting-bangladesh-and-why-it-matters/?utm_term=.eb0bacf35e21. Accessed May 28, 2019.

Aljazeera. (2018, April 15). *Myanmar's First Rohingya Repatriation 'Staged', Rights Groups Say*. https://www.aljazeera.com/news/2018/04/myanmar-rohingya-repatriation-staged-rights-groups-180415085630813.html. Accessed May 28, 2019.

Alsaafin, L. (2018, August 10). *Price hikes and jobs: How NGOs affect the economy in Cox's Bazar*. Aljazeera. https://www.aljazeera.com/indepth/features/price-hikes-jobs-ngos-impact-economy-cox-bazar-180810090248437.html. Accessed May 28, 2019.

BBC Media Action Translators Without Borders Internews. (2018). *What Matters? Humanitarian feedback bulletin on Rohingya response issue 07*. https://www.humanitarianresponse.info/en/operations/bangladesh/document/what-matters-%E2%80%93humanitarian-feedback-bulletin-issue-07. Accessed July 11, 2018.

Bangladesh Court Upholds Myanmar Rohingya Marriage Ban (2018, January 8). *BBC News*. https://www.bbc.com/news/world-asia-42612296. Accessed May 28, 2019.

Catholic Relief Services. (2017). *Little by little: Exploring the impact of social acceptance on refugee integration into host communities*. https://www.crs.org/our-work-overseas/research-publications/little-little-exploring-impact-social-acceptance-refugee. Accessed May 28, 2019.

Cheung, S. (2011). Migration control and the solutions impasse in South and Southeast Asia: Implications from the Rohingya experience. *Journal of Refugee Studies, 25*(1), 50–70.

Daily Sun. (2018, May 27). *Rohingya children get birth certificates, not citizenship*. https://www.dailysun.com/printversion/details/311635/2018/05/27/%E2%80%98Rohingya-children-get-birth-certificates-not-citizenship%E2%80%99. Accessed May 28, 2019.

Huang, C. (2018). *A Bangladesh compact: Beyond aid solutions for Rohingya refugees and host communities*. Centre for Global Development CGD Brief. https://www.cgdev.org/sites/default/files/bangladesh-compact-beyond-aid-solutions-rohingya-refugees-and-host-communities.pdf. Accessed May 28, 2019.

Human Rights Watch. (2000). *Burma*. http://www.burmalibrary.org/docs/Abrar-repatriation.html.

Human Rights Watch. (2013). *All you can do is pray: Crimes against humanity and ethnic cleansing of Rohingya Muslims in Burma's Arakan State*. https://www.hrw.org/report/2013/04/22/all-you-can-do-pray/crimes-against-humanity-and-ethnic-cleansing-rohingya-muslims. Accessed May 28, 2019.

Human Rights Watch. (2018). *Bangladesh is Not My Country: The plight of Rohingya refugees from Myanmar*. https://www.hrw.org/report/2018/08/05/bangladesh-not-my-country/plight-rohingya-refugees-myanmar. Accessed 28 May 2019.

International Crisis Group. (2017). *Myanmar's Rohingya crisis enters a dangerous new phase*.https://www.crisisgroup.org/asia/south-east-asia/myanmar/292-myanmars-rohingya-crisis-enters-dangerous-new-phase. Accessed May 28, 2019.

Inter Sector Coordination Group. (2018). *ISCG situation report: Rohingya refugee crisis-Cox's Bazar (covering 17th–30th July)*. https://reliefweb.int/report/bangladesh/iscg-situation-report-rohingya-crisis-coxs-bazar-02-august-2018-covering-17th-30th. Accessed August 2, 2018.

Inter Sector Coordination Group. *ISCG support to Bangladesh host communities in the Rohingya refugee response*. https://www.humanitarianresponse.info/sites/, www.humanitarianresponse.info/files/documents/files/2018.03.21_iscg_update__support_to_bangladesh_host_communities_in_the_rohingya_refugee_response_0.pdf. Accessed May 28, 2019.

Kiragu, E., Rosi, A. L., & Morris, T. (2011). *States of Denial–A review of UNHCR's response to the protracted situation of stateless Rohingya refugees in Bangladesh*. UNCHR, Policy Development and Evaluation Service. https://www.unhcr.org/4ee754c19.pdf. Accessed on May 28, 2019.

Knowledge, Evidence and Learning for Development. (2017). *Bangladesh Rohingya Crisis—Managing risks in securitisation of refugees*. https://reliefweb.int/sites/reliefweb.int/files/resources/224-Managing-risks-in-securitisation-of-refugees.pdf. Accessed October 20, 2017.

Loy, I. (2019). Briefing: How the Rohingya Crisis in Bangladesh is changing. *The New Humanitarian*. https://www.irinnews.org/analysis/2019/02/13/briefing-how-rohingya-crisis-bangladesh-changing. Accessed May 28, 2019.

Oxfam. https://www.oxfam.org.uk/what-we-do/emergency-response/rohingya-crisis.Accessed May 28, 2019.

Qayum, N. (2017, October 12). There's a massive Humanitarian Crisis in Bangladesh's Rohingya Refugee Camps. *The Washington Post*. https://www.washingtonpost.com/news/monkey-cage/wp/2017/10/12/theres-a-massive-humanitarian-crisis-in-bangladeshs-rohingya-refugee-camps/?utm_term=.935799ebf8d7. Accessed May 28, 2019.

Rozario, Rock Ronald. (2018, March 9). *Rohingya repatriation plan not sustainable: Plan to send refugees back to Myanmar lacks foresight as they are still unwelcome in Rakhine State*. UCANEWS. https://www.ucanews.com/news/rohingya-repatriation-plan-notsustainable/81611. Accessed May 28, 2019.

Sarkar, U. (2018, April 13). With no formal schools or jobs, Young Rohingya Left in Lurch. *Aljazeera*. https://www.aljazeera.com/indepth/features/formal-schools-jobs-young-rohingya-left-lurch-180413124136851.html. Accessed May 28, 2019.

Siddiqui, Z. (2018). *Bangladesh says start of Rohingya return to Myanmar delayed Thompson reuters*. https://www.reuters.com/article/us-myanmar-rohingya-repatriation/bangladesh-says-start-of-rohingya-return-to-myanmar-delayed-idUSKBN1FB0KG. Accessed January 22, 2018.

Socialist Republic of the Union of Burma. (1982). *Burma citizenship law*. http://www.refworld.org/docid/3ae6b4f71b.html. Accessed August 24, 2018.

Strategic Executive Group. (2018). *JRP for Rohingya Humanitarian Crisis March–December 2018*.https://reliefweb.int/report/bangladesh/jrp-rohingya-humanitarian-crisis-march-december-2018-0. Accessed May 28, 2019.

The Daily Star. (2018, January 7). *Rohingya camps: 48,000 babies to be born this year*. https://www.thedailystar.net/backpage/48000-rohingya-babies-be-born-year-1516156. Accessed May 28, 2019.

The Guardian. (2017 February 2). *Plan to move Rohingya to remote Island prompts fears of human catastrophe*. https://www.theguardian.com/global-development/2017/feb/02/bangladesh-government-plan-move-rohingya-remote-island-human-catastroph. Accessed May 28, 2019.

The World Bank. (2018). *The World Bank in Bangladesh*. http://www.worldbank.org/en/country/bangladesh/overview. Accessed May 28, 2019.

UN General Assembly Resolution 428 (V) of 14 December 1950. *Statute of the Office of the United Nations High Commissioner for Refugees*. http://www.unhcr.org/4d944e589.pdf. Accessed May 28, 2019.

UN Women and UNDP. (2017). *Rohingya Refugee crisis into Bangladesh: Rapid early recovery assessment of host community impacts, key findings and recommendations*.

UNDP Human Development Reports. (2018). *Bangladesh*. http://hdr.undp.org/en/countries/profiles/BGD. Accessed August 23, 2018.

UNFPA Bangladesh. (2018a). *One Year On-UNFPA's response to the Rohingya crisis in Bangladesh*. https://bangladesh.unfpa.org/en/news/one-year-unfpas-response-rohingya-crisis-bangladesh. Accessed May 28, 2019.

UNFPA Bangladesh. (2018b). *The Rohingya Crisis: Looking back, looking ahead*. 25 August 2018. https://bangladesh.unfpa.org/en/news/rohingya-crisis-looking-back-looking-ahead. Accessed May 28, 2019.

UNHCR The UN Refugee Agency. (2018a). *Bangladesh and UNHCR agree on voluntary returns framework for when refugees decide conditions are right*. http://www.unhcr.org/news/press/2018/4/5ad061d54/bangladesh-unhcr-agree-voluntary-returns-framework-refugees-decide-conditions.html. Accessed April 13, 2018.

UNHCR The UN Refugee Agency. (2018b). *Bangladesh refugee emergency-population info-graphic*. https://reliefweb.int/sites/reliefweb.int/files/resources/62881.pdf. Accessed May 28, 2019.

UNHCR The UN Refugee Agency. (2018c). *Refugee response in Bangladesh*. https://data2.unhcr.org/en/situations/myanmar_refugees. Accessed August 23, 2018.

UNHCR The UN Refugee Agency. *Rohingya emergency*. https://www.unhcr.org/rohingya-emergency.html. Accessed May 28, 2019.

UNICEF. *Rohingya Crises*. https://www.unicef.org/emergencies/bangladesh_100945.html. Accessed May 28, 2019.

UNICEF. (2019). *Rohingya refugee children face an unsafe future*. Patrick Brown and Olga Chambers. https://www.unicef.org/stories/rohingya-refugee-children-face-uncertain-future. Accessed May 28, 2019.

UNOCHA. (2018). *Rohingya refugee crisis*. https://www.unocha.org/rohingya-refugee-crisis. Accessed August 20, 2018.

Uttom, Stephan and Tock Ronald Rozario. (2018, January 11). Ban upheld for marriage between Bangladeshis and Rohingya. *UCANEWS*. https://www.ucanews.com/news/ban-upheld-for-marriage-between-bangladeshis-and-rohingya/81221. Accessed May 28, 2019.

World Vision. (2019). *Myanmar refugees in Bangladesh: Facts, FAQs, and how to help*. https://www.worldvision.org/refugees-news-stories/myanmar-refugee-crisis-facts. Accessed May 28, 2019.

Xchange Foundation. (2018a). *The Rohingya amongst us: Bangladeshi perspectives on the Rohingya crisis survey*. http://xchange.org/bangladeshi-perspectives-on-the-rohingya-crisis-survey/. Accessed May 28, 2019.

Xchange Foundation. (2018b). *Snapshot survey: An insight into the daily lives of the Rohingya in Unchiprang & Shamlapur*. http://xchange.org/snapshot-survey/. Accessed May 28, 2019.

Chapter 9
Women, Conflict and Conflict Reporting: The Deeply Gendered Discourse on the Rohingya Crisis in the News Websites in India

Ritambhara Malaviya

Abstract History shows how female bodies have been the site of contestation in violent conflicts across the world. There are innumerable instances of the use of rape as a systematic weapon for proving the superiority of one's own race during conflicts, for instance, during the Bosnian crisis, or even earlier during the 1971 war of independence of Bangladesh. While conflicts impact women and children especially because of their vulnerability, the very understanding of why and how the conflict happened is deeply gendered. The Rohingya crisis is a case in point. This chapter attempts to understand the gendered discourse underpinning the discussion on the Rohingya crisis in India through a study of some major news websites in India. As per the framework used by Galtung (The Missing Journalism on Conflict and Peace and the Middle East, 2005), news reporting in India on the Rohingya is split into two camps, the war/victory-oriented journalism and the alternative peace-oriented approach. This chapter notes that while war journalism draws upon concepts which are masculinist, the softer peace journalism resembles the approach of feminists towards conflicts and cooperation. Feminism has analysed how the categories like state, sovereignty, security and militarization are deeply gendered. The patterns of reporting, however, are seen to follow the mainstream masculinist framework. These masculinist lenses are seldom questioned, and how power operates through these categories is rarely the subject of reporting. Therefore, through a careful study of the news portals, the chapter tries to understand how the discourse on the Rohingya encompasses within it gendered stereotypes and power equations.

Keywords Rohingya · Gender · Power · Control · State · Conflict

Introduction

In an introductory chapter titled, "Gender makes the world go round", Cynthia Enloe begins with a question about a woman fleeing a violent conflict. She asks how the woman should feel in such a situation when her identity is lumped together with her

R. Malaviya (✉)
Department of Political Science, Kamala Nehru College, University of Delhi, New Delhi, India

N. Chowdhory and B. Mohanty (eds.), *Citizenship, Nationalism and Refugeehood of Rohingyas in Southern Asia*,
https://doi.org/10.1007/978-981-15-2168-3_9

children as "women and children" by aid workers (Enloe, 2014, p.1). Enloe tries to show that it is the working of these gendered frameworks in supposedly "trivial" or "local" conditions which explains a lot about international relations and foreign policy. Questions raised by feminist scholars succeeded to unsettle the complacency in the academic circles that the world of international relations had little to do with gender as a category of analysis. This chapter intends to build on this framework of the pervasiveness of gender in the way international relations operate, by probing into the coverage given to the Rohingya crisis by the media in India. It attempts to probe how the language and narratives about the Rohingya in the mainstream discourse are deeply gendered, reflecting the operation of power dynamics that privilege the masculinist assumptions over the alternative perspective. However, in questioning these mainstream assumptions of the statist security discourse, peace journalism stands very close to the feminist understanding of wars and conflicts. The chapter underscores how the mainstream masculinist assumptions that overshadow the peace-oriented approach in reporting on such matters.

The feminist scholarship in international relations (IR) has pointed out that the very conceptual foundations through which we understand international politics, issues of war and conflicts, security and national interest are deeply gendered (Tickner, 2001). War as an activity is about the masculine warrior as the protector or exploiter of the feminine (Youngs, 2004, p. 78). Similarly, the state, the main actor in IR, has also been seen as "manly" (Hooper, 2001), exercising control over its citizens and supposed to protect them as a patriarch. Youngs states succinctly, "The history of state formation and identity is therefore one of gendered (and other forms of) oppression" (Youngs, 2004, p. 81). When Enloe (2014, p. 9) posits "Marriage is political. Marriage is international", she implies how the gendered power dynamics within states determine who can acquire their citizenship after marriage. However, the relationship between the state and the citizens is also gendered. Feminists have problematized the concept of sovereignty and how it can become a masculinist framework for determining the identity of people. How the identity of people are determined by sovereign states, and how they are powerless without that identity is analogous to the way a woman always depends on a man for her identity, and the way her identity changes with marriage. Even the mainstream concept of security of borders which neglects the security of people and more so of women has been seen as deeply problematic by feminist scholars (Tickner, 1997, p. 625). It has also been underscored that wars and conflicts lead to disproportionate harm to women, in the form of overt violence, or by affecting the families economically or by turning them into refugees. Literature on conflicts has documented how rape becomes a tool in wars and conflicts to prove the superiority of a race or community over the other, for instance during the Bangladesh war of independence or the Bosnian crisis. Thus, Tickner (1997, p. 626) comments, rape is a "systematic military strategy" and Nancy Kelly claims that rape is a "weapon of war" (Kelly, 1993, p. 633). Drawing from this body of literature, this chapter probes into how the categories like state, security and militarization figured in the newspapers around the Rohingya crisis.

Chapter Outline

This chapter attempts to understand the debate on the Rohingya crisis in India through a study of the coverage given to the issue in the major news websites. As per the report of the Indian Readership Survey, with the rise of Internet users in India, the news websites have also shown an increased usage (MRUC, 2019). This chapter studies the news websites in India to capture not only the mainstream media coverage of the debate on conflicts, but also how the alternative media responds to these news. For understanding the debate, the websites of the four most popular newspapers in India in English and Hindi are studied. Based on the report of Indian Readership Survey (MRUC, 2019), the four most popular newspapers are *Dainik Bhaskar, Dainik Jagran, Times of India* and *The Hindu*. In addition, to capture the alternative views and debate on the web space, the chapter also studies an independent news website, which is not owned by an established corporate house—the website of *The Wire*. *The Wire* has been selected as it is regarded as a prominent news portal which has the reputation of covering news and views critiquing the mainstream discourse in India (Kohli-Khandekar, November 10, 2015).

The chapter examines the reporting on the Rohingya crisis in India in the year 2018. This year turned out to be a watershed for India's refugee discourse. This was the year in which seven Rohingyas were deported to Myanmar in October 2018, despite the objections raised by the human rights activists and the United Nations (UN). After their exodus from Myanmar in what was regarded as a "textbook case of ethnic cleansing" by the UN and various human rights organizations, the Rohingya took refuge in neighbouring states like Bangladesh, Indonesia and Malaysia. While they were considered by the UN as the most persecuted of people, a parallel discourse in India was gradually constructed which demonized them as dangers to national security and safety. The chapter studies the news coverage given to the crisis in the year 2018 in order to effectively capture the construction of this narrative, and the criticisms thereof.

On Conflict Reporting

Galtung (2005) explains two different ways of understanding international affairs: the security approach and the peace approach. The security approach looks at a conflict from the perspective of there being two clear sides, an evil and a virtuous. There is a threat of violence emanating from the evil intentions of the enemy and so strong measures are prescribed to defeat and deter the other party. On the other hand, the peace approach, according to Galtung, looks at conflict as a problem to be resolved or transformed through non-violent methods based on an empathic understanding of the problem. In contrast to the security approach which focuses on the imposition of one-sided solutions, the peace approach emphasizes creative and mutually acceptable solutions. Based on these two approaches, Galtung outlines two different styles of journalism: war/victory-oriented journalism and peace journalism. War-oriented journalism looks at conflict as a zero-sum game, while endlessly debating on who started the conflict first. It therefore finds violence as the solution, thereby beginning a cycle of blame game and retribution. It creates an "us-other" binary, thereby propagating on behalf of one party while dehumanizing and stereotyping the other. It is therefore propaganda-oriented and elitist. The emphasis is on defeating the enemy and achieving victory. On the other hand, peace journalism adopts a "win-win" approach towards conflict, focusing on the context and root cause of the conflict. It discusses the traumas and tragedies associated with wars and conflicts, instead of glorifying them. For creating an empathic understanding on the issue, it tries to give a "voice to all parties" while at the same time unmasking the false propaganda on both the sides. It is therefore people-centric and highlights the sufferings of the especially vulnerable like the women, children and the disabled, finally attempting to move the conflicting parties towards transformation and reconciliation (Galtung, 2005).

The concept of peace journalism stands very close to a feminist understanding of IR, where the mainstream statist discourses are problematized. As Tickner (1988) set the tone for a feminist reformulation of IR, it is this kind of approach which she emphasized. Tickner questioned the masculinist statist discourse and looks concept of national interest and proposed solutions based on cooperation rather than zero-sum solutions for resolving the problems of an increasingly interdependent world (1988, p. 438). Peace journalism challenges the robust, masculinist statist discourse and looks at conflicts through a humane approach, very close to how feminists question the statist biases. It is in this backdrop that this chapter attempts to understand the two different perspectives on the problem of refugees by studying the issue of Rohingya refugees in India.

The problem of Rohingya exodus from Myanmar can be traced back to the year 2012 when the problem of these people attracted the attention of the international media. While thousands of Rohingya got refuge in Bangladesh, many found their way to India and took refuge in Jammu and various other parts of the country. While some of them are registered with the United Nations High Commissioner for Refugees (UNHCR), many of them are not, thereby living as what is pejoratively labelled as "illegal immigrants" in the country. The debate on the Rohingya was very much about the exercise of power, the politics of control and the questions of identity, all of which showed how debate on the Rohingya in the Indian media was deeply gendered.

After a study of the newspapers, two kinds of discourses could be identified, one based on the pattern of the masculinist or war/victory journalism and the other based on style of the peace journalism. The different issues can be presented in a tabular form:

Masculinist/war journalism	Peace journalism
Rohingya as illegal immigrants or rather as intruders and not refugees	Emphasis on questioning the cold war definition of who a refugee is
Rohingya as the "other"	Rohingya as a part of the larger shared humanity
Stereotypes of the Rohingya and their dehumanization with accusations that they are "jihadis", terrorists, criminals, therefore, threats to national security and pests sucking off nation's vital resources	Rohingya as the "most persecuted" among the people escaping conflicts. Focus on their problems and plight
Focus on repatriating the Rohingya to Myanmar in the interest of nation	Rohingya as people needing aid and assistance: adhering to the humane principle of non-refoulement
Seeing the Rohingya as troublemakers and the solution in keeping them away from entering the borders by strengthening the border forces	Finding the root cause of conflict which led to the exodus of these people from Myanmar and finding solution in the cessation of violence and peace building

Projected Analysis

Intruders versus Refugees

The debate on the status of the Rohingya and their identity was perhaps the key to understanding the way power operates in international politics, thereby disempowering the most vulnerable and marginalized. The Rohingya are people who have not only been persecuted but have also been denied the very basis of existence—an identity by their home state. The process of their dehumanization begins where they become stateless people, claimed by none and thus deprived of the basic human need. Thereby, they are further weakened in their access to rights which other refugees enjoy. Discussing the international refugee law and the way numerous voices were excluded from the regime, Hathaway notes how the protection to refugees was prioritized over that of stateless persons, thus weakening the refugee regime (Hathaway, 2016, p. 349). Hathaway contends that in practice, the international refugee law is weak when it comes to protecting the forcibly displaced people. Rather, it enables the states to refuse protection to involuntary migrants as it "rejects the goal of comprehensive protection for all involuntary migrants" (Hathaway, 2016, p. 334). The refugee law has been criticized as state-centric, leaving it on states to determine who was to be granted the status of refugee and who was to be excluded from protection. This placed the national interest and strategic imperatives as the main factor deciding the destiny of refugees (Hathaway, 2016, p. 369). Further, criticizing the state-centred refugee law, Aleinikoff comments, "In short the modern world operates under the motto of a state for everyone and everyone in a state" (Aleinikoff, 2016, p. 386). How the manly states determine the identity and status of people becomes further evident when the relationship between the state and the refugee is compared to that of a woman inextricably linked to the patriarch and protector of a family, and the woman finding herself completely vulnerable with no social acceptance without a man to define her identity. Commenting on the refugee law, Aleinikoff writes, "Speaking the language of sovereignty and membership, it has viewed refugees as helpless objects of pity who must be assigned to some political community in order to have an identity at all (even the word "protection" suggests a paternalistic relationship between the powerful protector and the needy protected)" (Aleinikoff, 2016, p. 402). Therefore, for the empowerment of refugees, Aleinekoff suggests a bottom-up approach to the problem, so that refugees participate in defining both the "problem" and the "solution" (Aleinikoff, 2016, p. 403).

Statelessness thus drives the Rohingya into a perpetual state of marginalization. Drawing upon Arendt's work, Chowdhory discusses how the stateless people, because of having no citizenship, have no "rights to have rights" (cited in Chowdhory, 2018, p. 1). She emphasizes that this leads to a hierarchy of status and rights between the "insiders" or citizens and "outsiders" or non-citizens. Chowdhory sheds light on the marginalization of the refugees and the stateless and points out that their need to belong remains unfulfilled and the idea of their belonging is filtered through a state-centric lens which excludes non-citizens (Chowdhory, 2018, p. 16).

Refugee women bear the double burden of being refugees and women. However, they remain marginalized in the refugee law. It has been discussed how the evolution of regime on refugees and migration was a result of the Cold War politics. The definition of refugees emphasizes "persecution" due to five factors: "race, religion, nationality, membership of a particular social group or political opinion" (UNHCR, 2010, p. 14). It hence denies protection to those who have migrated because of economic reasons. A lot of scholarship now questions this definition of refugees. Scholars have pointed out that the emphasis on persecution was supposed to discredit the Soviet Union by providing refuge to their political dissidents. The refugee was thus supposed to be a person deprived of civil and political rights and not socio-economic rights (Karatani, 2016). Further, Kelly (1993) tries to show that this overemphasis on civil and political rights also resulted in gender being ignored in the refugee discourse.

Despite the fact that a majority of the refugees are women, concerns about gender are singularly lacking in the refugee law (Kelly, 1993, p. 625). Feminists have criticized the refugee law for being insensitive to the concerns of women. First, they raise concerns as to why the criteria for the determination of refugees do not include gender (Lambert, 1995; Indra, 1987; Kelly, 1993). Chimni also comments on this construction of the idea of a refugee by the countries of the North, "…an image of a 'normal' refugee was constructed—white, male and anti-communist—which clashed sharply with the individuals fleeing the Third World" (Chimni, 2016, p. 406). The argument about the inclusion of gender as a criterion in the definition can be seen in the light of how the refugee women remain especially vulnerable, "Women forced to flee their countries as refugees face continuing gender-related abuse including sexual harassment, rape, and torture by pirates, smugglers, border guards, camp administrators, and employers" (Kelly, 1993, p. 626). Some scholars have also given the idea of acceptance of gender-based refugee claims by recognizing women as a social group in the definition of refugees (Greatbatch, 1989). However, most of the states resist any such attempts.

The pictures of the Rohingya accompanying the news reports mostly depicted women and children in distress, affirming the disproportionate impact of the conflict on women (e.g. see Mishra, October 11, 2018). Some stories, like a report from Bangladesh in *The Wire,* on the completion of one year of the Rohingya fleeing Myanmar, tried to talk from the perspective of the lives of women, "A year since fleeing, Rohingya mother sees little hope for the future" (*The Wire*, August 25, 2018). Another example is a story in the *Times of India,* from this perspective, "Rohingya women struggle to come out of dark memories" (*Times of India*, September 2, 2018). However, oblivious to this plight, the mainstream discourse harped on how the Rohingya were not refugees but "illegal migrants", infiltrators or rather intruders with wicked designs. *Dainik Bhaskar* reported that around 40 thousand Rohingya intruders were living in India and there were instructions from the government to identify them, "भारत में करीब 40 हजार रोहिंग्या घुसपैठिए रह रहे हैं। हाल में केंद्रीय गृह मंत्रालय ने राज्यों से घुसपैठियों की पहचान करने को भी कहा है" (*Dainik Bhaskar*, October 4, 2018). The statist position affirmed that the Rohingya were not refugees but illegal infiltrators and hence were being sent back (see Rajagopal, October 5, 2018). Similarly, there were scares of Rohingya "intrusion" in different states. *Jagran* reported about the "Intrusion of Rohingya Muslims along with Bangladeshis in Aligarh" ("अलीगढ़ में रोहिंग्या मुसलमानों के साथ बंग्लादेशियों ने की घुसपैठ") (Srivastav, August 2, 2018) or "Intrusion of Rohingya in Uttarakhand" ("उत्तराखंड में भी रोहिंग्या की घुसपैठ!") (*Jagran*, August 2, 2018) and "Railway alert over influx of Rohingyas into Kerala" (*Times of India*, September 29, 2018).

A parallel development in India alongside the Rohingya debate was the controversy about the National Register of Citizens (NRC). The final draft of the updated National Register of Citizens containing the names of those who were to be counted as citizens of India in Assam was published on 30 July 2018 and raised a lot of controversy in the Indian media. Those who were to be excluded were mostly the illegal economic migrants from Bangladesh and therefore did not qualify to be called refugees and were considered unworthy of the host state's protection. However, to further complicate the matters, the central government, in the midst of this raging debate over the criteria of exclusion and inclusion in citizenship of Assam, tried to get a bill passed in the Parliament which called for conferring citizenship to minorities—Hindu, Buddhist and Sikh religions—fleeing persecution from other states. This brought into debate the question of religion as a criterion of granting citizenship to immigrants in the country. The Rohingya were clubbed together with the Muslim Bangladeshis as undesirable, while refugees belonging to some other religions were considered worthy of belonging to the country. There were calls for an NRC for different states like Delhi (*Jagran*, August 1, 2018a), Telangana (*The Hindu*, August 8, 2018) and even the whole of India (*The Hindu*, September 11, 2018) to drive away the "infiltrators".

The alternative discourse refuting this concept of "othering" came through the opinion pieces written by some journalists, academicians and human rights activists. In *The Hindu*, G. Sampath wrote a satirical piece on how the mainstream discourse

and economic opportunities, but as a criminal community undeserving of any hospitality. This dehumanization of the Rohingya in reporting thus created an image where they became the enemy or the evil party not deserving any sympathy.

The Rohingya were shown in numerous news items as problems for the economy, sapping the vital economic resources of the nation, and even changing the demographic composition of states (for instance, see *Times of India*, October 5, 2018a). The debate on the NRC conflated the problem with that of illegal immigrants from Bangladesh, and the discourse revolved around the statement that illegal infiltrators were like termites eating into the nation's resources (see *Times of India*, October 4, 2018a). Most prominently, a security threat was created around the Rohingya, and for the mainstream news, Rohingya remained a serious threat to national security. The construction of this security threat emanated from statements of politicians (an example is *Times of India*, October 4, 2018a), godmen (e.g. news about Baba Ramdev in *Jagran*, August 11, 2018) and events organized for this purpose (an example is the protest by an outfit in Jammu as described in *Jagran*, August 11, 2018). The news portals reported how a bomb blast in Bodh Gaya, the sacred Buddhist site, was perpetrated by Bangladeshi terrorists who wanted to avenge Myanmar government's atrocities against the Rohingya (see *Jagran*, October 1, 2018a; *Times of India*, 7 August 2018). Protest demonstrations were staged in Jammu against the Rohingya where they were called "ticking time bombs" (*Times of India*, August 1, 2018). A picture of a protest covered in the Jagran portal vividly illustrates this where demonstrators held placards saying that the Rohingya were "Jihadis" and therefore should go to Islamic countries (*Jagran*, August 11, 2018). As against this volley of news, very few news items attempted to cover the alternative view. For instance, there was a news item on how a UN functionary in Bangladesh said that the allegations on the Rohingya did not have evidence "There is no evidence of radicalisation in Rohingya camps" and further that "we mustn't taint a community that has fled such horrific violence", says UN's senior humanitarian coordinator (Haider, September 3, 2018). Here, reporting by alternative media showed a sharp contrast to the mainstream views. Raising the refugee voice that, "Why would we be against the country that gave us asylum?", *The Wire* had a report entitled, "Media, right-wing parties linking Rohingya to militant attack without evidence, refugees allege" (Javeed, February 19, 2018). Conversations with the Rohingya in a camp in Jammu were reported in this piece wherein the Rohingya said that they had escaped Myanmar because their women were raped and their lives were not safe, and so all they were looking for in India was to live peacefully, "They are using different tactics to deport us, but I want to tell them—kill us but don't defame us. We are not terrorists" (quoted in Javeed, February 19, 2018). The discussion can be seen in the light of a research on the politics of threat perceptions emanating from refugees. Mainstream news remained oblivious to the need of looking at the problem through a humanitarian lens. Savun and Gineste (2019) aver that the international discourse on the refugees as perpetrators of violence overlooks the violence against them (Savun & Gineste, 2019, p. 88). According to the authors, refugees often become scapegoats in the politics where the leaders are under pressure to show that they have improved the security of the state.

Refugees can be conveniently targeted as they are not voters and therefore "strategically attractive targets of repression" (Savun & Gineste, 2019, p. 90). The authors cite the UNHCR, "We are deeply disturbed by language that demonizes refugees as a group. This is dangerous as it will contribute to xenophobia and fear… Refugees should not be turned into strategic scapegoats and must not become the secondary victims of strategic events" (cited in Savun & Gineste, 2019, p. 92). In a similar vein, Karatani also argues that in wake of the 9/11 attacks, the rights of the migrants and refugees were further threatened by construction of a security threat by the states (Karatani, 2016, p. 27). The mainstream understanding of security in which security of the state seems to be endangered by external factors and "others", and the solutions come from eliminating this threat through the use of force, again shows the masculinist bias lurking within it. This lack of sympathy towards the plight of the Rohingya in the masculinist approach can be contrasted to the approach of peace journalism, which presents a humane picture of the Rohingya, thereby encouraging empathy and cooperation.

The Questions About Repatriation

The debate on the repatriation of seven Rohingyas is split into two distinct positions—the statist position on how the Rohingya had to be sent back in the interest of the nation, and the human rights discourse which invoked the principle of non-refoulement, contending that the international law does not approve of sending the persecuted people back to the place where their lives are under threat. The debate around deportation resulted in news portals reporting both the positions, but as the debate continued, the deportation of the Rohingya was increasingly linked with threats to law and order and security of the state. On the one hand, some reports narrated the account of the Rohingya living in wretched conditions in various camps and yet reluctant to return for threat of their lives (see *Times of India*, October 4, 2018b; October 5, 2018b); on the other hand, there was overwhelming coverage of the demands for increased surveillance of the Rohingya, for their identification and final deportation. This coverage overshadowed other news by the sheer strength of reporting on official statements, press conferences, parliamentary debates and administrative policies (for instance, see the report in *The Hindu* (August 1, 2018) which read, "Govt. has reports of their illegal activities, Kiren Rijiju tells Lok Sabha"). There were scares that the Rohingya were acquiring identification documents like the voter card and Aadhaar card and hence were getting entitled to the privileges of citizenship (some examples can be cited: "Three Rohingya nabbed with Aadhar card, PAN card and voter card, "आधार कार्ड, पैनकार्ड और वोटर कार्ड के साथ पकड़े गए तीन रोहिंग्या" (*Jagran*, August 11, 2018) and "Four Rohingyas held for illegally procuring Aadhaar cards" (*Times of India*, August 14, 2018). There were reports on instructions for recording the biometrics of the Rohingya (see *Jagran*, October 1, 2018b) along with reports on witch-hunts for them. The reports described the attempt to control their movement by trying to confine them to designated camps. All these reporting items showed how the state power was using the methods of surveillance and control. This can be seen through a reporting in the *Times of India* entitled, "Confine illegal Rohingya to designated camps: Centre to states" (*Times of India*, June 4, 2018) which read, "The Centre has asked Jammu & Kashmir and other states to confine illegal Rohingya settlers to pre-identified locations within their respective jurisdictions, record their personal particulars, including biometric details, and not to issue them Aadhaar number or any other identity proof". Prospects of being deported also provoked fear from this politics of confinement and control in Myanmar as well. *The Hindu* had a report entitled, "Rohingya will be safe in designated areas", on how the Army Chief of Myanmar had assured that, "Rohingya refugees who return to Myanmar will be safe as long as they stay in the model villages built for them" (*The Hindu*, May 6, 2018). The intensive surveillance and control exercised over the Rohingya again compares to how the women through history have been denied an identity without men, suspected and not allowed freedom of movement, their lives being totally subject to the control of men and their rule books. The case of Rohingya being denied a home and an identity by states is a similar exercise in the politics of surveillance and control.

Fortifying the Borders

The borders have always remained a prominent locus of the debate on the movement of people across the world. This debate between the statist position and the alternative discourse reflected in the media as well. While there were news items which affirmed and valourized border policing, there were discussions which questioned this politics of surveillance and control. The mainstream narratives regularly affirmed that the Border Security Force (BSF) was making all efforts to keep the Rohingya intruders away "रोहिंग्याओं की घुसपैठ रोकने के लिए तैनात किए गए बीएसएफ, असम राइफल्स के जवान" (*Jagran*, July 31, 2018), thereby valourizing a "strong state" capable of keeping off the infiltrators and flaying the soft stand of some politicians—"BSF के डीजी बोले- ममता सरकार अपना रही नरम रुख, पश्चिम बंगाल आ रहे रोहिंग्या घुसपैठिये" (*Jagran*, September 8, 2018). This binary between the soft and strong state cannot be missed for its gendered meanings.

On the other hand, there were some opinion pieces in *The Hindu* which questioned this "walling". Mini Kapoor, in *The Hindu*, questioned this restriction on the movement of people through her piece "Are we living in an age of walls" (Kapoor, May 20, 2018) where she commented on the history of walls in international politics and the strengthening of this trend in contemporary times with initiatives like that by the US President Donald Trump to fence off the "illegal immigrants" from Mexico. In context of this politics of expulsion, there was an article from the perspective of shared global bonds and solidarities titled, "Why I am not just an Indian". It discussed that,

> …being an Indian is carrying the history of being the largest colonised people. Being an Indian is thus, ironically, also not being an Indian, but being a part of the billions of colonised peoples across the world. Being an Indian means something that is greater than just being

> Indian; it means being against colonialism, both external and internal, against oppression of all kinds, and for equality and justice. (Mannathukkaren, August 21, 2018).

It might be noted that among the websites associated with the mainstream newspapers, most of the alternative discourse found its place in *The Hindu* portal, while the other portals gave a lopsided coverage to the mainstream narrative. Besides, *The Wire* consistently attempted to present the other side of the story and facts obfuscated by the mainstream discourse. This coverage, however, was overshadowed by the large amount of narratives coming through daily press briefings and official statements in the mainstream media. The mainstream media routinely covered the gendered politics of migration after having internalized these stereotypes, sometimes without even understanding the gendered nature of coverage and its implications for policy.

The Gender Lens and Reporting on the Rohingya

The analysis of the discourse in the news portals brings out starkly not only how the power dynamics in the Rohingya crisis were deeply gendered, but also how the reporting on the power dynamics is deeply gendered. In attempting to unveil the gendered patterns in reporting on the crisis, the chapter looks at how the language of the news portals is biased in favour of a statist lexicon which emphasizes a politics of security, surveillance and control. The news reports are oblivious of many of the gender stereotypes in the statist narratives.

A number of salient points raised in the chapter can be discussed. First, news reporting lacks an understanding of the gendered politics of determining who is a refugee. Based on official briefings, the news portals indiscriminately use the terms "intruders" and "illegal immigrants" for the Rohingya. This might be done consciously, but often the journalists simply lack the training in understanding the gendered implications of such a language. It goes unnoticed in course of a heated debate in the media that absence of the voice of the Rohingya in determining their fate and identity is analogous to the silence of women in matters of their identity or decisions affecting their lives. Second, the mainstream masculinist discourse is infused with a language based on binaries between "us" and the "other", "evil" and the "virtuous" or "protector" and the "protected". The feminist approach has always questioned these binaries and "othering", which also reflects in the more humane approach of peace journalism. Third, the chapter tries to analyse how the statist power operates through the construction of security threats and how the media helps in building up this narrative. The feminists hence question the language of securitization, identification, surveillance and control. They try to unravel how the "manly states" wield power in these matters. In coverage on the Rohingya attempting to acquire identity documents, or trying to find shelter in some other states, the newspapers neglect how the refugees are dependent on the states for their protection and identity. This is comparable to women dependent on men for the same, and there are parallels again in how both witness regimes of surveillance to control their movement. Finally, a majority of news items fail to note that the politics of securitizing the state by fighting the “enemy” is a replication of the traditional notions of strong men securing their families by exercising absolute control and power. A language valourizing militarized states again reflects a politics of power and control which feminists criticize by emphasizing solutions based on cooperation and empathy.

Conclusion

This chapter looks at how the coverage on the issue of the Rohingya immigrants in India was deeply gendered. Not only are the realities of conflict deeply gendered, the coverage on the conflict reflects these gendered realities. The chapter underscores how the very categories through which we look at the problems of refugees and illegal immigrants, like citizenship, state and security, are highly gendered. The status of the Rohingya in India, as the people deprived of an identity by the manly states, unable to “belong” anywhere, powerless to claim any rights, becomes analogous to the status that women have been relegated to in the history of patriarchal societies. Through an analysis of the news, it can be seen how the dominant masculinist notions of security privilege the concept of state security over that of the security of people. The Rohingya face various types of stigmas, stereotyping and “othering”, again reflecting how the masculinist assumptions of self-interest and gendered binaries dominate the debate. The chapter also notes how the “us-other discourse” and the construction of who is evil and who is good is played out on the bodies of women. Questioning the cycle of retribution flowing out of this masculinist discourse, the chapter suggests an alternative framework for understanding conflicts, emphasizing empathic responses to conflicts and their consequences for a durable solution to the problem.

References

Aleinikoff, T. A. (2016). State-centered refugee law: From resettlement to containment. In V. Chetail (Ed.), *International law and migration* (Vol. II, pp. 386–404). Cheltenham: Edward Elgar Publishing Limited.

Basu, A. M. (2018, November 14). It’s high time MPs around the world stand up for rights of women and minorities. https://thewire.in/rights/minority-women-rights. Accessed 24 May 2019.

Chimni, B. S. (2016). The geopolitics of refugee studies: A view from the south. In V. Chetail (Ed.), *International law and migration* (Vol. II, pp. 405–429). Cheltenham: Edward Elgar Publishing Limited.

Chowdhory, N. (2018). *Refugees, citizenship and belonging in South Asia: contested terrains*. Singapore: Springer.

Dainik Bhaskar. (2018, June 1). म्यांमार से भागते वक्त हिंदू लड़कियों को बंधक बनाकर ले गए रोहिंग्या, जान बचाकर भागी एक लड़की ने सुनाई आपबीती. https://www.bhaskar.com/news/report-claims-rohingya-militants-massacred-of-hindus-5885480.html. Accessed 14 May 2019.

Dainik Bhaskar. (2018, October 4). पहली बार 7 रोहिंग्या शरणार्थी म्यांमार को सौंपे गए, 6 साल से असम में रह रहे थे. https://www.bhaskar.com/national/news/government-deport-7-rohingya-from-assam-to-myanmar-0803899.html. Accessed 14 May 2019.

Dainik Bhaskar. (2018, December 21). 'हिंदुओं का मांस खा रहे रोहिंग्या...' इस मैसेज के वायरल हो रही तस्वीर, लेकिन झूठी है खबर, ये है सच. https://www.bhaskar.com/national/news/report-claims-rohingyas-are-eating-hindus-but-its-a-fack-news-viral-5997920.html. Accessed 14 May 2019.

Datta, S. (2018, November 24). The Rohingya in South Asia: People without a state' review: No place to call home. https://www.thehindu.com/todays-chapter/tp-features/tp-bookreview/no-place-to-call-home/article25589238.ece. Accessed 11 May 2019.

Enloe, C. (2014). *Bananas, beaches and bases: Making feminist sense of international politics*. Berkeley: University of California Press.

Galtung, J. (2005). The missing journalism on conflict and peace and the Middle East. https://www.transcend.org/files/article570.html. Accessed 28 Nov 2018.

Gopalakrishnan, A. (2018, August 5). If only hindus are natural citizens, it is a blow to India's idea of citizenship, says political theorist Niraja Gopal Jayal. https://timesofindia.indiatimes.com/home/sunday-times/all-that-matters/if-only-hindus-are-natural-citizens-it-is-a-blow-to-indias-idea-of-citizenship-says-political-theorist-niraja-gopal-jayal/articleshow/65273321.cms. Accessed 6 May 2019.

Greatbatch, J. (1989). The gender difference: Feminist critiques of refugee discourse. *International Journal of Refugee Law, 1*(4), 518–527.

Haidar, S. (2018, September 3). There is no evidence of radicalisation in Rohingya camps. https://www.thehindu.com/todays-chapter/tp-national/there-is-no-evidence-of-radicalisation-in-rohingya-camps/article24851005.ece. Accessed 11 May 2019.

Hathaway, J. C. (2016). A reconsideration of the underlying premise of refugee law. In V. Chetail (Ed.), *International law and migration* (Vol. II, pp. 331–385). Cheltenham: Edward Elgar Publishing Limited.

Hooper, C. (2001). *Manly states: Masculinities, international relations and gender politics*. New York: Columbia University Press.

Indra, D. (1987). Gender: A key dimension of the refugee experience. *Canada's Journal on Refugees, 6*(3), 3–4.

Jagran. (2018, May 26). रोहिंग्या आतंकियों द्वारा हिंदुओं के नरसंहार पर अमेरिका चिंतित. https://www.jagran.com/world/america-america-express-concern-over-the-killing-of-hindus-by-the-arakan-rohingya-salvation-army-as-amnesty-international-report-18001075.html. Accessed 16 May 2019.

Jagran. (2018, July 31). रोहिंग्याओं से मिली 29 लाख की नकदी, चार हिरासत में. https://www.jagran.com/politics/national-border-security-force-and-assam-rifles-are-deployed-to-stop-further-infiltration-of-rohingyas-says-rajnath-singh-18262249.html. Accessed 16 May 2019.

Jagran. (2018a, August 1). रोहिंग्याओं की घुसपैठ रोकने के लिए तैनात किए गए बीएसएफ, असम राइफल्स के जवान. https://www.jagran.com/delhi/new-delhi-city-ncr-manoj-tiwari-reaction-on-nrc-issue-demands-action-against-illegal-migrants-in-delhi-18267058.html. Accessed 16 May 2019.

Jagran. (2018b, August 1). मालगाड़ी से पेट्रोल-डीजल चुराने के आरोप में दो रोहिंग्या काबू. https://www.jagran.com/jammu-and-kashmir/jammu-robbery-rohingyas-18269896.html. Accessed 16 May 2019.

Jagran. (2018, August 2). रोहिंग्या बने देश के लिए सिरदर्द, बाबा रामदेव ने भी जताई चिंता, जानें क्या कहा. https://www.jagran.com/uttarakhand/dehradun-city-rohingya-intrusion-in-uttrakhand-18267782.html. Accessed 16 May 2019.

Jagran. (2018, August 9). चोरी की स्कूटी समेत रों¨हग्या युवक काबू. https://www.jagran.com/jammu-and-kashmir/jammu-rohingyas-get-cash-of-rs-29-lakh-four-in-custody-18296962.html. Accessed 16 May 2019.

Jagran. (2018, August 11). के डीजी बोले- ममता सरकार अपना रही नरम रुख, पश्चिम बंगाल आ रहे रोहिंग्या घुसपैठिये. https://www.jagran.com/politics/national-rohingya-made-headache-for-the-country-baba-ramdev-also-expressed-worry-what-did-he-say-18305572.html. Accessed 16 May 2019.

Jagran. (2018, September 7). रोहिंग्या से एकजुटता दिखाने के लिए हुआ था बोधगया विस्फोट: एनआइए. https://www.jagran.com/jammu-and-kashmir/jammu-rohingya-arrest-with-stolen-scooty-jammu-18398425.html. Accessed 16 May 2019.

Jagran. (2018, September 8). रोहिंग्या की पहचान के लिए राज्य सरकारें बायोमेट्रिक्स आंकड़े जुटाएं: राजनाथ सिंह. https://www.jagran.com/news/national-director-general-of-bsf-says-rohingya-intruders-are-going-to-west-bengal-18400868.html. Accessed 16 May 2019.

Jagran. (2018a, October 1). दिल्ली में भी उठी NRC की मांग, मनोज तिवारी ने कहा- घुसपैठियों को बाहर करे सरकार. https://www.jagran.com/news/national-nia-says-explosive-set-off-in-bodh-gaya-to-show-solidarity-with-rohingya-18486373.html. Accessed 16 May 2019.

Jagran. (2018b, October 1). उत्तराखंड में भी रोहिंग्या की घुसपैठ! https://www.jagran.com/west-bengal/kolkata-rajnath-singh-says-states-asked-to-identify-rohingya-refugees-and-collect-biometric-details-18485407.html. Accessed 16 May 2019.

Jagran. (2018, October 9). रहें सावधान, कहीं अंजान किराएदार रोहिंग्या मुसलमान तो नहीं. https://www.jagran.com/uttar-pradesh/agra-city-be-alart-for-giving-home-or-land-on-rent-18516235.html. Accessed 16 May 2019.

Javeed, A. (2018, February 19). *Media, right-wing parties linking Rohingya to militant attack without evidence, refugees allege*. https://thewire.in/politics/rohingya-refugees-militant-attack-jammu. Accessed 24 May 2019.

Kapoor, M. (2018, May 20). Along the borders. https://www.thehindu.com/opinion/columns/along-the-borders/article23938136.ece. Accessed 11 May 2019.

Karatani, R. (2016). How history separated refugee and migrant regimes: In search of their institutional origins. In V. Chetail (Ed.), *International law and migration* (Vol. II, pp. 3–27). Cheltenham: Edward Elgar Publishing Limited.

Kelly, N. (1993). Gender-related persecution: Assessing the asylum claims of women. *Cornell International Law Journal, 26*(3), 625–674.

Kohli-Khandekar, V. (2015, November 10). The online news experiment. https://www.business-standard.com/article/opinion/vanita-kohli-khandekar-the-online-news-experiment-115111001461_1.html. Accessed 25 May 2019.

Lambert, H. (1995, September 1). Seeking asylum on gender grounds. *International Journal of Discrimination and the Law*.

Mannathukkaren, N. (2018, August 21). Why I am not just an Indian. https://thewire.in/politics/indian-passport-narendra-modi-nationalism-bjp. Accessed 24 May 2019.

Mishra, S. (2018, October 11). सहमी मानवता की सिसकन का गवाह है बांग्लादेश का रोहिंग्या शरणार्थी कैंप. https://www.jagran.com/world/other-rohingyas-refugee-camps-of-bangladesh-ground-report-by-sanjay-mishra-from-cox-bazar-jagran-exclusive-18520366.html. Accessed 16 May 2019.

MRUC. (2019). Indian Readership Survey Q1, 2019, April 26, 2019. http://mruc.net/uploads/posts/8e428e54a95edcd6e8be593a7021a185.pdf. Accessed 22 May 2019.

Patel, A. (2018, June 14). The crimes of a few condemn the fate of many. https://www.thehindu.com/opinion/op-ed/the-crimes-of-a-few-condemn-the-fate-of-many/article24156601.ece. Accessed 11 May 11 2019.

Rajagopal, K. (2018, October 5) Deportation as per law, centre tells SC. https://www.thehindu.com/todays-chapter/tp-national/deportation-as-per-law-centre-tells-sc/article25127958.ece. Accessed 11 May 2019.

Sampath, G. (2018, August 5). Extend NRC to all of India. https://www.thehindu.com/opinion/columns/extend-nrc-to-all-of-india/article24604294.ece. Accessed 11 May 2019.

Savun, B., & Gineste, C. (2019). From protection to persecution: Threat environment and refugee scapegoating. *Journal of Peace Research, 56*(1), 88–102.

Singh, R. K. (2018, August 1). वोट बैंक की सियासत, दिल्ली में राजनीतिक पार्टियां दे रही हैं बांग्लादेशियों व रोहिंग्या मुस्लिमों को संरक्षण. https://www.jagran.com/politics/national-ncr-political-parties-are-giving-protection-to-the-bangladeshi-and-rohingya-muslims-18263513.html. Accessed 16 May 2019.

Srivastav, A. (2018, August 2). अलीगढ़ में रोहिंग्या मुसलमानों के साथ बंग्लादेशियों ने की घुसपैठ. https://www.jagran.com/uttar-pradesh/aligarh-city-bangladeshi-infiltrations-with-rising-rohingyas-in-aligarh-18270500.html. Accessed 16 May 2019.

The Hindu. (2018, May 6). Rohingya will be safe in designated areas. https://www.thehindu.com/todays-chapter/tp-international/rohingya-will-be-safe-in-designated-areas/article23789734.ece. Accessed 11 May 2019.

The Hindu. (2018, August 1). Centre tells states to count Rohingya migrants. https://www.thehindu.com/news/national/centre-tells-states-to-count-rohingya-migrants/article24566817.ece. Accessed 11 May 2019.

The Hindu. (2018, August 8). BJP demands NCR for Hyderabad. https://www.thehindu.com/news/cities/Hyderabad/bjp-demands-ncr-for-hyderabad/article24627252.ece. Accessed 11 May 2019.

The Hindu. (2018, September 11). Extend NRC to all states and seal border: Sonowal. https://www.thehindu.com/news/national/other-states/extend-nrc-to-all-states-and-seal-border-sonowal/article24920117.ece. Accessed 11 May 2019.

The Wire. (2018, August 25). A year since fleeing, Rohingya mother sees little hope for the future. https://thewire.in/south-asia/a-year-since-fleeing-rohingya-mother-sees-little-hope-for-the-future. Accessed 24 May 2019.

Tickner, J. A. (1988). Hans Morgenthau's principles of political realism: A feminist reformulation. *Millennium Journal of International Studies, 17*(3), 429–440.

Tickner, J. A. (1997). You just don't understand: Troubled engagements between feminists and ir theorists. *International Studies Quarterly, 41*(4), 611–632.

Tickner, J. A. (2001). *Gendering world politics: Issues and approaches in the post-cold war era*. New York: Columbia University Press.

Times of India. (2018, May 23). New evidence reveals muslim-majority Rohingya massacred 105 Hindus: Amnesty. https://timesofindia.indiatimes.com/world/south-asia/new-evidence-reveals-muslim-majority-rohingya-massacred-105-hindus-amnesty/articleshowprint/64293239.cms. Accessed 6 May 2019.

Times of India. (2018, May 24). Rohingya terrorists robbed & killed innocent villagers. https://timesofindia.indiatimes.com/world/south-asia/rohingya-terrorists-robbed-killed-innocent-villagers/articleshowprint/64296308.cms. Accessed 6 May 2019.

Times of India. (2018, June 4). Confine illegal rohingya to designated camps: centre to states. https://timesofindia.indiatimes.com/india/confine-illegal-rohingya-to-designated-camps-centre-to-states/articleshowprint/64441862.cms. Accessed 6 May 2019.

Times of India. (2018, August 1). Illegal immigrants 'ticking time bombs' in the country, just deport them: JKNPP. https://timesofindia.indiatimes.com/india/illegal-immigrants-ticking-time-bombs-in-the-country-just-deport-them-jknpp/articleshowprint/65230974.cms. Accessed 6 May 2019.

Times of India. (2018, August 7). NIA arrests 3 Bangladeshi terrorists. https://timesofindia.indiatimes.com/india/nia-arrests-3-bangladeshi-terrorists/articleshowprint/65303467.cms. Accessed 6 May 2019.

Times of India. (2018, August 14). Four Rohingyas held for illegally procuring Aadhaar cards. https://timesofindia.indiatimes.com/india/four-rohingyas-held-for-illegally-procuring-aadhaar-cards/articleshowprint/65400535.cms. Accessed 6 May 2019.

Times of India. (2018, September 2). Rohingya women struggle to come out of dark memories. https://timesofindia.indiatimes.com/india/rohingya-women-struggle-to-come-out-of-dark-memories/articleshowprint/65646463.cms. Accessed 6 May 2019.

Times of India. (2018, September 9). Madhya Pradesh: Rohingya hoax goes viral, cops issue advisory. https://timesofindia.indiatimes.com/city/bhopal/rohingya-hoax-goes-viral-cops-issue-advisory/articleshowprint/65737822.cms. Accessed 6 May 2019.

Times of India. (2018, September 29). Railway alert over influx of rohingyas into Kerala. https://timesofindia.indiatimes.com/city/chennai/railway-alert-over-influx-of-rohingyas-into-kerala/articleshowprint/66002636.cms. Accessed 6 May 2019.

Times of India. (2018a, October 4). 1st batch of 7 rohingya to be deported to Myanmar today. https://timesofindia.indiatimes.com/india/1st-batch-of-7-rohingya-to-be-deported-to-myanmar-today/articleshowprint/66060770.cms. Accessed 6 May 2019.

Times of India. (2018b, October 4). Deportation threat rocks new World Rohingyas built in India. https://timesofindia.indiatimes.com/city/delhi/deportation-threat-rocks-new-world-rohingyas-built-in-india/articleshowprint/66060523.cms. Accessed 6 May 2019.

Times of India. (2018a, October 5). BJP: Deportation to have far-reaching impact in Jammu. https://timesofindia.indiatimes.com/city/jammu/bjp-deportation-to-have-far-reaching-impact-in-jammu/articleshowprint/66083813.cms. Accessed 6 May 2019.

Times of India. (2018b, October 5). Life isn't easy in Mewat camps but few rohingya want to return home. https://timesofindia.indiatimes.com/city/gurgaon/life-isnt-easy-in-mewat-camps-but-few-rohingya-want-to-return-home/articleshowprint/66078119.cms. Accessed 6 May 2019.

UNHCR. (2010). Convention and protocol relating to the status of refugees. Geneva: UNHCR. https://www.unhcr.org/3b66c2aa10. Accessed 23 May 2019.

Youngs, G. (2004). Feminist international relations: a contradiction in terms? Or: why women and gender are essential to understanding the world 'we' live in. *International Affairs, 80*(1), 75–78.

Chapter 10
Radio in the Lives of Rohingyas in Camps in Bangladesh

Mafia Mukta

Abstract Rohingya refugees are a stateless Muslim community in Myanmar, bordering Bangladesh, fleing violence, and sought asylum in Bangladesh. A majority of them, in Myanmar and in Bangladesh, do not have access to modern education and remained unschooled for generations. Community Radio Naf, based in Teknaf, with technical support from DW Akademie—Germany's leading media organization funded by the German Foreign Ministry, provides training to group of youths, both from the Rohingya community and nearby host community, and designed a radio magazine show where their voices are heard. The radio show Voice of Palong gives voices not only to Rohingya but also gives spaces to various international humanitarian organizations who are in dire need to disseminate their own messages in the camp settlement.

Keywords Community radio · Human rights · Camp · Gender violence

Introduction

Just imagine, nearly 1.2 million people living in 34 camps, and only 40-kilometre south-east from the tourism city Cox's Bazaar, Bangladesh. They are Rohingya refugees—a stateless, persecuted and forcibly displaced Muslim community in Myanmar, bordering Bangladesh, fled violence and sought refuge in Bangladesh. The latest exodus, nearly more than 700,000 refugees have arrived in the first three months in 2017—according to UNHCR 55% of them are children. The UNHCR website says more than 40% are under the age of 12.

Rohingyas have been living in Myanmar for generations. They are a Muslim community from the Rakhine state, which is just beside the river Naf in Bangladesh's south-east tourism city Cox's Bazaar. They are regarded by Myanmar's Buddhists as illegal Bangladeshi migrants. The Myanmar government is repeatedly denying their citizenship for decades and all legitimate rights they should get as a national has been

M. Mukta (✉)
Mohammadpur, Dhaka, Bangladesh

N. Chowdhory and B. Mohanty (eds.), *Citizenship, Nationalism and Refugeehood of Rohingyas in Southern Asia*,
https://doi.org/10.1007/978-981-15-2168-3_10

denied to them. The Rohingyas began entering Bangladesh since the seventies. Nearly 250,000 took refuge in Kutupalong village in Cox's Bazar in 1990s. All Rohingya camps are situated alongside the Cox's Bazaar and Teknaf highway, which is parallel to the River Naf, next to the international borderline with Myanmar.

These refugees have been experiencing persecution for decades in their villages bordering Bangladesh. Hundreds of thousands of them fled persecution and took shelter in different countries. A big number of them took refuge in Cox's Bazar of Bangladesh. There are two registered refugee camps and a big portion of them are still living unregistered in Kutupalong village of Cox's Bazar. During the recent persecution in August 2017, according to UNHCR, more than 700,000 people crossed the border and headed to Kutupalong for shelter. Bangladesh Prime Minister Sheikh Hasina allowed Rohingyas' shelter generously and asked to opened the border for them.

But overcrowding and growing population have put tremendous pressure on Bangladesh's local infrastructure. Local administration was not prepared for this huge pressure. Lack of facilities, such as housing, sanitation, food storage, is very high, which Bangladeshi local population has been trying to allay happily. The local government was forced to allow Rohingyas cutting off trees in small hills in Kutupalong villages to build small shacks made of black plastic sheets and bamboo. A huge number of bamboo and plastic sheets became necessary but it became difficult to be arranged by the refugees. International organizations, partnering with local organization, responded quickly to support the government to organize the refugee crisis in that region within a very short period of time.

The waves of Rohingyas first arrived in Kutupalong village. After their arrival, the entire Ukhiya's Kutupalong village and nearby areas were gradually acquired to provide shelter to the refugees. At least over four thousand acres of land have been dedicated to host the Rohingyas. Their tiny little huts were made up of bamboo and covered with black poly sheets and were seen scattered around the places. They were suffocating huts without windows for proper ventilations. The summers and winters become unbearable. As a result, the entire green belt was lost. The area looked barren as trees were cut by the refugees to build the houses and by NGOs to build centres to help the refugees.

Since 2018, the government has been taking initiative to organize and develop this location. The present government has expanded the camp area towards the southwest direction to ease congestion, planned the house locations, widened roads inside the camp and constructed drains to drain out water to prevent water-logging during monsoon and heavy rain. The Rohingya settlement is situated in a cyclone-prone area. The necessity of constructing robust huts compelled the government to partner with the NGOs to provide safe shelter to the refugees. The government have adopted eco-friendly measures to prevent landslides in this areas. New learning centres facilitated Rohingya children to achieve standard education, medical centres and provide health facilities to refugees. The camp have a new look. There are patches of fruit bearing and woody trees. The government is assisting people to take land on lease near the hilly areas and promoting agriculture to sustain them as well as their livestocks. Markets are being developed and community centres for youths have been set up.

But it has not been a smooth task to manage everything to ensure basic human rights to a million refugees in the world's largest refugee settlement. In August 2017, over seven hundred thousand Rohingyas risked their lives, walked through jungles and hills for days, crossed the River Naf and took shelter in Bangladesh. They were injured, tired, ill and malnourished. Many youths arrived with bullet injuries had to run towards Bangladesh's border to survive. Pregnant women who while running for life gave birth on the way or on the boat. They all were in need of immediate medical attention. People, both young and old, were starving for days, they needed food. Many had escaped death, many had witnessed death of their husband, wife, brothers, sisters, sons and daughters. They had seen their home becoming pulverized within minutes and livestocks dying. Perpetrators set their houses on fire in the middle of the night, while they were in deep slumber. Many refugees are suffering from mental illness even after a year and a half has lapsed.

All their needs are now more or less taken care of with the contribution from the NGOs and help from the government and local people. The insurmountable task has been surmounted.

Palonger Hota (Voice of Palong)—A Radio Magazine by and for Bangladeshis and Rohingya

In Myanmar, the Rohingyas were almost disconnected, isolated from the modern world—a world which is abuzz with communicating networks of various kinds. Media provides information and knowledge about the world outside. One of the major things that Rohingyas were severely deprived of—among other basic needs—was news and information. They did not have access to any mass media such as newspaper, radio or television in their villages in Rakhine. Due to the lack of access to media information, Rohingya did not get to know how the rest of the world thought of them. How did people from the other part of the world eagerly awaited to read their stories. They had little idea of positive role the media would play in their new lives in Bangladesh.

This chapter is a case study of Palonger Hota (Voice of Palong) that examines the empowering role of the media on refugee women and youth in giving them an identity within the community. It provided them information as well as self-respect and dignity of livelihood. The media not only helped the refugees it also contributed substantially to providing employment to the unemployed youths of Bangladesh. By doing this, information and receptivity have become an integral part of the human rights that every government, host citizens as well as Rohingyas should realize. The information technology played an important role in changing their life.

Nowadays, however, there are some news and information websites on the internet which are trying to serve community interests. They are operated from abroad many by the Rohingyas themselves and some by their sympathizers. But Rohingyas in the refugee settlements in Bangladesh are not allowed to access these sites because

and rejected by Rohingya leaders, who said it does not address the concerns of their community. There is apprehension among the Rohingyas that upon their return to Myanmar they would lose their voices.

Chapter 11
New Faces of Statelessness: The Rohingya Exodus and Remapping of Rights

Nergis Canefe

Abstract This chapter analyses how the progressive erasure of citizenship of Rohingya shaped the gradual undoing of their livelihood in all of its aspects, with the result of legalization of the exodus of almost the entire population. I utilize lawfare and statelessness as related concepts in order to analyse the systemic nature of the factors fueling the Rohingya catasthropy. In the first two sections, I situate the Rohingya crisis within the broader politico-military context of post-colonial statehood in terms of redefining minority identity and international law debates on statelessness. I examine whether the legalized practices of violence and state-induced oppression exhibits a systemic character. In the last two sections, I trace how successive laws and policies then transformed the Rohingya into a de facto stateless population in the region. To this end, I critically evaluate the political and legal strategies, otherwise referred to as "lawfare", that led to the mass dispossession of the Rohingya first internally and then across the border with reference to the larger context of international law prescriptions on statelessness.

Keywords Erasure of citizenship · Belonging · Law fare · Post-colonial statehood · State-induced oppression · Statelessness

Introduction

Erasure of legal status delivered through statelessness entails acts of obliteration in their most extreme form (MacLean, 2018). And yet, this process always leaves a residue, if only in the form of memories of dispossession. In this chapter, I highlight the manner in which the progressive erasure of citizenship of Rohingya shaped the gradual undoing of their livelihood in all of its aspects, with the result being the largest crisis of de facto statelessness in Asia (MacLean, 2018).

The original version of this chapter was revised: This chapter has been revised in many places with new text. The correction to this chapter is available at https://doi.org/10.1007/978-981-15-2168-3_13

N. Canefe (✉)
York University, Toronto, Canada

N. Chowdhory and B. Mohanty (eds.), *Citizenship, Nationalism and Refugeehood of Rohingyas in Southern Asia*,
https://doi.org/10.1007/978-981-15-2168-3_11

Back in 2015, most estimates placed the total number of Rohingya in Northern Rakhine state at one million people.[1] By the end of 2018, after two years of acute violence, fewer than one-tenth of the Rohingya population are thought to remain in Myanmar and thus the number of displaced Rohingya in 2018 raised to 600,000.[2] The final number continues to escalate albeit at a diminished rate. No doubt these reported numbers are to be problematized in the context of the notorious unreliability of data in such mass and hybrid emergencies composed of internal and cross-border displacements. However, when considered together with qualitative data from international organisations responding to the humanitarian crisis and refugee testimonies, we could reliably conclude that the available quantitative data tells a story of a long drawn out conflict that includes not just displacement and dispossession but also mass sexual violence and ethnic cleansing in Rakhine state (Beyrer & Kamarulzaman, 2017).

In this larger context, in this chapter I utilize two central concepts, lawfare and statelessness, as related aspects of citizenship and "belonging" in the context of the contemporary Rohingya exodus (MacLean, 2018). In the first two sections, I situate the Rohingya crisis within the broader politico-military context of the post-colonial statehood in terms of redefining minority identity and international law debates on statelessness. I illustrate the ways in which the observed pattern of violence has been consistent with the practices the state-induced oppression not just against the Rohingya but against other ethnic minority populations across Myanmar and thus exhibits a systemic character. In the last two sections, I trace how successive laws and policies then transformed the Rohingya into the largest stateless population in the region if not the world and hence the application of the term "lawfare".[3] In the concluding sections, I summarize the strategies that were used to achieve full-scale dispossession of the Rohingya population in social, economic, political and legal terms.

'Rohingya' Minorities in Context

The Rohingya of Myanmar have been experiencing an alarming range of human rights violations and crimes including but not limited to the state-sponsored displacement and systemic ethnic cleansing (Ullah, 2016). As has already been widely argued, the genesis of the crisis lies in the denial of their legal status and granting citizenship would offer a solution if only there was a willing state on either side of Myanmar's borders. Apart from the legal dynamics affecting the Rohingya case,

[1] For the overall figures of displacement, see UNHCR's Rohingya Emergency Site at https://www.unhcr.org/rohingya-emergency.html. Accessed April 23, 2019.

[2] See Internal Displacement Monitoring Center data at http://www.internal-displacement.org/expert-opinion/how-many-internally-displaced-rohingya-are-trapped-inside-myanmar. Accessed April 23, 2019. Also note that IDMC states there is a considerable lack of credible data on displacement flows in this crisis, including very limited humanitarian access to verify any information coming out of Rakhine state.

[3] See Tiefenbrun (2010), MacLean (2018).

however, distinct historical aspects of this case require further analysis. The first question to be addressed is whether the Rohingya's identity as a minority constituted a key factor that led to their persecution. One complication in this regard is that their minority identity has been constructed and reconstructed during the colonial and then post-colonial history of Myanmar. The development of Burmese nationalism, hand in hand with the politicisation of Burmese identity and deepening ethnic divisions in Myanmar society, has all played significant roles in the formation of Rohingya identity as a minority. Ultimately, the community became targeted by a regime that gave rise to a type of citizenship in Myanmar, which fails to include not just the Rohingya but other select minorities within its ambit.

As an ethnic minority, the Rohingya have been steadily ostracized from the nation-building process, progressively persecuted in terms of denial of their legal rights and eventually became prime targets for strident state-sponsored abuses (Pittaway, 2008). The situation finally escalated to the level of humanitarian emergency, with the Rohingya recently experiencing violations arguably at the level of crimes against humanity (Alam, 2018). Furthermore, in spite of their significant historical presence in the country, the Myanmar government refuses to recognize them as citizens and as such, they are stateless.[4] Some argue that the genesis of the crisis lies in the denial of the legal status of the Rohingya, unanimously calling for the repeal or amendment of the 1982 Citizenship Law. The relevant provisions of the 2008 Constitution of Myanmar are also commonly identified as instrumental in stripping off the citizenship of the Rohingya and their eventual persecution as a minority.[5]

The dynamic relation between the state and minorities directly impacts the identity formation of the latter (Krasner, 2009). The development of minority identity is contingent upon political circumstances including domestic cultural background (Cohen, 1999). In such a conflicting circumstance, minority identity becomes contested and risky, and a collective identity develops on the grounds of contestation of a cultural and political heritage invented or imposed by the state. In terms of dominant religious identity, Myanmar is a Buddhist-majority country and Buddhism is professed by most Burmans, as well as several ethnic minorities—including most Shan, Mon and a majority of Karen.[6] There are Christian minorities, including most Kachin and Chin, and some Karen. Finally, there are significant numbers of Muslims and Hindus—many of whom are of Indian descent. In this regard, Rohingya are by no means the only or even the most predominant minority.

[4]The Citizenship Law 1982, the full text to be reached at http://eudo-citizenship.eu/NationalDB/docs/1982%20Myanmar%20Citizenship%20Law%20%5BENGLISH%5D.pdf. Accessed on May 19, 2019.

[5]Provisions of the 2008 Constitution of Myanmar, to be reached at https://www.wipo.int/edocs/lexdocs/laws/en/mm/mm009en.pdf. Accessed May 19, 2019. Also see Ghai (2008).

[6]Worthy of note is that the State Religion Promotion Act of August 1961, personally championed by Nu, was repealed by General Ne Win following his 1962 coup d'état. And yet, since 2011, the country has seen a significant rise in Burman-Buddhist nationalism. Monk-led groups such as "969" and the Organization for Protection of Race and Religion ("MaBaTha") enjoy strong popular support, with Muslims being identified as particular targets. In tandem, there has been repeated calls for laws to promote and protect Buddhism. See Horsey (2015).

The Rohingyas' current human rights violations and persecutions are often explained in terms of exclusionary legal instruments. However, we must also pay attention to the fluidity and dynamic character of identity formation in Southeast Asia (Gilmartin & Lawrence, 2000; Kertzer & Arel, 2002). In the context of Myanmar, the question to be posed is whether minority identity is still the most relevant determinant to understand the Rohingya's current status and suffering. In international law, the potential for preventing direct and structural violence traditionally hinges upon refining sovereignty as responsibility. That is the least likely scenario in contemporary Myanmar as far as the Rohingya are concerned. Overall, the citizenship crisis in Myanmar has multiple dimensions (Egreteau, 2016). Fragile civil liberties circumscribed political rights and limited social rights already lead to a broad curtailment of citizenship. Second, not only that Rohingya Muslims living mainly in Rakhine state are denied citizenship, other Muslims throughout the country are increasingly affected by a similar kind of legal denial of status. Compounding these two problems is the fact that designated ethnic minorities clustered in peripheral areas face targeted, specific restrictions of citizenship due to state security reasons. The cumulative result of these tensions is an ongoing, country-wide crisis of citizenship. Consequently, the transformation of a political system based on racial, religious and ethnic hierarchies to a model espousing democratic citizenship is yet a far cry.

In a regional context, the Rohingya crisis has long been a constant issue of discord in the bilateral relations between Myanmar and Bangladesh since the late 1970s. In a nutshell, the Rohingya problem is to be seen as composed of multiple episodes of past and present human rights violations in Myanmar contributing to a "non-traditional security crisis" in the borderlands of the two countries (Parnini, 2013). Forced migration of the Rohingya to Bangladesh has also the dimension of an internationalization process of a forced migration crisis. An optimist take may suggest that bilateral negotiations between Bangladesh and Myanmar as well as democratization in Myanmar to be accelerated by the concerted efforts of both local and international actors could eventually bring about a durable solution to the Rohingya problem. And yet, this instrumentalist viewpoint ignores the basic fact that forced migration, in particular the phenomenon of stateless refugees, has long been one of the most poignant and steady issues in the history of post-colonial states across the region. In other words, this is not just about Myanmar and Bangladesh.

Mapping Out "Statelessness"

This chapter examines how the Rohingya identity has been negotiated, mobilized and/or resisted and ultimately problematized vis-a-vis the notion of statelessness as the primary marker of their identity. In addition to scholars' and policy-makers' definitions of the problem of, and suggested solution to, their statelessness, in the following pages I will posit that statelessness is both a condition and a label that often erases the ability to speak and be heard. Perceptions of statelessness as markers of "rightlessness", "rootlessness" and "voicelessness", statelessness are then transformed into a paradigm of "threshold" above and beyond issues concerning rights, status, and condition. One remains "on the threshold of statelessness", as yet another example of the condition of permanent limbo in the context of forced migration.

Here, I would argue that the status and rights of non-citizens do not represent a special conundrum for scholarly disciplines and the international legal framework. A substantial body of literature addresses the position and increasing numbers of non-citizens that states declare that they have the obligation to protect under international law. Yet scholars, as well as policy-makers, have traditionally paid much less attention to this "non-citizenship position with no eligibility for rights".[7] According to the Convention Relating to the Status of Stateless Persons, and Convention on the Reduction of Statelessness, stateless persons belong to the non-citizenship category at least identified by international law. Similarly, in 2014, the UNHCR launched an #IBelong campaign and Global Action Plan to End Statelessness, leading to a wider consideration of what statelessness represents. But why did the United Nations General Assembly confers upon the Office of the United Nations High Commissioner for Refugees (UNHCR) a broad global mandate to address statelessness as late as 1995, that is, four decades after the Convention relating to the Status of Stateless Persons was adopted? The truth is UNHCR attempted to engage states on statelessness during the Cold War, exceeding its formal powers in doing so. And yet, states remained indifferent to or took a stance in opposition to UNHCR's efforts (Seet, 2016). After the Cold War, however, receiving states grew increasingly concerned with mass influxes of refugees resulting from large-scale situations of statelessness in Eastern Europe and began to pressure UNHCR to assume greater responsibility for averting such crises. By 1995, the location of the crises moved to Asia, Africa and the Middle East, and UNHCR was empowered to take "concrete measures" against statelessness. Hence, the agenda concerning statelessness in customary international law was and continues to be heavily political (Belton, 2016).[8]

The historical development of international law for the protection of stateless persons and its relationship with the international Status of Refugees, along with the prevention and Reduction of Statelessness, led to the emergence of significant bodies of international jurisprudence: the 1954 Convention on the Status of Stateless Persons and the 1961 Convention on the Reduction of Statelessness. Worthy of note is the fact that many of the contemporary challenges concerning the Prevention and Reduction of Statelessness, including the debate about whether statelessness is "de facto" or "de jure", lack of procedures for the determination of statelessness, and persistent gaps and discrimination in nationality laws, are beyond the mandate of UNHCR (Staples, 2017). Specifically, UNHCR's action agenda on statelessness focuses in particular on birth registration, documentation and discrimination, reflecting in each case on the politics of recognition of marginalized and excluded communities. In some states, the UNHCR is aware of statelessness and "risk of statelessness" but

[7]This gap was tackled profoundly by the recently published monograph entitled Understanding Statelessness edited by Tendayi Bloom, Katherine Tonkiss and Philip Cole.

[8]For a sentimental account of the UNHCR's role, see Belton (2016).

lacks reliable data, which then poses further challenges to address concerns or policies related to statelessness. Ironically, this problem is remedied as the stateless peoples start crossing borders and become at least temporarily visible. Regardless, there are a number of promising developments for progress in addressing statelessness, particularly the emerging role of human rights law in protecting the rights of stateless people and reducing statelessness as a permanent category.

Overall, understanding statelessness and the potential for limiting it or reversing it requires the dethroning of the myth that the contemporary state system can provide for even a basic level guarantee for the universality of human status. The complexity and plurality of political and legal forms of recognition and non-recognition of persons as members of a polity, in particular in states where law is not the primary constituent of personal status, provide ample support for this proposition.

The Reign of Law and Beyond

As I illustrated thus far, recent research on the Rohingya refugee situation has mostly concentrated on the political causes of the problem and failed to pay sufficient attention to either the socio-legal framework surrounding the issues or their long-term consequences. Refugee and forced migration movements emerge as a result of a combination of factors and relationships among different actors. The Rohingya refugees and stateless is a problem manifesting itself in multiple realms. It is a humanitarian and moral issue, a legal issue, a sociopolitical issue and to a growing extent it concerns environmental and natural resources. As such, the Rohingya crisis squarely fits the definition of a refugee problem that is both a "transboundary" and a "shared" problem (Milner & Wojnarowicz, 2017).[9]

Although there is little comprehensive research on the Rohingya problems, recent work especially by Bangladeshi scholars focused on the issues pertaining to their human rights violations, statelessness, critical repatriation and ongoing crisis in the border areas. Whether the scope of this work could be considered as transboundary, however, remains questionable. Indeed, a select group of legal experts urged the Bangladeshi government to submit documents and written observations about Myanmar's persecution on Rohingyas before the International Criminal Court (ICC). They came up with the call at a discussion titled "Accountability: ICC and the Rohingya Crisis" at Nawab Nabab Ali Chowdhury Senate Bhaban of Dhaka University. Centre for Genocide Studies of DU, Centre for Peace and Justice of BRAC University and ActionAid Bangladesh jointly arranged the discussion to sensitize the Bangladesh

[9]Milner and Wojnarowicz (2017).

The central question guiding the authors' inquiry is apt for the Rohingya context as well: "Can a more disaggregated understanding of power, sensitive to form and context of expression, open new areas of enquiry into the functioning of the regime and help explain its ability and inability to fulfil its core mandate of protection and solutions for refugees?" (p. 8).

government to put pressure on Myanmar over the plight of the Rohingya.[10] Similarly, the Global Rights Compliance currently representing the interests of 400 Rohingya women and girls, organized under the name "Shanti Mohila" (Peace Women) in the Cox's Bazar refugee camp, filed submissions to the International Criminal Court ("ICC") on behalf of Shanti Mohila in May 2018. The submissions for inquiry asked the Court to investigate and prosecute crimes of genocide, apartheid, deportation and persecution perpetrated against the Rohingya since August 2017 (Global Rights Compliance, 2018).[11] In response, on 6 September 2018, Pre-Trial Chamber I of the ICC granted the request of the Prosecutor seeking jurisdiction in relation to the deportation of the Rohingya from Myanmar to Bangladesh. The Chamber accepted arguments put forward by GRC on the possibility of the Court's jurisdiction extending to other crimes committed against the Rohingya, including state-sponsored persecution. As promising as these developments are, a singular focus on legal accountability determined by an international court risks overshadowing the need to bring about tangible improvements in Rohingyas' lives and the change of their status from a permanently stateless people.

The last question I will entertain in this final section concerns the presumed uniqueness of the Rohingya problem, in particular its almost permanent cross-border nature between Myanmar and Bangladesh. As a counter-point, let us consider the status of 198 political enclaves along the northern section of the border between India and Bangladesh. These enclaves may indeed provide the perfect background for a contextual analysis of the most current Rohingya exodus, though they themselves do not host the Rohingya (Jones, 2010). The enclaves are a remnant of the partition of British India in 1947 and they are effectively stateless spaces. Most are remarkably small and located several kilometres within their host country, which in turn has prevented the populations inhabiting them having any administrative contact with their home country. Ongoing border disputes prevented the normalization of their status for over 60 years. In addition to revealing deep-seated connections between bordering practices, and, de facto exclusion from citizenship and the excessive nature of sovereignty claims of post-colonial states, life in these enclaves also demonstrates the social and political benefits of the sovereign state system however limited as they may be, and the devastating consequences bordering practices cause by territorializing even the most basic of social protections. The continual failure to formalize the status of these enclaves, and thus, their inhabitants display the overcharged stance of nationalist homeland narratives concerning sovereignty and territorial integrity, at the expense of not just human rights but the most basic of them all, the right to life. In the case of the Rohingya, it is not the land that is stateless but the people themselves, and yet the treatment of their non-status positionality leads to very similar

[10]For an overall summary of such efforts, see https://harvardhrj.com/2019/02/atrocities-documented-accountability-needed-finding-justice-for-the-rohingya-through-the-icc-and-independent-mechanism-by-paul-r-williams-jessica-levy/. Accessed May 19, 2019.

[11]For a full text of these submissions, see http://www.globalrightscompliance.com/en/news/grc-files-submissions-on-behalf-of-400-rohingya-victims-at-the-icc. Accessed May 19, 2019.

consequences as that of those suffered by the inhabitants of the "stateless enclaves" (Chowdhory, 2016).[12]

As already covered in detail in previous sections of this chapter, the Rohingya crisis is rooted in the British colonial era that subsequently gained momentum through their gradual demarcation and marginalization first as an ethnic and later as a religious minority, their exclusion from the governmental institutions, and the ultimate deprivation of citizenship, effectively rendering them stateless. The major elements of the crisis from the colonial period to the present day could thus be summed up with a brief paragraph. What is unique about the Rohingya issue is the legalized nature of the crisis from the very onset and thus my resort to the notion of lawfare. The role of law in twenty-first-century conflicts and forced migration movements has been most decisive and legality, rather than illegality of violent practices is the determining feature of many of the contemporary waves of mass exodus. For international lawyers and others involved in national security matters, the transformational role of law is often captured under the aegis of the term lawfare. Meanwhile, perhaps as to be expected, lawfare has also generated its share of controversy.[13] In the specific context of the Rohingya crisis, I use the term with direct reference to the coercive use of legal instruments and in particular, the constitution, to create a real impact as well as threatened actions against select groups of citizens. In this regard, lawfare is an emerging domain of full spectrum warfare, and in the case of civil conflict, an important part of the spectrum of crimes falling under the aegis of crimes against humanity, which is either used in its own right to achieve the state's strategic objectives or as an enabler within the context of well-planned policies and plans.

It is well documented that to escape summary execution, indiscriminate rape and other human rights abuses nearly 700,000 Rohingya fled to Bangladesh by mid-August 2018 after a "clearance operation" carried out by Myanmar military on 25 August 2017 (UNHCR, 2018).[14] In the independent Myanmar, the Rohingya were also expunged in 1978, the early 1990s and 2012 (Holliday, 2014). These episodes of political violence bordering on state criminality no doubt go against the portrayal of Myanmar as a timeless place and a country of egalitarian Buddhist villages—which incidentally were ruled successively by different kings, British colonialists and most recently a military regime, and hence the dubious nature of the claim concerning the egalitarian history of the country's political culture. This potent mix of colonial legacy, decades of marginalization and oppression under authoritarian rule, combined with divisive social and religious factors discussed in the section on minorities, are directly associated with the unending Rohingya crisis (Freeman, 2017; Kyaw cited in Melissa Crouch, 2016).

[12]For a detailed analysis of such practices along the Indian border, see Chowdhory (2018). Also see her earlier work Chowdhory (2016).

[13]Dunlap Jr (2010) and Tiefenbrun (2010).

[14]See Report of the Independent International Fact-Finding Mission on Myanmar, HRC Res 39/64 of 2018, UN, 39th Sess, Agenda Item 4, UN Doc A/HRC/39/64 (August 24, 2018) (hereinafter "FFM Report") at https://www.ohchr.org/en/hrbodies/hrc/myanmarFFM/Pages/ReportoftheMyanmarFFM.aspx. Accessed May 19, 2019.

While "ethnicity" remains as a mutable concept and category in Myanmar, both colonial and post-colonial governments did create a clear distinction between the various Myanmar ethnicities commonly referred to as *taingyintha* or "sons of the soil" and Chinese and South Asians, the Rohingya being one group among them. Here, it is important to underline the fact that the post-colonial administration conformed to the classically racial physiognomy-based logic of the British census, and as is the story in many a post-colonial setting, since the British favoured the Rohingya economically, they became convenient objects of populist anger in the period of Independence. The genealogy of the term taingyintha clearly proves how it has become the precondition of belonging in Myanmar (Cheesman, 2017a). It is in this context that the most current constitution of the country puts being a taingyintha over and ahead of citizenship, subsequently addressing the political community not as an aggregation of citizens but as a conglomeration of "national races" (Cheesman, 2017b). Accordingly, the Rohingya came to possess the perceived characteristics of foreignness by negation as they cannot fit the demanding taingyintha status. These socio-historical constructs that eventually became "legal" factors, hence dictating distinctions made and hierarchies established between ethnicities, and leading to a jurisprudentially crowned construction of belonging versus foreignness. In summary, they constitute the foundational parameters of lawfare against the Rohingya in Myanmar.

The second dimension of the lawfare against the Rohingya is related to socio-economic policies. Although the majority of Myanmar's Muslims live in urban areas, speak Burmese, have Burmese names, and are Myanmar citizens, the Rohingya are quite different since most are Sunni Muslim and live in rural areas in Rakhine (formerly Arakan) (Anug-Thwin & Anug-Thwin, 2013). They traditionally lived in the country's north-west, speak a dialect of Bengali (Chittagonian) and have Muslim names. In Rakhine, prior to the latest exodus, it was estimated that 35.6% are the Muslim Rohingya, 59.7% are Buddhist and the remainder constitute other religious groups (Alam, 2011). Today, fewer than half a million currently reside in Myanmar while close to 2 million Rohingya have fled decades of repression and exclusion in several waves.

At this point, two additional colonial legacies must be mentioned which led to the most current of the ethnic minority crises including the Rohingya: the legacy of institutional weaknesses in terms of facilitating constitutional checks and balances, and the legacy of lack of legitimacy harking back to colonial institutions and carried forward in the post-independence period, in both cases leading to fractions rather than harmony in multi-ethnic Myanmar society. The independent Myanmar was shaped by these colonial legacies. Different laws, policies and governmental decisions made during the colonial times were precursors for the status and consequential suffering of the Rohingya. Although the Rohingya had been recognized as an ethnic group by the U Nu government in the 1950s, this has been denied by the subsequent governments. Their situation was further marginalized through the successive changes of the Constitutions of Myanmar. The first Constitution of 1947 recognized them as citizens; the 1948 Citizenship Law required specific conditions to be fulfilled before they could attain their citizenship status. The 1974 Constitution introduced much stricter conditions to prove citizenship. Finally, the latest constitution of 2008 also kept these onerous conditions to be fulfilled before the Rohingya can claim citizenship (Seekins, 2009). Thus, under the domestic legal framework of Myanmar, the Rohingya already became stateless.

Based on the example of the Rohingya's statelessness, this chapter is an invitation to reflect on the condition of statelessness above and beyond *ex post facto* state-specific solutions. The widespread nature of statelessness worldwide dictates the need for a more nuanced understanding of contemporary forms of membership and the interplay of different rights regimes above and beyond citizenship. While the Rohingya have been commonly characterized as undeservingly stateless with continually denied access to the procedure for status recognition, their experiences in the absence of any formal citizenship even back at home in Myanmar duly complicate Hannah Arendt's insightful characterization of stateless people as rightless from the point of their departure from homeland onwards (Sigona, 2016). Furthermore, their lack of any citizenship, Myanmarese or Bangladeshi in this instance, does not make the Rohingya the *prima facie* embodiment of bare life.[15] Giorgio Agamben's claim that refugees can be seen as the ultimate "biopolitical" subjects who are regulated and governed in a permanent "state of exception" has only limited applicability in this regard (Owens, 2009). Against it could be argued here that if refugee populations could reclaim the "bare life" by forging a public realm in the political world by way of being visible and present, and in some ways, ungovernable. In turn, this reverse interpretation of bare life reveals a potent political subjectivity as an embodied process, where subjects actively negate and negotiate their position in the world and vis-à-vis the state(s) making impositions upon them.

Redefining Bare Life

The Rohingya people are one of the most ill-treated and persecuted refugee groups in the world, having lived in the realm of statelessness for over six generations, and still doing so. Since 2017, more than 500,000 Rohingyas fled from Myanmar to neighbouring countries. Overall, the living conditions of Rohingya refugees inside the overcrowded camps remain dismal. Mental health is poor, malnutrition is endemic and physical/sexual abuse is high. In other words, they appear to be a prime example

[15] In her canonized discussion of the plight of stateless people, Hannah Arendt invokes the "right to have rights" as the one true human right. In doing so she establishes what Jacques Ranciere called "*aporia*". The question that remains with us post-Arendt is the following: if statelessness corresponds not only to rightlessness but also to a life deprived of public visibility and political presence, how could those excluded from politics possibly claim the right to have rights? Rancière's response to Arendt's aporetic account of human rights situates this question in relation to Arendt's conception of the political. According to Rancière, Arendt depoliticizes human rights in identifying the human with mere life (*zoë*) and the citizen with the good life (*bios politikos*). For him, politics is about contesting how that very distinction is drawn. For Rancière, "the human" in human rights does not refer to a life deprived of politics. In contrast to Arendt, Rancière's approach thus enables us to recognize contests over rights as part and parcel of social-legal struggles that are the core of political life. For further debate, see Rancière and Panagia (2000) and Schaap (2011).

of the bare life mentioned above. In this section, however, I will argue otherwise and suggest that the nation herself that creates such conditions of livelihood is a barren form of existence in toto and that there is agency involved in revealing the extent to which the deterioration of humanity has gone albeit through real human suffering.

As I argued elsewhere, colonial maps were potent political fictions (Canefe cited in Uddin & Chowdhory, 2019). The boundaries established henceforth reflected imperial desires for administrative expediency rather than political, economic and cultural realities of the colonized regions. The land once known as Burma and now as Myanmar as the military regime unilaterally changed the country's official name in 1989 is as much an invention as it is a historical entity. The three Anglo-Burmese Wars occurred during 1824–1826, 1852–1853 and 1885; each war incorporated new territory in what subsequently became the British-delineated Burma (Anug-Thwin, 1985). Instead, a diverse array of polities co-existed, tying the country to other polities in India, China and parts of mainland South-east Asia (MacLean, 2018). The Kingdom of Arakan (1430–1875), where large numbers of Rohingya historically resided, was just one of many of such polities. The original Kingdom, which extended far beyond the territorial borders that now demarcate Bangladesh from Burma/Myanmar, was a key node in trade networks of the colonial era. This situation changed only gradually after the experience of the British colonial state, which was administered from India until 1937. Military officials and colonial administrators managed the task of governance in such a way that the colonial state utilized direct rule in lowland areas where Burmans formed the majority, and indirect rule in upland areas where non-Burmans such as the Rohingya were the majority (MacLean ibid.). This sums up the experience of Rohingya in Northern Rakhine state under the colonial rule, albeit with one difference. During the colonial times as well as in the transition to independence, armed ethnic organizations attained a notable degree of political legitimacy among the populations they claimed to represent since they funded services such as education and health that the state would not. The most successful of these organizations also controlled access to valuable natural resources such as timber, jade, precious gems and opium in remote border regions, the profits of which underwrote the services they offered to the local population. In contradistinction, Rohingya political groups and military organizations did not have such resources at their disposal and thus could only provide limited protection and services (MacLean ibid.).

Specifically, the Rohingya Independence Force (RIF), created in 1963 to protest the 1962 military coup, demanded that the military regime's ban on Muslim organizations such as the Rohingya Students' Union and Rohingya Youth League be revoked.

In terms of political representation, in 1974, the Rohingya Patriotic Front (RPF) sought the creation of an independent Muslim state along the Bangladesh border (MacLean, 2018). This was followed by the Rohingya Solidarity Organization (RSO) established in 1982, and the Arakan Rohingya Islamic Front (ARIK). In 1995, the RSO and ARIK merged to form the Rohingya National Alliance Organization

(ARMO).[16] This sums up the Rohingya political organization in the country and none of the aforementioned ones provided the kind of political clout or services that other ethnic organizations managed in the country.

Against this background of fractured and ineffective political representation, British census practices, which were largely derived from those developed in India, had a marked impact on post-colonial understandings of Burmese and by derivation Rohingya identity. It is in this specific context that I posit we need to redefine what bare life means in the context of statelessness in Myanmar. These laws interwove prepositions about ancestry, genetics, territory and linguistic differentiation later combined with religious divisions (The Transnational Institute, 2014). Such imposed interconnections directly informed the country's discriminatory citizenship laws in the absence of effective political representation. In other words, there was a context that made the conditions of bare life possible before it was experienced by select communities. As the narrative goes, during precolonial times, the Rohingyas and Arakanese, the remainder of the population in Arakan, are believed to have lived in harmony. Only after colonization by the British and following the first Anglo-Burmese war in 1825, a rift is purported to appear as one side joined with the British and the other side with the Burmese. This rift further deepened during the Second World War, when the Rohingyas yet again declared their loyalty to the British, while the Arakanese sided with the Japanese. In return, during the Japanese occupation of Burma (including Arakan), the Rohingya population was targeted jointly by both the communalist (Buddhist) Rakhine and the Burma Independence Army, killing 100,000 Rohingya and exiling a further 50,000 towards the border to East Bengal (Selth, 1986). After Burma received independence in 1948, it was only to be expected that the anti-Rohingya campaign would persist.

By 1978, the anti-Rohingya sentiment culminated in a military junta operation to purge Burma of "illegal inhabitants", leading to the flight of a further 250,000 Rohingyas to Bangladesh. Faced by pressure from outside, a repatriation agreement was struck with Bangladesh the following year, resulting in the majority of Rohingyas returning to Burma. However, as will be discussed in detail in the next section, Burma then passed the 1982 Citizenship Law that categorically denied citizenship to Rohingyas, decreeing an estimated 800,000 Rohingyas in North Rakhine stateless and rendering their return from Bangladesh only three years ago a smoke screen. Completing the cycle, during military junta rule in 1988, the State Law and Order Restoration Council (SLORC) established a number of new military cantonments in the Rakhine state, focusing on the north where Muslims were situated (Rigg, 2004). Land was forcefully taken from the Muslim inhabitants without compensation, making the Rohingyas "homeless" in addition to "stateless". Branded as illegal residents, they were then denied access to education, health care, employment, freedom of movement, religion and limited rights to get married or to have children.

[16]Timeline: Being Rohingya in Myanmar, from 1784 to Now. *The Wire*, September 23, 2017, https://thewire.in/external-affairs/rohingya-myanmar-timeline. Accessed 19 May 2019. Also see MacLean (2018) for a very detailed analysis of political representation of the Rohingya.

Although Bangladesh has been the preferred destination for the majority of asylum-seeking Rohingyas, after 1992, Rohingyas entering Bangladesh were not officially recognized as refugees by the Government of Bangladesh (GOB). And yet, large numbers of Rohingyas arrived once again in Bangladesh during late 2016, then in 2018, following massacres in Myanmar where hundreds of Rohingyas were murdered, faced sexual violence and thousands of houses were burned down. With more than twenty years of continuous camp settlements, the current Rohingya refugee situation in Bangladesh has become one of the most protracted in the world (Cheung, 2011). This is despite the fact that in 2014, GOB announced its national policy for managing the Myanmar refugees, which is comprised of five elements: (i) preparation of a list of unregistered refugees; (ii) provision of temporary basic humanitarian relief; (iii) strengthening of border management; (iv) diplomatic initiatives with the government of Myanmar and (v) increasing national level coordination.

Whether Myanmar would consider taking a step back from the specific provisions of the 1982 Citizenship Law, which updated the definition in the 1947 Constitution, and undo the explicit ties between ancestry and territory is a question that far exceeds GOB's best intentions. The 1982 Law divided citizenship into three categories and assigned different rights for each of them, thus establishing a graded model of rights and belonging (MacLean, 2018). For our purposes here, it is this process of grading that makes production and reproduction of bare lives possible. These categories include full citizens who are defined as descendants of residents who lived in what is now Burma/Myanmar prior to 1823, associate citizens who acquired citizenship under the 1948 Union Citizenship Law, and naturalized citizens who had resided in Burma/Myanmar prior to 1948, but who had failed to apply for citizenship under the Union Citizenship Act (MacLean, 2018; Kyaw, 2015; Amnesty International, 2004). In all three cases, citizenship eligibility is limited to "national ethnic races" including Burman, Karen, Shan, Kachin, Chin, Mon and Arakanese (now Rakhine) but not the Rohingya.[17] The military regime conducted a new census in 1983, releasing a new list of 135 of these races, and the Rohingya were not among them yet again (Leider, 2014; MacLean, 2018).

According to state-sponsored and publicly consumed narratives of Burmese history, Rohingya are "Bengalis" who migrated from Chittagong in south-eastern Bangladesh after 1823 (Chan, 2005). Sadly, Rohingya advocates such as the Arakan Rohingya National Organization and the Rohingya National Council, both of which are based in the diaspora (London, UK), respond to this argument in terms of setting the "historical record straight" rather than refuting the imposition of such categories

[17]Department of Population Ministry of Labour, Immigration, and Population, The 2014 Myanmar Population and Housing Census: Census Report Volume 2-C (Naypyidaw: Ministry of Labour, Immigration, and Population, 2016), 12–5, reached at https://www.google.com/search?q=Department+of+Population+Ministry+of+Labour%2C+Immigration%2C+and+Population%2C+The+2014+Myanmar+Population+and+Housing+Census%3A+Census+Report+Volume+2-C&oq=Department+of+Population+Ministry+of+Labour%2C+Immigration%2C+and+Population%2C+The+2014+Myanmar+Population+and+Housing+Census%3A+Census+Report+Volume+2-C&aqs=chrome..69i57.335j0j7&sourceid=chrome&ie=UTF-8. Accessed 19 May 2019. Also see MacLean (2018).

of inclusion. They thus assert that their presence in Burma/Myanmar predates the 1823 cut-off and that they are a unique group linguistically and culturally distinct from "Bengalis" (Cheesman, 2017a). This troubling concept of "national ethnic races", which is accepted even by the Rohingya groups only to find a way to fit into the long list produced by the Myanmar government, reflects the belief that socio-cultural and linguistic differences are grounded in blood and kinship. Consequently, indigeneity is supposed to possess biological roots and it becomes a binary construct.

Accordingly, the 1982 Citizenship Law not only stripped the Rohingya of citizenship, but as stated above, the national census undertaken in 1983 did not even count them, as the binary logic counted them out. Some Rohingya were able to obtain national registration cards or temporary registration certificates, but none of these documents led to permanent legal status and related protections (MacLean, 2018). In short, the writing was already on the wall that they would eventually have to leave. This was further signalled by the military regime's launch of citizen verification programme in 1989 (Green et al., 2015). It is reported that non-Rohingya Muslims, who possessed registration cards or certificates, were encouraged to submit their documents, which were neither returned nor replaced (International Crisis Group, 2014). It is true that Rohingya refugees repatriated from Bangladesh during the early 1990s received yellow "returnees identity cards" from UNHCR. However, the military regime refused to grant any official status to these, either. Similarly, the UN-backed 2014 census did not count people who self-identified as Rohingya (Ferguson, 2015). The government's ban of the official use of the word "Rohingya", claimed to reduce tensions between the country's majority Buddhists and minority Muslims, led to more than one million people being uncounted (Amnesty International, 2017). As the final straw, the reformed Myanmar government introduced a pilot project in 2017 that would enable members of these uncounted populations to acquire a national verification card but with one caveat: the Rohingya had to provide that they registered as "Bengali" and list their religion (MacLean, 2018). This requirement resulted in widespread protests due to the fear that doing so would make it impossible to acquire citizenship in the future (Ken, 2019). These protests led to further violence, which then provided the background for the latest exodus. These repeated sequences of events prove my initial point that the bare life is not at the outside, at the margins, but in effect it constitutes a core element in the definition of a polity. It is not a thing, but a process, it is inter-relational and has far reaching consequences for the society and polity at large.

Conclusion

The decades-old Rohingya problem, which has affected not just Myanmar but also a number of other Southeast Asia countries, has long been defined in terms of forced migration, statelessness and humanitarian crisis. As the catastrophic chain of events involving Rohingya refugees, forced migrants and internally displaced persons is commonly associated with the discriminatory 1982 Citizenship Law, amending or repealing that law has often been proposed as the ultimate solution. Despite the law's several discriminatory provisions, in this chapter I argued that the real problem lies in the Rohingya's arbitrary deprivation of the right to nationality and citizenship documentation not just by Myanmar but also by the countries they arrive as displaced populations (Paxton, 2012). Furthermore, acknowledgement of statelessness not as a state of exception but as part of the tools of governance used by the post-colonial state in its dealings with minorities and identity politics would allow us to break down the grid of citizenship versus statelessness dichotomy. While forced migration scholars have turned to Arendt's analysis of statelessness time and again and superfluity to consider questions of immigration, "illegality", and the status of non-citizens, I believe Ranciere's account of political action offers a richer optic for considering the future of the Rohingya. Rather than defining "success" in terms of replicability or immediate legislative results of the Rohingya being accorded citizenship by Myanmar or any of the neighbouring states including but not limited to Bangladesh, the ongoing crisis concerning their legal status should be analysed in terms of the significance of non-citizens laying claims to the public realm. In line with Michael Warner's concept of "counter publics", the statelessness of the Rohingya could be understood as a moment of *initiation* to the politics of South Asia and an inaugural performance of the political to gain civic standing (Warner, 2002).[18]

South Asia is a principal source and host of refugees hosting more than 14% of the world's refugee population (Reliefweb, 2018).[19] The causes behind continual waves of displacement are many, including political instability, armed conflict, lack of resources and ethno-nationalist upsurges. Yet, none of the societies in South Asia have signed any major Convention or treaty at the international level in regard to refugees or the stateless.[20] Though this could be regarded as the ultimate decolonial/post-colonial strategy, this chapter demonstrated that the post-colonial arrangement in its South Asian form has failed to serve its supposed ultimate beneficiary, that is,

[18] Warner (2002). Warner's concept of counter publics illuminates the dynamic relationship between the realm of ideas, the social imaginary and the bodily habitus within which politics happens. Viewing statelessness from the lens of counter public highlights the significance of its changing temporalities, multiple social locations and the hybrid, fluid, nonlinear nature of post-colonial politics of belonging.

[19] See the Reliefweb report ISCG Situation Report: Rohingya Refugee Crisis, Cox's Bazar https://reliefweb.int/report/bangladesh/iscg-situation-report-rohingya-refugee-crisis-cox-s-bazar-15-November-2018. Accessed May 19, 2019.

[20] The majority of Asian states have not signed onto the major international refugee law instruments which promote refugee recognition and protection. Yet, second to Africa, the Asian region has had the highest number of refugees since the Second World War. The most commonly offered explanations in this regard are "economic costs" and "social disruption" arguments. An alternative explanation is of course how limited Asian involvement was in the drafting of international refugee law, which has led Asian states to reject refugee recognition practices and judicialization of the process as heavily Eurocentric. See Davis (2006) and Iskandar (2018). Iskandar's work takes this alternative argument even further. Accordingly, the Association of Southeast Asian Nations (ASEAN) as the only institutionalized transnational body in the region, not only embodies a political statement against the Western liberal order, but also keeps the spirit of the decolonization era alive by summoning Bandung's post-colonial ideals declaring the state is the only and ultimate agent in international affairs.

subaltern groups such as the persecuted Rohingya. The Rohingya have been denied their human rights not just by the colonialists but readily so by their post-colonial brothers as well. Celebrating the ingenuity of the Malaysian Human Rights Commission *Suruhanjaya Hak Asasi Manusia Malaysia* (SUHAKAM) and their call for an "indigenized pragmatism" embracing universal human rights that transcend the boundaries of colonial/post-colonial dichotomies rather than denying rights to refugees and stateless peoples due to their evocation of foreignness is apt (Iskandar, 2018). And yet, these genuine gestures of facing the realities of contemporary South Asia do not suffice to yield solutions to the problem at hand.

As yet, there is no national legislation or regional framework to deal with the issue of statelessness of the Rohingya. A comprehensive study focusing on the various dimensions of displacement in South Asia including refugees, migrants, stateless persons and internally displaced persons (IDPs) is imperative, though it lies beyond the scope of the present analysis. Meanwhile, how the stateless are perceived and governed in contemporary South Asian politics is not just a matter of keeping a tally of numbers. What sort of sovereign responses has been advanced to govern and discipline the movement of people without rights or status above and beyond the attributes associated with the "figure of the refugee" (Scheel & Squire, 2014)?[21] Do they fit into the generic description of the "abject masses from the Global South", or, do they not even enter the registers of such an already restricted category? I would argue that through the creation of new categories or legal *limits*, in the form of temporary protection statuses or de facto permits to remain for those perceived as passive victims, i.e. the stateless, the Rohingya have been pushed to the permanent background of South Asian regimes of border security, governance and supremacy of national sovereignty at times against the interests of the very people these states encapsulate. Whether to be labelled as "humanitarian immigrants" or "de facto stateless", Rohingya became a fixture of the forced migration landscape of the region. In keeping with the protracted conflicts in Myanmar and ongoing human rights abuses that span over at least four decades, such as forced labour, political persecution and mass sexual abuse since September 1988 declaration of power by the State Law and Order Restoration Council (SLORC), the Rohingya joined approximately one million Burmese nationals who have fled to neighbouring states (Bünte, 2009). In this regard, I would like to conclude with the statement that contextualization rather than isolation of the Rohingya problem is both a methodological and a political necessity.

References

Ahsan Ullah, A. K. M. (2016). Rohingya Crisis in Myanmar: Seeking justice for the stateless. *Journal of Contemporary Criminal Justice, 32*(3), 285–301.

[21] Scheel and Squire (2014). As Scheel and Squire argue, based on the severe limitations imposed upon their agency and choice, asylum seekers who are deemed as "deserving" refugee status are accorded at least a degree of legitimate existence.

Alam, M. A. (2011). *Marginalization of the Rohingya in Arakan state of Western Burma*. Kaladan Press.

Alam, J. (2018). The Rohingya of Myanmar: Theoretical significance of the minority status. *Asian Ethnicity, 19,* 180–210.

Amnesty International. (2004). *Myanmar, the Rohingya minority: Fundamental rights denied.* London: Amnesty International.

Amnesty International. (2017). *My world is finished: Rohingya targeted in crimes against humanity in Myanmar*. London: Amnesty International.

Anug-Thwin, M. (1985). The British 'pacification' of Burma: Order without meaning. *Journal of Southeast Asian Studies, 16*(2), 245–261.

Anug-Thwin, M., & Anug-Thwin, M. (2013). *A history of Myanmar since ancient times: Traditions and transformations*. Reaktion Books.

Belton, K. (2016). Ending statelessness through belonging: a transformative agenda? *Ethics & International Affairs, 30*(4), 419–427.

Beyrer, C., & Kamarulzaman, A. (2017). Ethnic cleansing in Myanmar: The Rohingya crisis and human rights. *The Lancet, 390*(10102), 1570–1573.

Bünte, M. (2009). The politics of refugees in and outside Burma/Myanmar. *Journal of Current Southeast Asian Affairs, 28*(2), 3–5.

Chan, A. (2005). The development of a Muslim enclave in Arakan (Rakhine) state of Burma (Myanmar). *SOAS Bulletin of Burma Research, 3*(2), 396–420.

Cheesman, N. (2017a). How in Myanmar 'National Races' came to surpass citizenship and exclude Rohingya. *Journal of Contemporary Asia, 47*(2), 14–15.

Cheesman, N. (2017b). How in Myanmar 'national races' came to surpass citizenship and exclude Rohingya. *Journal of Contemporary Asia, 7*(3).

Cheung, S. (2011). Migration control and the solutions impasse in South and Southeast Asia: Implications from the Rohingya experience. *Journal of Refugee Studies, 25*(1), 50–70.

Chowdhory, N. (2016). Displacement–A 'state of exception' and beyond: introductory remarks. *International Journal of Migration and Border Studies, 2*(2), 95–98.

Chowdhory, N. (2018). *Refugees, citizenship and belonging in South Asia: Contested terrains.* Springer.

Cohen, J. (1999). Changing paradigms of citizenship and the exclusiveness of the demos. *International Sociology, 14*(3), 245–268.

Constitution of the Republic of the Union of Myanmar. (2008). Provisions of the 2008 Constitution of Myanmar. https://www.wipo.int/edocs/lexdocs/laws/en/mm/mm009en.pdf. Accessed 19 May 2019.

Davies, Sara. (2006). The Asian rejection? international refugee law in Asia. *Australian Journal of Politics & History, 52*(4), 562–575.

Department of Population. Ministry of Labour, Immigration, and Population. (2016). *The 2014 Myanmar population and housing census: census report volume 2-C*, pp. 12–5. Naypyidaw: Ministry of Labour, Immigration, and Population. https://www.google.com/search?q=Department+of+Population+Ministry+of+Labour%2C+Immigration%2C+and+Population%2C+The+2014+Myanmar+Population+and+Housing + Census%3A+Census+Report+Volume+2-C&oq=Department+of+Population+Ministry+of+Labour%2C+Immigration%2C+and+Population%2C+The+2014+Myanmar+Population+and+Housing+Census%3A+Census+Report+Volume+2-C&aqs=chrome..69i57.335j0j7&sourceid=chrome&ie=UTF-8. Accessed 19 May 2019.

Dunlap Jr, C. J. (2010). Does lawfare need an apologia. *Case Western Reserve Journal of International Law*, 43, 121.

Egreteau, R. (2016). Embedding praetorianism: soldiers, state, and constitutions in postcolonial Myanmar. In M. Bünte & B. Dressel (Eds.), *Politics and constitutions in Southeast Asia* (pp. 131–153). Routledge.

Ferguson, J. (2015). Who's counting? ethnicity, belonging, and the national census in Burma/Myanmar, Bijdragent Tot De Taal-, Land- en Volkenkunde. *Journal of the Humanities and Social Sciences of Southeast Asia and Oceania, 171*(1), 1–28.

Ghai, Y. (2008). The 2008 Myanmar constitution: Analysis and assessment. Open Society Institute.

Gilmartin, D., & Lawrence, B. B. (2000). *Beyond Turk and Hindu: rethinking religious identities in Islamic South Asia*. Gainesville: University Press of Florida Press.

Global Rights Compliance. (2018). GRC files submissions on behalf of 400 Rohingya victims at the ICC. http://www.globalrightscompliance.com/en/news/grc-files-submissions-on-behalf-of-400-rohingya-victims-at-the-icc. Accessed 19 May 2019.

Green, P., Thomas MacManus, T., & de la Cour Venning, A. (2015). *Countdown to annihilation: Genocide in Myanmar*. London: International State Crime Initiative.

Holliday, I. (2014). Addressing Myanmar's citizenship crisis. *Journal of Contemporary Asia, 44*(3), 404.

Horsey, R. (2015). New religious legislation in Myanmar. In *Conflict prevention and peace forum*.

International Crisis Group. (2014). *The politics of Rakhine state*. Brussels: International Crisis Group.

Iskandar, P. (2018). Non-citizen rights in ASEAN: The need to chart a new course. *Social & Legal Studies, 27*(2), 180–199.

Jones, R. (2010). The border enclaves of India and Bangladesh. In A. C. Diener & J. Hagen (Eds.), *Borderlines and borderlands: Political oddities at the edge of the nation-state* (pp. 15-33). Lanham: Rowman and Littlefield Publishers.

Kertzer, D. I., & Arel, D. (2002). Censuses, identity formation, and the struggle for political power. *Census and Identity: The Politics of Race, Ethnicity, and Language in National Censuses, 1,* 1.

Krasner, S. D. (2009). *Power, the state, and sovereignty: Essays on international relations*. Routledge.

Kyaw, N. N. (2015). Alienation, discrimination, and securitization: legal personhood and cultural personhood of Muslims in Myanmar. *Review of Faith and International Affairs, 13*(4).

Kyaw, N. N. (2016). Islamophobia in Buddhist Myanmar: The 969 movement and anti-Muslim violence. In M. Crouch (Ed.), *Islam and the state in Myanmar: Muslim-Buddhist relations and the politics of belonging* (Chapter. 7). Oxford University Press.

Leider, J. P. (2014). Rohingya: The name, the movement, and the quest for identity. *Nation building in Myanmar* (pp. 204–255). Myanmar Peace Centre: Yangon.

MacLean, K. (2018). The Rohingya crisis and the practices of erasure. *Journal of Genocide Research, 21*(1), 83–95.

Milner, J., & Wojnarowicz, K. (2017). Power in the global refugee regime: Understanding expressions and experiences of power in global and local contexts. *refuge: Canada's Journal on Refugees, 33*(1), 7–17.

Owens, P. (2009). Reclaiming 'bare life'? *Against Agamben on refugees. International Relations, 23*(4), 567–582.

Parnini, S. N. (2013). The crisis of the Rohingya as a Muslim minority in Myanmar and bilateral relations with Bangladesh. *Journal of Muslim Minority Affairs, 33*(2), 281–297.

Paxton, A. (2012). Finding a country to call home: A framework for evaluating legislation to reduce statelessness in Southeast Asia. *Pac. Rim L. & Pol'y J., 21,* 623.

Pittaway, E. (2008). The Rohingya refugees in Bangladesh: A failure of the international protection regime. *Protracted Displacement in Asia: No Place to Call Home*, 83–105.

Prasse Freeman, E. (2017). The Rohingya crisis. *Anthropology Today, 33*(6), 1–2.

Rancière, J., & Panagia, D. (2000). Dissenting words: A conversation with Jacques Rancière. *Diacritics*, 113–126.

Reliefweb. (2018). ISCG situation report: Rohingya refugee crisis, cox's bazar. https://reliefweb.int/report/bangladesh/iscg-situation-report-rohingya-refugee-crisis-cox-s-bazar-15-November-2018. Accessed 19 May 2019.

Rigg, J. (2004). *Southeast Asia: The human landscape of modernization and development*. Routledge.

Rushing, E. J. (2017). How many internally displaced Rohingya are trapped inside Myanmar? Internal displacement monitoring center. http://www.internal-displacement.org/expert-opinion/how-many-internally-displaced-rohingya-are-trapped-inside-myanmar. Accessed 23 April 2019.

Schaap, A. (2011). Enacting the right to have rights: Jacques Rancière's critique of hannah arendt. *European Journal of Political Theory, 10*(1), 22–45.

Scheel, S., & Squire, V. (2014). Forced migrants as illegal migrants. In *The oxford handbook of refugee and forced migration studies* (pp. 188–99).

Seekins, D. M. (2009). Myanmar in 2008: Hardship compounded. *Asian Survey, 49*(1).

Seet, M. (2016). The origins of UNHCR's global mandate on statelessness. *International Journal of Refugee Law, 28*(1), 7–24.

Selth, A. (1986). Race and resistance in Burma, 1942–1945. *Modern Asian Studies, 20*(3), 483–507.

Sigona, N. (2016). Everyday statelessness in Italy: status, rights, and camps. *Ethnic and Racial Studies, 39*(2), 263–279.

Staples, K. (2017). Recognition, nationality, and statelessness: State-based challenges for UNHCR's plan to end statelessness 1. In T. Bloom, K. Tonkiss, P. Cole, *Understanding statelessness* (pp. 173–188). Routledge.

The Burma Citizenship Law 1982. http://eudo-citizenship.eu/NationalDB/docs/1982%20Myanmar%20Citizenship%20Law%20%5BENGLISH%5D.pdf. Accessed on 19 May 2019.

The Transnational Institute. (2014). *Ethnicity without meaning, data without context: The 2014 census, identity, and citizenship in Burma/Myanmar*. Amsterdam: Burma Center Nederland. https://www.tni.org/en/briefing/ethnicity-without-meaning-data-without-context.

The Wire. (2017). Timeline: Being Rohingya in Myanmar, from 1784 to Now. https://thewire.in/external-affairs/rohingya-myanmar-timeline. Accessed 19 May 2019.

Tiefenbrun, S. W. (2010). Semiotic definition of lawfare. *Case Western Reserve Journal of International Law, 43,* 29.

UNHCR. (2018). Rohingya emergency. https://www.unhcr.org/rohingya-emergency.html. Accessed April 23, 2019.

Uddin, N., & Chowdhory, N. (2019). *Deterritorialised identity and transborder movement in South Asia*. Springer Nature Singapore Pte Ltd.

UNHRC. (2018). *Report of the independent international fact-finding mission on Myanmar, HRC Res 39/64 of 2018, UN, 39th session, agenda item 4, UN Doc A/HRC/39/64*. https://www.ohchr.org/en/hrbodies/hrc/myanmarFFM/Pages/ReportoftheMyanmarFFM.aspx. Accessed May 19, 2019.

Warner, M. (2002). Publics and counter publics. *Public Culture, 14*(1), 49–90.

Williams, P. R., & Levy, J. (2019). Atrocities documented, accountability needed: Finding justice for the Rohingya through the ICC and independent mechanism. https://harvardhrj.com/2019/02/atrocities-documented-accountability-needed-finding-justice-for-the-rohingya-through-the-icc-and-independent-mechanism-by-paul-r-williams-jessica-levy/. Accessed May 19, 2019.

Chapter 12
Within a Legal Vacuum, Is Repatriation a Way Forward? Some Theoretical Reflections

Nasreen Chowdhory and Biswajit Mohanty

Abstract This chapter examines the way forward in the case of Rohingyas. While the literature on refugees grapples with the idea of finding a solution to the refugee question where repatriation is often viewed as the way forward. This chapter critically engages to suggest that despite attempting to end the question of refugee cycle, migration and refugee studies, it needs to re-look at the option of repatriation as a way forward. This question becomes more pertinent among the Rohingya refugees in Southern Asia where the original state and the host state refused to provide citizenship and asylum, respectively.

Keywords Asylum · Refugees · Repatriation · Rohingya · Legality

Introduction

States that have experienced colonialism in Asia, including Southeast Asia as well as Northern South Asia, have diverse trajectories of state formation. States in post colonial politics have had a different trajectory, and the focus on borders is very timely. Borders are among the most emblematic and visible symbols of the delimitations of a nation state. The idea of the state is reinforced via border-making, i.e. borders that engage, interact with extreme coercive power, yet constitute an integral part of the territorialisation process of the state. The most contested instrument of state power in the post-colonial project is the border, an important marker of state-making. A border tends to become the natural site of state control, with people residing along this line having the experience of the everyday effect of state policies, through police and other officials of the administration. Borders can be maintained only through intense bureaucratic effort, the legal presence of policing that deliberately includes the resident and excludes those who do not "belong" (Uddin and Chowdhory, 2019). Borders are part of a colonial product that impacts the post-colonial politics of everyday lives

N. Chowdhory
Department of Political Science, University of Delhi, New Delhi, India

B. Mohanty (✉)
Department of Political Science, Deshbandhu College, University of Delhi, New Delhi, India

N. Chowdhory and B. Mohanty (eds.), *Citizenship, Nationalism and Refugeehood of Rohingyas in Southern Asia*,
https://doi.org/10.1007/978-981-15-2168-3_12

of citizens. van Schendel (2013)[1] asserts that states in northern South Asia are unique as a result of uncertain sovereignty and "apprehensive territoriality" across borders. Therefore, borders in Southern Asia are a primary institution of the contemporary states, the construction of a geopolitical world of multiple states and the primary ethico-political division between the possibility of politics inside the state and the necessity of anarchy outside the state. As within all institutions, the inscription of the border and indeed the state requires the constant deployment of resources: the writing of the border, the state and the world again and again (Walker 2010). In this sense, governments, citizens and other agents perform the border, by which I mean that they enact and resist the dominant geopolitical narratives of statecraft as they cross, or are prevented from crossing borders.

States in Southern Asia share common borders, where populations on both sides share similar historical and cultural beliefs. Given the fact that such people have a common cultural underpinning based on cultural context, these countries have a prolonged history of receiving refugees. However, these countries also lack proper legislation that can protect refugees. In India, the categories of aliens, illegal migrants, and refugees are conflated. In the case of India, the decision of refugee determination is not based on either an individual or a group; rather, it is viewed as a bilateral issue between the country of origin and of asylum, for example, the Estate Tamils and the Chakma refugees in Assam prior to 1968. Most of these "refugees" are viewed as foreigners, and the UNHCR has the task of granting them assistance and protection.

India does not have any particular legislation that protects or assists refugees. In terms of determining rights and privileges, the Union Legislature (Parliament) in India has the sole jurisdiction over the subject of citizenship, naturalization and aliens. The official status of the refugee is interpreted under the Foreigners' Act of 1940 and is normally applicable to those who have entered India under false premises. India does not recognize refugees but has adopted a liberal viewpoint as stipulated in the Constitution of India—Article 14: the right to equality; Article 21: the right to personal life and liberty; and Article 25: the freedom to practice and propagate one's own religion, which are guaranteed to citizens and non-citizens alike. The Indian Supreme Court has ruled that the rights of foreigners/refugees are not to be limited to Article 21, to the "protection of life and personal liberty—no persons shall be deprived of his life or personal liberty except by procedure established by law".[2] In spirit, the Constitution of India provides adequate safeguards and upholds the principle of *non-refoulement*: "no refugee should be returned to any country where he or she is likely to face persecution or torture" (Chimni, 1998). As Article 21 of the Constitution assert that state shall not expel or return a refugee "in any manner whatsoever to the frontiers of territories where his life or freedom would be threatened on account of his race, religion, nationality, membership in a particular

[1] See Gellner (2013).

[2] See Saxena (1986). Chowdhory 2018b. Chowdhory 2007 (unpublished PhD dissertation, Belonging in exile and 'home': the politics of repatriation in South Asia, McGill University.

social group, or political opinion",[3] which reflects the spirit of the principle of *non-refoulement*.[4] Some refugees[5] have benefited from some of these rights enshrined in the Constitution of India, and a few cases exist where they were successful in drawing the attention of judiciary—a few of these cases were in the High Court of Madras.[6] The Supreme Court of India has also stayed orders of the deportation of refugees, for example, Maiwand's Trust of Afghan Human Freedom v. State of Punjab,[7] N. D. Pancholi v. State of Punjab and others.[8]

Even so, the application of these rights in the true sense has been difficult. The Indian state does not recognize the rights of non-citizens and has not stipulated any special rights. The rights of refugees, aliens and asylum seekers are not demarcated, and they are all viewed as "foreigners". Those belonging to the "non-citizens" category have few or no specific rights. But with the liberal interpretation of the Indian judicial system to act responsibly and effectively, some of these cases have been tried on a case-by-case basis.[9] One such case was heard during the time when the National Human Rights Commission (NHRC) had approached the Supreme Court under Article 32 of the Indian Constitution to argue that Articles 14, 21 and 25 were violated.

---

[3] Article 33, Paragraph (1) of the 1951 Convention on the Status of Refugees.

[4] The obligation of *non-refoulement* in part of Article 33 (1) of the 1951 Convention Related the Status of Refugee Determination.

[5] Gurunathan and others v. Government of India (WP No. S 6708 and 7916 of 1992); A.C Mohd. Siddique v. Government of India and others (1998 (47) DRJ (DB), p. 74).

[6] Two such cases exist where refugees were able to approach the court to argue against the issue of repatriation. The two unreported decisions of the Madras High Court in P. Nedumaran and Dr. S. Ramadoss v. The Union of India and the State of Tamil Nadu (1992) assessed the "voluntariness of repatriation process." In the case of P. Nedumaran v. Union of India, a Sri Lankan refugee appeared before the High Court of Madras and presented a *writ* of mandamus. It advised the Union of India and the State of Tamil Nadu to permit the UNHCR official to ascertain the voluntariness of "refugees going back to Sri Lanka" and to permit refugees to continue to stay in the camps in India. The court expressed the verdict "since the UNHCR was involved in ascertaining the voluntariness of the refugees' return to Sri Lanka, hence being a World Agency, it is not for the court to consider whether the consent is voluntary or not". The Court acknowledged the competence and impartiality of the representatives of the UNHCR. However, the case is pending before the National Human Rights Commission of India, 13 August 1997, cited from T. Ananthachari, "Refugees in India: Legal Framework, Law Enforcement and Security", in *ISIL Year Book of International Humanitarian and Refugee Law* 7 (2001). In the matter of Malavika Karlekar v. Union of India, the Supreme Court directed a stay on a deportation order of the Andaman Burmese refugees, since "their claims for refugee status were pending determination and a *prima facie* case is made out for grant of refugee status". Given these past precedents, in 1993, the Indian Supreme Court stated that the Chakma are not entitled to citizenship under Section 6-A of the Citizenship Act. However, in an earlier judgment, the Supreme Court in Luis De Raedt v. Union of India and State of Arunachal Pradesh v. Khudiram Chakma clarified that no one shall be deprived of his or her life and liberty without due process of law. Overall, the Indian judiciary has played a constructive role in protecting the rights of the refugees.

[7] Crl WP No. 125 and 126 of 1986.

[8] N. D. Pancholi v. State of Punjab and others [WP (civil) No. 1294 of 1987, unreported].

[9] Khudiram Chakma had approached the Supreme Court when his life was threatened within the state of Arunachal Pradesh. The Supreme Court observed that "the fundamental right of the foreigner is confined to Article 21 for life and liberty and does not include the right to reside and settle in

Some of these rights have been remedied by the enforcement of a few fundamental rights by the Supreme Court under Article 32[10] and by the High Court under Article 226. In one such case, when a Chakma refugee's rights were infringed upon by an activist student union, the court directed "relief on the basis of aliens under Article 14 and 21" (Chimni 2000, p. 492).[11] There have also been other situations in which the courts have prevented and "stayed" such deportation proceedings.[12]

The process of refugee determination has been quite indiscriminate. This process is determined neither by individuals nor groups; rather, it is based on specific evidence produced (by the refugee) to support his/her refugee claim. Each claimant has to bear the burden of proof until all the materials are collected and collated. Internationally acknowledged information is available on the region from which the claimant has arrived. In certain situations, the validity of the information obtained may be reconfirmed by the UNHCR office in the country of origin. The UNHCR office works on a limited mandate and capacity in India, providing a subsistence allowance to refugees on a case-by-case basis. Two of these specific cases concerned refugees who had illegally tried to leave the country and were apprehended—the case of Mehmud Ghazaleh[13] (an Iranian refugee) and Shah Ghazai and his minor son, Assadullah (two Afghan refugees). Ghazaleh was registered with the UNHCR and was illegally crossing over to Nepal through the Sonauli border in the district of Maharajgunj, Uttar Pradesh.[14] The Afghani refugees were apprehended near the Attari border in Amritsar, Punjab, while illegally exiting India for Afghanistan. These cases prove that refugees have limited or no rights other than the few rights provided to aliens in the Constitution of India, which does not acknowledge refugees as a category. Sometimes refugees may have valid documents while entering the country of asylum (more applicable to the case of South Asia) but fail to obtain an extension of a travel permit. Under such circumstances, refugees may be issued "leave India" notices. Allegations have arisen that refugees may be security threats to the "stability and integrity of the country" and have *mala-fide* intent to commit harm. A refugee's detention period is not well documented or recorded until authorities have proven credentials of the individuals concerned.[15] Under these circumstances,

this country as mentioned in Article 19 (1) (e) which is applicable only to citizens of this country". State of Arunachal Pradesh v. Khudiram Chakma 1994 Supp. (1) SCC 615.

[10]Article 32 of the Constitution of India delineates the Right to Constitutional Remedies. The Supreme Court has the power to issue direction, order writs, etc. for the enforcement of any rights as enshrined in Part III (Fundamental Rights) of the Constitution of India.

[11]See National Human Rights Commission v. Union of India, [(1996) 1 SCC 295; Khudiram Chakma v. Union of India (1994) Supp. 1 SCC 614].

[12]SAHRDC, Refugee Protection in India, October 1997. Writ Petition nos. 450/83; 605-607/84; 169/87; 732/87; 747/87; 243/88; 336/88.

[13]A. D. Cri No. 48 of 1994.

[14]The refugee was travelling with forged documents and was detained by authorities who discovered that his documents were forged. The refugee was arrested and placed in the local police station at Sonauli, and a case was registered of FIR u/s 419/420/468/471 IPC read with Sec 3/6 of the Passport Act and *Sec 14* Foreigners' Act.

[15]An Iranian refugee, Syed Ata Mohamadi, recognized by the UNHCR was arrested at the Bombay International airport en route to Canada. The refugee was detained for traveling under a false name.

each person is detained by officials and *prima facie* investigated. The longevity of these laws remains a question open to interpretation. Since these cases are tried on a case-by-case basis, an opportunity exists for partisanship and for overlooking the humanitarian aspect of refugee needs (Chowdhory 2018b).

Overall, the Southern Asia region lacks a consensus on the definition of refugee, and its states have made meagre attempts to address this issue. The basic principle underlying India's refugee policy is to view the problem strictly from a bilateral perspective. Therefore, in the absence of specific laws, all existing laws such as the Criminal Procedure Code, the Indian Penal Code and the Evidence Act apply to refugees, as well. As for the minimum standard of treatment of refugees, India has undertaken an obligation by ratifying the International Covenant on Civil and Political Rights and the International Covenant on Economic, Social and Cultural Rights to accord equal treatment to all non-citizens (on par with citizens) wherever possible. Presently, India, as a member of the Executive Committee of the UNHCR, has a responsibility to abide by international standards on the treatment of refugees. However, none of the countries in South Asia are signatories to the International Refugee Convention. India ratified the International Covenant on Civil and Political Rights (ICCPR) as well as the International Convention on Economic, Social and Cultural Rights (ICESCR) in 1976. India ratified the Convention on the Elimination of All Forms of Discrimination against Women (CEDAW) in 1979, under which Article 1 imposes legally binding obligations. In addition, India accepted the principles of *non-refoulement* as envisaged in the Bangkok Principles of 1966, which were formulated for the guidance of member states with respect to matters concerning the status and treatment of refugees. These principles also contained provisions relating to repatriation, the right to compensation, granting asylum and the minimum standard of treatment in the state of asylum (Chowdhory 2007).

While acknowledging that the Indian state does not give status to refugees, but its behaviour, activities, and functioning when it comes to treating refugees at par with rights given to the aliens or foreigners.[16]

Interestingly, the crossing of boundaries by individuals obliquely generates conceptualization of hospitality as the process spatially creates the categories of "host" and "guest" by virtue of the side of the border they belong to. As this passage across borders is "everyday practice" (Still, 2010), it provides a semblance of "universality" to the concept of hospitality. Even though extension of hospitality might be deeply entrenched in the cultural practices of many nations, the modalities of laws involved, regulations made and restrictions imposed create an inherent diversity in the way it is practised. Hospitality constantly negotiates the spatial factor where by "being inside" is privileged over "coming from outside" where inside and outside is constantly positioned against each other (Chowdhory, Hussain, & Kajla 2019). This brings us to Derrida's conceptualization where he projects the "law of unconditional hospitality" that permits complete openness compared to the "laws of hospitality"

After being detained for a month, the refugee was released only with the intervention of the Bombay High Court.

[16]See Chowdhory, Shamna, & Meghna Kajla (2019).

that conditions the access to entry through rules, norms and regulations (Derrida & Dufourmantelle, 2000). If one is permitting unconditional inclusion, the second is creating conditioned inclusion and in its fullest, exclusion. The transgression of borders permitted by the hospitality of the state creates "zones of coexistence in the inside" between insiders and permitted outsiders. The use of "laws of hospitality" to different groups of permitted outsiders manifests in the abstract creation of "good outsiders" and "bad outsiders" where state wields significant power in differentiating between the good and the bad.

Is Repatriation as Way Forward?

Few studies on refugees have focused on the repatriation (Rogge & Akol, 1989; Preston, 1993). The earlier approaches of the 1980s on refugees placed the responsibility on the host state to solve refugee problems rather than on states from which they had fled (Hansen, 1982; Harrell-Bond, 1986; Rogge, 1985; Desbarats, 1985; Conner, 1986; Kibreab, 1987). Previous approaches on refugee studies were reactive, exile-oriented and refugee-specific as opposed to the present discourse on refugees, which seems to be more proactive, homeland-oriented and holistic.

Most traditional academic research on refugees relates either to the causes of refugee flow or to the development of mechanisms to prevent the outflow of refugees to neighbouring countries. In view of the inherent inadequacies in such traditional research, scholars have studied the political context of refugees (Dillon, 1995; Xenos, 1996, p. 235).[17] Other scholars such as Bascom (1994, pp. 225–48) and Rogge (1994, pp. 14–49) have studied the socio-economic fallout of refugees. Scholars have also examined the perspectives of refugees' long-term interests and possible rehabilitation.[18] Few scholars have examined the motivations for the repatriation of refugees and their alleged ties or links to their countries of origin and their ability to regain status through repatriation. Few academic research focuses on the aspects of reconstruction and rehabilitation among returnee-refugees in their countries of origin.[19] Bascom (1994) analyses the dynamics of repatriation process of Eritrean

[17]See Xenos (1996, p. 235). Xenos discusses how refugees can be used as pawns in struggles between states, e.g. the Haitian boat people. He refers to them as "strategic human flows". The basis of these flows, Xenos maintains, "is the development of the state in terms of national identity and the social construction of a people within specific territory, the hyphenating of state within borders". Dillon, on the other hand, discusses "the scandal of the refugees", which is a reaction to being outside, of being "other" and part of "otherness". Dillon highlights the "otherness" of the refugees as being outside the fundamental "ontological determination of international politics and its exclusionary pressures". See Dillon (1995). The Scandal of the Refugees: Some Reflection on the 'Inter' of International Relations and Continental Thought. (Private paper copy with the author as mentioned in Warner (1999), Dillon (1995).

[18]Harrell-Bond (1989) and Allen & Morsink (1994) have argued that some international agencies encourage repatriation. Coles (1985, 1987, 1989, 1992a, 1992b) challenges his reader to re-think the "exilic bias" of resolving refugee problems in contemporary refugee law.

[19]With the exception of Laura Hammond and Barbara Harrell-Bond.

refugees from Eastern Sudan and contends that the mass movements of human beings symbolize a changing world order. Rogge (1991) emphasizes the importance of the social transformation of refugees in exile as a contributory factor in their repatriation. The variation in decision-making within two or three generations of refugee groups is significant. The fundamental preconditions for "voluntary repatriation", according to a minimalist interpretation, are the cessation of military conflict, regime change (where applicable) and the stability of the home government (Chowdhory 2018b).

The literature also tends to overlook the nexus between the legal position of refugees in their countries of asylum and their choice to repatriate. Therefore, it is imperative to understand the conditions for the "voluntary" repatriation of refugees. It is possible that refugees could return home after considering their options, but their repatriation would depend on their personal aspirations and the available information on the wider structural changes that may have occurred in their countries of origin; however, most refugees do not have the experience of such a balanced decision-making process when they repatriate (Chowdhory, 2018a). Stein et al. (1995) suggest a classification of repatriation along the continuum of conflict resolution in countries of origin. The different classifications are: ricochet repatriation, with almost immediate return; relocation-stimulated, when host governments try to move refugees into camps; alienated-induced, when some refugees cannot identify with the emerging refugee community; secondary relocation-stimulated, when host governments try to move refugees to settlements a long way from the border; and the major repatriation, where the UNHCR promotes mass return. The literature does not address the lack of political status of refugees in the countries of asylum and the consequences upon refugees' decisions to repatriate. The gap in the literature is manifested in several ways: first, the resolution to refugee crises seems to be more homeland-oriented, which means little to refugees; second, studies on repatriation have failed to address why refugees are inclined to repatriate; and third, the linkages between refugees as "temporary" exiles encourage notions of repatriation (Chowdhory, 2018a).

Repatriation can occur based on the terms and conditions involved in return. The decision to repatriate often requires a sense that the return would be long-lasting or durable. The durability of repatriation is due to a "change in circumstance in the country of origin" that would make repatriation a feasible and preferable option for refugees. However, certain assumptions are involved in the notion of "change" that can be difficult to ascertain, which leads to an emphasis on the "voluntariness" of return.[20] Scholars of international refugee law emphasize the changes in the historical and political context of the Convention to stress the importance of the "voluntariness" of repatriation. The notion of voluntary repatriation operates within the boundaries of refugee law (based on interpretation of both the Statute and Convention): it relies on the ability of the country of origin to use it to its own advantage. In its *Handbook for Emergencies*, the UNHCR asserts, "[a] voluntary repatriation program presumes there are refugees who return to country of origin based on change in conditions in their country".[21] Elsewhere, the UNHCR describes voluntary repatriation as "a

[20] See UN Doc. A/Res/38/121 (1983).

[21] UNHCR 1983 at 231.

practical technique for affecting the safe and dignified return of repatriation once the conditions that forced them to flee or to remain outside their country no longer exist".[22] The UNHCR can legally determine when repatriation will occur, and it can also send refugees back based on the provisions stipulated in cessation clauses. The UNHCR's *Protection Guidelines on Voluntary Repatriation* states, "the idea behind promoting and subsequently encouraging voluntary repatriation is to give the refugee an opportunity to voluntarily return home with UNHCR protection and assistance before he or she formally ceases to be a refugee".[23] The drive to resolve refugee problems is accomplished when refugees make a voluntary and conscious decision to return. The countries of asylum are obliged to help refugees repatriate in accordance with the accepted standards for voluntary repatriation. The concept of "safe return" has gradually replaced the concept of "temporary protection" that had legitimized instances of "involuntary return".[24] The idea of "safe return" in repatriation literature has a "lower threshold" than voluntary repatriation, so it is applied when countries of asylum seem inclined to apply the cessation clause and promote only safe return.[25] International norms require states to acquire voluntary consent from refugees prior to the repatriation process. The process begins with a visit by UNHCR officials to refugee camps; they request that the refugees fill questionnaires to verify their consent and the voluntary nature of their return. In some cases, refugees have affirmed their

[22]UN Doc. A/AC.96/815 (1993).

[23]According to the cessation clause, refugee status can be withdrawn when "situations have improved in the country of origin" and every other factor contributing to refugee's status ceases to exist. An interesting notion as in most situations, the timing of withdrawing the status is crucial as it is meant to act as a deterrent and refugee are encouraged to return with *slight* improvement in country of origin.

[24]The General Assembly of the United Nations resolved in the Resolution 8(1) of 1946: "[N] O refugees or displaced persons who have been finally and definitely, in complete freedom and after receiving full knowledge of the facts, including adequate information from the governments of their countries of origin express valid objections to returning to their countries of origin…shall be compelled to return to their country of origin. It was much later that the Statute establishing the Office of the UNHCR called upon the government to reiterate that repatriation had to be based on voluntary action of refugees. This was reaffirmed in the Conclusions adopted by the Executive Committee of the High Commissioner's Program. These have a binding character where the UNHCR is concerned, the texts of Conclusion no 18 (XXXI) and Conclusion No. 40 (XXXVI); both emphasize the voluntary character of repatriation itself. Likewise, Conclusion No. 40 states: The repatriation of refugees should only take place at their expressed wishes; the voluntary and individual character of repatriation of refugees and the need for it to be carried out under conditions of absolute safety, preferably to the place of residence of the refugee in his country of origin, should always be respected".

[25]The cessation clause can be divided into two broad sets: the first set comprises four clauses that relate to a change in personal circumstances of the refugee, brought about by the refugee's own act, and which results in the acquisition of national protection so that international protection is no longer necessary. The second set comprises of clauses that relate to the change in the objective circumstances in connection with which the refugee has been recognized, so that international protection is no longer justified (the ceased circumstances' cessation clause).

consent without being properly informed of the changes in their countries of origin or other such manipulation.[26]

Chimni (cited in Newman & Selm, 2003, p. 200) examines the shift in the focus of international agencies from voluntary repatriation to the concept of safe return; in doing so, he challenges the normative basis of voluntary repatriation. The author argues that voluntary repatriation has been replaced by "sustainable return", an expression that describes the status of refugees upon their return to the homeland. "Sustainable return" includes the physical and material security of returnees as well as their integration with the given civil society and state. The *Convention Relating to Status of Refugees* does not explicitly include provisions related to the "voluntary" nature of repatriation. Chimni claims that it was the Statute of the UNHCR that had some provisions, a claim supported by Hathaway (1997): "it is wishful legal thinking to suggest that a 'voluntariness' requirement can be superimposed on the text of the Refugee Convention" (Hathaway, 1997). Hathaway further opines, "once a receiving state determines that protection in the country of origin is viable, it is entitled to withdraw refugee status" (Hathaway, 1997, p. 553). Therefore, countries of asylum have their own impetus to create conditions for "safe return". Under these circumstances, refugees have no option but to follow the asylum state's bidding and "go back". The idea of return is based on subjective opinions of refugees living in countries of asylum. Goodwin-Gill (1997, p. 276) observed that such views "effectively substitute 'objective' (change of) circumstances for the refugee's subjective assessment, thereby crossing the refugee/non-refugee line" (Goodwin-Gill, 1997, p. 276). The assumption that repatriation occurs when all conditions are favourable is, in fact, how it is intended that asylum states should deal with refugees prior to the use of the cessation clause. In other words, it is assumed that the cessation clause will only be used by asylum states when "the circumstances in connection with which he has been recognized as a refugee have ceased to exist" (Article 1C (5) of the 1951 Convention). Thus, the criteria that must be understood for repatriation are as follows: first, there should be a decision made by refugees that is explicitly expressed to the host state to return; second, there should be certain minimum changes in the country of origin; and third, the UNHCR facilitates the return (which might go against the very tenets of its mandate).

The UNHCR determines the "voluntariness" of repatriation. The UNHCR acts in an advisory capacity, providing information and assistance to refugees, in order that they may make informed decisions, to facilitate, promote or certify self-repatriation.

[26]This was the case during the repatriation of Sri Lankan Tamil refugees in 1990–92 when UNHCR was accused of working against the interest of refugees. Some local NGOs in Tamil Nadu (India) questioned the role of UNHCR in ascertaining whether the refugees had voluntarily consented to go back. Most of the refugees were shown a video showing positive changes in Sri Lanka that enabled refugees to consent; in reality, the returned refugees failed to notice any distinctive change in circumstances. As asserted by refugee groups residing in open relief camps in Pessalai, located north of Sri Lanka.

The UNHCR defines modalities of assistance in guidelines[27] on voluntary repatriation, or what it calls "refugee-induced voluntary repatriation", indicating that its facilitation of voluntary repatriation is defined as:

> Assisting refugees, *in situations where UNHCR cannot [promote] voluntary repatriation* to make an informed decision reflecting their own priorities and standards and, once they decide providing them with the necessary support and guidelines so that they can achieve the goals of their decisions (Handbook on Voluntary Repatriation: International Protection, UNHCR Geneva 1996).

Initially, the UNHCR had been reluctant to facilitate repatriation of refugee groups who explicitly desired to return. However, officials who were then involved were convinced that "the overall assessment of the situations in the country of origin" was such that repatriation "is *not* in the best interest of the refugees concerned".[28] The initial mandate of the UNHCR changed in 1996, when repatriation was re-interpreted to respect "the refugees' right to return to their country at any time, UNHCR may *facilitate voluntary repatriation*...when refugees indicate a strong desire to return voluntarily...[and] it is safe for most refugees to return".[29]

The "promotion" of voluntary repatriation in the Handbook seems to represent an evolution of the UNHRC, with a move from an advocacy role, with "actions taken from the very outset of a refugee situation which could not foster a climate for return",[30] to one that promotes repatriation. The earlier definition was much more elaborate: "Furthering or advancing the development and realization of voluntary repatriation as a durable solution to the *refugee problem* on the basis of the principles of international co-operation and State responsibility to create conditions conducive to the safe and dignified return of refugees".[31] The concept of "promotion" now involves "planning and organizing the voluntary repatriation of refugees under conditions which are conducive to their safe return and durable reintegration".[32] Since

---

[27]Note that the following definition of "facilitating" voluntary repatriation is categorically different from that used in the past when it characterized UNHCR's role as regards voluntary repatriation at large a time, moreover when the major repatriation took place after clear-cut changes in the country of origin and the required assistance was of technical and financial nature.

[28]UNHCR Document. (1993). "Protection Guidelines on Voluntary Repatriation". (emphasis original) Note: facilitated repatriation can take place on the basis of either bilateral or tripartite agreements. Thus, there is a slight difference between facilitating and promoting repatriation. The difference is more in the nature of assistance and whether UNHCR has been instrumental in providing that exact nature of assistance. A case in point may be the Guatemalan refugees in Mexico.

[29]UNHCR Handbook. (1996). *Voluntary Repatriation: International Protection*. (emphasis original). UNHCR seems to confine its role in situations in which it considers repatriation premature to providing guidance and making its position known.

[30]UNHCR Handbook. (1996). *Voluntary Repatriation: International Protection*. (emphasis is original).

[31]UNHCR Document. (1993). *Protection Guidelines on Voluntary Repatriation*. (emphasis in original). Although there is no clear reference as to why the state has been given the responsibility and what the nature of the state is, it might be used in the context of liability and accountability for wrongful acts and their consequences, and it may be construed as such.

[32]UNHCR Handbook. (1996). *Voluntary Repatriation: International Protection*. Similarly: UNHCR Doc. (1993) (where these activities are discussed separately under the heading of "encouraging" voluntary repatriation: a heading that serves to underline that encouragement of the

the mid-eighties, the UNHCR's right to initiate the organization of repatriation was accepted and endorsed by the Executive Committee (and the General Assembly).[33] The 1951 *Convention Relating to the Status of Refugees*[34] and the 1967 *Protocol*[35] do not explicitly refer to the repatriation of refugees. Article 1(C) (4) of the 1951 Convention stipulates that refugee status ceases if refugees voluntarily re-establish themselves in their country of origin. Furthermore, the successful completion of a voluntary repatriation programme would indicate that the circumstances that caused the refugees to flee no longer exist. Voluntary repatriation can occur only when certain conditions have been met by countries of origin, which in turn facilitates the safe and dignified return of refugees. However, repatriation becomes a tool to suspend the status of refugees in asylum states, where a cessation clause may be applicable; it may also represent another way to prevent non-refoulement under Article 33, whereby the refugee status only ceases when there is either voluntary re-establishment (not just return), or when a change of circumstances has been shown to exist in the country of origin. In this process, states may find an ally in an unusual place, the UNHCR. The UNHCR has agency-based standards of repatriation that often conflict with the true meaning of cessation clauses. The UNHCR has adopted "a spectrum of institutional positions on repatriation which explicitly includes the facilitation of return 'even where UNHCR does not consider that objectively it is safe for refugees to return" (Hathaway, 2005). Zieck disagrees with Hathaway's argument of institutional over-reaching by the UNHCR but concedes that it might be possible. Zieck holds the Convention responsible for a lack of proper guidance in the modalities involved in voluntary repatriation. The 1951 Convention did not make any reference to voluntary repatriation, not in terms of solutions "for it can be argued that the fourth cessation clause is predicated on voluntary repatriation" (Zieck, 2005, pp. 217–48). Article 35 of the 1951 Convention provides a specific obligation on the part of states that accords certain *carte blanche* for the UNHCR. This article stipulates clearly that states need

solutions only takes place after its promotions have yielded the desired conditions "conducive to return". The Handbook retains a similar emphasis by its distinguishing between the promotion of solutions on the one hand, and the promotion of voluntary repatriation on the other).

[33]In addition, the perception of UNHCR's speaking "on behalf of the international community as a whole, representing an universal, non-political, humanitarian concern for refugees" could be adduced (Statement of the High Commissioner to the Third Committee of the General Assembly 1992; text printed in; 4 IJRL 1992 at 541). Recognition of this perception was formulated as a prerequisite for UNHCR's effectively extending international protection to refugees. An alternative characterization of UNHCR: "the High Commissioner is the embodiment of international refugee humanitarianism and the father of the world's refugee" (Kelley, 1990, p. 282).

[34]"As a result of events occurring before January, 1 1951, and owing to *well-founded fear* of being persecuted for reasons of race, religion, nationality, membership of a particular social group or political opinion, outside the country of his nationality and is unable or, owing to such fear, is willing to avail himself of the protection of that country; or who, not having a nationality and being outside the country of his former habitual residence as a result of such events, is unable or; owing to such fear, is unwilling to return to it" (emphasis added).

[35]The 1967 Protocol relating to the Status of Refugees removed the "temporal and geographical limitations" contained in the 1951 Convention. The Protocol was intended to broaden the basis of "refugee-hood" criteria.

to provide ultimate cooperation to facilitate the functions of the UNHCR. Article 2 of the 1967 Protocol also requires states to work towards complete cooperation with the UNHCR in matters related to refugee determination. In essence, Zieck disagrees with the concept of institutional overreaching but holds the Convention responsible for any misuse by the UNHCR (Chowdhory 2007).

The OAU 1969 *Convention Governing the Specific Aspects of Refugee Problems in Africa* is one of the binding documents between signatory countries and the international agency, the UNHCR, that explicitly treats some of the issues related to "voluntary repatriation". It recognizes the voluntary character of repatriation and specifies the responsibilities of both the country of asylum and the country of origin.[36] The Cartegena Declaration also includes provisions that relate to repatriation. The principle includes a range of issues such as the provisions of adequate information to refugees, freedom of movement, non-discrimination, access to means of subsistence and land, as well as access of the UNHCR to the returnees. None of the documents directly address the regional component of repatriation other than a few treaty provisions in the 1969 OAU Convention Governing the Specific Aspects of Refugee Problems in Africa,[37] which refers to "new circumstances prevailing in [the] country of origin" that enable refugees "to return without risk and to take up a normal and peaceful life without fear of being disturbed or punished".[38] But some of these changes in countries of origin are less discernible.

In relation to Rohingya refugees, the situation is quite complex. The country of asylum and origin appear to be contemplating repatriation as the way to end the refugee cycle. As indicated in all chapters in the volume, authors have explored the possibility of repatriation. However, in order to make repatriation success, it is critical that repatriation should be voluntary, and states abide by the principle of refoulement. Interestingly, countries in Southern Asia are not signatories to the Refugee Convention yet, though in practice states seem to be abiding by the principle of refoulement.

The phenomena of undocumented underclass, in legal parlance, termed as refugees and migrants, are the product of the internal politics of the sovereign states and their statelessness is a function of the dynamics of border and geopolitics at play. The sovereign states internally create conditions where people are governed through calibrated management and/or through confinement of human movement without any rights within a given geographic space. A community and concomitant cultural body is constructed through nationalism, religion and ethnicity discourses. Various geographic transversal forces enable purgation of the cultural community from their spatial habitations. The process of purgation leads to the origination of stateless people who move across the borders and live in a state of precarity. They become both analytical as well as legal categories. The rubric of explanations of refugee crisis spans

[36] See Article V of the 1969 OAU Convention Governing the Specific Problems of Refugees in Africa; see also CM/ Res. 399 (XXIV) Resolution on Voluntary Repatriation of African Refugees of the OAU Council of Ministers, Addis-Ababa, 1975.

[37] See Zieck (1999).

[38] Art. V (4).

different generative contexts—nationalism, ethnic cleansing, human rights, assimilation, gender and citizenship. The declaration of 1982 citizenship law in Myanmar and its ramification has outlawed Rohingyas from Rakhine state and rendered them stateless. The violence inflicted on Rohingyas in many instances is referred to as "nothing less than genocide" (The Guardian, May 31, 2015). This reflects on the ways in which Rohingya being an ethnic, linguistic and religious minority have perpetually been oppressed and mistreated both by the Burmese military and also by the larger Buddhist community in Myanmar.

The response of the Myanmar government and society to the plight of Rohingyas reflects the normalisation of organised structural violence against them. The contentious historical narrative of the Muslims in Rakhine, and sustained policies and statutory practices of discrimination and frequent episode of brutality and violence has relegated Rohingyas to physical, territorial and symbolic margins of Burmese society. The persecution of Rohingyas has constituted a continuum of violence that has escalated to one of the gravest human rights violation and humanitarian crisis of our times. The Rohingya crisis cannot be conclusively explained in its totality if we confine ourselves to the lens of citizenship as a legal status. The denial of citizenship is more than their deprivation that manifests as lack of birth certificates, absence of their names in the beneficiary list and the lack of identification documents that invalidates their existence. This structured exclusion means being born less than equal, being a foreigner in the only place one has ever known since birth, the inability to claim the very resources that one is entitled in their own land. Such exclusion shows the fear of potential discrimination and violent torture from the very state that should have ideally protected them. Bangladesh as the first country of asylum for Rohingyas finds it demanding to accommodate the increasing number of Rohingya refugees. Initially the government of Bangladesh was hesistant to receive aid and humanitarian assistance from various international organisations. The Bangladeshi officials feared that better facilities would induce a "pull factor" that will encourage more influx of Rohingyas to the state of Bangladesh. Mediated by China, and Myanmar, Bangladesh had entered into a bilateral agreement in January 2018 on the repatriation of refugees. According to the briefing given to United Nations by the Bangladeshi Foreign Minister in March 2019, such an effort to repatriate did not materialize as none of the Rohingya refugee did not consider Rakhine region to have a "conducive environment" necessary for them to return. In August 2019, the government of Bangladesh initiated a similar joint exercise with the UNHCR to regulate the modalities for offering the option of return to Myanmar for over 3000 documented Rohingya refugees. Eventhough UNHCR reiterates the primacy of 'voluntariness' in the repatriation process, it simultaneously asserts that the "eligibility for return" cannot be conflated with their individual choice of refugees to return. Various Rohingya advocavy groups had voiced their concern over such attempts of "premature repatriation" without taking into account the ground realities in Rakhine region. The lack of structured, systematic and transparent plan for repatriation along with reports of continued persecution of Rohingyas in Myanmar prevented attempts to initiate their voluntary return.

The asylum states can provide minimum assistance and protection to refugees, but they appear reluctant to institutionalize the role in terms of formal charters of rights. Refugees are suppose to encouraged to return to their country of origin, and in most instances, the country of asylum facilitates the process. The janus-face of the asylum state acts as a protector if need be, but it does not grant formal rights, tilts the balance of power in favour of state bureaucrats, who have a significant influence on the determination of the future of refugees, such as determining the timing of repatriation etc. Therefore, from the vantage point of the country of asylum, repatriation represents the end of refugee cycle which is rather difficult method as a way forward.

References

Allen, T., & Morsink, H. (Eds.). (1994). *When refugees go home*. Geneva: UNRISD.

Bascom, J. (1994). The dynamics of refugee repatriation: The case of Eritrean in eastern Sudan. In W. T. Gould & A. M. Findlay (Eds.), *Population migration and the changing world order* (pp. 225–248). New York: Wiley.

Chowdhory, N. (2007) (unpublished dissertation). *Belonging in exile and 'home': the politics of repatriation in South Asia*. Canada: McGill University.

Chowdhory, N. (2018a). *Refugees, citizenship and belonging, the contested terrains*. Singapore: Springer

Chowdhory, N. (2018b). *Citizenship, Refugees and Belonging in South Asia: A Contested Terrains*. Singapore: Springer.

Chowdhory, N., Shamna., T. P., & Kajla, M. (2019, August). The idea of protection: Norms and practices of refugee management in India. *Refugee Watch 53*, 36–55.

Chimni, B. S. (1994a). The legal conditions of refugees in India. *Journal of Refugee Studies, 7*(4).

Chimni, B. S. (1994b). Symposium on the human rights of refugees. *Journal of Refugee Studies, 7*(4).

Chimni, B. S. (1998). The geopolitics of refugee studies: A view from the South. *Journal of Refugee Studies, 11*, 350–375.

Chimni, B.S. (2000). Globalization, humanitarianism and the erosion of refugee protection. *Journal of Refugee Studies*, 13(3), 243–263. https://doi.org/10.1093/jrs/13.3.243

Chimni, B. S. (2003). Post-conflict peace building and the return of refugees: Concepts, practices and institutions. In Edward Newman & Joanne van Selm (Eds.), *Refugees and Forced Displacement International Security Human Vulnerability and the State*. New York: United Nation Press.

Coles, G. (1985). Voluntary repatriation: A background study. Paper prepared for the Round Table on Voluntary Repatriation. *International Institute of Humanitarian Law/UNHCR San Remo, Italy*.

Coles, G. (1987). The human rights approach to the solution of the refugee problem: A theoretical and practical enquiry. In A. Nash (Ed.), *Human rights and the protection of refugees under international law* (pp. 195–222). Montreal: Canadian Human Rights Foundation.

Coles, G. (1989). Approaching the refugee problem today. In G. Loescher & L. Monahan (Eds.), *Refugees and international relations*. New York: Oxford University Press.

Coles, G. (1992a). *Appeal to donor governments*. Asmara: Commission for Eritrean Refugee Affairs, Provisional Government of Eritrea.

Coles, G. (1992b). *Approaches and strategies in the repatriation of Eritrean refugees*. Asmara: Provisional Government of Eritrea.

Conner, K. (1986). Rationales for the movement of Afghan refugees to Peshawar. In G. Farr & J. Merriam (Eds.), *Afghan resistance: The politics of survival* (pp. 151–190). Boulder, CO: Westview Press.

Desbarats, J. (1985). Policy influences on refugee settlement patterns. *Kroeber Society Anthropological Papers,* 49–63.

Derrida, J. & Dufourmantelle, A. (2000). *Of Hospitality* (trans. R. Bowlby) (pp. 77–91). Stanford: Stanford University Press.

Dillon, M. (1995). *The Asylum Seeker and the Stranger: An other politics, hospitality and justice.* Paper presented in international studies association conference, Chicago.

Gellner, D. N. (2013). *Borderland Lives in Northern Asia.* Duke University Press: Durham and London.

Goodwin-Gill, G. (1997). *The refugee in international law* (2nd ed.). Oxford: Clarendon Press.

Hansen, A. (1982). Self-settled rural refugees in Africa: The case of Angolans in Zambian villages. In A. Hansen & A. Oliver-Smith (Eds.), *Involuntary migration and resettlement: The problems and responses of dislocated people* (pp. 13–36). Boulder, CO: Westview Press.

Hathaway, J. C. (1997). The meaning of repatriation. *International Journal of Refugee Law, 9*(4), 551–558.

Hathaway, J. (2005). *The Rights of Refugees.* Cambridge: Cambridge University Press.

Harrell-Bond, B. (1986), *Imposing aid: emergency assistance to refugees.* Oxford: Oxford University Press

Harrell-Bond, B. (1989). Repatriation: Under what circumstances is it the most desirable solution for refugees? An agenda for research. *African Studies Review, 1,* 41–69.

Kelley, N. (1990). Refugee women and protection: Criteria and practices for determining refugee status. Summary of comments made at the CRDD working group on women refugee claimants: Training workshop for members, RHO's and legal services. Toronto. Canada.

Kibreab, G. (1987). *Refugees and development in Africa: The case of Eritrea.* Trenton: The Red Sea Press.

Kunz, E. F. (1973). The refugee in flight: Kinetic models and forms of displacement. *International Migration Review, 7*(2), 125–146. https://doi.org/10.1177/019791837300700201.

Preston, R. (Ed.). (1993). *The integration of returned exiles, former combatants and other war affected namibians.* Windhoek: Namibia Institute for Social and Economic Research.

Rogge, J. (1977). A geography of refugees: Some illustrations from Africa. *The Professional Geographer, 24*(2), 186–193.

Rogge, J. (1985). *Too many too long: Sudan's twenty year refugee dilemma.* Totowa, NJ: Rowman and Allenheld.

Rogge, J. R. (1991). Refugees in Southeast Asia: An uncertain Future? *Canadian Geographer / Le Géographe canadien, 35,* 190–193. https://doi.org/10.1111/j.1541-0064.1991.tb01288.x.

Rogge, J. (1994). Repatriation of refugee: Not so simple 'optimum solution'. In T. Allen & H. Morsink (Eds.), *When refugees go home* (pp. 14–49). Trenton: Africa World Press.

Rogge, J. R., & Akol, J. O. (1989) Repatriation: Its role in resolving Africa's refugee dilemma. *International Migration Review, 23*(2): 184–200.

Saxena, J. (1986). Legal status of refugees, the Indian position. *Indian Journal of International Law, 26,* 501–515.

Schendal, V. W. (2013). Making the Most of 'Sensitive' Borders. In D. N. Gellner (Ed.), *Borderland lives in northern South Asia* (pp. 266–271). Durham, NC: Duke University Press.

Stein, B., Cuny, F., & Reed, P. (Eds.). (1995). *Refugee repatriation during conflict: A new conventional wisdom.* Dallas: The Centre for the Study of Societies in Crisis.

Still, J. (2010). Derrida and hospitality: Theory and Practice. Edinburgh: Edinburgh University Press.

Uddin, N., & Chowdhory, N. (2019). *Nasreen Deterritorialised Identities and Transborder Movement in South Asia.* Singapore: Springer.

Walker, W. S. (2010). *German and Bosnian Voices in a Time of Crisis: Bosnian Refugees in Germany, 1992–2002.* Indianapolis: Dog Ear Publishing.

Warner, D. (1999). Refugee state and state protection. In Frances N. & Patrick T. (Eds.), *Refugee Rights and Realities.* Cambridge: Cambridge University Press.

Xenos, N. (1996). Refugees: the modern condition. In Michael J. Shapiro & Hayward R. Alker (Eds.), *Challenging Boundaries: Global Flows, Territorial Identities*. Minneapolis: University of Minnesota Press.

Zieck, M. (1999). *UNHCR and voluntary repatriation of refugees: A legal analysis*. The Hague: Martinus Nijhoff.

Zieck, M. (2005). Vanishing points of the refugee law regime. Response to James Hathaway. *Ohio State Journal on Dispute Resolution, 20*(2), 217–284.

Correction to: New Faces of Statelessness: The Rohingya Exodus and Remapping of Rights

Nergis Canefe

Correction to: Chapter 11 in: N. Chowdhory and B. Mohanty (eds.), *Citizenship, Nationalism and Refugeehood of Rohingyas in Southern Asia*, https://doi.org/10.1007/978-981-15-2168-3_11

In the original version of the book, revised texts in many places are incorporated as post-publication corrections in the "Chapter 11". The chapter and the book now has been updated with changes.

The updated version of this chapter can be found at
https://doi.org/10.1007/978-981-15-2168-3_11

N. Chowdhory and B. Mohanty (eds.), *Citizenship, Nationalism and Refugeehood of Rohingyas in Southern Asia*,
https://doi.org/10.1007/978-981-15-2168-3_13

Index

N. Chowdhory and B. Mohanty (eds.), *Citizenship, Nationalism and Refugeehood of Rohingyas in Southern Asia*,
https://doi.org/10.1007/978-981-15-2168-3

The manufacturer's authorised representative in the EU is Springer Nature Customer Service Centre GmbH, Europaplatz 3, 69115 Heidelberg, Germany. If you have any concerns regarding our products, please contact ProductSafety@springernature.com

Printed and bound by CPI Group (UK) Ltd, Croydon, CR0 4YY
30/09/2026
02225253-0005